GIFTED, TALENTED, AND CREATIVE YOUNG PEOPLE

GARLAND REFERENCE LIBRARY
OF SOCIAL SCIENCE
(VOL. 120)

GIFTED, TALENTED, AND CREATIVE YOUNG PEOPLE
A Guide to Theory, Teaching, and Research

Morris I. Stein
Professor of Psychology
Department of Psychology
New York University

GARLAND PUBLISHING, INC. • NEW YORK & LONDON
1986

Library of Congress Cataloging in Publication Data

Stein, Morris Isaac, 1921–
    Gifted, talented, and creative young people.

    (Garland reference library of social science ; v. 120)
    Includes index.
    1. Gifted children—Education—United States—
Bibliography.   2. Gifted children—United States—
Identification—Bibliography.   3. Educational literature.
I. Title. II. Series.
Z5815.U5S73   1986 [LC3993.9]   016.37195'2   81-48419
ISBN 0-8240-9392-5

Cover design by Bonnie Goldsmith

Printed on acid-free, 250-year-life paper
Manufactured in the United States of America

Contents

Preface

The purpose of this book is to help cope with the information explosion in the literature on the gifted, talented, and creative, the excellent, student. This literature contains countless essays, research reports, curricular plans, instructional programs, procedures for stimulating creativity, etc., dispersed in untold numbers of books, monographs, journal articles and newsletters.

To get to know this literature is a formidable undertaking for those who want and need it most--students, teachers, researchers, counselors, school administrators, parents, school board members, governmental policy makers, and lay people--in short, anyone who is concerned with the identification and education of those young people, who, in the future, will make significant contributions to society.

To help make the literature more manageable I wrote this book. It contains summaries and annotations of a wide range of works in the field. They represent the major issues, orientations, research results, curricular and instructional programs, written by the major thinkers and investigators in the field as well as by lesser known persons who have also made significant contributions.

A broad time frame is represented in the works covered here. There are the classics, pioneering works in theory and research, published years ago whose influence is still felt. There are also representatives from contemporary literature: papers presented at conferences and symposia convened specifically for the rapid dissemination of information. Between the two extremes most attention is focused on the decade 1970-1980. Since a number of bibliographies in this book cover earlier periods and since some of the literature covered here was published after 1980, a reader has a resource that covers quite a span of history.

Readers acquainted with my previous bibliography concerning adults, *Creativity and the Individual: Summaries of the Psychiatric and Psychological Literature* published in 1960 with the late Shirley Heinze (which I hope will soon be back in print), will no doubt be aware of an important stylistic difference between this work on children and the earlier work on adults. The previous book contains *summaries* of the literature as its title says. This work contains some summaries (usually of classic works) but mostly annotations. The manuscript on the literature covered here, written in summary form, was one-third larger than the manuscript for this book. A book of that size was simply too large and too expensive to produce, hence this work.

The book starts with an introductory chapter that is divided into two sections. The first, *The State of the Art*, surveys where we stand now in the areas of identification and selection, education and training, and research. The second section, *A Look to the Future*, builds on current efforts and presents several organizational, methodological, and content suggestions to help make our work more effective in the future.

Each of the chapters that follows contains articles and books on a topic in gifted identification and education. Work selected for coverage met one of the following selection criteria: (1) A range of contemporary viewpoints and findings were to be covered. The major effort, as I said previously, concentrated on the decade 1970-1980. But this was an elastic time frame; some selections are earlier than 1970 and others were published after 1980. (2) To appreciate the history of the field and its development and to put contemporary issues in perspective, several works which were pioneering efforts when they were published were included. These classics set the tone for the field and their effects are still felt. (3) Some authors extend and modify their ideas over time in the light of new concepts and findings. To keep abreast of these developments and to provide a sense of continuity, both old and new publications are covered even at the risk of redundancy. (4) The vitality of this field and the drive it has to share information is reflected in the edited book, the multi-authored book, and the published proceedings of symposia. These works posed problems which I resolved in various ways. When I felt that a listing and perhaps a brief statement about the work was sufficient, I simply listed the participants and their offerings. In other instances, not only are the participants and their offerings listed but one or more pieces in the symposium are summarized. This occurred primarily when a specific idea or point of view had not been covered sufficiently. (5) When an author's ideas and findings are sufficiently discussed in an article it is presented and not the book which may also be cited. (6) Though I attempted to cover foreign literature it was not always available to me and coverage of this important area may be somewhat incomplete. I hope that colleagues in other countries will put me on their mailing lists so I will be aware of their contributions when I undertake a future work. (7) The most arbitrary decision I had to make was occasioned by the fact that there was a publishing deadline which could not be avoided. It was impossible to cover everything I wanted to cover and I am certain that I missed some very central works for which I am sorry. If there is a companion work to this volume I will correct my errors.

The books and articles presented here were selected to meet the needs of students who have educational and research requirements to fulfill. It is intended for predoctoral, postdoctoral, and professional researchers who want a rapid survey and introduction to the field. Teachers and counselors will find their fields covered as well. There are also chapters for those involved in the identification and selection of gifted, talented, and creative children and those who work with the gifted handicapped and the gifted poor. Instructors and professors will find this book valuable as a text or as a reference work in their courses on the gifted. The principal, the school board member, the policy maker, and the concerned citizen will also find information of interest and value here. For them as well as the others, an attempt was made to state results and issues separately from facts and aspirations in as straightforward a manner as possible.

As a further aid to the diverse members of the audience, the last chapter of the book is devoted to various resources in the literature and in the community that may be helpful. Names and addresses change so frequently that they need to be checked before using them. This last chapter plus the content of the preceding ones provide the reader with much coverage of the field.

   Within each chapter entries are grouped under brief headings
according to the major theme and are generally alphabetical by author's
last name. However, there are occasions when content takes priority.
If there was a development of a point of view over time then a chronological listing is used. If, however, there was a theme in the selection that did not follow a chronological order then the order is by
theme, not year of publication. Finally, where a contribution stirred
controversy and criticism, then the original work is followed by the
published criticism. This is especially true of the intelligence-
creativity controversy.

   I have occasionally listed *Suggestions for Further Reading* after
a selection, primarily after the work of a major contributor. These
are not annotated but are offered in order to be as inclusive as
possible. To gain maximum benefit from the material presented in
this book the reader should consult both the Author Index and the
Subject Index. The selections are usually so multifaceted they could
have multiple listings.

   There are three additional points I would like to make. First,
although this book is devoted to the gifted, talented, and creative
it should not be taken to mean that I favor the identification and
education of these children over and above others. For too long our
society has established adversary relationships between gifted,
talented, and creative children and other subgroups of children.
This is most unfortunate, for the education of *all* children is crucial
for our society and for the creative process to which every child and
every member of society has something to offer.

   Second, readers should know that I am a psychologist who has been
involved in studies of creativity in adults.* I have not been involved
in the education of young children. Only recently have I been involved
in research in this area. This I have carried out in a Saturday program for gifted children under the direction of Dr. Madelon Solowey at
C.W. Post College in New York. Being a newcomer to this field I have
had to proceed carefully and systematically, learning all the way.
I hope I have integrated my new and old knowledge in ways that the
reader will find illuminating and constructive.

---

*Those who want a more extended exposition of my point of view, theory,
methodology, and research findings might find it useful to consult my
two-volume work, *Stimulating Creativity*, *Vol. 1*, *Individual Procedures*
(1974) and *Vol. 2*, *Group Procedures* (1975) published by Academic Press,
Orlando, FL. My earlier works include: *Personality Factors in College
Admissions*, New York: College Entrance Examination Board, 1963; my
study of the first group of Peace Corps volunteers in Colombia, South
America, published as *Volunteers for Peace* by John Wiley, New York,
1966; and the studies of prediction at the college level with the late
George Stern and Benjamin Bloom which was published as *Methods in
Personality Assessment*, The Free Press, New York, 1956. There is a
small paperback that presents my ideas succinctly which is titled
*Making the Point: Anecdotes, Poems and Statements about the Creative
Process* which was published in 1984 by Bearly Limited at 149 York
Street, Buffalo, NY. The Center for Creative Leadership at P.O. Box
P-1 in Greensboro, NC 27405-1660, has available an audiotape of my
work titled, *Homo Transformare*, 1985, as well as a videotape titled
Stein on Creativity, 1985.

Finally, it should be pointed out that this book is being published at a time when the fate of gifted education is beset with uncertainties and threats to its existence. But this has happened before. Times will change and when they do, we should be prepared with new ideas and new plans. It is therefore hoped that this book will serve as a record of where we have been and as a source and a stimulus for creative ideas as we embark on a more fulfilling future.

I learned a great deal from the works I covered for this book. But, I learned even more from the friends I made as I joined those concerned with the gifted, talented, and creative child. These new friends, whom I knew first only through their publications, lived up to my expectations. They were most generous in sharing their time, knowledge, and experiences and were readily available to answer my questions. I consulted with them frequently so that I could make mid-course corrections in my work. Although many of my new friends adhere to theories, orientations, and methodologies that are different from mine, it made no difference in our discussions and relationships. I am most appreciative of the suggestions and guidance of my friends, but whatever shortcomings exist in this work are mine and not theirs.

I am especially grateful to: Abraham Tannenbaum, Harry Passow, Madelon Solowey, Irving Sato, Sandra Kaplan, Jim Curry, Sidney Parnes, Angelo Biondi, Donald Treffinger, Paul Torrance, Pansy Torrance, John Gowan, Joseph Justman, Mary Hunter Wolff, Dorothy Sisk, Ann Crabbe, Leonard Steinberg, Ed Tuttle, Scott Isaksen, Stan Gryskiewicz, and Nick Smith.

I am indebted to Prof. Richard Koppenaal of the Psychology Department of New York University for his helpfulness during various parts of this project.

A person who has to be singled out for special mention for her guidance and support throughout this work is my editor at Garland, Marie Ellen Larcada, to whom I am most indebted and grateful.

There are others whom I met only briefly at conferences, seminars, and colloquia who were also most helpful with their advice and suggestions. To them and to all others, mentioned and unmentioned, I express my appreciation and gratitude.

New York and Amagansett, 1985   Morris I. Stein

Introduction

THE STATE OF THE ART

Gifted, talented, and creative children are among our most valuable resources. They need the best of educational opportunities to fulfill their potentialities and to make their contributions to society. It is important, therefore, that we take stock from time to time of where we are educationally so that plans can be made for the future. No time is better for stock-taking than today, the mid-1980s. We have experienced a veritable explosion in this field. There has been enormous productivity in ideas, plans, curricula, tests, etc., that affect the lives of those we look to for excellence--the gifted, the talented, and the creative. Our prime purpose is to make much of it more manageable and accessible to the student, teacher, principal, superintendent, school board member, parent, and policy maker, and so to foster discussion and debate which will result in new and better plans for the future.

Society's concern with the gifted, talented, and creative is capricious. Although great strides have been made in this area in the recent past, there are currently problems which may prove to be serious stumbling blocks. Now, in the mid-1980s, the role of the federal government in gifted education has diminished and is becoming increasingly uncertain with the passage of time.

In the early 1970s, the federal government took a unique step and issued the Marland Report (1972),* a document which shaped the field for several years. Many ideas, plans, and hopes were enthusiastically received by those in the field and provided with financial support. There was even an Office of Gifted and Talented in the U.S. Department of Education.

In 1985, as this book is being published, the Office of Gifted and Talented no longer exists. At one point, the very existence of a separate U.S. Department of Education was debated. Currently, there are concerns about the financial support that will be available for educational programs. Some fear that if state and local taxes are no longer deductible from federal income taxes, state and local governments will not have the wherewithal to support education

---

*References in the text of this section that contain author and date are to be found in the text of the book. The other references have been listed at the end of this introduction under Notes. Some of these may also be found in the Suggestions for Further Reading lists that appear intermittently throughout the book.

properly. Furthermore, there is no indication of how much support
can be expected from the private sector. At present, the optimism of
the 1970s has been replaced by the uncertainty, if not the pessimism,
of the mid-1980s. Educators hope that there will be renewed leadership
at the federal level, but if it is not forthcoming, they hope that
leadership will come from the state and local levels.

If the past is any predictor of the future, it will not be too
long before the pendulum swings in a more positive direction once
again. When that time comes, we need to be ready with new ideas,
suggestions, and plans for the identification, selection, and education
of gifted, talented, and creative students. Let us learn from the experiences of those whose works are covered in this book so that we
will be able to participate creatively and effectively in the next
wave of educational developments.

In the chapters that follow, annotations and summaries of the
literature in a number of areas will be presented. The purpose of
this introductory chapter is to survey the state of the art in terms
of three subareas—identification and selection; education and training;
and research—and also to make some recommendations and suggestions
for the future.

Part 1
IDENTIFICATION AND SELECTION

The children discussed in this book are generally referred to as
gifted, talented, and creative. They have also been called supernormal, bright, precocious, brilliant, and "geniuses." When fine
distinctions are desired, the characteristics of the normal distribution curve are invoked and the children are referred to as the *highly*
talented, the *very* gifted, and the creatively *brilliant*. Each subgroup
is regarded as more rare and/or possessing more of the characteristic
under consideration. Whether such fine distinctions are possible or
even meaningful is an open question. But the fact remains that they
are made.

The words used to designate the groups that we shall consider go
in and out of fashion. When Cyril Burt was a young man, the preferred
word was *clever* rather than gifted (Burt, 1975). The use of *gifted*
to characterize supernormal students was introduced to the field by
Whipple[1] and became especially popular during World War I (L'Abate and
Curtis, 1975). In using this word, one should be aware that there are
113 definitions from which to select.[2] Gift and talent are used
synonymously in the field and in the literature. They are also used
interchangeably; the important center in gifted education at the University of Wisconsin refers to its Guidance Institute for the Talented
with the acronym GIFT.

Gift and talent may refer to different parts of the distribution
curve of IQ scores or they may be used to designate different areas of
outstanding achievement. In the latter case, gift would be used for
outstanding achievement in the verbal area and talent for outstanding
achievement in the non-verbal area (Gowan, 1978).

There is a good deal of variability in the terms that are used to
identify the children of interest. This can result in a great deal

of confusion, especially if one is interested in comparing results of different studies. In this case one must attend very carefully to the operations used to identify the students rather than depend on the terms. For example, Galton, in his classic study, *Hereditary Genius*,[3] called those persons geniuses who were regarded as one in 4,000 and who presumably had IQs of 150 and above. For his studies, Burt (1975) selected students who had IQs of 130 and above and who were regarded as among the brightest 2% of the elementary school population of the same chronological age. Finally Terman, for his classic studies of genius, focused attention on students whose IQs (the majority of which were 140 and above) placed them in the upper 1% of the child population.

The situation gets even more confusing when one adds those studies in which students are simply divided into groups of "high-IQ" and "low-IQ" and where the low group, on the average, has an IQ of 120. The problem is further exacerbated when researchers speak of high and low creativity and creativity does not mean what it does in studies of adults but instead refers to a test battery in which divergent thinking plays a major role.

There are many reasons for the proliferation of terms used, but one is especially noteworthy. There was a time when the primary or sole index of giftedness was a measure of IQ. But it was not long before there was much dissatisfaction expressed concerning the use of this measure. Because IQ alone overlooked many who were gifted, there were pressures to expand the definition of giftedness to include other factors.

The Marland Commission Report

At the level of the federal government, efforts to expand the concept of giftedness resulted in the Marland Commission Report to the U.S. Congress which was presented in 1972 by S.P. Marland, then the U.S. Commissioner of Education. The report called attention to the fact that there were young people in our country who required special educational programs if they were to realize their potential and make their individual contributions to society. Democracy, it was argued, would flourish when everyone was permitted and encouraged to develop according to their natural endowments. Without the proper educational environment, the gifted would not develop properly and society would lose in the long run.

The Marland Commission Report also contained a number of other statements that are germane to this presentation. The report contained a specific statement about the proportion of students in the general school population that should be involved in special education programs. The report recommended who was to do the selection, in what areas the selections were to be made, and the kinds of tests to be used. Since the Marland Report had such an impact on gifted education, these points will be used to structure the remainder of the discussion on identification and selection.

PROPORTION OF STUDENTS INVOLVED

With regard to the proportion of students to be involved in gifted education, the report selected a range of 3% to 5% of the general

school population. It has been estimated that in the 1970 census,
the 3% figure would have yielded approximately 1,935,000 boys and
girls. Although this may appear to be a large number, the recommended
proportion was a return to levels that existed prior to 1950. Before
1950, the term gifted identified only the upper 2% or 3% in intellectual ability in the general population. Later, the range was extended
to include practically everyone who had the potential for a college
education, i.e., 15% to 20% of the school population (De Haan and
Havighurst, 1961). The net was probably broadened as a result of
Conant's 1959 study of the high school in the U.S. Whatever the history of the changing proportion of the gifted, talented, and creative
in the general school population, the fact is that we are still dealing
with very large numbers.

SELECTORS

According to the Marland Report, selections for the special educational programs were to be made by professionally qualified persons:
principals, teachers, counselors, psychologists, and text administrators. These are still the primary selectors on the current scene.
Nominations, however, could come from a variety of sources, the aforementioned individuals as well as parents, people who know the child,
and even the child himself or herself.

Those doing the selecting used data collected through various
procedures, some of which will be considered at length shortly. They
include observations, interviews, checklists, rating scales, biographical questionnaires, and tests. More often than not, selections
were made on the basis of direct experience with the child or standardized procedure like a test. A standardized procedure frequently
has the value of objectivity and usually provides some supportive data
which could attest to the fact that the selector made a prudent decision
and did not play favorites or give in to subjectivity. Such evidence
may be necessary and desirable when questions are raised by parents,
school boards, or other community groups.

There are other practical considerations affecting the behavior
and decisions of the selectors, not the least of which are adequacy
of space, personnel, and funds. Since there are no absolute standards
as to who shall or shall not be selected, when there is an abundance
of space, personnel, and/or funds the cutoff point on a test or selection procedure may be lowered and in time of scarcity it may be raised.
Children who might be rejected at one time might have been selected at
another. To some, the procedures are so arbitrary that they would like
to see some relaxation of standards in ambiguous cases. Others, who
are even more generous, want all students admitted, with those who do
well allowed to continue.

Because of the serious nature of the decision, most selections
are made by committees who have access to information from a number
of persons and sources. Once again practical matters may play a role,
for the extent and nature of the selection conference can be affected
by the number of children to be evaluated for selection, the time
pressures, etc. Although there may be some kind of weighting system
in a conference approach and relative weights given to the opinions
of certain individuals (teachers as opposed to parents or teachers and
parents as opposed to tests) and procedures (rating scales as opposed
to tests), there is nothing systematic that is followed by all.

Those charged with the responsibility of identifying and/or selecting gifted, talented, and creative students are charged with a heavy
responsibiblity to the child, the school, the profession, and the society. If they make valid selections, all to the good. But if they
select students who cannot keep up with educational demands or, on the
other hand, if they reject students because they do not meet certain
standards and thus deprive them of appropriate educational opportunities, serious injustices have been done.

Unfortunately, records of deliberations and decision-making sessions
are not always kept so that it is difficult to know how various factors
are weighted in final decisions. Most attention has been paid to
teachers as selectors because of their central and responsible roles
in children's education. Yet, when research data are presented comparing teachers to other means of identifying students in this area,
teachers are often found wanting. In the area of creativity, for
example, it has been argued (Torrance, 1962) that teachers are apt to
miss a good number of students with creative potential. These students,
it is suggested, possess characteristics that are not likely to find
favor in their teacher's eyes and hence the student is not nominated
as creative. Teachers may be better able to identify intellectually
gifted students because they are usually convergent thinkers who do
not cause problems in the classroom, and they are often more appealing
to their teachers.

The current situation regarding selectors is such that one can
choose from among diverse people who work either individually or in
groups, and either with or without test data in the identification
and selection of gifted, talented, and creative students. There are
some persons who prefer to avoid the use of tests and suggest that
choices be made by observing which children do well when exposed to
the best of educational programs. There are still others who put the
most weight on tests alone, arguing that tests are more objective and
superior to decisions made by human judgment alone.

AREAS FOR SELECTIONS

According to the Marland Commission Report, selections were to be
made for six areas. The last of these areas was later dropped though
the use of five areas was an increase in the number of areas for which
the gifted were to be selected. The areas were: (1) general intellectual ability, (2) specific academic aptitude, (3) creative or productive
thinking ability, (4) leadership, (5) ability in visual and performing
arts, and (6) psychomotor ability (this last area was later dropped).

Procedures Used for Identification

Over the years, certain kinds of tests and procedures have been
used to identify children in these different areas. Intelligence
tests are used for general intellectual ability, special ability or
achievement tests are used for measures of specific academic aptitude,
and tests of creativity have been used for creative or productive
thinking ability. But otherwise, tests qua tests have not figured
much. For other areas and especially for ability in the visual and
performing arts, use is made of rating scales and reports of actual

performance measures (in or out of the school). As a matter of fact, these other techniques are often of particular use with students who are disadvantaged in various ways in being identified and/or assessed with the usual measures. Students who come from different ethnic backgrounds, students who are underachievers, students whose emotional and social problems interfere with how well they do in school, and students who are physically handicapped may fare better with identification that is based on the use of observational checklists, rating scales, inventories, and biographical questionnaires than they will with tests.

Although there is no lack of tests and procedures for identification purposes, the problem remains that many of those that are available are not very good because they are not valid or they are misused. Consequently many of the shortcomings pointed out by the Marland Commission Report in 1972 still persist. We are fortunate in having a report written by Richert and her co-workers in 1982 of an identification conference held in May, 1981. This is one of the best-balanced works available. It reports on possible areas of strength as well as the many weaknesses.

In the second chapter, entitled "National Survey of Identification Practices: Uses and Abuses of Identification Procedures," the authors write in their concluding paragraph:

> Apparently, the state of the art of identification of gifted and talented youth is in some disarray. It is common practice in the field to use tests/instruments in a manner which does not conform to what is intended and described in the published test manuals of those instruments. In many cases such use betrays an indiscriminate conflation of categories of the federal definition of giftedness; as in other cases it reflects confusion, if not ignorance, concerning the diversity and distinctness of identifiable different sets of abilities. There is a flagrant use of tests/instruments with populations on which they were not normed and for which they were never intended. Beyond the intellectual and academic categories there is a relative paucity of formal, not to mention validated, measures being used to identify gifted students. (Richert et al., 1982, p. 39)

The state of the art concerning identification is such that, "The emerging practices suggested some disturbing trends. Among the students who would most often be screened out on the basis of questionable assumptions and data were those who most *need* programs: the underachieving, handicapped, disadvantaged, bilingual, and exceptionally creative. Others regularly excluded from services were potential leaders and artists." (Richert et al., 1982, p. 39)

There is much that needs to be done in this area using the work of Richert et al. (1982). Meanwhile, there are a number of tests used to identify students in four areas, including intellectual ability; specific academic aptitude and achievement; visual and performing arts and leadership and psychosocial ability; and creativity. In discussing these areas the goal is not only to characterize the current state of the art, but also to highlight those areas that may prevent problems in future developments.

INTELLECTUALLY GIFTED

The most commonly used test to identify the intellectually gifted is the Stanford-Binet, though the Wechsler Intelligence Scale for Children-Revised (WISC-R) is a close second. The Stanford-Binet has been around for so long that when other tests are used, their scores are frequently restated in terms of Stanford-Binet equivalents. The Stanford-Binet and the WISC-R are individually administered tests which require training for their proper administration and, hence, are more costly than group administered intelligence tests. There are a number of group administered tests available which may be used in the identification and selection of the intellectually gifted. Local and/or state boards of education usually decide which of the available tests shall be used in any one situation.

A valid and reliable intelligence test is necessary in the selection of intellectually gifted children. As pointed out previously, it has been effectively argued that the use of intelligence tests in the selection of gifted children overlooks many gifted children. Hence, intelligence tests are now usually administered with an achievement test with appropriate cutoff scores. "Creativity" tests are also administered. The weights assigned to intelligence tests, other tests, teacher's ratings, and other ratings vary from situation to situation.

Terman's Work

It is impossible to discuss the identification and selection of the intellectually gifted student without also discussing Terman's contributions to the field. Although Terman's works were published some time ago, their impact continues to be felt. To convey the nature of Terman's contributions, each of the volumes reporting his work is presented in sequence and in detail in the text of this book. Terman's motivation, determination, and persistence in following his subjects and the quality of contact he maintained with them (which, no doubt, inspired them to stay in touch with him) is most impressive. In this regard, Terman is a model to be emulated.

Terman's Stanford-Binet not only became the instrument to identify the intellectually gifted, but also became the measure of intelligence for all kinds of groups and all kinds of purposes. The test became a model for other tests that were published later. In addition, Terman provided data on the characteristics of the intellectually gifted at different points in their life cycles. Never before had such systematic work been carried out on the intellectually gifted over such a long period of time.

Although we owe a lot to Terman, there are some shortcomings in his work that are often overlooked. Because of these shortcomings, the ways in which some people use Terman's legacy, the IQ, leaves much to be desired. Pauline Sears, who knows Terman's data well and who is responsible for publishing results which bring the studies up to 1972, has presented a balanced and concise statement which can serve as an excellent caution to anyone reading and using Terman's data. She points out that the samples in the studies were not random; the parents of the gifted had the benefits of better education when compared with the general population; Blacks and Mexicans were underrepresented and Jews were overrepresented, Chinese children were not sampled since, at the time of the study, they were attending special schools; the data are less useful for studies of group differences than they are for following the development of the subjects over the years; the myths about the gifted existent at the time were proven false with the use of averages and, for an individual child, the IQ was not a strong predictor of other qualities. Sears also points out that occasionally Terman "got carried away in his generalizations by his own hereditarian bias." Several points in this summary are so important that they require further discussion since their effects on the field are still felt today.

The hereditarian bias in Terman's work, which goes back to Galton and the beginning of the mental testing movement in 1870, continues to plague society in general (Gould[4]) and education in particular. The arguments between the hereditarians and the environmentalists are perennial even though each side frequently states that both heredity and environment are important in all behavior. While the arguments go on, there are practical decisions to be made which have serious consequences. In the field of the gifted, talented, and creative, test constructors and test publishers frequently argue that their tests favor no one group over another. Others argue, with equal vigor and lots of evidence, that the tests are biased against the economically disadvantaged and the culturally deprived. It is argued that children from these groups are rejected and denied the opportunity to participate in certain educational programs because the intelligence tests used are not fair to them. The irony of the situation is that there may in fact be no disadvantaged children, only "disadvantaged" tests (Richert et al., 1982). Tests can be constructed which members of the majority group in our society could fail because of their ignorance about how to get along in the barrio or survive in the streets.

Culture-fair tests have not met with much success, and it is possible that they cannot be further developed (Swanson and Watson, 1982). Tests that benefit only one part of society or only certain individuals should be labeled as such. Test constructors and test publishers should do everything in their power to prevent the misuse of tests by school administrators, school boards, and school personnel. For those students for whom the tests do not function validly, responsible identifiers and selectors must seek out more promising, valid, and reliable procedures.

Another important criticism of Terman's research is that he relied too much on teachers to select the students whom he studied. The teachers, with their own biases, were inclined to favor the pleasant, well-behaved, and properly disciplined child. They may well have overlooked the withdrawn student who had to be called upon to reveal his or her original ideas, or the inquisitive and creative student who interrupted class with original comments. Consequently, Terman's data and the value of the IQ test for identification and selection purposes may be quite limited. An IQ test may be good for identifying the intellectually gifted but it may not recognize the creative student; this matter will be examined in the next section. Others argue that the well-rounded psychological characteristics that Terman reported for the intellectually gifted do not characterize the upper range of IQ scorers, but are limited to those whose IQs hover around 140. This group, it has been said, does not include the "true geniuses" who have IQs of 180 or more (Hollingworth, 1926, 1942). If Terman had had a good sampling of these students in his study, the overall picture would not have been as healthy psychologically as the image formed by studying those with IQs of 140 or so. By not focusing on the very

highest IQs Terman may have been able to deal with some of the negative myths about the gifted child. Yet, the picture he painted about
how well adjusted this child was, did an injustice to the children with
the higher IQs who might indeed have had problems with which they
needed help and counseling. These same children may have been responsible for some very important contributions to society and many
more of them might have been able to do so if their problems (whether
they were their own doing or resulted from their environments) were
acknowledged and dealt with.

The IQ level that one uses to decide whether a child is gifted or
a genius is a rather serious issue. Prior to Terman, there were
several writers (covered in Stein and Heinze, 1960) who might be called
"pathographers of genius." They argued that persons of acknowledged
genius had physical as well as psychological problems. Terman's work
made an important contribution by going against this orientation.
Terman argued that the young people he called gifted or whom he included in his studies of genius, were very healthy, both physically
and psychologically. Despite the importance of this contribution,
others argued, as we have just seen, that Terman found such a healthy
group of students because the IQ level for giftedness in his study
was too low. Had he raised the IQ level in his study, he would have
found, it was argued, the presence of psychological problems and even
pathology. In addition, it was also argued that the issue was not
simply a matter of finding or not finding pathology, but that at the
lower IQ level, one could not find the true geniuses who make the truly
important contributions to society. The counter-argument to this last
point claimed that while it is true that among Terman's subjects one
does not find anyone of the caliber of a Shakespeare or an Einstein,
one does find persons who make impressive contributions to society.
It also has to be acknowledged that one intelligence test, administered
rather early in the lives of these people, does not always pick them
out.

The matter of where one sets the IQ level for identifying the
gifted also has many practical consequences. It is an important
factor in determining the number of students in the general population
of students who are identified and selected for gifted programs. On
an individual level, it has a serious impact on the child who is rejected from a gifted education program because of a lower than desirable
intelligence test score. This can be terribly ironic, especially in
those cases where a student could do well on another test, such as one
that measures creativity.

Support for the suggestion that IQs of around 140 may be too high
for the identification and selection of gifted children comes from
studies of creative adults. Evidence obtained from studies of adults
who are creative in various fields of endeavor, by MacKinnon and his
associates at the Institute for Personality Assessment and Research
(IPAR) at Berkeley, indicate that these adults, on the average, do not
have IQs as high as those used in some schools as cutoff points in the
selection of students for gifted programs. The average IQ of persons
regarded as creative in these and other studies is about 120. It is
usually necessary to have an IQ in this range to get through college.
It has also been argued that intelligence, as measured by intelligence
tests, may be important in getting the opportunity to be creative,
though once one has the opportunity it takes more than just IQ to make
the most of it.[5] The results of studies of the intelligence of creative

adults also reveal that intelligence test data are better for screening out people who will not be creative than for predicting who will
be creative.

The practical results of all of the above arguments is that gifted
educational programs accept children with IQs lower than 140; they
accept children with IQs of 127 and lower. Programs try not to miss
those children who would not be picked up by a high IQ score by also
checking other test scores and other characteristics. A very highly
regarded educational program that selects students on the basis of such
combinations is Renzulli's program. In Renzulli's (1977) Triad approach, children are admitted to a gifted educational program if they
have "above average intelligence" and "above average creativity."
In addition, they need to possess "task commitment."

Factor Analysis and Guilford

In addition to the criticisms already mentioned, that focus on
Terman's hereditarian bias, the biased character of the sample used,
the problem of using teacher's nominations for selection of students
to be studied, and the IQ cutoff point, there also has been criticism
on theoretical grounds from the factor analysts who argue that Terman's
conceptualization of intelligence was in error. For the Stanford-
Binet test, intelligence was regarded theoretically as composed of a
general or g factor and a specific or s factor.[6] Others have conceptualized intelligence differently. Thurstone[7] regarded intellectual
functioning as composed of group factors which include: verbal, number,
special word fluency, memory, and vocabulary ability. More recently,
Guilford (1967) regarded intellect as composed of specific factors.
For Guilford the structure of the intellect is regarded as being composed of three major categories of factors--operations, contents, and
products--each of which is further divided into subclasses. In Guilford's system, there are 120 different abilities which make up the
structure of the intellect. An intellectual factor in this system is
composed of one operation combined with one content and one product.

Just as Guilford has been critical of Terman's conceptualization
of intelligence so other factor analysts who are concerned with
theoretical issues are critical of Guilford. Specifically, they
(e.g., McNemar[8]) were critical of Guilford for having so many factors
(120) in his structure of the intellect. These many factors, they
argued, made the structure of the intellect meaningless. Practitioners,
those involved in the day-to-day concerns of working with gifted
children, paid little attention to such theoretical matters; they are
pragmatic and want something that helps them to fulfill their responsibilities. Before leaving Guilford's work on the structure of the
intellect, it should be noted that his work has become not only the
starting point for those who study the intellect and those who wish
to develop creativity tests, but it has also become a model for curricular development (Meeker, 1969). In Meeker's program, children are
educated and trained so that they develop properly, as defined by some
of Guilford's factors.

New Developments

The question of how to identify and select the intellectually
gifted does not end with Guilford's contributions. For an excellent
critique of existing tests and approaches, as well as a survey of new

approaches and promising ideas, the reader may wish to consult
Swanson and Watson's book, *Educational Psychological Assessment of
Exceptional Children: Theories, Strategies, and Applications*.[9]
Specific mention has to be made of two major programs that are pur-
suing new approaches to intelligence. One is by Gardner who is de-
veloping a conceptualization that involves multiple intelligences.[10]
The other is by Sternberg who is developing a componential theory of
intellectual giftedness[11] and a triarchic theory of intelligence.[12]

The Use of the IQ

Before concluding this discussion of the use of intelligence
tests for identifying and selecting the intellectually gifted, a word
has to be said about the use of intelligence tests for predictive
purposes. The IQ, the concept of "intelligence," and the intelligence
test are important developments and crucial factors in the study of
the gifted. But, like all such important developments, they can be
and have been misused. As mentioned previously, practitioners want
methods that work and they want to have numbers which can be used for
decision-making purposes. They believe that with numbers, they will
not have to tolerate any ambiguity. They also want a test that is
economical in time, money, and training. Therefore, for them, the best
test is one that takes the least time to administer (usually a frac-
tion of a class period), the least amount of money per student (group
administered paper and pencil tests), and the least amount of training
and experience for administration, scoring, and interpretation (self-
administered tests that are machine scored). With such requirements,
it is surprising that intelligence tests work as well as they do in
the identification and selection of gifted students. Likewise, it is
not surprising that there has been so much criticism about misidentified
children.

The concept of intelligence has become reified; intelligence is
no longer simply a concept but something almost tangible and capable
of being "contained" in an IQ score. All kinds of myths regarding IQ
and intelligence prevail; IQs have developed lives of their own.
Responsibility has been ceded to test developers. Practitioners have
put logic and rationalism aside in overlooking the content and
psychological processes that are tested for in intelligence tests
and concerning themselves only with the numbers that make up the IQ.
Consequently, they forget that the IQ is a measure of a child's rate
of development. When the IQ is used for identification and selection
purposes, it is implicitly being used for predictive purposes. The IQ
will predict well if the psychological processes measured in the test
are related to the criterion (e.g., grades) which it is predicting
(Stern, Stein, and Bloom, 1956).[13] A child's IQ is not all that one
should know about the child. Among other things, one needs to know
whether a child will make effective use of his or her IQ and for this,
one also needs to know, from observation or test, something about the
child's personality and motivation.

SPECIFIC ACADEMIC APTITUDE AND ACHIEVEMENT

Achievement tests are usually the tests used to identify and/or
select students who, in the Marland Commission Report, are referred
to as the academically gifted. Generally, achievement tests concern

themselves with the facts and information that a student has learned
in a specific area and his or her score is compared to that achieved
by his or her peers. "They usually have less to do with analytical
functions such as the ability to organize and evaluate. Moreover,
they usually do not measure a student's ability to see relationships
and meanings. Their emphasis is upon the ability to recall facts"
(Richert et al., 1982, p. 61). Achievement tests such as these are
regarded by the conference participants, reported on by Richert et al.,
as good for screening students and for nominating them as part of a
talent pool. There are also diagnostic tests which can help point to
a student's strengths and weaknesses so that a proper curriculum can
be designed.

In general practice, practitioners who have to make decisions
about accepting or rejecting students for gifted programs usually
accept students who score at a level which is at least two grades
higher than their actual grade placement. Achievement tests are best
used with other test data and information. They are abused when
teachers teach for the achievement test and when they are used to
exclude students from a broad-based talent pool (Richert et al., 1982,
p. 61).

Stanley

One program that bears watching is the one developed by Stanley
(George et al., 1979; Colangelo and Zaffrann, 1979) at Johns Hopkins
University. Tests of increasing difficulty are used in a sequential
manner to identify and select students for gifted programs in mathematics and in the verbal area. The tests are, essentially, a series
of filters which lets only the very best students through. For example, the SAT mathematics test is administered to students and those
who pass it at a high enough level can then take the Differential
Aptitude Test. Qualified students are then highlighted for admission
to the Johns Hopkins or related programs. This process of successive
filtering bears watching. If follow-up data bear out Stanley's expectations, then others may want to emulate his procedures. However,
one cannot help but wonder if putting so much weight on the SAT as the
first hurdle in the selection process and not using other psychological
measures that relate to creativity is a wise course.

In terms of evaluation, this means that the Johns Hopkins program
should not only gather data on how well those they select perform, in
the program and afterwards, but they should also gather follow-up data
on persons whom they reject for their program. All too often programs
are evaluated solely in terms of the accomplishments attained by those
within the program. In this instance, because the filtering system
of testing is an integral part of the program and because it is conceivable that at least one test may exclude desirable students, it is
critical that data be collected on rejectees, whether they made a
career of mathematics or not.

VISUAL AND PERFORMING ARTS AND LEADERSHIP/PSYCHOSOCIAL ABILITIES

For the visual and performing arts the Richert et al. report does
not endorse any specific testing instrument. Conference participants
focused on the evaluation of a student's portfolio. In other words,
they opted for a performance-based criterion. Some instruments "were

seen as having some usefulness for documenting an aptitude for, or
ability in, some talent areas" (Richert et al., 1982, p. 67).

In the conference reported by Richert et al. the discussion of
the leadership area was regarded as "the most inconclusive." On the
one hand, there were those who felt that giftedness could occur in
any area and that this category was "too limiting rather than too
broad." There was another group who objected to this area and felt
that giftedness should be reserved for a certain "level of general or
specific academic ability." Another objection raised to the leadership category came from those who felt that creativity was a criterion.
It was also suggested that the leadership category "be redefined as
psychosocial ability which would include such human relations talents
as leadership, management, counseling and teaching. The social value
of these abilities was emphasized." The conference group did not
recommend any test instrument to identify leadership or psychosocial
giftedness.

There was no formal consideration at the conference of psychomotor
ability. "Yet, from the informal comments on this subject during the
conference, it seems that the perspectives on this category are similar
to those on leadership. Some would exclude it if it meets no intellectual or creative criterion. If criteria for excellence within the
fields of athletics, dance, mechanical abilities, etc., are met, then
others see no reason for exclusion. Furthermore, there is a recognition that there are psychomotor components in the performing arts
(acting, dance, mime). If these are included, why not include gym-
nastics, skating, etc.?" (Richert et al., 1982, p. 68)

CREATIVE OR PRODUCTIVE THINKING

One of the more complicated charges in the Marland Commission
Report was to identify, select, and educate "children with *demonstrated*
and/or *potential* high performance" in the area of creative or productive thinking. It has been difficult enough to work on the creativity
and productive thinking of adults; one can imagine what it must be like
working with children in either of these areas. In the adult area there
are many theories and hypotheses but no consensus. In addition, there
are as yet no agreed upon body of tests that are easily available or
which might serve as a model. Furthermore, while there has been some
experience with programs and techniques for stimulating creativity at
the adult level, there are no hard data as yet as to how good these are
and who might profit from them. And certainly, there are no educational programs to provide the necessary guidelines.

The area is most important and continues to be complicated and
controversial. In working with children there have been no major
breakthroughs in theory, although there have been research studies in
the area as well as tests. The tests originated with Guilford's 1967
work on the intellect and the most popular ones at the present time
are those developed by Torrance (1966). Creativity tests have their
protagonists but they also have their critics. There are those who
believe that the only criterion for creativity is manifest creativity
as one finds with adults; the available tests with children do not all
meet this criterion. There are others who feel that there are studies
under way which are promising and which eventually will provide the
necessary data. There are some who feel that creativity is multi-
dimensional and that its appropriate study involves a consideration

of both intellectual abilities and personality traits. Others disagree. While some feel reasonably good about how the intellectual
abilities and personality traits involved in creativity are measured,
there are others who are quite unhappy about this state of affairs.

In view of the lack of consensus and the lack of clarity about
the various controversial issues, some believe that a great deal of
caution should be exercised in using tests in this area and that
judgments should be withheld until all the requisite validation data
are in. This group might like to see the tests in use today limited
to research purposes. Others are confronted with practical needs and,
consequently, tests are recommended and used.

The choice of testing materials can have serious consequences.
On the one hand, if one admits children to gifted programs on the
basis of intelligence tests alone, one might overlook a good number
of gifted and creative children and deprive them of the educational
opportunities they deserve. On the other hand, if creativity tests
are used for selection and prove to be invalid, one might do certain
children an injustice by putting them into learning situations which
they cannot handle. To provide the reader with basic information
about the issues involved, we shall first consider some historical
background which concerns Guilford's work. Then we shall proceed with
a discussion of three pioneering works that focus on what has been
called the "intelligence/creativity controversy."

A Bit of History--Guilford

Educators and psychologists became interested in creativity and
creativity tests as a result of Guilford's presidential address to
the American Psychological Association in 1950 on creativity, and
because of his important work on the structure of intellect (Guilford,
1967). In his address, Guilford said, "We must look well beyond the
boundaries of the IQ if we are to fathom the domain of creativity"
(p. 448). He argued against the IQ as a measure of creative talent
and said that to account for creative talent in terms of high intelligence or IQ "is not only inadequate but has largely been responsible
for lack of progress in the understanding of creative people" (p. 454).
For Guilford, although the Stanford-Binet test includes a variety of
tests, it still does not measure adequately the kinds of abilities
that may be involved in creativity. As pointed out earlier (p. xxiv)
Guilford disagreed with Terman about the factor structure of intelligence. In his own work on the structure of the intellect, Guilford
presented the factors that he regarded as related to creativity as
well as those related to other measures of intelligence. For example,
one of the factors in Guilford's structure of the intellect is convergent thinking, that is, the thinking involved in responding to
questions that have one correct answer. This factor is involved in
tests like the Stanford-Binet. Questions that require creative
thinking are those with multiple possible answers; Guilford called
the thinking involved in responding to such questions and the various
abilities associated with it divergent thinking. Although Guilford's
divergent-production abilities are probably the best known of the
abilities tested for in seeking creative children, Guilford himself
pointed out that the divergent-production abilities were not the only
factors involved in creativity. He said:

> Although the most obvious aspects of creative thinking appear
> to depend on the abilities to do divergent-productive thinking

and the abilities to effect transformations of information,
with the abilities fluency, flexibility, elaboration, and redefinition playing significant roles, with creative thinking
put in its larger context of problem solving, we see that any
or all kinds of abilities represented in the structure of intellect can play their useful roles directly or indirectly.
(p. 11)

Guilford supported his statements with empirical data and tests.
Nevertheless, major factor analysts disagreed with him; they felt
that 120 factors were too many to account for the structure of the
intellect. For many of those involved with the gifted, Guilford's
view prevailed. During the 1960s, three major studies were published
(Getzels and Jackson, 1962; Wallach and Kogan, 1965; and Torrance,
1966) which had profound effects on the field despite published
criticisms of statistical problems.

The fundamental issue posed by Guilford and the fundamental issues
in the aforementioned studies were whether intelligence and creativity
were correlated or not. If they are significantly correlated, the
tests which presumably measure each of them separately are measuring
the same psychological variable. If intelligence and creativity are
not correlated and are in fact independent of each other, separate
tests are required to measure them.

Guilford essentially argued that intelligence and creativity were
independent of each other. For example, he argued that the typical
intelligence test, like the Stanford-Binet, contains questions with
single correct answers. To arrive at such answers requires convergent
thinking. However, questions which require creativity are questions
for which there are no immediate single correct answers; one has to
consider several possibilities. For this, convergent thinking alone
is not sufficient; one also needs to be capable of divergent thinking.
But, creativity involves even more than just divergent thinking, for
example, transformation factors are also required. Though these other
factors have not received much consideration, much attention in the
field has been directed to divergent thinking.

The studies that were carried out in the 1960s on the relationship
between intelligence and creativity argued that the two were independent. In another study, statistical reanalysis of the original data
disputed the researchers' claims regarding the independence of creativity and intelligence. Oddly enough, despite the fact that the basic
arguments revolved around statistical issues, and the fact that eminent
statisticians demonstrated that the findings did not stand up under
analysis, there was an enormous groundswell of support in favor of
the creativity tests. Much time, effort, and money were expended on
additional studies using so-called creativity tests and practical
decisions were made about young people on the basis of the data. Yet,
in a major conference held approximately twenty years after Guilford's
studies, it was concluded that the entire matter might have been a
tempest in a teapot, for only some of these efforts received recommendations which were cautious and lukewarm.

Getzels and Jackson

The first major study to attract attention in the field was that
of Getzels and Jackson (1962) which was conducted at a midwestern
university's secondary school. IQ scores were obtained for 449
adolescents which were based on the Stanford-Binet or, if other tests

were used, the scores were converted to Binet IQ equivalents. The creativity test battery consisted of five tests: word association, uses of things, hidden shapes, make-up problems, and fables. A score was obtained for each test and the scores were added to yield a single creativity score. With arrays of scores available for both the IQ and creativity measures, Getzels and Jackson then established cutoff points on each measure to indicate where the upper 20% of the students fell in each case. Then they established two major subgroups. In one were those students who scored above the 20% mark for IQ but below the 20% mark for creativity. In the other group were those students who scored above the 20% mark for creativity but below the 20% mark for IQ.

In other words, they referred to one group as high on IQ but not as high on creativity and to the other group as high on creativity but not as high on IQ. This was a rather unfortunate designation since the field is more accustomed to referring to comparison groups as a high group and a low group. As a result the Getzels and Jackson designation of "high, but not as high, etc." usually results in the erroneous transformation either in the literature or in discussion as "high creativity/low intelligence" or "low creativity/high intelligence." The terms high and low IQ are especially confusing since the average IQ of the high group was 150 and the average IQ for the low group was 127--an IQ score which is not very low, even though, as the authors point out, the difference is 23 IQ points.

The results of this study were quite intriguing. For example, although the two samples of subjects differed from each other by 23 IQ points, they did equally well in measures of scholastic achievement, and both groups did better than their classmates. It had been expected that the high IQ group would do better than the high creativity group on an achievement test since IQ is usually positively correlated with such tests. It was of further interest that the high-creative group did better than the high-IQ comparison group on tests requiring imagination. In addition, it was found that teachers preferred the high-IQ group to the general population of students and to the high-creatives. This finding may have satisfied those who believe that teachers discriminated against the high-creatives.

In sum, the important thing about this study was that the authors interpreted their results as arguments against the use of the IQ score in the selection for giftedness. In a paper that preceded their book the authors (Getzels and Jackson, 1958) wrote that they conclude that "high academic performance of ... creative children coupled with the related lack of recognition which they may receive from teachers points to the problem of expanding the present conception of 'Giftedness,' and of breaking the bonds that the IQ has on this concept in the school situation" (p. 77). By breaking the hold of the IQ on selection for giftedness, the numbers of available gifted students could be increased and admitted to the proper educational programs.

The floodgates were open; numerous studies followed to investigate the relationships between IQ tests and tests of creativity. Some supported the initial findings and others did not and we shall consider a number of these later. As one might suspect, the floodgates of criticism were also opened.

One body of serious criticism was developed on psychometric grounds. The force of the Getzels and Jackson argument was based on the intercorrelations they obtained. For creativity and intelligence to be independent, which was crucial for their argument, it was necessary for the creativity measures to intercorrelate highly and significantly with each other and more highly than they would with the intelligence measures in the test battery. The same should hold true for the intelligence measures in relation to the creativity measures. This did not happen with the necessary consistency; the argument is best summarized by Ward (1968, p. 738) who says that:

> It is necessary to at least demonstrate that so-called creativity tests measure something in common, that their shared variance cannot be accounted for by relation to other dimensions. In particular, it must be shown that creativity tests are something other than unusual and relatively unreliable measures of IQ. The analysis of a number of studies suggests that these minimal conditions for the usefulness of the construct have not often been achieved--either creativity measures have shown little relation to one another, or they have intercorrelated to about the same degree that they have correlated with IQ scores. Typical of the former finding is the study by Flescher (1968) where the average intercorrelation among creativity measures was .11; the latter pattern was exemplified in the work of Getzels and Jackson (1962) where the creativity scores correlated on the average .30 with one another and .27 with IQ. Additional analyses with similar results have been reported by McNemar and Ward (1966).

Questions were also raised about the procedure that Getzels and Jackson used to obtain a single score. They summed the creativity measures and argued that it was permissible to do so because the creativity subtests correlated significantly and positively with each other. However, Thorndike[14] pointed out that the range of correlations on the creativity tests for the boys and for the girls was not different from the respective ranges of the correlations between IQ and the total test battery. Wallach (1970) argued that if the creativity and intelligence tests had been administered at the same time, then the obtained differences between the two sets of data might have disappeared. Using chi-square analysis to reanalyze the Getzels and Jackson study led Marsh (1964) to say that intelligence and creativity were not really independent in the original study.

Sampling in the original study was also criticized. It was argued[15] that only in a group with high test scores, such as those found in the Getzels and Jackson group, might one find a difference between creativity and intelligence. In an unselected group the two variables might well overlap.

The Getzels and Jackson study was criticized on various grounds, including the lack of independence of creativity and intelligence test scores, inadequate sampling, tests selected, procedures for dealing with test scores, inappropriate interpretation of results, and the problem of non-replication. Any one of these criticisms might have stopped the effects of such a study, yet it has had amazing effects. The reasons for this influence are suggested by the following points. (1) There had been growing dissatisfaction with the IQ as the sole measure of giftedness. (2) Guilford had pointed out that it was necessary to go beyond the IQ to understand creativity. (3) Guilford had distinguished between convergent and divergent thinking. The latter was part of creativity, though not the only part. (4) Convergent

thinking had been an important variable in the usual measures of intelligence. Teachers were likely to select students high on convergent thinking when they were asked to select their best students;
these students were likely to be obedient and conforming but not
necessarily creative. Divergent thinkers were likely to be nonconforming and autonomous and were less likely to be selected by
teachers as their best students. (6) The 1960s was a decade in
which independent, autonomous, and even counter-culture behavior was
emphasized and valued. Those who favored the Getzels-Jackson study
and its results had everything going for them except the statistical
data that reflected the independence of intelligence and creativity
tests.

Wallach and Kogan

The Getzels and Jackson study was not the only one that studied the
IQ/creativity issue. The study conducted by Wallach and Kogan (1965)
had a different theoretical orientation than that adopted by Getzels
and Jackson. Getzels and Jackson followed Guilford and cited the
psychoanalyst Kubie (1958) for their theoretical orientation. Whereas
Getzels and Jackson represented the dynamic point of view, Wallach and
Kogan represented the associationistic point of view following Mednick's theoretical orientation and his Remote Associates Test (RAT).[16]
Wallach and Kogan used ideas from associationism as they searched
for the best conditions under which to collect data from children.
If children are to do their best, they must have the opportunity to
work in game-like, non-evaluative conditions. Following an associa-
tionist theoretical orientation, Wallach and Kogan argued that the
increase in frequency of associations occurs early in a data-gathering
session. Unique responses occur late in the series of a subject's
associations. Hence, they argued that when a divergent thinking test
is administered with a short time limit, it arouses anxieties which
constrain thinking and inhibit novel responses. The negative effects
of a short time limit can be alleviated if the test occurs in a non-
evaluative and game-like atmosphere.
Consequently, Wallach and Kogan administered their tests to 151
ten and eleven year old children in the kind of environment that they
wanted. They used divergent thinking tests (not the RAT) which included both verbal and visual material. The verbal tests included
instances, alternate uses, and similarities. Among the visual tests
were pattern meanings and line meanings. The tests were scored for
number and uniqueness of response.
The results of the Wallach and Kogan study showed that their
divergent thinking tests correlated well with each other and sufficiently so as to indicate that they were part of a unitary factor.
Also, when the divergent thinking data were correlated with measures
of convergent thinking, like subscores on the Wechsler Intelligence
Scale for Children (WISC), they found that, by and large, the two
measures were independent of each other. Thus, they could argue that
they had indeed found intelligence and creativity to be independent
of one another.
Again, it was not long before questions were raised about the
Wallach and Kogan results. Some questioned the value of the game-like
conditions and even found evidence that conventional test conditions
could provide the best results.[17] Tannenbaum's (1983) review of a
number of studies found that the Wallach and Kogan tests were better

for concurrent validity than for predictive validity. While some investigators have replicated the Wallach and Kogan findings with some age groups, there are others working with children at the kindergarten level whose tests do not yield definitive results. In these studies, replications are found with tests of semantic content but not with tests of figural content.

The most telling criticism of all came from Cronbach (1968) whose status in the field as a statistician is widely acknowledged. Cronbach reanalyzed the original Wallach and Kogan data which he obtained from the authors, and concluded that the data do not support their conclusions. Cronbach's paper is rarely cited with reference to the Wallach and Kogan data and for all intents and purposes, to the best of our knowledge, it has been ignored but not rebutted.

Once again the field is divided. Some believe that the results support the independence of intelligence and creativity and acknowledge the importance of relaxed testing conditions. Critics do not regard the data as supporting the independence of intelligence and creativity and they do not see much significance in using game-like conditions in administering tests to children. Interestingly enough, the tests that were unique to both the Getzels and Jackson and the Wallach and Kogan studies have not often been used for the identification and selection of creative children. The Torrance Tests of Creative Thinking are the most popular in this regard.

Torrance

Paul Torrance is another of the pioneers in the study of the relationship between intelligence and creativity. Torrance, who has made many other contributions to our knowledge and understanding of the gifted and their education, followed Guilford's orientation and developed what are probably the most frequently used of the so-called creativity tests for children (Torrance, 1966). These tests measure four factors: fluency, flexibility, originality, and elaboration. There are verbal and figural tests. For each set of tests, single test scores are provided based on the sum of the subtests involved. Thus, for each subject there are both a verbal score and a figural score. The Torrance test battery has received a recommendation, with note of some cautions that need to be exercised in administration, by the conference group reported on by Richert et al. (1982). Torrance is working on the measurement of some additional variables, "resistance to premature closure, richness of imagery, fantasy, extending or breaking of boundaries, and unusual visual perspective" (Torrance & Hall, 1980); but these await further refinement before they are included in the published manual.

Among Torrance's contributions are his work on: the importance of the distinction between intelligence and creativity, the conditions under which the Getzels and Jackson results were obtained, the fairness of the test to minority groups, and the prediction of creativity. But, as with other studies in this area, they do not escape criticism or skepticism.

In 1962, when Torrance reported on some of his earlier research with children at all educational levels, he pointed out that if only tests of intelligence were used in their identification, more than 70% of them who scored in the upper 20% on creativity measures would have gone unrecognized.

Torrance has also reported on the important matter of the predictive value of his tests. In 1959, Torrance collected data on the IQ of 392 high school students, which included their scores on the variables in the Torrance Tests of Creative Thinking and peer judgments. In 1966, he collected criterion data for 46 subjects, and in 1971, he collected criterion data for 52 subjects. These subjects provided works which were rated for their creativity by advanced students in classes on creativity. These ratings constituted the criteria. In other words, data were gathered from high school students in 1959 and were compared, 7 and 12 years later, to judgments of the quality and quantity of works that these later students had done in areas ranging from poems and books published to research grants received and business enterprises initiated. On the basis of this study, Torrance (1977) reports that his tests either equal or are superior to intelligence tests in predicting creative achievements later in life. He also notes that their predictive validity gets better as the student-subject matures.

Another predictive study that is based on data collected over a longer time period is also reported by Torrance (1981). From 1958 to 1964, Torrance collected data from all the pupils in grades one through six in two elementary schools. In 1979 and 1980, he collected follow-up data from 211 of the subjects, 116 women and 95 men from 24 to 32 years of age. He collected self-report data on five indices of creative achievements which included such matters as the number of creative achievements in high school and the number of "creative life style" achievements that were not publicly recognized. The results of correlating test data with these criteria yielded statistically significant correlations in all instances. The correlations ranged from .38 to .58. A multiple correlation of .62 was obtained using a stepwise regression analysis.

While Torrance's work is quite impressive, it has also been subject to criticism. For example, while the tests of fluency, flexibility, and originality intercorrelate rather well, elaboration seems to be unrelated to the other factors.[18] This is rather important since the Torrance battery is unique in the creativity test area because it attempts to get data on elaboration which is part of Transformation in the Products category of Guilford's system. Guilford considers Transformation to be one of the more important factors insofar as creativity is concerned. In another study, Crockenberg[19] compared the extent to which the subtests on fluency intercorrelated with the extent to which IQ subtests intercorrelated. The former were fairly low compared to the latter, which raises some question as to how strong the factor is.

Some people have reanalyzed Torrance's data. In one instance, the data were reanalyzed in terms of aesthetic judgments. In this study,[20] it was found that the students whose work was rated highest were not the ones who were most fluent, flexible, original, or elaborative on the tests.

Although the data that Torrance presents on Black students is an agreeable finding to many people, one needs to bear in mind that although Black students excel on tests with figural content, tests with verbal content are usually the ones that predict academic achievement best. This is not meant as a criticism but as a caution for those who might be guided by the reported results and want to put them into practice.

Tannenbaum (1983) is dismayed at Torrance's report "that there is no evidence of heritability or of racial and socioeconomic bias in the abilities measured by his instruments. This has curious implications, for it amounts to saying that some of the most powerful elements of the genotype and the phenotype have no bearing on creativity. It is hard to imagine any test of creative performance, let alone potential, in which the results are entirely unaffected by hereditary factors or by forces in the environment that are so prominent in determining racial or socioeconomic status. What else is there to account for human variability?" (Tannenbaum, 1983, p. 277).

With regard to the predictive studies, Tannenbaum (1983, p. 275) asks for large sample replications with the subjects stratified by age, sex, and socioeconomic status. Studies should concern themselves with whether or not "there is a consistent, predictable relationship between scores on specific tests and specific criteria for creative accomplishment. In other words, can we generally expect that scores on verbal inventiveness and on flexibility in imagining consequences in improbable situations will forecast success in creative writing with correlations on the order of .6, as Torrance discovered for his 1960 sample? Equally important, how much of the variance in these relationships can be explained independently by measures of divergent thinking? What would happen to Torrance's .6 coefficients if assessments of convergent thinking, such as IQ, were partialed out?" (Tannenbaum, 1983, pp. 275-276).

To summarize, Torrance, a pioneer contributor to this field, has developed what is currently the most widely used creativity test battery, the Torrance Tests of Creative Thinking. Torrance believes that his measures of creativity are independent of intelligence, fair to minority groups, and predictive of students' future accomplishments. Others criticize the level of the correlations between creativity and intelligence and between subgroups, and they are skeptical that the tests are fair to Blacks. There is also a call for more systematic and better controlled predictive studies. Despite these reservations, the conference reported on by Richert et al. (1982) gave the Torrance tests a cautious recommendation. Work on the use and predictive value of the tests has provided evidence which some regard as positive. Others await more data before making a final commitment. With this overview of Torrance's work, the presentation of the pioneering studies of the intelligence/creativity controversy and the development of the so-called creativity tests is concluded.

Summary

Creativity tests have their protagonists as well as their critics. Protagonists insist that their tests measure creativity independently of intelligence; they define creativity as a factor sufficiently different from intelligence that a separate test battery is needed to measure it. They believe that if the identification and selection of creative students for special educational programs were based solely on the use of intelligence tests, a large number of creative students would be rejected. The protagonists continue to attempt to add new variables to both their test batteries and to their methods of collecting validation data. They are also engaged in longitudinal studies oriented to investigating the development and contributions of their creative subjects over long periods of time.

Creativity tests have also had their critics. Tannenbaum (1983) surveyed the creativity/intelligence literature and pointed out that the correlations between creativity tests and intelligence tests vary widely. He also felt that it is not certain that "divergent thinking tests can help us to discern talent that other instruments would overlook." Tannenbaum's criticism of the divergent thinking tests of creativity has been bolstered by a review of the use of these tests with creative adults. Generally speaking, the divergent thinking tests have been found to be wanting. Barron[21] reported a positive relationship between some measures of divergent thinking and a criterion of originality in a study of Air Force officers. But other studies with other kinds of subjects did not report such positive results. Divergent thinking tests did not correlate well with creativity criteria in studies of artists,[22] architects (MacKinnon, 1961), or research scientists.[23]

Although Guilford may well have been pleased with the effects on creativity of his work on the structure of intellect, his writings also indicate concern with the fact that creativity tests put undue emphasis on divergent thinking. Guilford (1975) pointed out that two of his product abilities, Transformation and Implication, respectively, "change in meaning and ... interpretation" and "anticipation and predictions," were more important than divergent thinking abilities. The field, however, has concentrated much more on divergent thinking abilities than on the other abilities. Torrance's test battery does include some measure of transformation ability as it is represented by a measure of elaboration. But, as reported above,[18] this measure is not as strongly related statistically to the other measures in the test battery. It seems, therefore, that for more complete measures of creativity, more reliable and valid measures of transformation and implication are still required.

It has been suggested that while it may be wrong to call the current test batteries, which are so heavily loaded with tests of divergent thinking, tests of creativity, there is nothing wrong, and possibly something worthwhile, in calling the tests by their designated names--tests of divergent thinking, tests of fluency, tests of ideational productivity, etc.[19] These tests should be studied in relation to other tests and criteria to determine what their contributions could be to the identification and selection of gifted, talented, and creative children. The test measures might also be studied to determine what they reflect about a student's cognitive style in order to learn how it, too, might be related to a student's giftedness, talent, or creativity.

Other criticisms of creativity tests include the following points. It has been asserted that the tests contain only cognitive material. Others state that studies of the tests' predictive value should have a better balance of diverse groupings of subjects than is now the case. Another criticism is that where the tests are correlated against criteria, the criteria should include not only the classroom type contributions that characterize so many studies today, but they should also, eventually, include data on how well the tests predict future socially significant creative contributions. There has also been criticism of the intent to predict a child's creativity from cognitive tests alone. Creativity, it is argued, is more than cognitive. If one is to be manifestly creative and make a significant contribution to society, one needs to possess appropriate motivational, personal, and social characteristics in addition to appropriate cognitive characteristics.

Readers confronted with the need for creativity tests for identification and selection purposes will want to evaluate the material
presented here and the material covered in the test manuals. Broad
overviews of the field are not terribly sanguine about the available
tests. Petrosko[24] analyzed more than 100 creativity tests for elementary school children using more than 36 criteria to evaluate the
educational and psychometric value of the tests. He found that there
was a real lack of information on their reliability and validity. He
also thought that it would be difficult to meet psychometric standards
in the development of creativity tests.

The more recent conference reported on by Richert et al. (1982)
claimed that measures of creativity might be useful indicators in the
identification and selection of creative students if they were used
as part of a total assessment and identification process. The conference also made some carefully qualified recommendations; the reader
should read what Richert et al. (1982) have to say before making a
decision. The recommended tests and other instruments were: Torrance
Tests of Creative Thinking, the subtests of the Structure of the Intellect Learning Ability Test, Guilford's Creativity Tests for
Children, the Khatena-Torrance Creative Prescription Inventory, the
Renzulli-Hartman Scales for Rating the Behavioral Characteristics of
Superior Students, the Biographical Inventory, the Preschool Talent
Checklists, and the Test for Creative Potential. In this list of
recommendations, readers should note that there are tests and instruments other than those discussed in this text. Though the so-called
creativity tests have dominated the field, people concerned with the
identification and selection of creative students should give serious
thought to these other instruments and methods.

It is apparent that the ambiguity regarding creativity-testing
instruments is a reflection of the ambiguity and difficulties that
exist on the theoretical level. For evidence on this score we turn
once again to the Richert et al. (1982) report. According to this
report, the conferees called attention to the following points.
There is (1) a need for a more precise definition of creativity in
different areas. (2) There are differences in the field concerning
concepts of creativity, specifically, "which abilities are involved,
how they are related to other intellectual abilities and personality
traits, how these should be measured and whether they predict adult
creativity." (3) Some participants questioned whether creativity
could be measured by a single instrument. There was also a feeling
in the group that the accurate prediction of adult creativity was yet
to be demonstrated but that Torrance's studies were promising in this
regard. (4) There were some who supported the idea, set forth in the
Marland Report, that creativity is a separate category of giftedness.
Others felt, however, that creativity, as manifest in specific content
areas, is also a manifestation of giftedness.

CONCLUSIONS

To identify and select the intellectually gifted child, well-
constructed individual and group intelligence tests are used. However,
studies show that if children are selected using intelligence tests
alone, children with different talents and creativity may be overlooked.
Consequently, other tests, questionnaires, and rating scales are also
used, either in conjunction with intelligence tests or separately. It

has also been suggested that all children be allowed to participate in educational programs for the gifted so that use can be made of the child's behavior in these programs as a means of identification and selection.

Where there is a desire to identify and select academically gifted students, use is made of valid and reliable achievement tests. Students who score two grades or more above their current grade level are usually identified as academically gifted. They may be admitted to appropriate educational programs, either on the basis of the achievement test alone or the achievement test plus high scores on intelligence tests. No tests are used systematically for the visual and performing arts or for identifying and selecting students with high psychosocial and leadership skills. In these instances, evaluation may be based on a student's portfolio or on rating scales which are devised by observers of the student's behavior.

A great deal of work has gone into the attempt to settle the intelligence/creativity controversy and into the development of creativity tests. There are those who strongly favor these tests though most researchers acknowledge that more work is necessary for their further development. Others are quite critical of the tests. An invaluable aid in deciding which creativity test, questionnaire, or rating scale to use is the report by Richert et al. (1982). This report is useful in the identification and selection of gifted and talented as well as creative children.

Part 2
EDUCATION AND TRAINING

Behavior is a function of the transactional relationships between an individual and his or her environment. Consequently, the students identified, assessed, and selected according to procedures discussed in the previous section have to be provided with the proper educational environment if their gifts, talents, and creativity are to be properly nurtured and if they are to fulfill their potentialities. Not all people agree with this point of view. They argue that gifted children can "take care of themselves" and if they "really have it" they will come through. They also argue that providing special education programs for the gifted, talented, and creative smacks of elitism or deprives the retarded of their due. The counter-argument notes the enormous loss that society endures if it does not cultivate the resources it possesses in its gifted, talented, and creative young people Without the proper educational environments these children wither on the vine. Moreover, the elitism issue can be seen as a red herring, for the "equal treatment of unequals is unequal" (Brandwein, 1981a). The amount of educational opportunities provided for the gifted, talented, and creative waxes and wanes. Its status usually depends on how well those who favor it are able to marshal their forces in the political arena.

In the current state of the art, there is a veritable cornucopia of riches available for the education, training, and stimulation of the gifted, talented, and creative young people in our society. The Marland Report (1972) was an important catalyst in this regard. It

alerted society to the losses it would suffer and the problems that
the gifted suffered when they were not provided with appropriate educational environments. The educational community, acutely aware of
the problems, responded with a bonanza of alternatives (not all of
which were specifically designed for the gifted but which could contribute to their education nevertheless). Numerous programs were
developed with varied content, procedures, and techniques. There were
countless opportunities to fulfill diverse standards, requirements,
and student needs. They are inherently valuable but their ultimate
effectiveness depends on how well they are backed up by the values
and funds of their communities and local, state, and federal government agencies.

There are programs which favor acceleration and others which favor
enrichment. Both are designed to give the gifted, talented, and
creative student more--either in quantity, depth, or quality. Since
acceleration provides more by moving the student ahead (in terms of
grade) faster than other students, it can be referred to as vertical
enrichment. If one bears this in mind, it facilitates communication
since all educational programs can then be described as enrichment
programs.

It should be apparent at the outset that there is no single
educational program for the gifted, talented, or creative. There
are models (Maker, 1982b) or paradigms (Tannenbaum, 1983) which are to
be adapted to the student's individual needs and requirements. Two
of the paradigms have been specifically designed for gifted students.
One was designed by Renzulli (1981, and Renzulli et al., 1982) and the
other by Tannenbaum (1983). There are other educational programs
based on the works of a variety of people including: Bloom and Krath-
wohl, Bruner, Guilford, Kohlberg, Parnes, Taba, Taylor, Treffinger,
and Williams. All of them have been reviewed by Maker (1982a) and
Tannenbaum (1983). Approaches that select and combine features of
these different programs also have been presented (Maker, 1982b, for
example).

The aforementioned programs are visible when they are adopted.
But there is another choice for those who believe that students who
have not necessarily been identified as gifted, talented, or creative
can also profit from curricular programs for the gifted. Such a program, which blends with the educational programs already existent and
thus has the added advantage of not being as visible, is also presented
(Treffinger, 1981).

For students who do not get the proper education or enough stimulation during regular school hours there are after-school programs,
Saturday programs, and summer programs. To further motivate children
and capture their imaginations there are problem-solving competitions
and an Olympics of the Mind which is, in a sense, modeled after the
sports olympics.

Educational programs of the type to be described cannot be effective without the implicit or explicit support of the community, including school boards and local, state, and government agencies. This
we can only mention in our survey, as a complete discussion would take
us far beyond our purposes. There is another group, which includes
schools, principals, etc., that deserves more discussion because of
the critical role it plays in the education of the gifted. Unfortunately, this group is so critical that it does not get much attention in
this regard. Teachers, on the other hand, have come in for more

attention. One is more concerned with their motivations and attitudes to the different kinds of students to whom they are exposed. Here, use is being made of some of the basic research in social psychology to help teachers understand their "culturally disadvantaged" (really economically poor) students (Sisk, 1981) and their female students who are afraid of success. Teachers' roles are currently undergoing change. The knowledge explosion is such that the number of facts is overwhelming, and, consequently, it is deemed important to provide the students with strategies rather than facts. The teacher is no longer limited to imparting knowledge but is also a facilitator. In this regard, attention must also be paid to the computer. The computer has only just made its debut on the contemporary scene and its effects are likely to be far-reaching. Whether it will enhance the development of the gifted, talented, and creative student or not is a matter to be decided in the future.

In the current state of the art increasing attention is being paid to the role of parents and relationships between the child and his or her parents. The research in this area is not as widespread or as intense as it should be. Parents are seen as critical and political advocates for gifted education; ways to stimulate their interest and motivation are discussed.

On the contemporary scene, there is increasing awareness of and communication with programs in other countries, especially as a result of the activity and reports of international organizations.

Things do not always go as one would expect with some students; consequently, there are opportunities for mid-course corrections through student counseling. In the current state of the art, discussions are devoted to the specific problems of gifted, talented, and creative students and their parents. For the mid-course corrections necessary for educational programs, formative evaluation procedures have been developed. In addition, the importance of summative evaluation at the end of a period during which a program has been used has been acknowledged.

This, in broad strokes, characterizes the current state of the art insofar as education and training are concerned. There are at least two final cautionary points to keep in mind. The educational programs which are available are focused on the needs and requirements of the students whose gifts, talents, and creativity they want to nurture and develop. Yet, the question remains as to whether educators and teachers really know enough about their students to provide them with the educational environments they need and the educational stimulation that suits them best. It seems, from what we have learned about identification and selection, that many persons use procedures that are limited to measuring cognitive characteristics such as fluency, flexibility, originality, and elaboration. However, school administrators and teachers also need to know their students' learning styles and motivational and personality characteristics. At present, programs are constructed so that one need not worry about this; if one provides enrichment and lets the child select his or her own diet of courses under the guidance of facilitators, the results are assumed to be positive. But, at this time, and this is the second caution, there is no research concerning the benefits of this procedure. The field is caught up in the process of developing new, "better," and "richer" opportunities. Eventually, the time will be ripe for a serious evaluation.

A Bit of History

Passow, a profound thinker and an important contributor to the field, provides some interesting background history. Passow (1979) quotes from the Twenty-third Yearbook of the National Society for the Study of Education (1924) and we cite the quotation.

> It is quite evident that the most unique aspects of the gifted child problem do not lie in the field of formal organization of the school. Grade skipping, segregation, grouping within a class, sectioning according to ability within a grade are simple enough to manage. There is increasing agreement on the desirability of enriching the experience, rather than speeding the rate of the capable children through the all-too-meager offerings of the school years. The biggest question and the most difficult of solution is undoubtedly recognized as this: "How shall their superior powers be challenged, and how shall curriculum and schoolroom procedure be modified to meet more fully the rightful demands of superior endowments?" (pp. 63-64)

Thus, it was known, certainly as far back as 1924, what needed to be done. It was not done for many reasons; one of them is acknowledged by the Committee for the Yearbook by Passow who quotes the Committee as saying that "it was certainly a fact that there is much administrative timidity before the problem of organizing and conditioning practice to meet the newly conceived needs of superior children" (p. 49). Programs then, as now, that encounter administrative timidity are unlikely to see the light of day.

In 1958, when Passow surveyed the various approaches to gifted education, he wrote (Passow, 1979, pp. 97-98):

> I reviewed various approaches to providing for gifted students. Administrative adaptations, including enrichment in the regular classroom, special groupings, and various kinds of acceleration, were discussed in terms of their potential for helping gifted children attain desired goals. After noting that particular modification seemed to be of value for specific kinds of achievement, I concluded that "no single administrative plan has provided a 'package formula' for all schools to use with equal effectiveness for the variety of talents among its students." (p. 201)

Today, as then, there is no single package though there are many options and alternatives available for differentiated curricula (Gallagher, 1981, and Passow, 1982) and individual educational programs (Butterfield et al., 1979). It is again impossible to cover all that is available; therefore, what follows focuses on major or representative programs.

Acceleration

According to the advocates of acceleration, a gifted, talented, or creative student may be so advanced in a particular area that he or she will be bored and learn very little if he or she is kept in grade according to age. Consequently, it is necessary to accelerate

the child. The child is placed in an advanced grade which is considered commensurate with its knowledge and ability so that it can be
appropriately challenged. The old-fashioned term for acceleration
was "skipping" and the newer word is "vertical enrichment."

There are various concerns about the use of vertical enrichment/
acceleration. Some revolve around the subject matter and some revolve
around what such programs do to children who are chronologically
younger than their classmates. Specifically, the concern is that they
will lose out on their social skills. This, plus the concern about
too much homework and pressure, which can result in superficial
learning, have been among the factors that have led some to be critical of the acceleration approach.

On the positive side, the favorable arguments have included the
suggestion that by grouping gifted children with their peers they are
allowed to proceed at their own level and to have an enriched experience. This makes teaching easier, and it helps the non-gifted
for they are not swamped by their gifted peers. For further argument
for and against acceleration, the reader is referred to Passow (1958),
Fox (1979), and Tannenbaum (1983) and for a related approach to
ability grouping, to Findley and Bryan.[25]

The current protagonist of the acceleration approach is Stanley
(1977, 1979) whose orientation is reflected in the program he directs
for the Study of Mathematically Precocious Youth (SMPY) at Johns
Hopkins University. The program has been extended into the verbal
area as well. Students are selected on the basis of very careful and
systematic testing of their abilities (verbal or mathematical), starting with the Scholastic Aptitude Test (SAT) and continuing through
more difficult procedures that are appropriately selected. They are
then accepted for appropriately designed advanced educational programs.

Some of the evaluations of the program have yielded positive results. Stanley (1976) reports better than expected advancement in
mathematics, positive feelings of self-regard, more interest in
hobbies, less boredom, and other positive personality developments.
Cohen[26] also reports positive developments, with the boys showing advances in mathematical knowledge and social skills and the girls
giving more attention to peer relationships than to their academic
subjects.

This program will certainly bear watching to see if the students
in the program do indeed contribute to the field of mathematics in
the future or excel in it and related fields. We have expressed
concern (cf. p. xxvi) about the possibility that starting with the SAT
will exclude "creative personalities" and encourage an undue emphasis
on tests in a society that is already so overwhelmed by the importance
of tests for future educational opportunities that it is willing to
pay for tutoring. One hopes that future studies will follow up on
"good bets" that did not get selected for the program.

Enrichment

SPECIALLY DESIGNED

Renzulli

One of the best known and most widely used models of the enrichment approach is that developed by Renzulli (1977). Like other similar
programs, it provides the student with more and richer experiences at
his or her level than is available in a traditional program. Renzulli
believes that the opportunity to enter enriched programs has to be
restricted to superior students. He looks for three characteristics:
above-average intelligence, above-average creativity, and task commitment. Children then are exposed to an Enrichment Triad composed of
three types of activities: Type 1, general exploratory activities,
Type II, group training activities, and Type III, individual and small-
group investigation of real problems. The model is based on an understanding of what goes on in the creative contributions made by adults.
Teachers, prepared properly with numerous techniques and procedures
supplied by Renzulli, facilitate the student's progress through the
various activities. The student attends when he or she is ready with
something to work on and leaves when he or she is finished. Thus the
students go through a "revolving door" (Renzulli et al., 1981). The
emphasis is on accommodating the educational program to the child's
needs. The child designs the program with the help and guidance of
the teacher and takes responsibility for the directions and outcome
of the program. Projects can be part of the general classroom activity or some separate facility; there is great freedom in this regard.

Maker (1982b) points out that, while this approach is based on
much research about effective teaching and programs, the Enrichment
Triad model itself, as a total package, has not yet been evaluated.
Parts of it have been examined with positive results (Renzulli and
Gable),[27] but there are unanswered questions according to Maker
(p. 231). For example, "Do the parts fit well together? Does it
work with young children? What is the best administrative structure
to facilitate its success? Are there adequate measures of task commitment at early ages? Do those who show task commitment in school turn
out to be task-committed adults? Do those who do not show task
commitment in school turn out to be task-committed adults?" For Maker,
the most important advantage of the Renzulli program is that it was
designed specifically for gifted children and based on research on
gifted children. It is also an advantage that this model takes into
account the regular curriculum that is in use.

Maker has concerns about a number of disadvantages. One disad-
vantage is the lack of research to evaluate the approach. Consequently,
there is a related concern. Maker writes, "Since it is the only
framework designed specifically for use with gifted students, educators have jumped on the bandwagon without seriously considering the
philosophical approach necessary for its implementation. Everyone
has adopted the framework and incorporated existing curricula into it.
Educators have made a few changes to make it all fit together, but
they have not made the philosophical and programmatic commitments
that will make it work. The philosophy is apparently hidden to some,
but is clear to others" (p. 232). Other potential disadvantages are

that the three-ring model used to select children is based on research with adults and it is not known how effective the approach is
in selecting children and that selecting students for task commitment i
difficult. In addition, the model is deceptively simple and teachers
are not necessarily sufficiently or properly trained to carry out
their responsibilities.

Tannenbaum (1983, p. 424) sees positive and negative effects of
the Renzulli program. He writes:

> The advantages are that moving gifted children into time-limited
> projects of their own choosing takes care of their individual
> enthusiasm, yet reduces the possible adverse effects of sepa-
> rating them from peers and conventional school activities.
> However, there is always the danger of regarding special
> projects as "icing on the cake," rather than as part of the
> basic meal for those capable of digesting it. Also, if the
> "revolving door" method is poorly administered, it will serve
> only the self-starting, independent-minded children who pursue
> their interests doggedly, while neglecting those who rely on
> external stimulation.

While Renzulli's approach is the best known and most popular at the
present time, there are other approaches which are more recent and
still others which contain ideas for new combinations. These shall
be considered shortly.

Treffinger

Treffinger's approach is the self-directed learning experience in
which students benefit from teachers' experience and guidance which,
in turn, helps them develop into persons who are capable of directing
their own activities, managing their own time, and taking responsibility for themselves. Thus, the teacher moves from providing options, to
being a resource person, and then on to the role of facilitator. The
student, on the other hand, moves from passive recipient who has to
select from the presented options, to diagnostician, to director of
learning, and on to self-evaluator. It is apparent that Treffinger's
approach is desirable in the development of positive characteristics.
It is also valuable for all students, whether they are in gifted programs or not.

Treffinger believes that it is possible and worthwhile to blend
gifted and regular programming. He does not think that these programs
have to be made visible, but, rather, that they should be subtly inter-
woven with regular programs (Treffinger, 1982). He has developed
indices for knowing when such programming is successful (Treffinger,
1983).

Aside from one study by Barton (1976), which has reported positive
results using Treffinger's approach, Maker does not report having
found more which would be desirable. Nevertheless, she reports
(Maker, 1982b, p. 368) that the approach is practical, it can help
other approaches become more successful, it is based on a knowledge
of students' characteristics, and it builds on student strengths.

As to its disadvantages, Maker (1982b, p. 369) believes that the
approach may not be able to stand alone. Students may not want to be
self-directed over the long run and it may take a particular teacher
to be able to fulfill the requirements of the teaching role. Parents

may also want teachers to direct their children's learning rather than
to just provide them with the freedom to direct their own learning.

Tannenbaum

The Enrichment Matrix recommended by Tannenbaum (1983) is designed
to cope with one of the concerns just mentioned. Tannenbaum is concerned that when the teacher becomes facilitator and oriented to
helping the student sharpen his or her abilities, the teacher gives
a secondary role to the matter of dispensing knowledge to the student.
He writes:

> An alternative approach would be to establish a greater balance
> between the two roles, with the understanding that *what* to learn
> has to be given as much attention as *how* to learn. The proposed
> enrichment matrix is an attempt to bring about such a balance
> by amalgamating elements of existing paradigms and adding com-
> ponents that are deemed essential to differentiated programs
> for the gifted. (p. 422)

To achieve his goal, he recommends a common core that all students
would have to take, whether gifted (those who frequently miss out on
some basic training) or non-gifted. It would consist of "skills,
knowledge, insights, and opportunities for creative initiative that
all students need in order to appreciate and function well in the
world they inhabit" (p. 424). Beyond the common core, which is represented figurally as the circle in the Japanese flag, there is an area
of enrichment experience. Students can enter this on a trial basis
and stay in it if they can and prefer to do so. Thus, for the gifted
there would be a content area of basic work and the conventional disciplines like language arts, mathematics, social studies, and the
performing arts. But there would also be at least one supplementary
area that is not included in the precollege curriculum. This could
be cultural anthropology, geopolitics, psychology, etc. There would
also be interdisciplinary area choices.

To visualize what Tannenbaum has in mind, these content areas and
disciplines can be placed as the rows on a chart; the columns constitute what he calls content adjustment which involves the presentation
of the content to the student. This may involve "telescoping the
common core," "expansion of basic skills," etc. There are, then, two
more columns. One of these is for cognitive processes and refers to
the need to develop high-level cognitive processes in the student as
he/she relates to each of the content areas. The last column, Social
and Affective Consequences, relates to the consequences of being a
high-level producer. The section in which this last item is discussed
is appropriately titled Enrichment with a Conscience. Though it is
still too early for any evaluations of Tannenbaum's program to have
appeared, it bears watching.

NON-SPECIFIC MODELS FOR THE GIFTED

While the models we have just discussed are designed specially for
the gifted or with the gifted primarily in mind, there are other educational models that have appeared in the literature which have much
to offer and from which teachers can select to develop differentiated
and individualized programs for their students. Maker (1982b) has an

excellent review of a number of these programs (as well as of others previously mentioned) and points out various ways in which they might be used with the gifted. For example, she cites Bloom's and Krath-wohl's taxonomies as two good sources for variables in the evaluation of higher and lower thinking processes and affective processes in gifted programs. She calls attention to the importance of Bruner's emphasis on the student as an inquirer and cites Guilford's work (and its development by Meeker) for its potential value as diagnostic aids in determining the strengths and weaknesses of a gifted child that can be attended to in educational programs. Maker's work also con-tains a discussion of programs that focus their attention on the im-portance of ethical behavior and moral development in students' edu-cation. Hilda Taba's work on Strategies and their potential usefulness for gifted students are also discussed, as is Calvin Taylor's em-phasis on the idea that students have more talent than they can use and Frank Williams's approach which calls attention to the point that optimum learning is an outcome of the pupil's characteristics, the nature of the curriculum, and the characteristics of the teacher.

Maker

There is much to pick and choose from on the current scene in creating the appropriate curricular program to meet the needs of the pupil, the requirements of the school, and the abilities of the teacher. The diversity can be overwhelming. Help can be obtained in getting through the different programs by consulting two of Maker's (1982a and b) books. A thorough analysis of 11 programs is presented by Maker (1982b) which is based on variables discussed in (1982a). Briefly, the variables are (Maker, 1982b, p. 414): "(a) involvement of the key individuals who assess the situation in assisting in de-velopment of goals and in the program development; (b) development of a definition of giftedness; (c) assessment of the needs of the stu-dents; (d) development of a philosophy; (e) development of program goals; (f) choice of teaching-learning models; (g) development of objectives and strategies; (h) development of evaluation procedures; and (i) development of a plan for implementing the curriculum." These variables can be very important in developing a curriculum to meet one's own situation and Maker's books can be of valuable aid.

In closing this section on programs, it seems appropriate as a fitting summary to quote the last paragraph of Maker's second book (Maker, 1982b), in which she says:

> In this volume a wide range of teaching-learning models have been presented that can be helpful in developing a compre-hensive curriculum for gifted students. All were designed for different purposes and have different strengths and weaknesses when considered as comprehensive approaches. All also have different advantages and disadvantages in a practical sense. Few have been validated through research as effective programs, and even fewer as effective models for use with the gifted. No comparative research indicates which models may be more appropriate than others, but many practitioners are sold on one or more of the approaches. In this collection, I hope that all of you will find *at least one* that works for you and your children! (p. 452)

MORE SOURCES AND RESOURCES

There are countless other sources and resources that school administrators, teachers, parents, and other interested persons may
wish to consult to nurture, educate, and train gifted, talented, and
creative students. It is absolutely impossible to cover all of them.
We shall cover a good number of them in the text at somewhat greater
length, but in this brief overview, we mention a few just to indicate
the range, variety, and richness of the materials and sources available. These are not limited to what students can experience only
within school buildings during regular school hours.

Curricular Planning

For more information on curricular planning and teaching strategies, the reader may wish to consult the work of Sato et al.,
*Developing a Written Plan for the Education of Gifted and Talented
Students*.[28] Sandra Kaplan has provided much information on
curricula and teaching aids; for programs one may wish to consult
her *Providing Programs for the Gifted and Talented: A Handbook*
(Kaplan[29]) and for insights and ideas, there is Gallagher's
(1985) *Teaching the Gifted Child*.

Procedures for Stimulating Creativity

There are a variety of programs and techniques that readers may
wish to consult and to use. They can be used as training programs or
as ideas for training programs. Parnes and his co-workers have developed a program called Creative Problem Solving (Parnes et al.,
1977); numerous works based on this approach have been developed for
use at all grade levels. A recent development on this topic is a
work by Isaksen and Treffinger.[30] Synectics is an approach in which
the metaphor plays a critical function in the creative process as
conceived by Gordon (1961). Various adaptations of the basic orientation have appeared in publications by Gordon and Poze (1980) and in
Synectics Educational Ststems (SES Synectics, Inc., 1971). DeBono
has extended his work on lateral thinking (1967, 1970) with other
books like *PO: Beyond Yes or No* (DeBono, 1972) and *Teaching Thinking*
(DeBono, 1978). There is another integrated program for creative
thinking and creative problem solving which has tapes, exercises, and
the like. It is the Purdue Creativity Training Program which has
been described by Feldhusen and his associates.[31]

For source books on the above one should consult: Noller, Parnes,
and Biondi's (1976) *Creative Actionbook* and Parnes, Noller, and Biondi's
(1977) *Guide to Creative Action*. There is also a work which brings
these first two as up to date as 1982 by Treffinger (1983); this is
Appendix A of Tannenbaum's (1983) book. Treffinger's work is titled
*Methods, Techniques and Educational Programs for Stimulating Crea-
tivity: 1982 Revision*. For additional techniques there is the work
by VanGundy (1982). For a presentation of individual and group procedures used primarily at the adult level, which contains research
data on the assumptions as well as the evaluations of the various
procedures, readers may wish to read Stein's (1974, 1975) two-volume
work, *Stimulating Creativity*.

Saturday and Summer Programs

To augment the opportunities available for gifted education, one can also take advantage of Saturday programs.[32] For a description of a summer program there is the work at the University of Denver.[33]

National Competitions

In the current state of the art, there is not only much that can be done for educating and stimulating the gifted, talented, and creative child at the local level, there is also planned activity at the national level. One of these is the Future Problem-Solving Program (Torrance, 1978, and Torrance et al., 1978). Another of these is the Olympics of the Mind in which students are presented with realistic problems which are to be solved and presented in competition; the work is under the direction of Creative Competitions.

Foreign Efforts

Much work is going on in England, Russia, Europe, Israel, Japan, and various other countries around the world. Some of these programs are designed to help those who have been called disadvantaged, but other programs have been designed to stimulate the gifted, talented, and creative children in those countries. Much is to be learned from these various procedures and programs. Fortunately, we have been able to draw on the published proceedings of international meetings for citations in the text.

Teachers

Up to this point, attention has been focused on the student and the programs, with their related sources and strategies. All of these have to be eventually delivered by the teacher. The teacher is such a critical factor in the total picture that one can only wonder why there is not more definition of the teacher's professional status. There are those who insist that everyone can teach and that everyone can teach the gifted. Obviously, there are strong adherents to each point of view and one hopes that progress will be made in this area in the future.

There are studies[34] which have concerned themselves with teacher effectiveness, pointing to their critical role. Teachers who want to learn more about their own teaching styles and find diagnostic information might find it helpful to consult Mosston's paper[35] and the paper by Treffinger and Barton.[36]

Knowledge of one's own teaching style can be worthwhile in its own right but it has increased value if it is considered in conjunction with the learning styles of one's students. In this regard it may be worth one's while to consult various methods and techniques for gathering the necessary information. Helpful sources are: Dunn and Dunn[37] and Gregoric.[38]

Teachers can also profit from work going on in academic areas where the work is related to the interactions, and hence the effectiveness, of teacher and pupil. For example, reports concerning the effects of teachers' attitudes (Purkey, 1978; Perrone and Male, 1981) can alert the teacher to the prejudices which can stymie the development of students. Concepts like the fear of success can improve our

understanding of why girls (and even boys) may be afraid to do well
in school. More and more knowledge is also becoming available on the
backgrounds and characteristics of minority, disadvantaged, or culturally deprived students (Passow, 1972, 1975; Sisk, 1981). The
overt manifestations of the minority child's behavior may not mean
the same things in the child's culture as they do in the white culture.
For example, the white, middle class teacher who expects the disciplined child to look him or her in the eye may be surprised when con-
trite children from a Spanish culture show their shame and contrition
by looking at their feet.

Of course, the teacher will find that he or she exists as part of
a total system. Try as he or she might to be a creative teacher, who
has responsibility for gifted, talented, and creative children, these
efforts will prove most effective only if they occur in a context
where the school administration and the community share and are
supportive of the same values.

Counseling and Guidance

No matter how good the intentions and efforts of everyone involved, and no matter how finely one tries to tune the relationships
between students and programs, unforeseen problems and difficulties
may arise. These have to be dealt with; they require mid-course help
and mid-course correction.

Gifted students are quite diverse and frequently require individual attention through counseling and guidance. "One of the
main purposes of counseling and guidance in schools is to discover
unique patterns of individual characteristics--interests, aptitudes,
abilities, values, motives--and to assist the individual to determine
the meaning of these characteristics in relation to educational,
career, and life-style opportunities. A corollary purpose is to
assist the teaching staff in utilizing individual characteristics
in generating appropriate developmental experiences" (Sanborn, 1979,
p. 425). With this statement of overall purpose in mind, there is
much to be gained from reading about counseling and guidance in the
Sanborn (1979) article just cited, a contribution to the Seventy-
eighth Yearbook, the edited work by Colangelo and Zaffrann (1979),
and to the special issue of the *Roeper Review* devoted entirely to
"Counseling Gifted Persons: A Lifelong Concern."[39]

Parents

Parents are most critical to the nurturing and development of
gifted, talented, and creative children. Unless parents work in
concert with teachers and the schools, there is much that is lost.
But when a real partnership develops, as reflected in the study by
Bloom and Sosniak (1981) of accomplished pianists, swimmers, and
mathematicians, there is much to be gained. Colangelo and Dettman
(1983) believe that there is still insufficient research on parents
and their roles in this area.

Among studies that have been done, we find, in addition to such
classics as Roe (1952, 1958), Goertzel and Goertzel (1962), and other

omnibus studies in which parent characteristics were included, studies of underachievement (summarized by Tannenbaum, 1983) in which patterns are suggested as the factors which yield apparently contradictory results in studies. There are also studies of the relationship between parents and children which show little warmth in the lives of creative subjects (Siegelman).[40] There is work on the similarity or differences between creative test patterns of children and their parents (Wallinga and Sedahlia, 1979) in which children's scores on some of the Torrance Tests correlated with some of the fathers' scores on the same tests but not with the mothers'.

There is also information available on how parents may help to organize themselves as advocates (Boehelt, 1979; Buisman, 1979; Delt and Martinson, 1977; and Nathan, 1979). There is material that provides parents with advice and information (e.g., Ebeling, 1979 and Sieghart, 1981). A good survey is provided by *Parents of the Gifted and Talented Child* by Callahan (1982). Parents who want information on other sources may want to consult books like Freeman (1981) and Freeman and Stuart (1979) and even find suggestions on how to read aloud to their children (Trelease, 1982).

Finally, parents today are being bombarded with information about computers. They are becoming ubiquitous on the educational scene and parents often wonder what to do about purchasing one for their daughter or son. There is information available about this from industry sources (e.g., Electronic Industries Association, 1983) and consumer organizations (*Consumer Reports*, 1983a and 1983b).

Additional Information

Libraries are excellent sources for tracing and developing bibliographies on various topics of interest. Librarians like Stievater (1980) have provided suggestions for journals, books devoted to test reviews, and lists of publishers that professionals in the field, parents, and students may wish to consult. There are newsletters that are available for the rapid dissemination of information as well as agencies at the local, national, and international levels that one may wish to join.

Evaluation

It goes without saying that all of the above programs are relatively new. It is most important that they be evaluated so that we can learn how truly effective each of them is for the individual child who is trained and educated under various circumstances. Evaluations can take place during the course of a program and allowances can be made for mid-course corrections. Evaluations can also be made at the end of a period of time. Whatever the case, it is important to learn about the educational effects and achievements in the various areas of an individual student's life. It is also important to have information on the cost effectiveness of a program. Local, state, and federal agencies that are responsible for funding are often concerned with the "bottom (financial) line." It is best if evaluators provide such information rather than leave the determination to those who read

the reports. Many of the major programs considered above (e.g., Renzulli, 1977) provide for evaluation. There are other places, like the
Northwest Regional Laboratory (Smith, 1981 and 1982), who provide a
variety of evaluation procedures that can be utilized or adapted
(through comparison with other areas) to individual needs.

SUMMARY

There are currently numerous curricular programs that educators
can select from to further the education and training of gifted,
talented, and creative children. For regular school programs, curricula are oriented around acceleration or enrichment. There are also
after-school programs, Saturday programs, and summer programs as well
as national competitions. Students not only compete in these competitions but they receive special training for them.

Many resources are available to teachers to help them plan curricula, learn about creativity stimulating procedures, and learn about
programs in foreign countries. There are numerous evaluation procedures
to learn about the effectiveness of educational programs which can be
used during a school year. One hopes that in due time, more and more
evaluations will be carried out so that we may learn not only how effective the programs are in and of themselves, but also, which teachers
are best with which programs and with which students. Until such
specific information is available, there is much work to be done concerning teacher effectiveness and the importance of different teaching
styles. To further help the gifted, talented, and creative student,
there are counseling and guidance programs to deal with both the problems that are unique to them and those which affect all children.

The effectiveness of educating the gifted, talented, and creative
is not only dependent on teaching programs, teachers, and students,
but also on parents. There are many resources and advocacy groups
that parents have started to make their wishes and needs known and to
increase their effectiveness. For all persons involved in the identification, selection, education, research, and training of gifted,
talented, and creative students, there are numerous organizations,
agencies, and publications which can be of much help.

Part 3
RESEARCH

The first section of this survey focused on the identification and
selection of gifted, talented, and creative students for special educational programs. The second part focused on the programs themselves
and discussed the various kinds of training, education, nurture, and
guidance that is available to the children so that they can make the
most of their potentialities and abilities. We turn now to a charac-
terization of the research that typifies the current state of the art
which is oriented to providing a better understanding of the gifted,
talented, and creative student. Our thoughts are discussed best in
terms of three dichotomies: empirical/theoretical; historical/ahistorical;
and cognitive/non-cognitive, with two specific content areas: the peren-
nial--nature/nurture--and a more recent area of interest--split brain
research.

Empirical/Theoretical

In the current state of the art, a large body of important work falls into a category that is affected by an orientation called "dustbowl empiricism." Many of its current adherents trace their intellectual heritage to the University of Minnesota and its well-known MMPI (Minnesota Multiphasic Personality Inventory). In the creativity area the approach is best represented by Harrison Gough of IPAR (the Institute for Personality Assessment and Research) at the University of California, Berkeley. This approach is manifested in his well-known Adjective Check List which has been used with adults in studies of creativity as well as in numerous studies of gifted, talented, and creative children.

This brand of empiricism has been extremely productive. It is also an approach that is attractive to many researchers for it is simple to follow. For example, tests or techniques are administered to two groups of subjects who differ on some basis, then, through the use of appropriate statistics, differences are tested for significance and results are reported. The procedure is very straightforward. Sometimes a rationale is presented in which lip-service is given to some theoretical idea like self-concept, openness to experience, or self-actualization. But it is often only lip-service and one has the impression that the work would have been carried out regardless. Basically, theory does not figure in this approach.

One of the problems with the empirical approach of the dustbowl variety is not so much the approach as how it is used. Specifically, these empirical studies are not replicated as often as they should be. One is left with a finding that can be quite intriguing but one does not know just how general it is, whether it will stand up over time, or how it is affected by various conditions.

Not all research in the field is of the empirical variety just described. Some investigators draw on Piaget, Kohlberg, Gowan, Freud, and others for the hypotheses and ideas which shape their work. We have seen how Wallach and Kogan derived their hypotheses about test administration conditions from associationism and the work of Mednick. Theory may also be used to pull together an existing body of empirical data. At the moment, the best example of this is to be found in the literature on adult creativity. I refer here to MacKinnon's[42] tour de force which uses Rankian theory to integrate results obtained in the studies of architects at IPAR.

As an aside, MacKinnon points out that his colleagues at IPAR would have been very surprised to see their empirical data contribute so well to the tests of hypotheses derived from Rankian personality theory. One hopes that there will be more such work, not only with data collected from adults, but also with data collected from gifted, talented, and creative children.

Historical/Ahistorical

Much contemporary research in this field is ahistorical in nature. Children are described in terms of their current status and their current talents and abilities. The children appear to be two-dimensional, as it were. What is lacking is depth, a third dimension that would

make them more meaningful and believable to the reader. It would also
provide the reader with necessary information so as to speculate about
the child's future development.

Students, no matter how young, have histories. They have histories
of interpersonal relationships with parents, siblings, peers, and
adults outside of school. Then, of course, they also have histories
with principals, teachers, and classmates in school. They have histories of physical development and psychosexual, intellectual, perceptual, and personality histories. All of these are well recognized in
the important theories of child development. One wants to know, not
only how children's studies shape up in terms of normative variables,
but also something of the continuities or discontinuities in development, as well as the varieties of subgroups that may be found in terms
of developmental characteristics as in *Cradles of Eminence* (Goertzel
and Goertzel, 1962).

There are studies here and there which purport to gather data on
students' life histories. But, if one takes a close look at them,
one finds that they contain many more questions about the student's
current life and interests than they do about how the present life and
interests developed. Family history is sometimes weak and one does
not learn as much as one would like about the child's parents and even
grandparents. With the change in life styles nowadays and with the
increasing number of divorces, attention might have to be paid to new
areas of questioning. New information will have to be gathered about
parent surrogates and the resources in the community that might or
might not be available to a child.

Both longitudinal and cross-sectional studies can yield valuable
data in this regard. Terman's studies are models to be emulated in
this regard. Biographical studies of children are not only important
in their own right, they are also necessary as a means of checking
data collected from adults who have made creative contributions but
whose reports, especially of their early lives, may have been negatively affected by the problems of recall.

Cognitive/Non-Cognitive

It is a truism that educators and psychologists are interested in
the whole individual, whether child or adult. Each person is seen as
composed of several transacting systems; one system can dominate the
others, compensate for the others, or all systems might be equal. In
all cases, there is an integration which is seen as the whole individual. Nevertheless, the state of the art is such that the emphasis
is on one aspect of the person, usually on the person's cognitive
characteristics.

The emphasis is obviously in line with mainstream psychology which
also emphasizes the cognitive characteristics of the individual. In
mainstream psychology, the individual is seen primarily as an information processing organism; non-cognitive factors, if they are studied
at all, are usually regarded as noise in the system. One cannot help
but wonder if this emphasis is more a function of partisan psychological affiliations than something required for a complete understanding of the problem itself. To avoid a complete understanding of non-
cognitive characteristics or even of cognitive characteristics and
the transactional relationship between them is to focus only on partial
aspects of the problem.

The importance of non-cognitive characteristics in the study and understanding of the gifted, talented, and creative has been pointed out in numerous instances. Especially noteworthy in this regard is the early work of Catherine Cox (1926) who, in her study, *The Early Mental Traits of Three Hundred Geniuses* (which was part of Terman's *Genetic Studies of Genius*), says with emphasis, "*that high, but not the highest intelligence combined with the greatest degree of persistence, will achieve greater eminence than the highest degree of intelligence with somewhat less persistence*" (p. 187).

In concluding her work, Cox also emphasizes the importance of non-cognitive characteristics when she says, "That all equally intelligent children do not as adults achieve equal eminence is in part accounted for by our last conclusion: *youths who achieve eminence are characterized not only by high intellectual traits, but also by persistence of motive and effort, confidence in their abilities, and great strength of force of character*.... The appearance in childhood of a combination of the highest degree of general ability, special talent, seriousness of purpose, and indomitable persistence may well be greeted as indicating a capacity for adult achievement of the highest rank" (pp. 218-219).

Even before Cox, Galton[3] cited the importance of non-cognitive factors. He believed there were three main aspects of mental activities—knowing, feeling, and willing—which we would refer to today with the terms cognitive, affective, and conative. As for the importance of non-cognitive factors, Galton believed (according to Burt [1975], p. 29) that "those who may be accounted of outstanding achievement are distinguished, not merely by high intellectual capacity, but also by a keen emotional interest in what they may have taken in hand, and by a resolute will to work harder, intently and persistently."

Many workers in this field today would agree with the orientation set forth above, that intellectual ability or information processing ability, alone, is insufficient for outstanding achievements or for creative contributions. It is best to consider the total individual and obtain data on both cognitive and non-cognitive characteristics. Nevertheless, the old attitude persists and attention is focused primarily on cognitive factors.

This one-sided attitude has a long tradition. While Galton was aware of the importance of non-intellectual factors, he, nevertheless, elected to concentrate his efforts on intellectual matters and thus, set a precedent that others have followed. Galton believed that intellectual factors set an upper limit on what an individual could achieve. For Galton, knowing, feeling, and willing (cognitive, affective, and conative) were each "largely 'an award of inheritance,' but the decisive factor was 'the gift of high ability'" (Burt, 1975). Much of this attitude was later held by Terman and others and, thus, there has been a long tradition of emphasizing cognitive factors in this field.

There are difficulties confronting persons who are interested in investigating the importance of non-cognitive factors among gifted, talented, and creative children. Not the least of these involve problems in developing reliable and valid tests. Not only is the content area difficult to study, but children, not yet mature, are likely to be inconsistent and to fluctuate in their behavior a good deal. All of this poses enormous problems in measurement, but no "good" problem is easy. Consideration may have to be given to adapting tech-

niques usually used with adults such as more frequent measurements.
It certainly will require resourceful and creative theoreticians and
psychometricians. In combining cognitive and non-cognitive characteristics attention should be given not only to the more usual multiple
regression techniques but also to the development of typologies.

Nature/Nurture

To give something more of the flavor of the current state of the
art, we shall look at two content areas. One, nature/nurture, is a
matter of long standing and the other is a relatively recent problem
that has attracted much attention. There are papers published peren-
nially on the nature vs. nurture controversy and the relative contribution of hereditary or environmental factors to the understanding of
giftedness, talent, and creativity in children. Arguments are presented
and attitudes are manifest in subtle and not so subtle ways. Arguments
in favor of hereditary factors were presented as far back as 1870 in
Galton's *Hereditary Genius*. Hereditary and racial bias was also manifest in Terman's work. The effects of bias in this area were manifest
in the ways that intelligence test data were utilized in the formula-
tion of federal immigration laws that limited the number of immigrants
who entered the United States.
It may be argued that the current use of the words "gift" and "talent" reflect an orientation in favor of heredity. In Webster's una-
bridged dictionary (ed. Neilson, 1953), the first definition for gifted
is: "1. Endowed by nature with some gifts or a gift...." In its third
usage, gift is described as, "Some quality or endowment given to man
by God or a deity...." Talent is defined in its fifth sense as, "The
abilities, powers and gifts, bestowed upon a man, natural endowments,
thought of as divine trust (as in the parable of the Talents in the
New Testament—Matthew 25: 4-30)."
With a belief in a God-given source, it is understandable that
many would object to special programs for the gifted. From their
point of view, gift or talent "will out" and if the boy or girl "has
it in them" they will come through no matter what. What is somewhat
more surprising is that educators and psychologists who do not put
much weight on hereditary factors still persist in using words like
"gift" and "talent" instead of a word such as "excellence."
People are in such awe of their fellow human being's unique and
original accomplishments that they assume that no one could attain
such heights with learning alone and without the help of a deity or
a special inheritance. This is manifest in the amazement experienced
when youngsters achieve and accomplish without prior learning, experience, or models. To fill in the gap occasioned by our ignorance,
we look to a powerful outside source. Even a psychological determinist
like Freud tells us that when it comes to understanding the behavior
and works of creative individuals, even psychoanalytic theory has its
limitations. Psychoanalytic theory, according to Freud, can help to
a certain point but there is a jump when talent takes over and enables
the creative person to do his or her outstanding work. Before this
talent, psychoanalytic theory lays down its armaments.
Implicit in the counter-argument of the environmentalists is a
belief that, if this ignorance exists, we can live with it and until
it is clarified, there is no reason to discriminate against those who

do not have the necessary hereditary qualifications. An argument such as this also goes back into the history of the work in this area. At least as far back as Constable,[43] we find an argument against Galton's data pointing out that no man who had been a genius left an heir who was also a genius if he did not also leave his heir lots of money.

The environmentalist position is reflected in the development of innovative educational programs and procedures for nourishing and stimulating the capacities of children at all levels throughout the educational system. Those who damn the use of tests in this area and argue in favor of giving every child a chance to show what he or she can do in an educational program are arguing in favor of an environmentalist position.

The nature/nurture controversy has been going on for a long time with great expenditures of time and energy on both sides. It has continued during the decade covered by the literature presented in this book. In the current state of the art, arguments are so overheated and intense that one symposium suggested a most unusual procedure. Since it seemed that a cool intellectual debate was not possible, the leader of the symposium suggested that a moratorium on discussions of the controversy be called. Passions have become so intense that we have to acknowledge that prejudices may have won out over clear heads. No doubt, this is not the first time in history that this has occurred. But, certainly, during the decade under review here, a low point on this matter was reached.

The Split Brain

A relatively recent research area that has attracted a great deal of attention is the work on the split brain. Since Roger Sperry[44] reported important differences in the functions and behavior associated with the left and right sides of the brain, the work has attracted a great deal of attention. Research in the area increased at an enormous pace with countless reports of the differences found between left-brain dominant and right-brain dominant individuals.

In addition, there has been much associated work on how to diagnose or determine whether an individual is left- or right-brain dominant. This information has had the implicit value of making it possible to select an individual to solve problems which require one or the other side of the brain to find the best solution. Such selection possibilities have made it possible to select individuals to work together. Obviously, if a person is dominated by one side of the brain and he or she is teamed up with an individual who is dominated by the other side of the brain, they could make an unbeatable team.

Needless to say, as in so many other areas, no sooner had it become known that differences existed and that it had become possible to diagnose for the differences, than one found persons who were willing to train others in how to use the dominant sides of their brains with maximum effectiveness or to improve the less dominant side. Not much later, the evidence began to come in that most people could and should use both parts of their brain to maximize the effectiveness of their problem-solving abilities.

No one can deny the importance of the work in this area as a contribution to the understanding of human behavior. It is important to know as much as we can about the different parts of the brain as they function separately and in concert. But it has begun to concern some persons that a fad-like quality characterizes much of the interest and work being done by those who presumably have as their major interest, the gifted, talented, and creative child. Because some significant findings about the split-brain had been reported, some people had to demonstrate that their fields, too, could provide supportive evidence.

It seems as if investigators did not trust their previous observations of the children with whom they had worked. They seemed to feel better when they had some physiological basis for their work. True, such bases are indeed important, but the attitude smacked more of scientism than science. One has the impression that the workers had known all along of the importance of intuitive and creative behavior. They also knew the importance of analytical and linear thinking, as well as intuition and related matters, in the creative solution of problems. Yet, one feels that they might have disregarded such beliefs were it not for the fact that they had found support in the split-brain research.

SUMMARY

Research in this area comes from a tradition of dustbowl empiricism. While it is primarily atheoretical, there are some important theoretically based studies which might be models for future research. The research that has been carried out is largely ahistorical in two senses. First, researchers do not necessarily cover or give due credit to the efforts of investigators who have preceded them. Second, they do not get much involved in the developmental histories of their subjects so that the picture of how they developed over time is lacking, as is the effect of their transactions with their siblings, parents, and grandparents. Current research concerns itself largely with cognitive variables, and since relatively little is done with personality factors, one rarely gets the picture of the total child. One hopes that future efforts will combine both cognitive and noncognitive variables to provide a picture of the total student.

The age-old problem of nature vs. nurture still occupies some investigators; unfortunately, they make no more progress with it than others did before them. With varying degrees, both are important. The field also tends to go through fads as reflected in its interest in split-brain research. While there is much of scientific value that has been done with this problem, there is also much in this field that smacks of scientism. At times, it appeared as if the field were lopsided in favoring one side of the brain over the other, forgetting that both sides are important in different ways to gifted, talented, and creative students and adults.

A LOOK TO THE FUTURE

We face a future whose social, economic, and political environment is hardly positive and encouraging. Our society has been characterized as litigious; we are more politically conservative than ever; we may be coming out of an economic decline but there are questions as to whether the rise can be maintained; worker productivity is frequently

questioned; educational programs for the young are in constant danger
of being cut; our youth are characterized as narcissistic; our aged
are worried about how well they will fare during their declining
years; and support for the arts and humanities and for basic research
is questionable. Fundamentalism, dogmatism, and traditionalism are
the by-words of the day. The times are uncertain and dark shadows
hang over the field of gifted education. The difficult situation
cannot last forever; when it changes, we must be ready with new plans,
ideas, and results. Toward this end I would like to make several
recommendations and comments on topics in three areas--organization,
methodology, and content.

ORGANIZATION

A Consortium

The first recommendation that I have is that a consortium be
created. This cooperative organization would involve educators and
researchers who would exchange ideas, plans, and results. The consortium would collate the works of all those involved and determine
which kinds of children or situations would be served by the results.
The consortium would have a continuing role in surveying the field
and in calling the attention of educators and researchers to gaps in
knowledge and to problems which require attention. The consortium
would integrate and focus all of our efforts so that the knowledge we
would gain would have both theoretical and practical significance.
A model for the creation of a consortium exists in the "Consortium
for Longitudinal Studies."[45] This consortium pooled the work of 14
longitudinal research and demonstration projects on the long-term
effects of early education on children from low income families.
This consortium was so successful that its efforts had significant
effects on both Democratic and Republican administrations in securing
funds for Head Start. The achievement of this goal took lots of
effort, a desire to share ideas, a capacity to overcome resistance,
and a willingness to compromise. "It took an enormous amount of time,
effort and compromise to reach the general solution just outlined.
We were all frustrated by the degree to which discussions of organizational principles threatened to dominate Consortium meetings, at the
expense of scientific issues that also needed discussion. However,
in retrospect, it seems that the decisions made were almost always the
best ones. If we all had to do it over, I believe we would not only
agree to do it, but also to do it in much the same way" (Darlington,
1981; p. 4). A consortium composed of educators and researchers can
be equally effective in working on the problems of the gifted, creative, and talented.

A Bureau of Standards

The second recommendation is for a bureau of standards. This
bureau would be charged with the responsibility for collating and
evaluating data on the reliability and validity of available tests

in the field. In carrying out this responsibility, the bureau would
have to make certain that it did not construct formidable obstacles
to new developments. In this regard, the bureau would have to work
closely with test developers, offering suggestions and expertise when
required. In the long run, the purpose of the bureau would be to keep
the field informed as to the appropriate uses of available tests.
Once again, a model for such a bureau already exists. In this instance, the model is the conference that was assembled to prepare the
basic evaluations for the report published by Richert et al. (1982).
Periodic meetings of such a conference would go a long way in fulfilling the functions of a bureau of standards such as the one proposed here.

METHODOLOGY

Cumulative Studies

Many of the studies in this field were conducted in one school
setting with a relatively small number of students. This situation
is understandable, for access to larger groups is not necessarily
available and when it is, there are problems with insufficient funds
and lack of personnel. Nevertheless, it is critical that we learn
just how far we may generalize with our results. Though it is very
tempting to apply exciting results immediately, it is better to apply
them only after they have been replicated in several situations.
With this in mind, it is important to caution one's colleagues to
hold off on broad application until more opportunities are available
to conduct and report replicated studies.

Laboratory Experiments and Case Studies

Together with field data, laboratory studies can be valuable in
helping investigators become aware of the relationships between
variables in the field. When other field opportunities are not
available to study these relationships, it is often worthwhile to
study these phenomena under laboratory conditions or in intensive
case studies.

Environmental Measures

If data are to be collected in different educational settings,
it is important to be certain that settings are grouped together only
if very critical characteristics are similar. To do this, it is important to use and, if necessary, to develop appropriate environmental
measures.

Pupil Types

Just as it is important to collate data collected from different
educational settings in terms of environmental similarities, it is
also important to establish subgroups, or typologies, of pupils.
Pupils differ not only on specific variables, but also in how they
stand on a number of different variables considered at the same time.
Their psychological structures are not reflected in the nomothetic
single variable approach, and the case study approach is too detailed
and too cumbersome for research purposes. The typological approach
is somewhere between the two and can serve our purposes admirably.
Although not all ingredients are in place at the present time for a
typological approach with young people, it is nevertheless worth considering.

Longitudinal Studies

Almost all studies reported in the literature present criterion
data collected concurrently with other data, or they present predictive data with criterion data of very short duration. Long-term
follow-up data are needed, perhaps following the model of Terman's
studies. It would be desirable to have several decades of follow-up
data on the techniques developed since Terman's work. Torrance has
been a pioneer in this regard and more of us need to follow in his
footsteps. In addition, we should follow not only those students who
met our criteria but those who did not. The latter group may surprise
us with their contributions and extend our view of the validity of
our instruments.

Evaluation

It is already somewhat customary to build evaluation procedures
into tests which are known as a test's reliability and validity. But
curricular and other similar programs do not necessarily have these
built-in evaluation procedures. If we are to benefit from each other's
contributions to curricular programs and teaching techniques, it is
critical that evidence be presented not only on how well a program
worked but also for whom it worked, under what conditions it worked,
and possibly some consideration as to why it worked. In addition, to
complete the picture it would be important to indicate, if it is
possible to do so, the characteristics of the student for whom the
program might not work and the characteristics of the teacher and
school that might not want to consider the program.

CONTENT

A Moratorium on the Words
"Gifted," "Talented," and "Creative"

There are times during the problem-solving process when the words that one has been using become obstacles to the solution. The very words that may have been helpful at the beginning of the process may have to be set aside for a while if one is to achieve a proper and creative solution. This may be true of the words "gifted," "talented," and "creative." At one time, they may have been important in designating a group of students or an educational program. But, over time, they seem to have become encumbered with surplus and even erroneous meaning and they have begun to have negative effects. Let us drop them for awhile and become more operational in our definitions and in our use of words. If tests are used for selection purposes then let us refer to our students as students who have been selected by "Test A," "Test B," or "Test C."

The moratorium and the return to operational definitions may not only make our communications less confusing, but it may also make it easier for us to take stock of where we have been, where we are, and where we are going. For example, we might try once again to open our so-called gifted programs to all students in an effort to learn how many of them respond in gifted, talented, and creative ways. Perhaps we would not exclude some who might not have passed the hurdles of the various selection tests currently in use.

Research Content

In the section on research (pp. li-lvii), several content areas were discussed. To avoid being redundant, let us say that it is hoped that the future will see more studies derived from theory with more emphasis on the transactional relationships between cognitive and non-cognitive variables. One hopes that investigators will also be more aware of the historical precursors of their research efforts as well as the historical antecedents of their students' current behavior.

Curriculum and Learning

There is a veritable cornucopia of curricula available for teaching the gifted, talented, and creative. Let us hope that even when these programs live up to their promises, researchers will not become complacent but will continue to investigate and determine the basic learning principles which are characteristic of the students. In the past, we witnessed occasions when some curricular programs were instituted because they were thought to be good for the students, even when their value and effectiveness did not live up to the promises. A good curriculum should be based on principles that are congruent with the students who learn. Those who teach the gifted, talented, and creative are in the best position to bring these principles to light.

The "Other" Students

As we continue to identify, select, and educate the gifted,
talented, and creative student let us not forget the other students.
These other students are also entitled to the best education that is
available so that they, too, can make the best use of their potentialities.   Therefore, as we discover valid principles of educating the
gifted, talented, and creative let us make certain that we transmit
this information to the broader educational community.   This will
have at least four effects.   It will foster the development of all
students' potentialities; it might dispel some of the criticism of
elitism; we might discover gifted, talented, and creative students
whom we might otherwise have overlooked; and the sharing of the best
educational practices would be consistent with the concept of *con-
tricipation,*[46] that is, the ability either to contribute or appreciate.
People with something new to offer need others who are willing to
accept their contributions.   People who, for one reason or another,
do not offer something new need these original people to improve and
enrich their lives.

SUMMARY

The current state of the art is dynamic, energetic, vibrant, and
extremely productive although not yet up to the standard that one would
like.   To describe and assess its status, the literature presented in
this book is collated into the following major areas: identification
and selection, education and training, and research.
Identification and selection received both stimulation and structure from the Marland Commission Report (1972) which discussed the
proportion of students to be identified and their selection, the persons to do the selection, the fields in which the selection was to
take place, and, implicitly, some of the procedures to be used.   Since
the report, the structure of the field has become quite elastic.   The
gifted, talented, and creative students are referred to with a multitude of terms which is confusing.   While there has been a proliferation
of procedures, they seem to have been developed without an adequate
awareness of their antecedents (an awareness which might have saved
much time and energy) and are oft-times without proper professional
responsibility.   While there are many techniques to select from, there
are no guidelines as to which are best for which students
under which conditions.
Education and training programs exist in abundance; teachers,
administrators, etc., have a wide range of procedures and schedules
from which to select.   It would appear that we devote energy to training for something we do not quite understand.   Fortunately, techniques
are available which are used with increasing frequency to help evaluate that which exists, so that it will be possible to zero in on
desired goals in the future.   One hopes that evaluations will make it
possible to introduce and make these special programs available to all
children so that they will have a chance to *contricipate* (Stein, 1984),
i.e., either contribute or appreciate, to the fullest.   Advances are
evident in work with the disadvantaged in this area and, as more work
is carried out, progress will occur.   With the advent of computers,
the importance of the school as a system has been discussed and atten-

tion has been called to challenges confronting the field. Specifically, caution has been recommended in embracing technology too quickly and without a plan. Otherwise, we might experience the failures that were attendant upon other recent educational innovations.

Research is discussed in terms of pairs of variables. In the empirical/theoretical dimension, the current status is largely characterized as manifesting the effects of dustbowl empiricism with theory not completely overlooked. It appears that theoretical formulations and experiments derived from theory are on the rise. When considered in terms of the historical/ahistorical dimension, contemporary research is largely ahistorical. Although historical approaches yield anecdotal data that are quite rich, the antecedents of subjects' current behavior does not seem to get the attention it deserves. Contemporary research emphasizes cognitive factors and non-cognitive factors do not get the attention they deserve. In this day of computer availability, it is not necessary to focus on single variables and one hopes that researchers will overcome their bias against non-cognitive variables and incorporate them with cognitive variables in multivariate studies.

To further characterize contemporary research, attention is called to the fact that the perennial problem, nature vs. nurture, is still with us. On occasion, it has heated up to such an extent that some feel a moratorium is necessary, certainly an odd mechanism for dealing with a research problem. A more recent and more popular problem is that of the split brain. The literature survey, with its emphasis on left brain or right brain, reflects more scientism than science. It also calls attention to the fact that the field is subject to fads which take up much time and energy while not necessarily having the desired payoff.

The most critical event that occurred during the decade to which this book is devoted is hardly covered by an annotation or a summary. This event is the change in the role of the federal government in the identification, selection, and training of gifted, talented, and creative children. In the early years of the decade, the federal government played a critical leadership role. But immense changes took place in the middle of the decade and there is much uncertainty about the future. One wonders whether the federal government will take an active role again or whether state and local governments will take over, aided perhaps by the private sector. These are critical questions that still have no answers. But we have been through such times before, and new leadership is bound to arise. When it does, it is necessary to be ready with ideas, suggestions, and plans. There is much in current work that should be discussed and understood. It should be supplemented with novel ideas and educational programs for gifted, talented, and creative children as well as for all other children.

NOTES

1. T.S. Henry, *Classroom Problems in the Education of Gifted Children. The Nineteenth Yearbook*, Part II (Chicago, IL: National Society for the Study of Education, 1920).

2. W. Abraham, *Common Sense About Gifted Children* (New York: Harper and Brothers, 1958).

3. F. Galton, *Hereditary Genius* (New York: Appleton, 1870, 390 pp.).

4. S.J. Gould, *The Mismeasure of Man* (New York: W.W. Norton, 1981).

5. B. Meer and M.I. Stein, "Measures of Intelligence and Creativity." *Journal of Psychology* 29 (1955): 117-126.

6. C.E. Spearman, *Abilities of Man: Their Natures and Measurement* (New York: Macmillan, 1927); P.E. Vernon, *The Structure of Human Abilities* (Rev. ed., London: Methuen & Co., 1960).

7. T.G. Thurstone, *Primary Mental Abilities* (Chicago: University of Chicago Press, 1938).

8. Q. McNemar, "Lost: Our Intelligence, Why?" *American Psychologist* 19 (1964): 871-882.

9. H.L. Swanson and B.L. Watson, *Educational Psychological Assessment of Exceptional Children: Theories, Strategies, and Applications* (St. Louis: Mosby, 1982).

10. H. Gardner, *Frames of Mind: The Theory of Multiple Intelligences* (New York: Basic Books, 1983). Readers may also be interested in two other books by Gardner, *Art, Mind, and Brain: A Cognitive Approach to Creativity* (New York: Basic Books, 1982) and *The Mind's New Science: A History of the Cognitive Revolution* (New York: Basic Books, 1985).

11. R.J. Sternberg, "A Componential Theory of Intellectual Giftedness." *Gifted Child Quarterly* 25 (1981): 86-93.

12. R.J. Sternberg, *Beyond IQ: A Triarchic Theory of Human Intelligence* (New York: Cambridge University Press, 1986).

13. See note on p. xiii of Preface for full reference.

14. R.L. Thorndike, "The Measurement of Creativity." *Teachers College Record* 64 (1963): 422-424.

15. P. Hasan and H.J. Butcher, "Creativity and Intelligence: A Partial Replication with Scottish Children of Getzels and Jackson's Study." *British Journal of Psychology* (1966): 129-135.

16. For his idea on theoretical orientation see his "The Associative Basis of the Creative Process." *Psychological Review* 69 (1962a): 220-232. For the RAT: *Remote Associates Test* (Ann Arbor, MI: University of Michigan Press, 1962b). This test is a one-solution problem. In this test, a person is presented with three words and is asked to come up with a word, which is the solution, that relates to all three. For example, the subject is presented with "bitter," "sixteen," and "heart." The correct response is "sweet" which is associated with all three as in "bittersweet," "sweet sixteen," and "sweetheart." The associations may be forward as in "sweet sixteen," or backward as in "bittersweet." In assessing the RAT with high school children Richert et al. (1982, p. 369) say, "There is not sufficient evidence to indicate that the RAT does measure the ability to think creatively. Cautious use is recommended." And later they added, "Validity is insufficient."

17. J.A. Hattie, "Conditions for Administering Creativity Tests." *Psychological Bulletin* 84 (1977: 1249-1260; J.A. Hattie, "Should Creativity Tests Be Administered Under Test-like Conditions?" *Journal of Educational Psychology* 72 (1980): 87-98.

18. V.G. Cicirelli, "Form of the Relationship Between Creativity, IQ, and Academic Achievement." *Journal of Educational Psychology* 56 (1965): 303-308.

19. S. Crockenberg, "Creativity Tests: A Boon or Boondoggle for Education?" *Review of Educational Research* 42 (1972): 27-45.

20. D.H. Feldman, B. Marrinon, and S. Hartfeldt, "Usualness, Appropriateness, Transformation, and Condensation as Criteria for Creativity." Paper presented at the annual meeting of the American Educational Research Association, New York, February, 1971.

21. F. Barron, "The Needs for Order and Disorder as Motives in Creative Activity." In C.W, Taylor and F. Barron (eds.) *Scientific Creativity: Its Recognition and Development* (New York: John Wiley & Sons, 1963), 153-160.

22. K.R. Beittel, "Creativity in the Visual Arts in Higher Education." In C.W. Taylor (ed.) *Widening Horizons in Creativity* (New York: John Wiley & Sons, 1964), 379-395.

23. H.G. Gough, "Techniques for Identifying the Creative Research Scientist." In *Conference on the Creative Person* (Berkeley: University of California, Institute for Personality Assessment and Research, 1961).

24. J. Petrosko, "Measuring Creativity in Elementary School: The Current State of the Art." *Journal of Creative Behavior* 12 (1978): 109-119.

25. W.G. Findley and M. Bryan, "Ability Grouping: 1970 Status, Impact and Alternatives." (Athens: Center for Educational Improvement, University of Georgia, 1971).

26. S.J. Cohen, "Two Components of the Study of Mathematically Precocious Youths' Intervention Studies of Educational Acceleration: Chemistry and Physics Facilitation and Longitudinal Follow-up." Unpublished doctoral dissertation, Johns Hopkins University, Baltimore, Maryland, 1980.

27. J.S. Renzulli and R.K. Gable, "A Factorial Study of the Attitudes of Gifted Students Toward Independent Study." *Gifted Child Quarterly* 20 (1976): 91-99.

28. I. Sato, M. Birnbaum, and J.E. LoCicero, *Developing a Written Plan for the Education of Gifted and Talented Students* (Los Angeles, CA: National/State Leadership Training Institute on the Gifted and the Talented, 1974).

29. S. Kaplan, *Providing Programs for the Gifted and Talented* (Los Angeles, CA: National/State Leadership Training Institute on the Gifted and the Talented, 1974).

30. S.G. Isaksen and D.J. Treffinger, *Creative Problem Solving: The Basic Course* (Buffalo, NY: Bearly Limited, 1985).

31. J.F. Feldhusen, D.J. Treffinger, and S.J. Bahlke, "Developing Creative Thinking: The Purdue Creativity Program." *Journal of Creative Behavior* 4 (1970): 85–90; J.F. Feldhusen, S.M. Speedie, and D.J. Treffinger, "The Purdue Creative Thinking Program: Research and Evaluation." *NSPI Journal* 10 (1971): 5–9; S.M. Speedie, D.J. Treffinger, and J.F. Feldhusen, "Evaluation of the Components of the Purdue Creative Thinking Program: A Longitudinal Study." *Psychological Reports* 29 (1971): 395–398.

32. J.F. Feldhusen and A.R. Wyman, "Super Saturday: Design and Implementation of Purdue's Special Program for Gifted Children." *Gifted Child Quarterly* 24 (1980): 15–21; J.F. Feldhusen and L. Sokol, "Extra-School Programming to Meet the Needs of Gifted Youth. Super Saturday." *Gifted Child Quarterly* 26 (1982): 51–56; Teachers College, Columbia University, *Saturday Enrichment Courses for Children* (New York: Teachers College, Columbia University, 1983); University of Southern Mississippi, *Saturday Gifted Studies Program* (Hattiesburg, MS: University of Southern Mississippi, 1983); University of Virginia, *Satureday Seminars for Gifted Students* (Charlottesville, VA: University of Virginia, 1982).

33. K. Seeley, E. Katz, and T.W, Linder, "The University as a Community Resource for Gifted: The University for Youth." *Gifted Child Quarterly* 25 (1981): 3.

34. D.J. Veldman and J.E. Brophy, Measuring Teacher Effects on Pupil Achievement." *Journal of Educational Psychology* 66 (1974): 219–324; F.J. McDonald and P. Elias, "Report on the Results of Phase III of the Beginning Teacher Evaluation Study: An Overview." *Journal of Teacher Education* 27 (1976): 315–316.

35. M. Mosston, *Teaching: From Command to Discovery* (Belmont, CA: Wadsworth, 1972).

36. D.J. Treffinger and B.L. Barton, "Fostering Independent Learning." *G/C/T* (March–April 1979).

37. R. Dunn and K. Dunn, *Teaching Students Through Their Individual Learning Styles* (Reston, VA: Reston Pub., 1978).

38. A.F. Gregoric, *Learning/Teaching Styles: Student Learning Styles: Diagnosing and Prescribing Programs* (Reston, VA: National Association of Secondary School Principals, 1979), 19–26.

39. J.R. Delisle (ed.), Special Issue: "Counseling Gifted Persons: A Lifelon Concern." *Roeper Review* 8 (1985): whole issue.

40. M. Siegelman, "Parent Behavior Correlates of Personality Traits Related to Creativity in Sons and Daughters." *Journal of Consulting and Clinical Psychology* 40 (1973): 43–47.

41. C. Wallinga and J.C. Sedahlia, "Parental Influence on Creativit of Fifth Grade Children." *Gifted Child Quarterly* 23 (1979): 768–777.

42. D.W. MacKinnon, *In Search of Human Effectiveness* (Buffalo, NY: Creative Education Foundation; and Great Neck, NY: Creative Synergetic Association, 1976).

43. F.C. Constable, *Poverty and Hereditary Genius: A Criticism of Mr. Francis Galton's Theory of Hereditary Genius* (London: Arthur C. Fifield, 1905. 149 pp.).

44. R.W. Sperry, "Mental Unity Following Surgical Disconnection of the Cerebral Hemispheres," *The Harvey Lectures*, Series 62 (New York: Academic Press, 1968).

45. R.B. Darlington, "The Consortium for Longitudinal Studies." *Educational Evaluation and Policy Analysis* 3 (November–December 1981): 37–45.

46. See M.I. Stein, *Making the Point: Anecdotes, Poems and Illustrations for the Creative Process* (Buffalo, NY: Bearly Limited, 1984), where the word was coined and the concept described.

Gifted, Talented, and
Creative Young People

Chapter 1

HISTORY

ISSUES IN HISTORICAL PERSPECTIVE

The Gifted and the Talented

--Witty, 1958
--De Haan and Havighurst, 1961
--Passow, 1979a
--Passow, 1979b
--Passow, 1983
--Gold, 1982
--Jackson, 1983
--Tannenbaum, 1979

The Creative

--Torrance, 1962
--Gowan, 1978

FEDERAL AND STATE PROGRAMS IN HISTORICAL REVIEW

--Marland, 1972
--Sisk, 1974
--Jackson, 1979
--Lyon, 1980
--Zettel, 1979
--Mitchell, 1982

IMPACT ON PUBLIC POLICY

--Takanishi; DeLeon; and Pallak, 1983
--Zigler and Berman, 1983

ISSUES IN HISTORICAL PERSPECTIVE

The Gifted and Talented

Witty, P. "Who Are the Gifted?" In Henry, N.B. *Education for the Gifted. The Fifty-seventh Yearbook of the National Society for the Study of Education.* Chicago: University of Chicago Press, 1958. 41-63.

In this early paper, attention is called to the fact that gifted-ness can be found in areas other than the intellectual. Limitations of intelligence tests are pointed out, as is the means of identifying gifted children in other areas.

A society's values and the regard it places on different activities and attainments affect its concept of giftedness. Witty points out that educational opportunities for the gifted are frequently affected by the socio-political orientation of the society. In the United States there is the belief that educational opportunities should be equal. But teachers are aware of differences in learning rates among students. While retarded students receive special education, the gifted child is "often unrecognized and frequently ignored."

The author then speaks of the importance of intelligence tests in selecting students who will do well in school. Witty also comments on those students who are selected as gifted but who are not very successful; he considers two factors to be of "unusual significance." "The first [of these] is associated with the failure of the home and the school to offer challenging educational opportunities and stimulation; the second is lack of pupil interest."

When a child enters school, the teacher should have information concerning the child's ability and development. Among the most useful is intelligence test scores. But test scores must be used in conjunction with other data about home environment and personal and social development.

Witty then discusses the characteristics of the gifted child in abstract intelligence and science. Some gifted children can be identified by an intelligence test. But some abilities can be recognized chiefly by their performance. Thus our definition of giftedness must be broadened beyond the intellectual and our dependence on intelligence tests lessened. The author then discusses creativity in writing and creative ability in music, painting, drawing, dancing, dramatics, and potential physical skills. The characteristics that teachers might utilize to recognize gifted students in some of these areas are pointed out.

De Haan, R.F., and Havighurst, R.J. *Educating Gifted Children*. Revised and enlarged edition. Chicago: University of Chicago Press,
1961. 362pp.

First published in 1957, this book is among the works that had an
early impact on the field. It contains material on the early history of the field and an overview of the early situation insofar as
identification and curriculum objectives were concerned and a discussion of the roles of administrators, teachers, and family. There
are numerous practical suggestions as well as a presentation of
critical material for evaluation and research.

Passow, A.H. "Perspective on the Study and Education of the Gifted
and Talented." In Passow, A.H. (Ed.). *The Gifted and the Talented:
Their Education and Development*. *The Seventy-eighth Yearbook of the
National Society for the Study of Education*. Part I. Chicago:
University of Chicago Press, 1979a. 1-4.

There were three previous yearbooks devoted to the gifted. The
first, published in 1920, was edited by Henry; the second, published
in 1924, was edited by Whipple; the third, published in 1958, was
edited by Havighurst.
In the 1924 volume, Whipple noted that Dr. William T. Harris,
Superintendent of Schools in St. Louis, had what was perhaps the
first systematic approach for dealing with "bright pupils." In
Harris' reports of 1868-69 and 1871-73, he "commented on the advantages of promoting pupils at short intervals, as short as five
weeks in the lower grades, and of accelerating gifted pupils through
the grades. He noted that the plan provided gifted pupils with more
challenging work and prevented them from acquiring habits of lazi-
ness."
Whipple noted that the yearbook committee was in agreement on how
the gifted should be educated, the selection of gifted pupils, and
the "administration of their training." Proponents of different
points of view had to prove their own cases.
By 1924, the yearbook included an annotated bibliography of some
453 items, among the earliest of which was an article by Terman (1906
on "Genius and Stupidity."
The 1958 yearbook dealt with curriculum and education of the
gifted. This work was planned before Sputnik, which provided a
powerful stimulus to gifted education. Again, the editor wondered
if the yearbook committee would agree with the presentations of all
the contributors. The yearbook, however, was viewed as stimulating
more advances in the education of the gifted.
The seventy-eighth yearbook, authorized in 1975 and published in
1979, "looks at the problem of educating the gifted and the talented
in the light of significant developments that have taken place in
the past two decades."

Suggestions for Further Reading

Yearbooks of the National Society for the Study of Education:

Henry, T.S. (Ed.). *Classroom Problems in the Education of Gifted
    Children*. *The Nineteenth Yearbook of the National Society for the
    Study of Education*. Part II. Chicago: University of Chicago
    Press, 1920.

Whipple, G.M. (Ed.). *The Education of Gifted Children. The Twenty-third Yearbook of the National Society of Education.* Part I. Chicago: University of Chicago Press, 1924.

Havighurst, R.J. (Ed.). *Education for the Gifted. The Fifty-seventh Yearbook of the National Society for the Study of Education.* Part II. Chicago: University of Chicago Press, 1958.

Yearbooks of Education:

Bereday, G.Z.F., and Lauwerys, J.A. (Eds.). *Concepts of Excellence in Education. The Yearbook of Education 1961.* New York: Harcourt, Brace and World, 1961.

————. *The Gifted Child. The Yearbook of Education 1962.* New York: Harcourt, Brace and World, 1962.

Passow, A.H. "A Look Around and a Look Ahead." In Passow, A.H. (Ed.). *The Gifted and the Talented: Their Education and Development. The Seventy-eighth Yearbook of the National Society for the Study of Education.* Part I. Chicago: University of Chicago Press, 1979b. 439–456.

The author surveys the history of the field, indicates its current status, and takes a look at the future. The historical survey begins with the *Twenty-third Yearbook* in which there were studies of the gifted, plans for ability grouping or acceleration, and Rugg's contributions. Rugg divided the gifted into the verbally, socially, mechanically, and aesthetically intelligent. He also broadened the concept of giftedness to involve different aspects of culture, highlighted the differences in ability between the genius and the others, and suggested the numbers that might be involved.

While interest in the gifted was at a low ebb at the end of World War II, by the 1950s there was renewed concern because of the cold war, manpower shortage, and a reappraisal of educational programs. Sputnik only intensified matters. In the *Fifty-seventh Yearbook*, there were chapters on motivation, creativity, and social leadership of gifted children. In the early 1960s, there was a decline of interest in the gifted.

The federal laws from 1969 to 1975 are reviewed as are Marland's contributions, the development of the Office of Gifted and Talented, and the government program of the National/State Leadership Training Institute on the Gifted and Talented in the 50 states. The increase in spending is also pointed out.

The author pulls together 17 principles that can help in the development of differentiated curricula for various groups of talented and gifted children. He talks about curricular requirements, parents' contributions, evaluation, and funding. The author is also concerned about the gifted not being served properly, the need for new educational models, the need for new ways to identify the gifted, the need to satisfy the needs of minority groups, the need for additional resources, etc. Despite all this, the author is optimistc about the future.

Suggestions for Further Reading

Goldberg, M.L.; Passow, A.H.; and Justman, J. *The Effects of Ability Grouping.* New York: Teachers College Press, 1966.

Passow, A.H. *Educating the Gifted*. Cambridge, MA: New England
    School Development Council, 1961.

————. *Education for Gifted Children and Youth—An Old Issue—A
    New Challenge*. Ventura, CA: Ventura County Superintendent of
    Schools Office, 1980.

————. "Fostering Creativity in the Gifted Child." *Exceptional
    Children* 43 (1977): 358–364.

————. "The Gifted and the Disadvantaged." *The National Elementary
    Principal* 51 (1972): 24–31.

————. *The Gifted and the Disadvantaged. Notes and Working Papers
    Concerning the Administration of Programs under Title III*, EASEA
    (PL 89-10), Subcommittee on Education, Committee on Labor and
    Public Welfare, U.S. Senate. Washington, DC: U.S. Government
    Printing Office, April 1967. 215–229.

————. "There is 'Gold in Them Thar Hills.'" In Addison, L., et al
    (Eds.). *Balancing the Scale for the Disadvantaged Gifted*. Ventura
    CA: Ventura County Superintendent of Schools Office, 1981. 1–26.

————. The Nature of Giftedness and Talent." *Gifted Child Quarter-
    ly* 25 (1981): 5–10.

————. "Program Alternatives for the Gifted/Talented." In Gallag-
    her, J.J., et al. (Eds.). *Issues in Gifted Education*. Ventura,
    CA: Ventura County Superintendent of Schools Office, 1979. 27–46.

Passow, A.H.; Goldberg, M.L.; Tannenbaum, A.; and French, W. *Plan-
    ning for Talented Youth: Consideration for Public Schools*. New
    York: Teachers College Press, 1955.

Raph, J.B.; Goldberg, M.L.; and Passow, A.H. *Bright Underachievers*.
    New York: Teachers College Press, 1966.

Passow, A.H. "A Universal View of Gifted and Talented Programs."
Paper prepared for the Second Plenary Session of the Fifth World
Conference on Gifted and Talented Children. Manila, The Philippines,
August 2–6, 1983.

Results of a survey questionnaire from 35 countries around the
world are presented. Seventeen specific points are made which are
summarized in the following two points: (1) Gifted education, in
many countries, has a cyclical history. (2) The education of the
gifted "in too many countries seems to be an esoteric endeavor
rather than part of the educational mainstream.... What is clearly
needed is total school planning for the pursuit of excellence and
the nurturance of individual talent potential."

Gold, M.J. *Education of the Gifted/Talented*. Los Angeles, CA:
National/State Leadership Training Institute on the Gifted and the
Talented, 1982. 508pp.

This book was published in 1965 under the title, *Education of the
Intellectually Gifted*, and is brought up to date by the 29-page
Epilogue, 1965–1982. It is part of the series published by Irving
Sato of the National/State Leadership Training Institute on the

Gifted and Talented. This book presents a survey of the field up to 1965 in a very systematic fashion, bringing the field up to date in the last chapter. Hence, it fulfills the purpose of the series which is described by Sato as follows: "The purpose of this series of publications, entitled *A Perspective Through a Retrospective*, is to make available once again the concepts, principles, and applications which are a part of our heritage and, thus, to encourage a better understanding of the present in gifted/talented education through a reexamination of the past."

To characterize Gold's perception of the state of the field in 1982 compared to 1965 when the book was first published, he says "education of the gifted/talented appears to be on a firmer footing than in 1965." There are problems with obtaining financing at the federal and state levels but "There is growing awareness that greater differentiation is needed for young people at the extreme ends of ability spectra, and substantial theoretical constructs and teaching materials are now available both for children and teachers. Genuinely differentiated curricula have begun to appear. Research on early childhood, brain physiology, and the structure of intellect now underpins significant advances for the gifted, and for education as a whole. Earlier studies of creativity are finding increased application in the classroom. A broader definition of giftedness with more open identification methods permits recognition of previously neglected talents and produces a new awareness of giftedness among women, minorities, and the handicapped. More and more teachers are learning how to work with gifted children. Education of the gifted has experienced more 'ups' and 'downs' than most school programs. This epilogue is written in an 'up' period, with the hope that the curve will continue to ascend."

Jackson, P.W. "The Reform of Science Education: A Cautionary Tale." *Daedalus* 112 (Spring 1983): 143-166.

The three decades from World War II through the 1970s are evaluated. Two movements are seen in federal intervention in educational reform: horizontal (which involved movement toward equity and social justice) and vertical (which involved excellence and achievement). Most reforms were closer to the vertical than the horizontal. The curricular reform movement, however, did not live up to its expectations because of: "(1) the level of difficulty of the material produced; (2) the complexities of their dissemination; and (3) the ambiguities surrounding federal policy with respect to curriculum development." In orienting themselves to the future, there is an emphasis on science and mathematics in our schools with a different kind of science instruction at all levels. These are complex goals which have to be considered in the context of the total educational system. "What is needed is a sense of partnership, an awareness of common cause uniting *everyone* who seeks to see our schools become better than they are."

Tannenbaum, A.J. "Pre-Sputnik to Post-Watergate Concern about the Gifted." In Passow, A.H. (Ed.). *The Gifted and the Talented. Their Education and Development. The Seventy-eighth Yearbook of*

the National Society for the Study of Education. Part I.   Chicago:
University of Chicago Press, 1979.   5-27.

There are two peaks of interest in gifted and talented children.
One of these was in the half-decade following Sputnik in 1957 and
the other was in the last half-decade of the 1970s.   Between these
points, attention was devoted to the "low functioning, poorly motivated, and socially handicapped children in our schools." The
"cyclical nature of interest in the gifted is probably unique in
American education.   No other special group of children has been
alternately embraced and repelled with so much vigor by educators
and laymen alike."

The period from the 1950s through the 1970s is reviewed; the author
concludes with the thought that the gifted may be rescuing public
education.   "The presence of the ablest is beginning to make a difference in the total school atmosphere, which demonstrates that they
are capable of enhancing all of education if their learning capacities are properly respected.   This truism may turn out to be the
most important lesson learned from our experience with gifted and
talented children in the 1970s."

The Creative

Torrance, E.P. *Guiding Creative Talent*. Englewood Cliffs, NJ:
Prentice-Hall, 1962.   278pp.   (Especially 1-43).

In the first 43 pages of this book, the reader will find a review
of research and non-research literature that antedates some of the
major developments in the work on intelligence and creativity to
which the author has been a major contributor.   The author regards
creative thinking abilities as important contributors to the acquisition of knowledge.   While intelligence tests serve certain functions
they do not cover those functions covered by creative thinking
tests.   If one were to identify the gifted solely by the use of intelligence tests, one would eliminate approximately 70 percent of
the most creative.

The author covers two important conferences held in the early days
of the work on intelligence and creativity; one was held at the
University of Minnesota and the other at the University of Utah.
In addition, the Minnesota Tests of Creative Thinking, which the
author developed early, and the newer Torrance Tests of Creative
Thinking are described.   This book also discusses issues involved
in identifying the gifted, the development of thinking abilities,
and the common problems of the highly creative.   From these bases,
the author presents his orientation to and suggestions for counseling
and guidance.

Gowan, J.C. "Creativity and Gifted Child Movement." *Journal of Creative Behavior* 12 (1978): 1-13.

The historical relationships between the gifted child movement and
the creativity movement are discussed and put together in their
proper perspectives in humanistic psychology.   The seven topics

considered are: (1) broad humanism, (2) measurement, (3) intelligence, (4) gifted children, (5) creativity, (6) development and parapsychology.

Humanistic psychology values the individual as an end and not as a behavioristic means. Measurement assumes that individuals have different talents that can be measured. In the relationship between intelligence and gifted children, there have been changes from unifactor to multifactor views, from seeing the gifted child as an abnormal genius to seeing the child as a pool for potential creativity, and from a mechanistic view of intelligence to one where it is perceived of as composed of transformations, implications, and a more creative consciousness.

Suggestions for Further Reading

Gowan, J.C. *An Annotated Bibliography on the Academically Talented.* Washington, DC: National Education Association, 1961.

————. *Annotated Bibliography on Creativity and Giftedness.* Northridge, CA: San Fernando Valley State College Foundation, 1966.

————. *The Development of the Creative Individual.* San Diego: Knapp, 1972.

————. "The Education of Disadvantaged Gifted Youth." *California Journal of Instructional Improvement* (December 1969): 239-251.

————. "Issues in the Education of Disadvantaged Gifted Students." *Gifted Child Quarterly* 12 (1968): 115-119.

————. *Operations of Increasing Order.* Westlake Village, CA: John Curtis Gowan, 1980.

————. "The Relationship Between Creativity and Giftedness." *Gifted Child Quarterly* 15 (1971): 239-243.

————. "Some New Thoughts on the Development of Creativity." *Journal of Creative Behavior* 11 (1977): 77-90.

Gowan, J.C., and Demos, G.D. *The Education and Guidance of the Ablest.* Springfield, IL: Charles C. Thomas, 1964.

Gowan, J.C.; Demos, G.D.; and Torrance, E.P. (Eds.). *Creativity: Its Educational Implications.* New York: Wiley, 1967.

Gowan, J.C.; Khatena, J.; and Torrance, E.P. (Eds.). *Educating the Ablest* (2nd ed.). Itasca, IL: Peacock, 1979.

FEDERAL AND STATE PROGRAMS
IN HISTORICAL PERSPECTIVE

Marland, S.P., Jr. *Education of the Gifted and Talented.* 2 vols. *Report to the Congress of the United States by the U.S. Commissioner of Education.* Washington, DC: U.S. Government Printing Office, 1972.

This is the classic federal report that set the standards for identifying gifted/talented children and the areas in which such identification should take place. Professionally qualified persons should identify gifted and talented children. These children have outstanding abilities, are capable of high performance, and require differentiated educational programs, not usually provided in regular educational programs, to fulfill their contributions to themselves and society. These children have demonstrated ability or potential in the following areas: "(a) general intellectual ability, (b) specific academic aptitude, (c) creative or productive thinking, (d) leadership ability, (e) visual and performing arts, (f) psychomotor ability."

The first volume contains background material for the commissioner's report as well as his findings. It focuses on matters such as the characteristics of gifted and talented children and asks the following questions. Can the gifted and talented be identified? How good are the screening tests? Do the tests also work with minority group children and children of different cultures? How many gifted children are there? How can they be defined? The first volume also discusses the characteristics of a good educational program and the issues involved in planning it. Case studies are presented.

The second volume is composed of the following appendices: Research on the gifted and talented: Its implications for education; An analysis of problems and priorities; Advocate survey and statistical sources; Analysis of hearing held by regional commissioners of education; State laws for education of gifted children; Comparisons of gifted and average students in the project TALENT population; Case studies of four states with programs for the gifted and talented populations; Assessment of present United States Office of Education delivery system to gifted and talented children and youth.

Sisk, D. "Educational Planning for the Gifted and Talented." In Kauffman, J.M., and Hallahan, D.P. (Eds.). *Handbook of Special Education*. Englewood Cliffs, NJ: Prentice-Hall, 1981. 441-458.

In 1958, Congress passed two educational measures: the National Defense Education Act and the National Science Foundation program. These programs provided financial assistance to the states and local educational agencies for various programs for the gifted and talented. But this activity diminished when the initial reaction to the space race calmed down and emphasis shifted to support for the disadvantaged.

In 1969, Congress amended the Elementary and Secondary Education Act. Public Law 91-230 allowed that Title III funds sent to state and local agencies could be used for the gifted and talented and that Title V money could also be used for this purpose. Title III funds sent to state and local agencies could be used for the gifted and talented, as could Title V money. Title III money was used for new programs in science, art, music, and foreign languages. With Title V money, some states hired consultants for the gifted programs or technical advisors. P.L. 91-230's most important contribution was to commission the Marland Report.

The Marland Report indicated that only 20% of the states used Title III funds for the gifted and talented; only nine states had used Title V money to make stronger programs for the gifted; and fewer than 15% of the states were spending Title I funds for gifted and talented students from deprived areas.

In 1974, the Elementary and Secondary Act was amended by Public
Law 93-380 to allow more direct assistance for the education of the
gifted and talented. Congress appropriated $2.56 billion and es-
tablished an administrative unit, a national clearinghouse, state
and local educational assistance, model projects, and traditional
grants. This law also established the Office for the Gifted and
Talented in the U.S. Office of Education. Sixty percent of P.L.
93-380 funds were earmarked to strengthen state efforts, since
studies had indicated that where states had a full-time coordinator
of gifted education, they had more successful programs. Six model
projects were funded for handicapped preschool gifted, preschool
gifted, arts for the disadvantaged, scientifically talented, handicapped leadership, and the gifted and talented in rural areas.
There were also training grants for teacher training, national
leadership training institutes, and internships. In 1978, P.L.
95-561 continued P.L. 93-380 but changed the delivery mechanism.

Jackson, D.M. "The Emerging National and State Concern." In Passow,
    A.H. (Ed.). *The Gifted and the Talented: Their Education and
    Development. The Seventy-eighth Yearbook of the National Society
    for the Study of Education*. Part I. Chicago: University of Chicago
    Press, 1979. 45-62.

As a result of the efforts of Congressman John Erlenborn of Illinois, an important step was taken at the federal level affecting the
education of the gifted and talented. The Marland report (Marland,
1972) submitted to the Congress on Oct. 6, 1971, made a number of
important recommendations and advocated a number of "firsts" in the
education of the gifted, talented, and creative.
    Among the results was a shift from advocacy by the federal govern-
ment to the allocation of categorical funds to the states; this
occurred in 1975 under the provisions of Special Projects of P.L.
93-380, Section 404. The funding represented the interaction of
both federal- and state-level thinking.
    The author discusses the importance of the ERIC Clearinghouse on
handicapped and gifted children. ERIC (Educational Resources and
Information Center), a subdivision of the National Institute of
Education begun in 1972, is operated by the Council for Exceptional
Children. The clearinghouse gathers and disseminates information
on all aspects of gifted education; publishes manuals and reports;
conducts computer searches on special topics; sponsors workshops
for users of the ERIC system; and answers questions on all aspects
of gifted education.
    The author also discusses the National/State Leadership Training
Institute on the Gifted and Talented (LTI), established in August
1972. Funded through a federal grant, it is administered by the
Ventura County (California) Superintendent of Schools. The LTI
serves as a bridge to the states and is oriented to developing awareness of the educational needs of gifted and talented children, training leaders in the area, and planning for the children's educational
needs.
    At the state level, activity was initially limited to six states--
California, Connecticut, Florida, Georgia, Illinois, and North Carolina. At the time the chapter was written, 38 states had provisions
for the gifted and talented in their legislation, but only since

1971 have eight of the states instituted their policies of funding local programs. In 1971, one-fifth of the states had full-time coordinators for gifted education. By 1977, this was true of one-half of the states.

In closing, the author is optimistic about the future: "The end is not yet in sight, but the emerging national and state concern for the gifted and talented is encouraging enough to prompt the wager that an ineluctable beginning has been made."

Lyon, H.C. "The Federal Perspective on G&T." *Journal for the Education of the Gifted* 4 (1980): 3-7.

The author presents a historical overview of what has occurred with education for the gifted and talented over the past twenty years, citing both crucial socio-political events as well as the kind of progress achieved over the years. In conclusion, the author, a former Director of the Office for the Gifted and Talented, U.S. Office of Education, cites several studies he feels should be integrated into work in this area.

The National Defense Education Act in 1958, the first large-scale federal program involving aid to the gifted, had as its goal the upgrading of education in chemistry, physics, mathematics, biology, and economics. But after the space race was won, interest subsided until the advent of the congressionally mandated Marland Report that "thoroughly detailed the widespread ignorance and abuse which marked gifted programs in the early 1970's." In 1972 the Office for the Gifted and Talented was established in the U.S. Office of Education to advocate the needs of the gifted at the national level.

The degree of progress that has been achieved in the field is reflected in a survey by the Office of Civil Rights which "revealed that approximately 35 percent of the gifted population were being served. Further, 40 states now have full-time consultants for the gifted with the remaining 10 having at least part-time coordinators. Additionally, approximately 37 universities have graduate programs specializing in gifted education, which is up from a decade ago."

Today there are still myths and prejudices about the gifted:
(1) The gifted will do fine on their own without special attention.
(2) The gifted are already an elite and receive special attention.
(3) "One other misconception is more difficult to correct because historically it has contained more than a kernel of validity. This refers to the charge of racial discrimination in gifted programs. Over the years, groups have been excluded from gifted programs because of faulty identification procedures and biased programming." Federally funded programs have sought to eliminate such bias and the federal government's commitment to minority participation is strong.

Three research studies are cited by the author as especially noteworthy. (1) Aspy and Roebuck carried out research based on Carl Rogers' work with successful therapists. They found that the same traits that were reported as being characteristic of successful therapists were characteristic of successful teachers. The characteristics included genuineness, empathic understanding, and prizing (caring). More of this study and its replication in Germany by Tausch will be reported in a forthcoming book by Lyon and Rogers entitled *On Becoming a Teacher*.

(2) Burton White's research on curiosity in the child between 8 and 22 months of age is also cited. This curiosity is regarded as the foundation for creativity. Parents can discourage this curiosity, but White has suggested means of developing stimulating environments for these children.

(3) Joseph Chilton Pierce conducted a study of African mothers who practiced natural childbirth. When the child was born, the parents massaged the child from head to toe before the umbilical cord was cut. Child development occurred faster than in the U.S. and "incredibly intelligent and bright children" resulted.

Zettel, J. "State Provisions for Educating the Gifted and Talented." In Passow, A.H. (Ed.). *The Gifted and the Talented: Their Education and Development. The Seventy-eighth Yearbook of the National Society for the Study of Education.* Part I. Chicago: University of Chicago Press, 1979. 63-74.

In 1977, the Office for the Gifted and Talented of the U.S. Office of Education made a grant to the Council for Exceptional Children to conduct a nationwide survey of what state agencies were doing for gifted and talented youth. This chapter is a summary of those findings and contains such matters as the statutory descriptions of gifted and talented, the types of screening and identifying procedures for the gifted and talented, state activities in support of the gifted and talented, etc.

Mitchell, B.M. "An Update on the State of Gifted/Talented Education in the U.S." *Phi Delta Kappan* 63 (1982): 357-358.

This is an update of a survey published by the author in 1980. (Mitchell, B.M. "What's Happening in Education in the United States Today?" *Kappan* [1980]: 563-564). The earlier survey showed that support for gifted/talented education was increasing nationally. But, since then, fiscal conservatism has spread across the nation and, hence, it could be expected that gifted/talented education might suffer at federal, state, and local levels.

In the current survey, 11 states, up from 10 in the previous study, have or are developing certification requirements for teachers of the gifted. Three states, Georgia, Idaho and Ohio, require special coursework and 36 states, down from 40 in 1978-1979, require no certification or course work.

The most frequently mentioned foci in gifted/talented programs for 1980-81 were, in order: creative problem solving, Renzulli's enrichment triad model, the development of higher level thinking skills, and computer education. Other types of independent learning activities followed.

Property tax ceilings on the funding of education for the gifted, talented, and creative did not seem to have much effect. Directors of programs felt that adequate funding was the most serious problem, followed by the training of qualified teachers. The development of comprehensive programs for the whole K-12 expanse was the third most pressing problem. Inadequate programming for the culturally different child was also an issue. The priorities, in terms of improvements, were: funding, in-service training for teachers, and

more comprehensive programming. Three states, California, Massachu-
setts, and Michigan, expressed concern about the future.

This update suggests that, in the field of gifted education,
everything is "alive and well" but, at the same time, there is a
concern about adequate funding.

IMPACT ON PUBLIC POLICY

Takanishi, R.; DeLeon, P.H.; and Pallak, M.S. "Psychology and Public
Policy Affecting Children, Youth and Families." *American Psychologist* 38 (1983a): 67–69.

This is the lead article which precedes several papers that concern themselves with the relationship between psychology and public
policy insofar as the education of children is concerned. In one
of the papers (by Maccoby, Kahn, and Everett), there is a consideration of several critical factors which need to be considered if one
wishes to have an impact on public policy. They are: (1) consisten-
cies and inconsistencies in research findings, especially where
early results are greatly modified or even reversed by later ones;
(2) cases in which documentation of a problem is not accompanied by
information on the costs and benefits of possible remedial measures;
(3) in evaluation research, failure to monitor the implementations
as well as the expected outcomes of the interventions; and (4) dis-
junctions in timing between the appearance of a research finding
and congressional schedules, executive decision processes, and the
agendas of interest groups. Other matters that are stressed are the
political climate and the need for researchers to know the right
times and right places for introducing their information to the
right people.

Takanishi, R.; DeLeon, P.H.; and Pallak, M.S. "Psychology and Education: A Continuing, Productive Partnership." *American Psychologist*
38 (1983b): 996–1000.

This article, part of a feature in *American Psychologist* called
"Psychology in the Public Forum," is an introduction to statements
by three national figures on the educational enterprise: Willard
McGuire, President of the National Education Association; U.S. Representative Pat Williams; and Myron Thompson, a trustee of the Bishop
Estate in Hawaii, which is involved in the educational programs that
are part of the Kamehameha Schools/Bishop Estate.

The paper makes a number of points regarding the present relationships between psychology and education. A number of comments which
characterize the current *zeitgeist* are cited.

The authors indicate that education is currently seen as "an instrument of economic recovery and progress." Concern is being expressed about declining or untapped human capacities.

In a piece by McGowan in the *New York Times* (McGowan, 1982) the
cost of functional illiteracy in incompetence, lost tax revenues,
crime, income maintenance programs, and remedial education is pointed
out.

The National Commission on Excellence in Education in 1983 issued
a report entitled *A Nation at Risk: The Imperative for Educational
Reform*. This report stated: "If an unfriendly foreign power had
attempted to impose on America the mediocre educational performance
that exists today, we might well have viewed it as an act of war....
We have, in effect, been committing an act of unthinking, unilateral
educational disarmament."

The authors then cite the following points from the above report:
(1) There are 23 million functionally illiterate adult Americans.
(2) Thirteen percent of all 17 year olds are functionally illiterate;
illiteracy may run as high as 40% among minority youth. (3) "Over
half the population of gifted students do not match their tested
ability with comparable ability in school." (4) "Many 17-year-olds
do not possess the 'higher order' intellectual skills we should expect of them." (5) "Business and military leaders complain that
they are required to spend millions of dollars on costly remedial
education and training programs in such basic skills as reading,
writing, spelling and computation."

In discussing some of the contributions of psychology to education
the authors cite a number of sources. For controversies in the field
about the validity of research, the authors cite Cronbach (1975).
For the influence of psychological research on education, the authors
cite the work of Cronbach and Suppes (1968) and Suppes (1978). For
the role of psychologists in developing and evaluating programs for
school-age, low-income children in the Follow Through Planned Variation study, the authors cite Rhine (1983). And for the long-term
effects of the Head Start program, they cite Lazar, Darlington,
Murray, Royce, and Snipper (1982).

The authors note that the National Institute of Education (NIE)
was established in 1973. Education has received federal support for
only 20 years while agriculture and medicine have received support
for 100 years. The NIE and the National Science Foundation have
supported efforts in the "young field of cognitive science, which
has considerable potential for designing more effective instruction
in mathematics and science" (Resnick, 1983). These important contributions of psychology to education have occurred although "less
than 5% of all federal funds allocated for education are spent on
research relevant to understanding education."

The authors conclude: "Although the relationship of economic productivity and education has been discussed often, the focus of that
discussion has been on the development of cognitive and work-related
capacities. The role of educational settings in developing attitudes that lead individuals to be economically productive and politically active members of a society has remained in the background.
The importance of motivational factors may well be an area in which
psychological knowledge could make important contributions."

Suggestions for Further Reading

Cronbach, L.J. "Five Decades of Public Controversy over Mental
   Testing." *American Psychologist* 30 (1975): 1-14.

Lazar, I.; Darlington, R.B.; Murray, H.; Royce, J.; and Snipper, A.
   "Lasting Effects of Early Education." *Monographs of the Society
   for Research in Child Development*, Serial No. 195 (1982).

McGowan, W. "Illiterasee att Wurk." *New York Times*, August 19,
   1982, p. 20.

National Commission on Excellence in Education. *A Nation at Risk: The Imperative for Educational Reform.* Washington, DC: U.S. Department of Education, 1983.

Resnick, L. "Mathematics and Science Learning: Some New Conceptions." *Science*, April 29, 1983, pp. 477-478.

Rhine, W.R. "The Role of Psychologists in the National Follow Through Project." *American Psychologist* 36 (1983): 288-297.

Suppes, P. (Ed.). *The Impact of Research on Education: Some Case Studies.* Washington, DC: National Academy of Education, 1978.

Zigler, E., and Berman, W. "Discerning the Future of Early Childhood Intervention." *American Psychologist* 38 (1983): 894-906.

The focus here is on the success of the Head Start program. While other educational programs have been cut, the Reagan administration increases the support of this program. In no small measure, the success of this program was positively affected by the cooperative endeavors of researchers who not only accumulated evidence to respond to possible negative criticism, but also shared knowledge and experience. They reinforced each other and made plans for future research.

The field of gifted, talented, and creative education would do well to emulate the cooperation of Head Start researchers who worked as a consortium. While the illustration of this point is the main reason for presenting this selection here, readers will also find an excellent review of the different theoretical models that have been used to study the effects of early educational intervention. The article also discusses the effects of the media, factors involved in the study of intervention programs, and evaluation.

Chapter 2

THEORY

GENERAL

--Busse and Mansfield, 1980
--Stein, 1974
--Stein, 1982
--Treffinger; Isaksen; and Fierstien, 1982

EDUCATIONAL THEORISTS, EDUCATIONAL PSYCHOLOGISTS
  AND EDUCATORS

--Clark, 1979
--Dewey, 1934
--Gowan, 1972
--Gowan, 1979
--Gowan, 1977
--Passow, 1981
--Piechowski, 1979
--Pulvino and Perrone, 1979
--Tannenbaum, 1983
--Torrance, 1979
--Torrance, 1982

PSYCHOANALYSTS

--Adler, 1930
--Eissler, 1971
--Freud, 1910
--Freud, 1948
--Jung, 1928
--Jung, 1946
--Kris, 1953
--Kubie, 1958
--MacKinnon, 1976
--Rapaport, 1950

PSYCHOLOGISTS

--Amabile, 1982
--Amabile, 1983a
--Amabile, 1983b
--Barron, 1953
--Barron, 1958
--Davidson and Sternberg, 1984
--Gardner, H., 1982
--Gardner, J.W., 1961
--Guilford, 1950

--Guilford, 1970
--Guilford, 1977
--Hebb, 1958
--MacKinnon, 1976
--MacKinnon, 1978
--Maslow, 1958
--May, 1975
--Murray, 1959
--Rogers, 1959
--Stein, 1953
--Thurstone, 1950
--Torrance, 1962
--Vernon, P.E.; Adamson; and Vernon, D.F., 1977
--Wertheimer, 1945
--Woodworth, 1934

OTHERS

--Cannon, 1940
--Poincaré, 1913
--Wallas, 1926

GENERAL

Busse, T.V., and Mansfield, R.S. "Theories of the Creative Process:
A Review and a Perspective." *Journal of Creative Behavior* 14 (1980):
91-103, 132.

The authors group theories of creativity and theorists into seven
categories: Psychoanalytic--Kris and Kubie; Gestalt--Wertheimer;
Association--Mednick; Perceptual--Schachtel; Humanistic--Rogers;
Cognitive-developmental--Feldman; and Composite theories--Hadamard,
Koestler, Gruber, and Haslerud.

In conclusion, the authors present their own view of the creative
process as consisting of: selection of the problem, extended effort
to solve the problem, setting constraints on the solution of the
problem, changing the constraints and, finally, verification and
elaboration. They consider that this process "most probably is not
applicable to nonscientific areas in which the validity of ideas
depends more on subjective and aesthetic criteria."

Stein, M.I. *Stimulating Creativity.* Vol. 1: *Individual Procedures.*
New York: Academic Press, 1974. 348pp. Vol. 2: *Group Procedures.*
New York: Academic Press, 1975. 306pp.

Stein defines creativity as a process that results in novelty that
is accepted as useful, tenable, or satisfying by a group of significant others at some point in time. The process itself is divided
into: hypothesis formation, hypothesis testing, and the communication
of results. It calls attention to the various sub-processes that
occur at an intrapersonal level as well as those that occur at an
interpersonal level. With regard to the latter, it becomes apparent
that creativity occurs in a social context; consequently, one must
consider the effects on creativity of the *zeitgeist*, geographic,
socio-economic, philosophic, and other forces within the society.
One also needs to consider the important roles played by intermediaries (curators of museums, peer review committees, granting
agencies, etc.) as well as the characteristics of the audience
(which may vary in size) as it accepts or rejects a creative work.

For an understanding of the intrapersonal factors involved in the
creative process one must study the individual's history, risk-
taking ability, attitudes, values, motivations, personality characteristics, etc. One should also study the creative individual's
problem-solving characteristics. But creativity is not to be
limited to problem solving since creativity includes both the
rational and non-rational and problem solving is usually limited to
the more rational aspects of an individual's behavior.

The stages of the creative process, hypothesis formation, hypothesis testing, and communication of results are used to provide a dis-

cussion of various techniques for stimulating creativity in the two
volumes cited above. A summary of some of Stein's empirical findings may be found in the Borgatta and Lambert book, described below.

Suggestions for Further Reading

Stein, M.I. "Creativity." In Borgatta, E.F., and Lambert, W.W.
    (Eds.). *Handbook of Personality Theory and Research*. Chicago:
    Rand McNally, 1968.

Stein, M.I. "Creativity Research with Adults and Children." In Sato,
    I. (Ed.). *Creativity Research and Educational Planning: Selected
    Proceedings of the Second National Conference on Creativity and the
    Gifted/Talented*. Ventura, CA: National State Leadership Training
    Institute on the Gifted and Talented/Ventura County Superintendent
    of Schools Office, 1982. 31-39.

Six major criteria of creativity are used in studying adults:
generally acknowledged creativity; representation in secondary
sources; expert judgment; quantity of products; psychometric tests;
and the creative process itself. In studies of children, judgmental
data may also be used but in many cases there is a dependence on
test data.
    In the adult literature, there is little support for the relation-
ship between tests of divergent thinking and creativity; in the
American child literature, tests of divergent thinking are regarded
as tests of creativity. British psychologists, however, regard the
tests as tests of divergent thinking and not of creativity.
    In the adult area, studies of needs, anxiety, ego strength, values,
attitudes, etc., have contributed to our understanding of adult
creativity; this information is not yet as complete in studies of
children because tests of these different variables are not as yet
fully developed for children.
    Biographical data have been collected on adults and children.
For adults there is much interesting information but we cannot
assess the effect of recall problems. In the case of biographical
data on children, it may be valid because the subjects are closer
in age to the recalled events. Coordination between adult and child
studies may yield much valuable information in the future.
    Studies of creative adults are sometimes carried out in real-life
situations so that the effects of environmental factors on their
creativity can be studied. Some similar studies of children have
been carried out.
    Stein concludes that there are many similarities and some differen-
ces in creativity research on adults and children. It is regrettable
that few investigators have experience with both groups. It would
be instructive to conduct some studies of children and adults using
the same techniques.

Treffinger, D.J.; Isaksen, S.G.; and Fierstien, R.L. (Eds.). *Handbook
    of Creative Learning*. Vol. 1. Williamsville, NY: Center for Crea-
    tive Learning, 1982. 5-17.

In this selection, "Creative Learning: Nature and Definition,"
the editors collate theories and approaches to creativity into five
major categories:

I. *Cognitive, Rational and Semantic*: Problem-solving (phases/ stages)--Wallas, Rossman, Dewey, Osborn, Parnes, et al.; Cognitive abilities--Bruner, Guilford, Torrance; Associative--Maltzman, Mednick, Koestler; Gestalt--Kohler, Koffka, Wertheimer.

II. *Personality and Environmental*: Personality traits or characteristics--Anderson, Barron, Crutchfield, MacKinnon; Parental practices, Social/Cultural setting--Crutchfield, Eisner, Stein; Transactualization--I. Taylor; Affective/Cognitive interaction--Williams; Stimulus/Response (Behavioristic)--Hull, Skinner, Staats.

III. *Third Force Psychology (Mental Health and Psychological Growth)*: Self-actualization and psychological growth--Fromm, May, Maslow, Rogers; Biological and personal growth mechanisms--Land, Sinnott.

IV. *Psychoanalytic or Psychodynamic*--Classical Freudian emphasis on conflict and sublimation--Freud; Emphasis on regression and preconscious--Kris, Kubie; Perceptual dynamics--Schachtel; Aesthetic-- Jung.

V. *Psychedelic*--Existential non-rational--Barron, Weil, Houston; Altered states of consciousness (through drugs)--Harmon, Tart, Aaronson and Osmond, Lilly, Masters and Houston, Leary; Expansion of consciousness (non-drug)--Erickson, Naranjo and Ornstein, Karlins and Andrews, Payne, Gowan.

EDUCATIONAL THEORISTS, EDUCATIONAL PSYCHOLOGISTS,
AND EDUCATORS

Clark, B.   *Growing Up Gifted*.   Columbus, OH: Charles E. Merrill, 1979. 467pp.

This textbook brings together contemporary theory (Jung, Maslow, and others), research and practice to encourage parents, educators, and others to provide the gifted with a "better growth experience" and enable them to actualize their potential.

Dewey, J.   *Art as Experience*.   New York: Menton, Balch, 1934.   355pp.

There is in life "a rhythm of loss of integration with environment and recovery of union"; equilibrium is achieved out of, and because of, tension.   The artist cultivates this tension, since it may bring to consciousness a total and unified experience.   The scientist is involved in the tension between thought and observation.   The difference between the esthetic and the intellectual is the placement of emphasis in the rhythmic interaction between individual and environment.

The artist carries within him/her "the attitude of the perceiver while he works.   The doing or making is artistic when the perceived result is of such a nature that *its* qualities *as perceived* have controlled the question of production."

Although the idea for the work of art is private, its content is public.   Communication with others is not a necessary part of the artist's intention, but he can never escape the possibility of an audience.   The function and consequence of the artist's expression

is "to effect communication, and this is not by external accident--
but from the nature he shares with others."
     Appreciation for the final product, like the development of the
product itself, involves "a series of responsive acts that accumu-
late toward objective fulfillment. Otherwise, there is not perception but recognition."
     Most of us are not artists because we lack the "capacity to work
a vague idea and emotion over into terms of some definite medium."
Between conception and the final product, there is a long period of
gestation during which "the inner material of emotion and idea is as
much transformed through acting and being acted upon by objective
material as the latter undergoes modification when it becomes a
medium of expression."

Gowan, J.C. *Development of the Creative Individual.* San Diego, CA:
     Robert Knapp, 1972. 153pp.

     This book scrutinizes "the process of individual development,
with special attention to the development of the superior individual,
and [attempts] to justify inclusion of creative production as a
process in that developmental escalation."
     Chapter 1 reviews the literature on development and creativity.
The stage aspects of development are emphasized and it is seen as
"improvement and change through evolution." Five categories are
identified for the literature of creativity.
     Chapter 2 focuses on "the existence and periodicity of eight
developmental stages." Of special importance are the creative aspects of Erikson's Stage 3 Initiative and Stage 6 Intimacy.
     Chapter 3 concerns itself with the "important concept of escala-
tion, with its five attributes of succession, discontinuity, emergence, differentiation and integration." These processes are discussed with regard to concept formation; the discussion includes
both cognitive and affective factors, which are precursors of creativity in the child. The "objective of escalation is seen as creative performance in the individual." Chapter 4 centers on creativity
and focuses specifically on its preconscious sources in relation to
the developmental stages. Chapter 5 looks at the environmental
stimulation for creativity at every level, and includes a section
on parental stimulation and teacher and counselor stimulation.
Chapter 6 discusses problems of and penalties for being noncreative.
The problems range from complete immobilization and psychosis "to
the lotus-land happiness of the merely uncreative" (p. 110). The
final chapter, Chapter 7, focuses on the process of self-actualization as it relates to the last three adult developmental cognitive
stages--creativity, psychedelia, and illumination.

Gowan, J.C. "The Use of Developmental Stage Theory in Helping Gifted
     Children Become Creative." In Gallagher, J.J., et al. (Eds.).
     Issues in Gifted Education. Ventura, CA: Ventura County Superinten-
     dent of Schools, 1979. 47-77.

     This article overlaps with others of Gowan's publications, to
which the reader may wish to refer:
     "The Organization of Guidance for Gifted Children." *Personnel and
Guidance Journal* 39 (1960): 275-279.

The Development of the Creative Individual. San Diego: R. Knapp, 1972.

The Development of the Psychedelic Individual. Buffalo, NY: The Creative Education Foundation, 1974.

"Incubation, Imagery and Creativity." *Journal of Mental Imagery* 2 (1978): 23-43.

"Education for the Gifted in Utopia." *Mensa Research Journal* 8 (1978): 2-11.

This paper focuses on the application of developmental stage theory to the problems of the gifted and to helping them become creative adults. Special guidance procedures are presented and emphasized.

Gowan sees development as consisting of a series of discrete, discontinuous stages. Gowan draws on the work of Erikson and Piaget but extends their works with ideas and concepts of his own. For Gowan most gifted children do not make the jump from Piaget's stage of formal operations to the stage of creativity, and therefore are lost to creativity. He suggests that this loss can be prevented by encouraging right-hemisphere function, preserving creative fantasy, using science to avoid the drop in creativity at the 4th-grade level and using writing assignments to stimulate verbal creativity in adolescents.

The central characteristics of the model are as follows: (1) It combines cognitive material from Piaget and affective material from Erikson. (2) Piaget's five stages are extended to eight. The added ones are creativity, psychedelia, and illumination. (3) There is periodicity of three in the tables and hence similarity between Stages 1 (trust vs. mistrust, etc.), industry vs. inferiority, etc.) and 7 (generativity vs. stagnation, etc.). (4) Five components of escalation are emphasized: discontinuity, succession, emergence, differentiation, and integration. (5) Dysplasia (a malformation in development) is manifest in the splitting of the cognitive and affective levels in malfunctioning individuals. (6) To escalate into higher levels, self-actualization is emphasized.

Within a stage, development occurs as a result of escalation, which possesses five attributes: succession, discontinuity, emergency, differentiation, and integration. The environment may have maximal or minimal effects depending on the individual's position in the cycle.

Considering the modifications that must be made in this model for the gifted, Gowan suggests two major departures in guidance approaches: guidance should start earlier and extend later in the lifetime of the individual; and guidance should include not just traditional guidance workers but all persons who come into contact with the exceptional child.

In working with a gifted child, guidance has a twofold function: "first, to assist in personality development and the removal of emotional or environmental handicaps; and second, to aid and advise in the maximizing of achievement and college placement which will facilitate his progress to a professional career" (p. 60). Gowan asserts that both these tasks should be pursued aggressively.

To help establish verbal creativity in adolescence; to help students not to get lost to creativity; and to help them make the jump from formal operations to creativity, Gowan recommends: "(1) a dedicated teacher, (2) a segregated seminar, (3) maintenance guidance

and (4) continual pressure to produce creative writing via a journal."

In conclusion Gowan says:

"1. Giftedness is mere *potentiality*....

"2. To make the gifted child creative, we must understand developmental stage theory with its blending of Piagetian (cognitive) and
Eriksonian (affective) levels ... right-hemisphere functions
[should] not be lost so that some imagery may be preserved.

"3. There are three developmental stage levels where the baby can
be thrown out with the bath water.

"4. The continued understimulation of the potential talents of
gifted students is stupidity ..." (p. 71).

Gowan, J.C. "Creative Inspiration in Composers." *Journal of Creative
Behavior* 11 (1977): 249-255.

While talent and training are necessary for all kinds of creative
products, it is necessary to distinguish between products which are
creative only for the artist and those which have timeless and
universal appeal. Therefore, the author sought out composers' own
descriptions of the creative. Among the composers covered are:
Brahms, Richard Strauss, Puccini, Wagner, Mozart, and Tschaikowsky.

For most of the composers covered, the creative process consists
of three phases: "(1) the prelude ritual, which may be conscious or
unconscious, ending often with an invocation; (2) the altered state
of consciousness, or creative spell, during which the creative idea
is born, starting with vibrations, then mental images, then the flow
of ideas which are finally clothed in form. This syndrome often
proceeds with extreme and uncanny rapidity in what is always referred
to as a trance, dream revery, somnambulistic state, or similar
altered condition; and (3) the postlude in which positive emotions
about the experience suffuse the participant." All of the steps
did not occur in any one of the reports.

Passow, A.H. "The Nature of Giftedness and Talent." *Gifted Child
Quarterly* 25 (1981): 5-10.

After discussing various definitions of giftedness and creativity,
the author summarizes what is known about giftedness and talent and
suggests how the gifted and talented might be identified. He says,
"The gifted and talented come in a tremendous variety of shapes,
forms, and sizes. Some gifted youngsters are slightly above average
with respect to the criteria applied while others are so unusual as
to be extremely rare; some individuals are gifted/talented
in a single area, while others seem to be unusually able in practically any area. Some individuals who seem to have outstanding
ability have relatively little motivation or interest in developing
that potential while others are both highly talented and highly
motivated. Some are high achievers and quick absorbers of information while others utilize knowledge in new and different ways.
Some are basically consumers of knowledge while others are potentially outstanding producers as well as consumers. Some are especially precocious, manifesting unusual potential at early ages
while others are 'late bloomers' and do not show unusual potential

or performance until much later. There are cultural differences with respect to which talent areas are more likely to be rewarded and, consequently, which will be nurtured...."

Not all students identified as gifted possess all the characteristics usually ascribed to gifted students. In some cases a single characteristic may be sufficient to identify a gifted student. Various procedures should be used to identify the gifted student. The author prefers a method where sufficient opportunity is provided for a student to identify himself or herself on the basis of products and performance. This is a continuous process.

Piechowski, M.M. "Developmental Potential." In Colangelo, N., and Zaffran, R.T. (Eds.). *New Voices in Counseling the Gifted.* Dubuque, IA: Kendall/Hunt, 1979. 25-57.

To broaden the concept of giftedness to include more than test [IQ] scores, the author presents a model in which giftedness is regarded as being made up of other than testable skills. The model is based on the idea of developmental potential, which consists of "readily identifiable components: special talents and abilities and five forms of psychic overexcitability: psychomotor, sensual, intellectual, imaginational, and emotional" (p. 25).

The model can be used in various ways, one of which is to evaluate various checklists for identifying gifted students. Those evaluated in this manner were found wanting in imaginational and emotional factors. Such checklists gather data on intellective factors. The model is also used to compare creative and noncreative profiles. The former is high on emotional factors and the latter is low on intellectual and imaginational factors. The usefulness of the model for counselors and educators is discussed.

(The concept of developmental potential is based on work to be found in other sources, including:

Dabrowski, K. *Positive Disintegration.* Boston: Little, Brown, 1964.

Dabrowski, K., and Piechowski, M.M. *Theory of Levels of Emotional Development.* Vols. 1 and 2. Oceanside, NY: Dabor Science, 1977.)

Pulvino, C.J., and Perrone, P.A. "A Theoretical Perspective for Understanding the Gifted and Talented Child." In Colangelo, N., and Zaffran, R.T. (Eds.). *New Voices in Counseling the Gifted.* Dubuque, IA: Kendall/Hunt, 1979. 1-24.

This paper contains the theoretical orientation underlying the work of the Guidance Institute for Talented Students at the University of Wisconsin. Its three major components are the organism, goals, and the system.

Concern with organism focuses primarily on mental development, although social and physical development are also important for the development of the total organism. The organism tries to achieve a balanced relationship with the environment moving between field-dependence and field-independence. Further development increases in a stimulating and trusting environment. Emphasis is placed on the action of both brain hemispheres; maximal functioning of the left brain occurs through sound and touch and the functioning of

the right is developed through sight. The authors also subscribe
to Maslow's need hierarchy.

For goals, the authors focus on Bloom's taxonomy as reflecting
the "structures through which the organism gains knowledge from
various fields." The authors also draw on Land's article, "Grow or
Die" (1973), with its theory of knowledge acquisition.

As to system, the authors see the organism and the environment
forming a relationship that is "both freeing and controlling."
"Throughout, we find the various stage theories applicable and thus
hypothesize that 'understanding' a person involves recognizing that
the life-space of an individual involves many person-environment
interactional sectors, each processing somewhat unique data, in
somewhat unique ways (levels). Yet the organism acts in a singular
fashion, thus masking much of what's really happening and allowing
us only to infer from distilled behaviors" (p. 5).

Tannenbaum, A.J. *Gifted Children: Psychological and Educational Perspectives.* New York: Macmillan Publishing Co., 1983. 527pp.

This book comprises both an intensive and thorough survey of the
field, including the author's own contributions and special point
of view. The book is made up of 6 parts including a total of 23
chapters and 3 appendices. Part I, on the history of interest in
the gifted, "deals mainly with ambivalent attitudes toward encouraging
the fruition of human talent." Part II covers different ways of
characterizing the gifted. This part also includes the author's
definition. He begins by classifying talent into four categories:
scarcity, surplus, quota, and anomalous types of talent. He concludes with his own social-psychological approach, which links
promise and fulfillment through five factors: superior general
ability, special aptitudes, nonintellective facilitators, environmental influences, and chance factors. These five factors are then
discussed and elaborated upon in Part III of the book. In this
part, related theory and research are discussed and the works of
such investigators as Terman, Hollingworth, Thurstone, and Guilford
are covered. This leads to an extensive and critical review of the
work on creativity in Part IV.

In Part V, the author deals with the education of the gifted and
concerns himself with identifying the gifted, educational enrichment
paradigms, and methods of evaluating programs for the gifted.

Part VI contains an epilogue and in the last chapter the author
presents a "Bill of Rights" for the gifted.

Three important appendices complete this book. The first covers
the matter of stimulating creativity and presents techniques, methods
and educational programs. The second contains "books about the joys
and travails of achieving excellence." The third contains a survey
for gathering data on attitudes toward the gifted and the kinds of
education they receive.

Torrance, E.P. "Unique Needs of the Creative Child and Adult." In
Passow, A.H. (Ed.). *The Gifted and the Talented: Their Education
and Development. The Seventy-eighth Yearbook of the National Society
for the Study of Education.* Chicago: University of Chicago Press,
1979. 352-371.

"At the 1967 annual meeting of the National Association for Gifted Children, it was proposed that the creative gifted be designated a new category in the field of Special Education-Exceptional Children." Although things have improved somewhat for creative children and adults, there is still much to be done in this area. Toward this end, the author discusses a list of suggested policies and practices. The author discusses the use of a combination of tests and observations to identify creative children and adults. Torrance points out that creativity tests can be categorized into two types--those that focus on cognitive-affective skills (e.g., Torrance Tests of Creative Thinking) and those that tap a personality syndrome (e.g., Alpha Biographical Inventory)--and argues that both types of tests are valuable when used in conjunction with each other.

Also discussed is the creativity-intelligence distinction; the author points out that confusion has been created by attempts to distinguish clearly between the two. The author himself has never tried to make such a distinction and believes that both kinds of processes are involved in creative problem-solving activities. Thus he does not think one should replace intelligence tests with creativity tests but rather that a wider range of tests should be used.

Another matter discussed is how measures of intelligence and creativity behave differently. For example, there are measurable differences related to race and socio-economic status in measured intelligence, but no racial and socio-economic differences were reflected on the Torrance test results in the studies reviewed. While evidence for heredity has been found with intelligence tests, no such evidence appears in studies using the Torrance tests. Tests should not be the sole means of identifying the creative child. "Tests *can* help, however, in making educators aware of creative potentialities that might otherwise go unrecognized and unacknowledged."

Still other policies and practices that the author recommends include: creative children and adults need a refuge in the system because their creativity frequently sets them apart. Creative children and adults need sponsors and patrons. Creative giftedness has to be recognized and acknowledged. Creative people have to be helped to understand their creativity and need opportunities to express themselves and their ideas in acceptable ways. Schools are not the only resources for creative children and adults: "policies and practices are needed at all levels--community, city, county, regional, national and international--that facilitate access to the resources needed by creative children and adults."

Torrance, E.P. "Misperceptions about Creativity in Gifted Education: Removing the Limits on Learning." *Curricula for the Gifted: Selected Proceedings of the First National Conference on Curricula for the Gifted/Talented.* Ventura, CA: Ventura County School Office, 1982. 59-70.

The author presents and responds to 10 misperceptions about creativity in gifted education. Some of these, the author says, occur among experts such as Hagen (1980), Keating (1980), Rice (1980), Spillane (1980), and Stanley (1980).

"1. The scientific study of creativity dates from J.P. Guilford's 1950 presidential address to the American Psychological Association." In the United States and in Western countries there has been research in this area since the late 1800's and earlier in some Eastern cultures.

"2. Curricular materials designed for teaching creative thinking and problem-solving are devoid of academic or artistic content." The author and others have advocated teaching creativity techniques as a part of every course.

"3. Creativity research has been concerned almost exclusively with divergent thinking." Some critical researchers in the field have always emphasized that divergent thinking is not all there is to creativity, and more than divergent thinking has been incorporated into training materials.

"4. (a) Creative thinking is a rational cognitive process; (b) Creative thinking is something wild and unstructured, and involves clairvoyance, telepathy, and other psychic abilities." Torrance counters, "Genuine creative achievements require great persistence and discipline, but also involve going beyond the rational" (p. 62).

"5. Creativity teaching in education is responsible for the drops in SAT scores in recent years." The author cites a number of studies which found nothing to support the accusation. He also cites a study (Allen, 1969) in which training in creative dramatics increased reading comprehension more than did instruction in remedial reading.

"6. Creativity and practice skills are antithetical." No one involved in the development of instructional materials and curricula would deny the importance of drill and practice.

"7. Creativity tests have no validity (Hagen, 1980; Spillane, 1980) and creativity experiments involving their use consequently have no validity (Crockenberg, 1972; Mansfield, Busse and Krepelka, 1978)." The author points out that many validity studies have been conducted.

"8. The longer the time period for which you try to predict future behavior, the less accurate the predictions are." This may hold true for some tests and some criteria but not for the Torrance Tests of Creative Thinking. Researchers did not pay adequate attention to persistence and were in too much of a hurry to complete their prediction studies.

"9. Creativity test scores are inappropriate for use in multiple screening for special gifted programs." The strongest evidence for using creativity tests for multiple screening purposes "is a set of studies spanning 22 years, indicating that creatively gifted student who fall short of the IQ screening criterion for giftedness (130 or higher) achieve just as well as those who pass this criterion...."

"10. Black and other disadvantaged children identified as creative gifted are not really gifted. This is just a convenient way of 'letting them into' gifted programs." A lack of racial and socio-economic bias is characteristic of the Torrance Tests of Creative Thinking (Torrance, 1964, 1971, 1977) and a Torrance test for pre-primary children called Thinking Creatively in Action and Movement (Torrance, 1981).

The author concludes that "Serious limits have been placed on gifted education through our identification methods. In general, our search for giftedness has been too passive, too white, and too middle class. We have been too obsessed by a single concept of giftedness and have been too slow in adopting a multi-criteria approach to identification" (p. 70).

Suggestions for Further Reading

Allen, E.G. "An Investigation of Change in Reading Achievement, Self-concept and Creativity of Disadvantaged Elementary Children Experiencing Three Methods of Training." Doctoral dissertation, University of Southern Mississippi, 1969. *Dissertation Abstracts International* 29 (1969), 3032. University Microfilms Order No. 69-4683.

Crockenberg, S.B. "Creativity Tests: A Boon or Boondoggle for Education?" *Review of Educational Research* 42 (1972): 27-45.

Cropley, A.J. "Some Canadian Creativity Research." *Journal of Research and Development in Education* 4 (1971): 113-115.

DeBono, E. *Thinking Course for Juniors.* Dorset, United Kingdom: Direct Education Services, 1974.

DeBono, E. *Think Links.* Dorset, United Kingdom: Direct Education Services, 1975.

DeBono, E. *Thinking Action.* Dorset, United Kingdom: Direct Education Services, 1976. (Pupil's Book, teacher's book, and pupil leaflets.)

Getzels, J.W., and Jackson, P.W. *Creativity and Intelligence.* New York: John Wiley, 1962.

Hagen, E. *Identification of the Gifted.* New York: Teachers College Press, 1980.

Howieson, N.A. "A Longitudinal Study of Creativity." *Journal of Creative Behavior* 15 (1981: 117-134.

Kamin, L.J. *The Science and Politics of I.Q.* New York: Wiley, 1974.

Keating, D.P. "Four Faces of Creativity: The Continuing Plight of the Intellectually Underserved." *Gifted Child Quarterly* 24 (1980): 56-61.

Lozanov, G. *Suggestology and Outlines of Suggestopaedy.* New York: Gordon and Breach, 1978.

Majumdar, S.K. "Creative Abilities in the Making of Scientists." Report for the National Council of Educational Research and Training, New Delhi, India, 1979.

Prichard, A., and Taylor, J. *Accelerating Learning.* Novato, CA: Academic Therapy Publications, 1980.

Rice, B. "Going for the Gifted Gold." *Psychology Today* 13 (1980): 55-58, 67.

Spillane, R.R. Letter to E. Paul Torrance, dated October 24, 1980. The State Education Department, Albany, NY.

Stanley, J.C. "On Educating the Gifted." *Educational Researcher* 9 (1980): 8-12.

Torrance, E.P. *Guiding Creative Talent.* Englewood Cliffs, NJ: Prentice-Hall, 1962.

Torrance, E.P. "Identifying the Creatively Gifted Among Economically and Culturally Disadvantaged Children." *Gifted Child Quarterly* 8 (1964): 171-176.

Torrance, E.P. *Encouraging Creativity in the Classroom*. Dubuque, IA: William Brown, 1970.

Torrance, E.P. "Are the Torrance Tests of Creative Thinking Biased Against or in Favor of Disadvantaged Groups?" *Gifted Child Quarterly* 15 (1971): 75–80.

Torrance, E.P. "Can We Teach Children to Think Creatively?" *Journal of Creative Behavior* 6 (1972a): 114–143.

Torrance, E.P. "Predictive Validity of the Torrance Tests of Creative Thinking." *Journal of Creative Behavior* 6 (1972b): 236–252.

Torrance, E.P. "Career Patterns of and Peak Creative Achievements of Creative High School Students Twelve Years Later." *Gifted Child Quarterly* 16 (1972c): 75–88.

Torrance, E.P. *Torrance Tests of Creative Thinking: Norms--Technical Manual*. Bensenville, IL: Scholastic Testing Service, 1974a.

Torrance, E.P. *Sociodrama in Career Education*. Athens: Career Education Project, College of Education, University of Georgia, 1974b.

Torrance, E.P. *Discovery and Nurturance of Giftedness in the Culturally Different*. Reston, VA: Council for Exceptional Children, 1977.

Torrance, E.P. *The Search for Sartori and Creativity*. Great Neck, NY: Creative Synergetic Associates, 1979a.

Torrance, E.P. "A Three-Stage Model for Teaching for Creative Thinking." In Lawson, A.E. (Ed.). *The Psychology of Teaching for Thinking and Creativity*. Columbus: ERIC Clearing House for Science, Mathematics and Environmental Education, Ohio State University, 1979b.

Torrance, E.P. "Predicting the Creativity of Elementary School Children (1958–80)." Paper prepared for presentation at the annual meetings of the National Association for Gifted Children, Minneapolis, October 30, 1980.

Torrance, E.P. *Administration, Scoring and Norms--Technical Manual for Thinking Creatively in Action and Movement*. Bensenville, IL: Scholastic Testing Service, 1981.

Torrance, E.P., and Gupta, R.K. *Programmed Experiences in Creative Thinking*. Minneapolis: Bureau of Educational Research, University of Minnesota, 1964.

Torrance, E.P., and Hall, L.K. "Assessing the Further Reaches of Creative Potential." *Journal of Creative Behavior* 14 (1980): 1–19.

Torrance, E.P., and Myers, R.E. *Creative Learning and Teaching*. New York: Harper and Row, 1970.

Torrance, E.P., and Wu, T.H. "A Comparative Longitudinal Study of the Adult Creative Achievement of Elementary School Children Identified as Highly Intelligent and as Highly Creative." *Creative Child and Adult Quarterly* 6 (1981): 71–76.

Torrance, E.P.; Sandwith, N.; and Horng, R.Y. *Cumulative Bibliography on the Torrance Tests of Creative Thinking*. Athens: Georgia Studies of Creative Behavior, 1981.

PSYCHOANALYSTS

Adler, A. *Problems of Neurosis*. New York: Cosmopolitan Book Corp., 1930. 244pp.

Genius involves a socially affirmative response to both hereditary and environmental factors. The manner in which it is expressed will be conditioned by the greatest defect of the organism. The effect of psychic compensation for organ inferiority is manifest in the lives of great men.

Fear of death as a motivating factor in the lives of some poets and philosophers is also discussed. Fear of death stems from early experiences with illness or with death. One way of dealing with such fear is to determine to make one's influence felt at some future time through one's creations.

Eissler, K.R. *Talent and Genius: The Fictitious Case of Tausk contra Freud*. New York: Quadrangle Books, 1971. 403pp. (Especially Chapter VII, Talent and Genius, 248-320.)

This book argues against various attempts to defame Freud's personality and to denigrate his contributions. Specifically, it focuses on a book by Paul Roazen entitled *Brother Animal*, which presents Freud's relationship with Tausk and suggests that Freud was responsible for Tausk's death.

Eissler considers Freud a genius and devotes a sizable part of the book to this thesis. Chapter VII, Talent and Genius, contains a number of points that are relevant to this book, with Eissler supporting his theories by examples from Freud's life and experiences.

Paradigms, following Kuhn, are produced by geniuses and the talented "modify or employ the paradigm that a genius has produced." A genius' achievements cannot be grasped right away; those of a talent can be grasped quickly. The bizarre behavior, etc., observed in genius is not common psychopathology "but rather manifestations of the creative act or its prerequisites." The genius has an extraordinary ability to bear pain and frustration. The phantasies of the creative child have a "propulsive force" (a term coined by Greenacre).

While it has been argued that the energy available for sublimation is pregenital in nature and that genital libido is exempt from sublimation, Eissler doubts that this may be the case in genius. When a genius completes his work he falls into a tranquil mood comparable to that which follows sexual gratification. The author suggests that genius produces creative work when there is maximal frustration together with "maximal directedness toward the world." Rescue fantasies appear more frequently among the talented than among the geniuses.

Talented people do not succeed in harnessing the unconscious as geniuses do. With regard to genius and suicide Eissler says that in general, a true genius will commit suicide--if he does so at all-- only when the pathway to creative acts is permanently blocked. The genius becomes involved in doing and undoing but talent does not have the need to undo.

Another difference between talent and genius is "inequality in the level of inner strength." Thus, the genius can overcome his

intense anguish. Whereas the talented person needs to resolve the
Oedipal conflict, the genius not only has the strength to endure
conflict but also needs it "in order to be incited over and over
again to renewed accomplishments." The genius initially is involved
in a great deal of internalization but gradually creativity becomes
increasingly autonomous and object-independent.

Freud avoided severe psychopathology because he carried out a
partial self-analysis and because he had a great deal of self-
discipline. Conditions in society have to favor the development
of genius. In Freud's case, it was the important effects occurring
in Victorian society.

Freud, S. *Three Contributions to the Theory of Sex*. New York: Nervous
and Mental Disease Publishing Co., 1910. 117pp.

Sublimation involves the diversion of sexual motive powers from
sexual aims to new aims. These new aims are cultural accomplishments or accomplishments of a higher order. Sublimation forms one
of the sources of artistic activity. Depending on how complete the
sublimation is, the psychoanalysis of the character of gifted and
artistically disposed individuals "will show any proportionate
blending between productive ability, perversion, and neurosis."

When the sexual life of the child reaches its first peak, from the
ages of three to five, it begins to manifest activity related to the
impulse for knowledge and investigation. Psychoanalysis believes
that children's inquisitiveness is attracted to sexual problems
quite early and intensively, and perhaps it may first be awakened
by sexual problems.

Freud, S. "The Relation of the Poet to Day-dreaming." In Riviere, J.
(Trans.). *Collected Papers*, Vol. IV. London: Hogarth Press, 1948.
173-183.

Daydreaming in the adult is a substitute for play in the child's
life. Analysis of this activity may lend some insight into the
creative process. The motivating factors for adult phantasy are
unsatisfied wishes. The dynamics of phantasy are related to the
present, past, and future, and are worked out as follows. Something
in the present which aroused an unfulfilled wish goes back to the
past where the wish was fulfilled. Then a situation is created in
the future in which the wish can be fulfilled.

For his analysis, Freud selects not those writers who are highly
esteemed by critics but those who create spontaneously and are the
writers of romances and novels that are read rather widely. For
these people "imaginative creation, like day-dreaming, is a continuation of and substitute for the play of childhood."

The creative person is ashamed of his/her phantasies but his/her
artistic technique enables him/her to overcome feelings of revulsion
Artistic technique makes the material more palatable, and there is
an esthetic pleasure in the presentation of the material. The real
pleasure comes in the release of tensions. The audience is also
allowed to enjoy its own daydreams without feeling reproach or shame

Jung, C.G. "On the Relation of Analytical Psychology to Poetic Art."
In Jung, C.G. *Contributions to Analytical Psychology*. New York:
Harcourt, Brace, 1928. 225-249.

Jung differentiates between two types of art work. In one, the
artist intends a specific effect and the material is subject to the
artist's purpose. The other type, which he calls extroverted art,
involves an experience where the artist obeys what seem to be foreign
impulses that have a power over him/her and the work then flows
spontaneously from his/her pen. Extroverted art is more symbolic
than introverted art. Symptomatic art involves the personal unconscious and symbolic art the unconscious.
For Jung the creative process is an "autonomous complex." It
starts with stirrings from the unconscious and then spreads to
other associations. The artist shapes the archetype and, by bringing it into relation with conscious ideals, makes it possible for
every man to find "the deepest springs of life which would otherwise
be closed to him." In this lies the social importance of art. And
in this, the artist is the "educator of his time."

Jung, C.G. *Psychological Types*. New York: Harcourt, Brace, 1946.
(Especially Chapter X, General Description of Types, 412-517.)

Jung's typology, consisting of eight major kinds of people, stems
from the combination of two major attitudes--extroversion and in-
troversion--and four major functions--thinking, feeling, sensation,
and intuition.
The eight types are:
1. The extroverted thinking type. This individual utilizes intellectual function with external data. He/she is productive and
a synthesizer in his judgment.
2. The extroverted feeling type. People of this type go to the
theater, concerts, etc. Fashions depend on them and they support
social, philanthropic, and cultural enterprises.
3. The extroverted sensation type. This person seeks out experiences with external objects. It is important to sense objects
and to enjoy sensations.
4. The extroverted intuitive type. This person opens situations
with his/her intuition. This person is constantly looking for new
possibilities, new situations, objects, etc. This person may be a
promoter or initiator of enterprises and can inspire others.
5. The introverted thinking type. This person is directed to
subjective ideas and facts. This type formulates theories and
questions, opens up prospects but has the facts.
6. The introverted feeling type. This type manifests its creativity in "intimate poetic forms" that are guarded from others.
7. The introverted sensation type. For this person, the external
object serves as a release for subjective responses. Painters of
this type possess an unconscious which changes sense impressions in
accord with subjective material.
8. The introverted intuitive type. This person regards images in
terms of the unconscious. Mystical dreamers, seers, and the artistic
fall into this category. The artist in this category can do extraordinary things. Those who are not artists may be unappreciated
geniuses, great men "gone wrong," etc.

Kris, E. "Psychoanalysis and the Study of Creative Imagination."
   Bulletin of the New York Academy of Medicine 29 (1953): 334-351.

   Creativity consists of three phases--inspiration, elaboration,
and communication. In the first phase, the individual is "driven;
he is in an exceptional state. Thoughts or images tend to flow,
things appear in his mind of which he never seemed to have known."
The second phase is characterized by labor, concentration, and endeavor; here, the creator looks on his/her work from the outside.

Kubie, L.S. *Neurotic Distortion of the Creative Process.* Lawrence:
   University of Kansas Press, 1958. 151pp.

   Conscious symbolic processes are anchored in reality, and this
limits their free imaginative play. In the unconscious, the relationship of symbol to what it represents is impaired, distorted, or
actually lost. Since "by the creative process, we mean the capacity
to find new and unexpected connections," the free play of preconscious symbolic processes is essential to the creative activity.
   Additional educational methods either tie preconscious processes
prematurely to reality or leave them to the distorting influences
that stem from unresolved unconscious conflicts.
   The author does not believe that sublimation of unconscious
processes is necessary to understand creativity. Indeed, since the
concept of sublimation was formulated before the workings of the
preconscious system were understood, the concept of sublimation may
be misleading.

MacKinnon, D.W. Chapter 11. "Personality and the Realization of
   Creative Potential." *In Search of Human Effectiveness.* Buffalo,
   NY: Creative Education Foundation; and Great Neck, NY: Creative
   Synergetic Associates, 1976. 136-151.

   MacKinnon first briefly summarizes Rank's orientation and applies
it to his study of three groups of architects, differentiated in
terms of their creativity.
   Rank conceptualizes that human beings go through three stages in
arriving at their own individuality and realizing their creative
potential. Sometimes these stages are also conceptualized as personality types: the adapted type, the neurotic type, and the creative
type. They might also be referred to as the average or normal person, the conflicted or neurotic person, and the artist or person of
will and deed.
   People, according to Rank, move through life from trauma of birth
to trauma of death. Their personalities are developed by the interaction and strength of two basic and opposed fears: the fear of life
and the fear of death. Psychological development depends on the
individual's capacity to integrate the conflict between the two
fears.
   The integrative capacity of the individual is called "will."
Historically, the will develops as "counterwill," a resistance to
demands and pressures from others. In following the counterwill
the child experiences guilt as the separation from others. If the
family accepts the child's behavior and accepts the child as independent of them, then the child can develop his/her own individuality.

This results in the development of the creative type. The adapted
type identifies *early* with the will of the parents and so experiences
little pain in the development of his/her own independence. This
type experiences no strong motivation for individuation and feels
no conflict about complying with social norms. The neurotic type
does not have a sense of independence from society nor is it sufficiently developed to enable the individual to express his/her own
individuality creatively.

MacKinnon applies Rankian theory to the three groups of architects
studied at the Institute for Personality Assessment and Research
(IPAR). Group I, the most creative, was intensively studied in the
IPAR assessment program. Groups II and III filled out forms and
questionnaires at home. Differences found among the three groups,
in a *post hoc* study, differentiated among them in line with Rankian
theory.

Evidence presented from Gough's Adjective Check List is also in
line with Rankian Theory. MacKinnon also mentions the Freudian
concepts of the three groups of architects.

Rapaport, D. "On the Psychoanalytic Theory of Thinking." *International Journal of Psychoanalysis* 31 (1950): 161-170.

Thought processes, according to the psychoanalytic view, are
motivated by instincts, and thinking "is a detour from the direct
path towards gratification." Genetically, two processes are distinguished: the primary process and the secondary process. The
former operates with mobile cathexis, strives for complete and
immediate discharge of tensions, and is regulated by the pleasure
principle. The secondary process operates with small amounts of
bound cathexis, does not discharge tension before experimental action
indicates that tension reduction is possible, and is regulated by
the reality principle. Topographically, thought processes may be
conscious, preconscious, or unconscious. The idea that the unconscious operates in terms of the primary process, and the preconscious and conscious in terms of the secondary process, is
somewhat arbitrary. Kris has indicated that the ego may use primary
processes for its own purposes, as in art and inspiration. This
area still requires clarification.

Structurally speaking, thought processes are related to ego-
development. From an economic point of view, thought processes are
discussed in terms of counter-cathexis, hyper-cathexis, attention
cathexis, and in terms of delibidinized, or sublimated, energies.
From a biological point of view, Rapaport says that "thinking is
experimental action with small amounts of energy. Thinking explores
the possible pathways of action to find the one of least resistance,
least danger, and greatest directness, while preserving almost intact the energy necessary for motor action."

PSYCHOLOGISTS

Amabile, T. "Social Psychology of Creativity: A Consensual Assessment
Technique." *Journal of Personality and Social Psychology* 43 (1982):
997-1013.

Amabile, T. "The Social Psychology of Creativity: A Componential Conceptualization." *Personality and Social Psychology* 45 (1983a): 357-
376.

Amabile, T. *The Social Psychology of Creativity.* New York: Springer-
Verlag, 1983b. 245pp.

For the author, the most appropriate definition of creativity is
that it be based on the product that is produced. Hence she defines
it as "the quality of products or responses judged to be creative
by appropriate observers, and it can also be regarded as the process
by which something so judged is produced" (Amabile, 1982, p. 1001).
She sees three major components in creativity: (1) domain-relevant
skills, including knowledge and skills required to work in a specific
area. These depend on the individual's innate cognitive and perceptual and motor skills as well as the individual's formal and informal education; (2) creativity-relevant skills, including cognitive style, knowledge of the "heuristics for generating novel
ideas" and a "conducive work style." These depend on training in
idea generation and the individual's personality characteristics;
(3) task motivation, including the individual's motivation for undertaking the task and his/her perception of his/her own motivation
for undertaking the task. These depend on the intrinsic motivation
for the task, the "presence or absence of salient constraints in
the social environment," and the "individual ability to cognitively
minimize extrinsic constraints."

The creative process consists of: problem or task presentation,
preparation, response generation, response validation, and outcome.
The three components previously described operate on different
stages of the process. A major difference between this approach
and others "is the prominence given to task motivation and the
presentation of specific propositions concerning the detrimental
effects of extrinsic motivation on creativity."

Barron, F. "Complexity-Simplicity as a Personality Dimension."
Journal of Abnormal and Social Psychology 48 (1953): 163-172.

This is a report of a study of preference for complexity as
measured by preferences for asymmetrical line drawings in the
Barron-Welsh Art Scale and the psychological correlates thereof.
The subjects were 40 male graduate students from several different
departments at the University of California. The study was conducted
at the Institute for Personality Assessment and Research (IPAR) at
the University of California, Berkeley.

Complexity was positively related to IPAR staff ratings on such
variables as personal tempo, verbal fluency, effeminacy, sentience,
and sensuality. The correlations were negative with constriction,
good judgment, rigidity, conformity, and submissiveness. Complexity
also correlated positively with faculty ratings of originality and
negatively with self-ratings on conformity.

It is suggested that the preference for complexity discussed here
may be related to orality and its derivatives (originality, artistic
creativeness, acceptance of femininity in men, etc.) It is also regarded as related to impulse acceptance and the absence of repression

Barron, F. "The Psychology of Imagination." *Scientific American* 199 (1958): 150-166.

This is an overview and integration of research conducted at the Institute for Personality Assessment and Research (IPAR). Original people are regarded as able to deal with the imperfections and imbalances in nature. They are challenged by the unusual and the irregular. For them, "disorder offers the potentiality of order." Creative individuals receive satisfaction of an aesthetic sort from their synthesizing abilities. The synthesizing disposition of creative people is regarded as a reflection of their striving to integrate diverse phenomena into "an elegant new order more satisfying than any that could be evoked by a simpler configuration."

With regard to creativity and mental health, Barron believes that whereas the creative individual may often appear to be unbalanced, in fact he/she is too healthy for society's norms. The appearance of instability is related to the creative individual's being hypersensitive to the complexities of life. The creative individual is also observant of the world, has a high energy level, and is very much in contact with his/her unconscious and therefore gives the appearance of being "odd." The ability to synthesize complexity is the mark of the creative individual.

Suggestions for Further Reading

Barron, F. *Artists in the Making.* New York: Academic Press, 1972.

————. *Creative Person and Creative Process.* New York: Holt, 1969.

————. *Creativity and Personal Freedom.* New York: Van Nostrand, 1968.

Davidson, J.E., and Sternberg, R.J. "The Role of Insight in Intellectual Giftedness." *Gifted Child Quarterly* 28 (1984): 58-64.

The authors argue that the usual measures of intelligence may mask certain skills that distinguish the intellectually gifted from the intellectually average and subaverage. Insight is one of those skills and this paper consists of a series of experiments on three psychological processes related to insight—selective encoding, selective combination, and selective comparison. The results of the various studies provide evidence in support of the authors' hypothesis. A training program designed to improve children's insight is also presented.

Suggestions for Further Reading

Sternberg, R.J. *Beyond IQ: A Triarchic Theory of Human Intelligence.* New York: Cambridge University Press, 1986.

————. "Intelligence and Nontrenchment." *Journal of Educational Psychology* 73 (1981): 1-16.

————. "Testing Intelligence without IQ Tests." *Phi Delta Kappan* 65 (1984): 694-698.

Sternberg, R.J., and Davidson, J.E. "Insight in the Gifted." *Educational Psychologist* 18 (1983): 51-57.

Gardner, H. *Art, Mind and Brain: A Cognitive Approach to Creativity.*
New York: Basic Books, 1982. 371pp.

   This book presents and discusses several crucial sources for the
author's thinking and contributions to "Project Zero." Project Zero
was founded by the Harvard philosopher Nelson Goodman, who noted
that "next to nothing" was known about "the nature of artistic
thinking" and sought to learn about it through this project, which
coordinated both philosophical and psychological perspectives on
the arts.
   The book is divided into five parts: Part I--Masters--discusses
the works of Piaget, Chomsky, Lévi-Strauss, Cassirer, Langer, Goodman
and Gombrich. Part II--Artistic Development in Children--discusses
children's artistic creativity, including the matter of development
in specific artistic media (including the development of the metaphor in children). This section concludes with two chapters on
exceptional children--one on the case of an autistic child, Nadia,
and the other on child prodigies.
   Part III--On Education and Media: The Transmission of Knowledge--
focuses on television and its effects. Part IV--The Breakdown of
the Mind--discusses such topics as brain damage and loss of language.
Part V--The Heights of Creativity--contains one chapter on adult
creativity and another on Mozart.

Gardner, J.W. *Excellence: Can We Be Equal and Excellent Too?* New
York: Harper and Brothers, 1961. 171pp.

   "This is a book about excellence, more particularly about the conditions under which excellence is possible in our kind of society;
but it is also inevitably a book about equality, about the kinds of
equality that can and must be honored, and the kinds that cannot be
forced."
   The book is divided into four parts: Part One--Equal and Unequal,
Part Two--Talent, Part Three--Individual Differences, and Part Four--
The Ingredients of a Solution.
   Among Gardner's conclusions are that "excellence implies more than
competence. It implies a striving for the highest standards in
every phase of life. We need individual excellence in all its forms-
in every kind of creative endeavor, in political life, in education,
in industry--in short, universally." He further concludes, "Free
men must set their own goals.... They must be quick to apprehend
the kinds of effort and performance their society needs, and they
must demand that kind of effort and performance of themselves and of
their fellows."

Guilford, J.P. "Creativity." *American Psychologist* 5 (1950): 444-
454. (Guilford's *The Nature of Human Intelligence* is presented on
p. 144.)

   In this paper, Guilford's presidential address to the American
Psychological Association, Guilford points out his examination of
the 121,000 titles published in the *Psychological Abstracts* for the
23 years since its inception showed that only 186 were indexed as
"definitely bearing on the subject of creativity." Of the textbooks
on general psychology only two had separate chapters on creativity.

The topic may have been neglected because of the belief that genius is largely a matter of IQ, because the criterion issue is so difficult to resolve, because creativity cannot be measured by tests designed as tests of intelligence which demand objectivity and scoring convenience, and because learning research has been limited to animals, in whom signs of creativity are almost nonexistent.

For Guilford, "creativity refers to the abilities that are most characteristic of creative people. Creative abilities determine whether the individual has the power to exhibit creative behavior to a noteworthy degree. Whether or not the individual who has the requisite abilities will actually produce results of a creative nature will depend upon his motivational and temperamental traits." Creativity can be expected in all people.

Guilford considers it unfortunate that "genius" is associated with high IQ. He is critical of Terman's work, and observes that there is little evidence of creativity among Terman's high IQ group.

The content of intelligence tests reveals little that has to do with creative behavior. Most intelligence tests measure only about a half-dozen intellectual factors, whereas many more surely exist. Also, some of the abilities related to creativity are not intellectual, but perceptual.

There is a major section on the use of factor analysis and one headed "Specific hypotheses concerning creative abilities." These hypotheses concern sensitivity to problems, fluency, existence of novel ideas, flexibility, synthesizing ability, analytical ability, reorganization or redefinition, complexity, and evaluation.

Regarding validity, Guilford says that the factorial study of the tests alone is a validation. The second issue is the relationship between the tests and the creativity of people in everyday life. In everyday life, creativity is likely to be dependent on primary traits other than such abilities as motivation and temperament. Hypotheses regarding these need to be developed.

In concluding, Guilford notes that once we have identified the factors that predict creativity, we can select individuals with creative potential. We then need to know how to foster and increase this potential through education.

Guilford, J.P. "Creativity: Retrospect and Prospect." *Journal of Creative Behavior* 4 (1970): 149-168.

Guilford reviews the history and developments to mid-century and presents data reflecting the large increase in publications in the area of creativity since his 1950 paper. Guilford then reviews some of the work that has been done and reflects on it. Some of the reflections follow.

For Guilford, "creativity is not any one thing; it is many things and takes many forms."

If one chooses only one test for creativity one may make an error. For example, if the test is Mednick's Remote Associates Test, one may be using a test of convergence rather than divergent thinking. Also, in evaluating any training program one should analyze with great care the instruments and exercises used to determine precisely what factors may be involved and what tests to use. Superficial analysis may be misleading. Changes in test conditions can bring about unexpected results.

Another ability that has been neglected is transformation. Transformation abilities provide a basis for intellectual flexibility which is important in creativity.

The earlier "sensitivity to problems" is now "cognition of semantic implications."

The operation evaluation has also been neglected in research. Evaluation can occur in all stages of problem solving and there is an opportunity for evaluation even in Osborn's brainstorming procedure.

Regarding education, Guilford says that to produce skilled problem solvers "we should see that developing individuals encounter the experiences that will exercise the functions in all categories.... I have often recommended another step, and that is to acquaint the learner with the nature of his various intellectual resources as early as he is ready to understand this information."

There is a readiness for change in society and a tolerance for experimentation in higher education. Colleges devoted to creative education can play crucial roles in this regard.

Guilford indicates that of the 120 possible Structure of Intelligence (SI) factors 98 have already been demonstrated.

Guilford, J.P. *Way Beyond the IQ: Guide to Improving Intelligence and Creativity.* Buffalo, NY: Creative Education Foundation; and Great Neck, NY: Creative Synergetic Associates, 1977. 192pp.

Written for the serious general audience, this book presents Guilford's views as they developed over the years.

The reader is introduced to the idea that intelligence is not regarded as measurable by a single value. All the factors are liberally illustrated with many examples; on some of them the reader can try his/her own skill. There are suggestions of how the factors appear in daily life and how they may be developed, as well as exercises for the reader and suggested readings.

There are three dimensions to Guilford's model: contents, operations, and products. In other words, there is a content that the individual works on with various operations to produce certain products. Within each dimension are various categories. For contents there are five: visual, auditory, symbolic, semantic, and behavioral. For operations there are five: cognition, memory, divergent production, convergent production, and evaluation. For products there are six: units, classes, relations, systems, transformations, and implications. Thus there are a total of 150 factors (5 x 5 x 6).

Analyzing the Stanford-Binet Intelligence Scale to determine how many of the Structure of Intelligence (SI) abilities it contains, Guilford reports that of the 140 problems, only 28 Structure of Intelligence abilities were "represented each by at least one problem." Instead of a single IQ score, "What is needed is a profile of scores, in which the individual's strengths and weaknesses are displayed."

In the last chapter Guilford discusses how various combinations of SI abilities operate in problem solving and creativity. The point is made that the problem with Binet-type tests is that they test for comprehension or understanding rather than productive thinking, and productive thinking is more important in problem solving. Similarly, in educational settings, it has been found that much time is spent with cognition and memory rather than production and evaluation. Divergent production and transformation are essential to critical thinking.

In this chapter, Guilford presents his problem-solving model based on his structure of intellect. Memory underlies everything and contributes to everything that goes on. The problem-solving process begins with input from the communication system, from the environment, and from the soma, which includes the bodily parts. In this manner, Guilford takes care of the input from feelings and emotions that may initiate problem solving in producers of art in any form.

The environmental information goes through a "filtering process." The nervous information that gets through begins the process of cognition. This involves an awareness of the problem and comprehension of the nature of the problem. Cognition continues to operate in the diagnosis of the problem. Then one is at the solution-generation stage; to seek solutions, one is involved in divergent production, which involves searching one's memory store. If the search had not been so broad, the individual would have been involved in convergent production.

Ideas are evaluated along the way. Some divergent production may avoid evaluation as in Osborn's idea of "suspended judgment." There is always a backing and filling. The lack of solution of a problem may indicate that the problem was inappropriately cognized and the individual has to go back and start again. Creativity in the model takes place wherever divergent production occurs. "Activities in the model are also creative where transformations occur."

The remainder of the chapter is devoted to how various other factors may facilitate or hinder the creative process. He considers such matters as: environment, motivation, store of information, flexibility versus rigidity, group thinking, criticism, attitudes, and emotions. Then he discusses a variety of strategies and tactics in the creative process such as broadening the problem, asking questions, and suspending judgment.

Hebb, S.O. "Problems Relating to Thought." In Hebb, D.O. *A Textbook of Psychology*. Philadelphia, PA: W.B. Saunders, 1958. 200-219.

In a chapter entitled "Discovery, Invention, and Logic," Hebb distinguishes between "(1) discovery or invention, the attaining of new ideas, and (2) verification, the process of testing, clarifying, and systematizing them." A new idea is a recombination of "mediating processes," and these processes are, in turn, a product of sensory data and the immediately preceding central processes. The thinker does not know what combination he/she is looking for. After exhausting the alternatives presented by logical analysis, he/she may turn to a more or less "blend" manipulation of the problem elements. Here, chance plays a role in determining when the appropriate combination will appear.

Hebb points out that some of the most brilliant contributions to science do not involve any intellectually difficult ideas. "The great scientist is not always one who thinks at a more complex level. He is great frequently because his thoughts somehow have avoided the complexities in which others are bogged down, because he sees the relevant issues, and often enough with no logical justification except that in the end it works--because he had pushed apparently

contradictory data to one side, leaving them to be explained later."
The reason that the scientist is able to temporarily ignore contradictory data is that his thought encompasses the prospect of future
change in knowledge as well as present data.

MacKinnon, D.W. "Assessing Creative Persons." In Biondi, A.M., and
Parnes, S.J. (Eds.). *Assessing Creative Growth--The Tests--Book
One*. Great Neck, NY: Creative Synergetic Associates, 1976. 27-43.

This paper describes some of the essential characteristics of the
approach of the group at the Institute for Personality Assessment
and Research (IPAR) to the study of creativity. It is based on the
approach developed by Murray for the Office of Strategic Services
(OSS) during World War II and described in *Assessment of Men* (OSS
Assessment Staff, 1948). It has been used successfully at IPAR and
flourished there despite Cronbach's (1956) pronouncement that
assessment was dead.

Assessment involves the psychological evaluation of individuals
based on the following: "(1) the testing and observing of individuals
in a group setting, (2) with a multitude of tests and procedures
(3) by a number of staff members who through (4) a pooling of test
scores and subjective impressions sought to formulate psychodynamic
descriptions of the assessed subjects which would permit (5) prediction of the assessees' behavior in certain types of roles and situations."

The emphasis is on "(1) an attempt to delineate the 'personality
as a whole' (not the 'whole personality' which is something different
and, I am afraid, impossible to achieve), (2) a concern with the
more favorable and positive aspects of personality and its potentialities for effective functioning in demanding roles and situations,
and (3) a serious attempt to validate the predictions concerning the
current or future behavior of assessed subjects."

Assessors at IPAR record their impressions in both quantitative
and qualitative ways. They write out reports and complete a 100-
item check list covering the subject's life history, behavior during
the interview, speech, reaction to the interview and interviewer,
etc. Assessors check their impressions on the Gough Adjective
Check List (Gough, 1960; Gough and Heilbrun, 1965). They also use
100 statements for a Q-Sort (Block, 1961). A third technique is to
rate each subject on 20 to 30 traits, and then average the ratings.

One of the problems with assessment centers is the expense involved
in supporting an assessment staff and in bringing subjects in for
assessment.

High standards have been set for assessment programs, but critics
of these programs (who have concentrated on low predictive validities)
have overlooked the important objective of the program in discovering
what goes with what in personality structure, and of determining
more specifically the distinguishing characteristics of those who
score high or low on the various scales of standard personality tests
and inventories.

To cut down on expense the assessment center does not invite all
groups to the center for study; other groups are studied through
mailed questionnaires and tests.

Data may be analyzed by correlating ratings and scores with a criterion, but also by stepwise regression analysis.

Suggestions for Further Reading

Block, J. *The Q-sort Method in Personality Assessment and Psychiatric Research*. Springfield, IL: Charles C. Thomas, 1961.

Cronbach, L.J. "Assessment of Individual Differences." *Annual Review of Psychology* 7 (1956): 173-196.

Gough, H.G. "The Adjective Check List as a Personality Assessment Rsearch Technique." *Psychological Reports Monograph Supplement* 2,6 (1960): 102-107.

Gough, H.G., and Heilbrun, A.B., Jr. *Adjective Check List Manual*. Palo Alto, CA: Consulting Psychologists Press, 1965.

MacKinnon, D.W. *In Search of Human Effectiveness*. Buffalo, NY: The Creative Education Foundation; and Great Neck, NY: Creative Synergetic Associates, 1978.

The first director of the Institute for Personality Assessment and Research (IPAR) at the University of California, Berkeley, presents the Institute's orientation, methods of research and results in the study of creativity among adults in this book written for the serious lay reader. Acknowledging "that there is no single mold into which all who are creative will fit," the author presents the following as characteristics of creative individuals: "effective intelligence," "openness to experience," "freedom from crippling restraints and impoverishing inhibitions," "aesthetic sensitivity," "cognitive flexibility," "independence in thought and action," "unquestioning commitment to creative endeavor," and "increasing striving for solutions to the ever more difficult problems that he constantly sets for himself." Issues for future research are also presented.

Maslow, A.H. "Emotional Blocks to Creativity." *Humanist* 18 (1958): 325-332.

Maslow distinguishes between primary and secondary creativeness and discusses the interaction between them that is a requisite to growth, maturity, and true creativity. He is particularly concerned with the way in which rationality, though necessary for secondary creativity, can, if relied on excessively, establish blocks to creativity.

Primary creativeness is the "source of new discovery, of real novelty, of ideas that depart from that which exists at the point." It comes out of the unconscious, from primary process material, and is the source of play and fantasy as well as creativeness. Secondary creativeness, on the other hand, is "a kind of rational productivity demonstrated by many capable, functional, successful people." These people may be good scientists; the kind of scientific research at which they would excel would require the patient accumulation and painstaking analysis of great quantities of statistical data. Carried to extremes, however, this personality characteristic turns into an obsessive-compulsive neurosis.

Creativity is blocked when the individual's access to primary process material is blocked. Social adjustment may interfere with

the individual's acceptance of the data and of experiences provided
by his/her own primary processes. "Healthy, creative people are
able to be childlike *when they want to be*; this is 'regression in
the service of the ego.' These same people can afterward ... become
grown up, rational, sensible, orderly, and so on; and examine with
a critical eye what they produced in a great burst of enthusiasm and
creative fervor. A truly integrated person can be both secondary
and primary; both childlike and mature."

May, R. *The Courage to Create*. New York: W.W. Norton, 1975. 143pp.

   The title for this book comes from Paul Tillich's *The Courage to
Be*. May points out that "one cannot be in a vacuum. We express
our being in creating. Creativity is a sequel to being.... The
word *courage* in my title refers ... to that particular courage
essential for the creative act. This is rarely acknowledged in our
discussions of creativity and even more rarely written about."
The courage referred to here is not the opposite of despair but
"the *capacity to move ahead in spite of despair*."
   For the author, the creative act is the result of processes involved in the struggle of human beings "with and against that which
limits them." Nevertheless, "*creativity* itself requires limits."
The creative process expresses human "passion for form" which brings
order out of chaos and success in the struggle against disintegration. Through this struggle there is brought "into existence new
kinds of being that give harmony and integration."

Murray, H.A. "Vicissitudes of Creativity." In Anderson, H.H. (Ed.).
Creativity and Its Cultivation. New York: Harper, 1959. 96-118.

   Creativity is a process that results in a composition that is
new and valuable. The requirements for creation the author discusses include: a great store of contents in the preconscious and
unconcious, as well as a great fund of knowledge of the external
world; availability of "passionate psychic energy"; permeability
between the boundaries that separate the conscious and unconscious;
the ability to evaluate properly so that appropriate factors are
incorporated and superfluous ones are discarded; a process of putting
the intellect in order; and the relish for novelty. The creative
person is committed to a selected aim.
   The ego itself, although it plays an important role, is limited
in the creative process. It cannot force creation. It can only
preside "over an interior transaction which may or may not come out
with something that is worth seizing."
   Creation usually starts in the unconscious of one or more people,
and usually arises out of the suffering and estrangement they have
experienced. If others share this suffering and the final work is
"engagingly represented in other words or enacted in deeds," it will
be accepted and assimilated by others.
   Murray also considers creativity in interpersonal relationships
and illustrates it in the example of marriage. Finally, creativity
in different cultural epochs is considered.

Rogers, C.R. "Toward a Theory of Creativity." *ETC: A Review of General Semantics* XI (1954): 249-260. Also in Anderson, H.H. (Ed.). *Creativity and Its Cultivation.* New York: Harper, 1959. 69-82.

Rogers defines the creative process as "the emergence in action of a novel relational product, growing out of the uniqueness of the individual on the one hand, and the materials, events, people, or circumstances of his life on the other." People are motivated to create because of their tendency to actualize and become their potentialities.

There are three inner conditions for creativity: (a) "openness to experience," which includes "lack of rigidity," and "tolerance of ambiguity"; (b) "an internal locus of evaluation"; and (c) "the ability to toy with elements and concepts" and to combine them in new ways. Creativity may be fostered by conditions that facilitate "psychological safety" and "psychological freedom."

Rogers presents a number of hypotheses designed to give operational form to the theory and discusses ways in which his hypotheses may be tested.

Stein, M.I. "Creativity and Culture." *Journal of Psychology* 36 (1953): 311-322.

The nature of creative products is analyzed and inferences are drawn concerning the psychological processes involved in their creation. The author discusses the ways in which a variety of cultural factors may influence these psychological processes and the evaluations of the product.

The creative product is defined as "a novel work that is accepted as tenable or useful or satisfying by a group at some point in time." "Novel" means a deviation from the status quo. It represents a reintegration of existing materials or knowledge for the production of something new. It is a consequence of interaction between a creative individual and his/her environment. The psychological characteristics which distinguish the creative individual are: (a) heightened sensitivity to gaps or disequilibria in the environment; (b) a capacity to tolerate ambiguity, or to "live with" the disequilibria until they can be effectively resolved; (c) the capacity to generate hypotheses toward the resolution of the problem (which is in turn dependent on the effective communication between the individual and his/her environment and between some or all of the inner personal regions; (d) the capacity to test the hypotheses generated; and (e) the ability to communicate the results to others.

The terms "tenable or useful or satisfying" refer to the realm of ideas, things, and aesthetic experiences, respectively. Results of the creative process must be communicated to others. Thus, the creative person needs to possess two characteristics: (a) he/she must have mastered a means or medium of communication, and (b) he/she must have eliminated from the creative product those elements that are completely idiosyncratic.

The creative work "resonates" with the needs and experiences of an audience. The condition that the creative work be accepted "at some point in time" provides for the fact that products may be evaluated differently in different time periods. Cultures exert a variety of forces on creative works. Critics within a culture serve

as intermediaries in the creative process. Valuable lessons may be
drawn from the "non-appreciators" in the culture.

Thurstone, L.L. *Creative Talent*. "Reports from the Psychometric
Laboratory," No. 6. Chicago: University of Chicago Press, 1950.
10pp.

Thurstone suggests a number of hypotheses for the study of creative talent. If creative talent is qualitatively the same at all
levels, then problem solving at the professional level is different
from the work of genius only in degree. Professional work habits
might yield additional clues that should be followed up. Creative
talent and intelligence are not the same, but the two are undoubtedly
positively correlated. Likewise, creative talent is not the same as
scientific talent.

The main characteristic of creative work is the moment of insight
that differentiates it from the usual problem solving. From an
educational point of view, it is important to learn how, through
selecting students and through the proper curriculum, such original
thinking can be encouraged. There is a need to study what kinds of
mental work are done best under conditions of tension and concentration and which are done best under conditions of relaxation.

Studies of creativity, like studies of intelligence, might well
begin with attempts to determine whether there is a general factor,
different factors for different fields, or a group of factors.
Cognitive as well as temperamental characteristics have to be
studied.

The group selected for study should be equated for scholarship,
intelligence, professional prestige, and ability for critical ap-
praisal. Grades will correlate imperfectly with judgments of
originality because customary academic judgments are different from
those involved in judging originality.

Insofar as the selection of candidates for scholarship programs
designed to produce future leaders is concerned, the author proposes
that candidates fulfill minimal requirements for eligibility, present
evidence of marked attainment in one field, and present evidence
that the candidate for eligibility has produced something on his
own initiative. He believes it would be an error to award university scholarships on the basis of uniform national examinations.

Studies of creativity should include objective tests of temperament
and tests of the primary factors (the two closure factors, the
several space factors, the inductive factors, and several memory
factors). In addition, it may be valuable to study perceptual functions and perseveration.

Thurstone also points to the value of studying individual differences in learning before insight, and suggests experiments in this
area. Finally, he suggests that, "It is conceivable that we may
discover how to select people with creative talent before we can
learn much about the nature of that kind of talent."

Torrance, E.P. *Guiding Creative Talent*. Englewood Cliffs, NJ: Prentice-Hall, 1962. 278pp.

Torrance defines creative thinking "as the process of sensing gaps
or disturbing, missing elements; forming ideas or hypotheses concern-

ing them; testing these hypotheses; and communicating the results, possibly modifying and retesting the hypotheses."

Torrance began his studies of creative thinking in 1958 while at the Bureau of Educational Research of the University of Minnesota. He sought a set of tasks that would be applicable from kindergarten through graduate school. Alternate forms of some of Guilford's tests were developed, and in working out adaptations, content more appropriate to children was used. Other tasks were also developed, but in them Torrance followed an orientation that was different from Guilford's. "An attempt was made to construct tasks which would be models of the creative process, each requiring several types of thinking.... Perhaps the greatest divergence is from Guilford's insistence that predictor measures should represent single factors...."

At the University of Minnesota Laboratory Elementary School, Torrance administered his creativity tests and the Stanford-Binet to the children. He established a highly creative group that was in the upper 20% in creativity but not in intelligence, and a highly intelligent group that ranked in the upper 20% in intelligence but not in creativity. Students who were high in both measures were eliminated. Then he noted that "if we were to identify children as gifted on the basis of intelligence tests, we would eliminate from consideration approximately 70 percent of the most creative." He further noted that although there was a difference of 25 IQ points between the highly creative and the highly intelligent students, there were no statistically significant differences between them on achievement tests. This was similar to results reported by Getzels and Jackson for a secondary school. These results were not confirmed in a parochial school and in a small town elementary school where the emphasis was on teaching "traditional virtues in education." Torrance accounted for this by suggesting that in learning situations where students are taught to learn creatively, creative-thinking abilities are important, whereas in schools where teaching is authoritative, emphasizing memory and conformist behavior, highly intelligent students will perform better than the highly creative.

Teacher ratings were obtained for both groups of children. Teachers rated the highly intelligent children "as more desirable, better known or understood, more ambitious, and more hardworking or studious." This, Torrance interprets to mean that the highly creative learn as much as the highly intelligent but they do not appear to work as hard.

For the eight groups he studied, correlation between intelligence and creativity was little more than would be expected by chance.

Torrance considers that an increase in IQ over 120 makes little difference, and that above this point creative-thinking abilities become important. Torrance concludes "that we need to consider different kinds of achievement and develop measures to assess" them.

Torrance also reports data and results from other populations and studies. Summarizing these studies Torrance says, "The tasks discriminated industrial arts students rated as highly creative from those rated least creative, saleswomen who sell most from those who sell least, and saleswomen who work in creative departments from those who work in routine departments."

The book also contains much of Torrance's early work and his thinking on identifying the creative personality and creative development

(which includes discussions of the stages of development during the
preschool years, elementary years, high school, and after high school)
There are chapters on problems in maintaining creativity, problems
that may arise when creativity is repressed, goals for guiding creative talent, relationships with creative talent, a chapter for counselors, teachers, and administrators, and an appendix on administering the Minnesota Tests of Creative Thinking.

Vernon, P.E.; Adamson, G.; and Vernon, D.F.   *The Psychology and Educa-*
tion of Gifted Children. London: Methuen and Co.; and Boulder, CO:
Westview Press, 1977.   216pp.

Since 1960, much has been learned about the nature of intelligence
and its development. Although during childhood it varies a great
deal and is dependent on environmental factors, there is also a
hereditary component in both general and specialized abilities,
which are considerably more diverse than previously realized. There
is much interest in creativity "and a good deal of confusion between the creative production of outstanding artists or scientists,
and the rather trivial results of so called creativity, or divergent
thinking tests." In Britain, there is increasing criticism of and
decline in secondary (eleven-plus) education, and attacks on stream-
ing (ability grouping or homogeneous grouping). In North America,
support for gifted education is difficult to obtain because of
charges of elitism. There are different approaches to the education
of the gifted, each with its pros and cons. "Other trends which
need to be taken into account include computer managed instruction;
curricular developments, particularly in mathematics and science;
and the advocacy of what is called normalization in the education of
exceptional children."
The introductory chapter of this non-technical book for teachers
of the gifted gives a historical overview. The authors then turn to
giftedness and intelligence. Giftedness is broader than IQ; there
are gifted children with high IQs but also children with specialized
abilities whose IQ's may not be very high but are "usually well
above average."
The authors believe there is some justification for earlier testing of children who appear to be gifted--at three-and-a-half to four-
and-a-half years--since their Binet IQ's could be at 5 years old or
better. This chapter also presents and criticizes Terman's work.
In Chapter 3 the authors focus on intelligence, heredity, and environment, making use of Hebb's distinction between Intelligence A
and Intelligence B. The former "is the basic potentiality of the
organism whether animal or human, to learn and adapt to its environment." It is genetic and is mediated by the central nervous system;
the extent to which it develops depends on environmental stimulation.
"Intelligence B is the level of ability that a person actually shows
in his behaviour...." We cannot measure Intelligence A, and Intelligence B is not a single entity. The skills which make up Intelligence B reflect the culture in which the individual was reared.
To these two types of intelligence Vernon adds Intelligence C
which refers to intelligence test scores. Psychologists, according
to the authors, are often unclear whether they are "referring to
all-round thinking capacities (B), or to scores or IQs, obtained from
a particular test (C), or the basic genetical potential."

The authors suggest that giftedness and high intelligence depend largely on heredity, but because of genetic diversity many of those with high intellectual potential will come from average or sub-average families. Their potential will only be realized in an appropriate environment. Many potentially gifted children will be lost because their environment is not sufficiently nurturant.

In education, diversity of methods and content of instruction are needed to suit individual talents. Since gifted children are already high in conceptual ability, they could more profitably develop their skills and abilities in special areas of interest to them through "more flexible techniques of exploration and study than the ordinary classroom encourages."

The authors suggest that an IQ of 130 be used as a cut-off for selecting students for special educational programs. However, they emphasize that the IQ should be utilized quite flexibly and that "All those whose abilities are much superior to the average of their classmates should come under review, and arrangements made according to individual needs."

The authors distinguish between creativity of adults and creativity of children. They discuss various personality characteristics that have been associated with creativity among adults; these must be taken into account in dealing with the amateur whose works have to be distinguished from those of more creative individuals. After reviewing a number of studies that have utilized the divergent thinking tests, the authors conclude that these tests are "disappointing." Biographical questionnaires are more useful than divergent thinking tests for indicating giftedness. It is possible in grades 5 to 9 to pick out most of the intellectually gifted children (by using a well-chosen group test, teacher ratings, and consultation with parents.) The authors suggest that a trained psychologist also be involved. The main difficulty of this scheme is expense.

One chapter discusses the home life of gifted children. The authors make the point "that gifted children are children first and foremost: they should be valued and treated as such, rather than just for their achievements." The chapter concludes that parents must be prepared to compensate through home activities for the shortcomings of the school environment.

The authors consider the advantages and disadvantages of acceleration, segregation, and enrichment and conclude that the need for better facilities is increasingly being recognized by school boards. Such school programs do not create an elite group; they simply acknowledge the presence of the gifted minority.

Wertheimer, M. *Productive Thinking*. New York: Harper, 1945. 224pp.

Problems possess structural requirements which need to be understood by the problem-solver before they can be solved. A problem-solving situation may, in general, be divided into two parts: S1, in which the thought process begins; and S2, in which the problem is solved. The structural features of S1 set up stresses, strains, and tensions, which yield vectors "that in turn lead to the steps and operations dynamically in line with the requirements. This development is determined by the so-called Prägnanz principle, by the tendencies to the good gestalt, by the various gestalt laws." In S2, there is harmony between the mutual requirements, in which the parts are determined by the whole and the whole by its parts.

A factor that may interfere with an individual's capacity to follow the structural requirements of a problem is his/her inadequate view of the situation. Another possible interference may arise if the individual is seduced into accepting shortcuts. Since the individual and his/her personality are also part of the total problem-solving field, there may be other characteristics in him/her that interfere with the capacity to determine the structural requirements of the problem.

The book includes discussion of a problem solved by Gauss, Galileo's discovery of the law of inertia, and the thinking that led Einstein to the theory of relativity.

Woodworth, R.S. *Psychology*. 3rd ed. New York: Henry Holt, 1934. 517pp.

Four stages of the creative process are described. It is uncertain whether unconscious work goes on in the incubation phase. "In the preparatory period the necessary cues have been assembled along with much irrelevant material which is an interference as long as it possesses 'recency value.' When this recency value has evaporated with the lapse of time, and when the individual makes a fresh attack, the whole matter is clear. This theory is at least as probable as the theory of subconscious work."

OTHERS

Cannon, W.B. "The Role of Chance in Discovery." *The Scientific Monthly* 50 (1940): 204-209.

The focus here is on serendipity, a term proposed by Horace Walpole after reading the fairy tale "The Three Princes of Serendip." The princes were constantly traveling and "making discoveries, by *accident* or *sagacity*, of things they were not in quest of."

The author stresses the point once made by Pasteur, "In the field of observation chance favors only the minds which are prepared." To be "prepared," two conditions are necessary: (a) knowledge of the past--since this knowledge enriches the meaning of present experiences, and (b) an open mind--an ability to weigh ideas on their merits and judge them fairly and critically. "Regard for learning of the past, tolerance and free discussion of novel suggestions, and readiness for cautious experimenting when opportunity offers--these features are typical of the prepared mind."

Poincaré, H. "Mathematical Creation." In Poincaré, H. *The Foundations of Science*. New York: Science Press, 1913. 383-394.

Poincaré presents his observations of the process of mathematical creation as it occurred in his own experience. Mathematical demonstrations consist of syllogisms "*placed in a certain order*, and the order in which these elements are placed is much more important than the elements themselves."

Not all individuals have this feeling or intention of mathematical order, but those who possess it can create. Mathematical creation does not consist in the making of all possible combinations of available elements, but in making those combinations that are useful.

The author describes how he wrote his first memoir on Fuchsian functions, and then forms certain hypotheses as an explanation for these experiences. Days of conscious effort produced no results, but during a sleepless night, "I felt them [ideas] collide until pairs interlocked, so to speak, making a stable combination." By morning he had established the existence of a certain class of functions and had only to write out the results, which took just a few hours. More conscious and deliberate work followed, elaborating these results.

In seeking to explain how, from the many combinations which occur in the unconscious, the fertile ones come to consciousness, Poincaré suggests that the most likely evaluation of these phenomena may be found in a hypothesis which sets up "esthetic sensibility" as a sort of delicate sieve, admitting from the unconscious only those combinations which fit harmoniously and are most beautiful.

Wallas, G. *The Art of Thought*. New York: Harcourt, Brace, 1926. 314pp.

The stages of forming a new thought are: (a) preparation--the stage in which the problem is investigated from all directions; (b) incubation--the stage during which the individual is not consciously thinking about the problem; (c) illumination--the stage during which the "happy idea" occurs, together with the psychological factors that immediately preceded and accompanied its appearance; (d) verification--in which the validity of the idea is tested, and the ideas reduced to exact form. Although these four stages can be distinguished from each other, they do not fit into a "problem and solution" scheme.

Some habits that may facilitate the art of thought are: (a) arranging hours for intellectual work; (b) preceding work with a "warming up" period; (c) not becoming upset if the process is slower some days than others; (d) having a specific place to work or an arrangement of working materials; (e) noting ideas as they occur so they can be more easily recalled; (f) marking the passage if an idea occurs while reading.

The individual should be the master, not the slave, of his/her habits, for change may be necessary, "Without industry great intellectual work cannot be done, yet mere industry may prevent creation."

Chapter 3

IDENTIFICATION AND SELECTION

DEFINITIONS AND ISSUES

--Bagley, 1979
--Bradley, 1970
--Comte, 1981
--Crabbe, 1970
--Gallagher, 1979
--MacKinnon, 1978
--Newland, 1976
--Stein, 1983

IDENTIFICATION

--Baker, 1978
--Ciha; Harris; Hoffman; and Potter, 1974
--Foster, 1979
--Foster, 1981
--Fox, 1981
--Hagen, 1980
--Kough and De Haan, 1955
--Lawless, 1977
--Martinson, 1973
--Perrone; Karshner; and Male, 1979
--Richert; Alvino; and McDonnel, 1982
--Robinson; Roedell; and Jackson, 1979
--Tannenbaum, 1983
--Torrance, 1974
--Torrance, 1979

DEFINITIONS AND ISSUES

Bagley, R., et al. "Identifying Talented and Gifted Students." Oregon
State Department of Education: Northwest Regional Educational Laboratory, 1979. 77pp.

Characteristics of talented and gifted pupils are described so
that learning situations can be developed for them. Oregon's guidelines for selecting gifted and talented pupils and programs for
teaching are presented. Special areas discussed include: culturally
different talented and gifted, underachieving talented and gifted,
general intellectual ability, specific academic aptitude, creative
and productive thinking, visual and performing arts, and leadership
ability. Information on special bibliographies, tests, and forms
for identifying the gifted are also presented.

Bradley, R.C. (Ed.). *The Education of Exceptional Children*. Texas:
The University Press, 1970.

This edited textbook for beginning courses contains papers on the
exceptional child--the retarded, blind, physically handicapped, etc.
--in which the self-concept serves as an organizing concept. There
are chapters on the intellectually gifted, "children with original
and novel ideas--the creative," and "children with high exploratory
drives--the curious." Methods and techniques for identifying such
children and measuring their capacities are discussed. Characteristics of the gifted are presented as are methods for stimulating and
fostering their development.

Comte, M.M. "Revisiting the Concept of 'Giftedness' in Relation to
Recognition of Musical Talent in the Very Young." In Kramer, A.H.,
et al. (Eds.). *Gifted Children: Challenging Their Potential--New
Perspectives and Alternatives*. New York: Trillium Press, 1981.
196-211.

The role of research on musical talent is discussed as is the role
of musical talent in the prodigy, the composer, the conductor, and
the performer. Seashore's measures of musical aptitude and Gordon's
Musical Aptitude Profile are critically evaluated. Educators in
the field of music and psychologists need to engage in cooperative
research that would include longitudinal studies as well as studies
of non-musical traits such as character, temperament, intelligence,
and creativity.

Crabbe, A.B. "Characteristics and Identification of the Gifted."
Lincoln, NE: Nebraska Department of Education, 1977. 6pp. Mimeo.

With some modifications, the author presents characteristics of the gifted in six areas based on the De Haan and Kough (1956, p. 58) book. The areas considered and some of their associated characteristics are: (1) intellectual ability--learns rapidly, uses common sense, is original, alert, and observant; (2) academic achievement--expresses self very well in writing and speaking, has a high level of abstract ability; (3) creativity--has new ideas, is inventive, uses materials in new ways, is experimental, and has curiosity; (4) leadership ability--is liked and respected by peers, influences others, is regarded as a leader by others; (5) ability in visual and performing arts--draws or paints, develops stories; and (6) psycho-motor ability--has mechanical and physical skills, works on craft projects, is interested in mechanical gadgets, understands mechanical problems. For physical skills, attention needs to be paid to whether the pupil enjoys competitive games, likes sports, and is coordinated physically.

Gallagher, J.J. "Research Needs for Education of the Gifted." In Gallagher, J.J., et al. (Eds.). *Issues in Gifted Education*. Ventura, CA: Ventura County Superintendent of Schools, 1979. 79-91.

The following areas are in need of further work: (1) the definition of giftedness and the development of procedures to identify the gifted; (2) the effect of environmental factors on intellectual giftedness; (3) the stimulation to be provided for the culturally different gifted child; (4) the underachieving gifted; (5) an evaluation of work on creativity to date, with a plan for future work; (6) curricula for the gifted; and (7) attitudes of society toward the gifted.

The support system for creativity is discussed and the need for the following indicated: in-service training for teachers, leadership training, research and development on curricula, and assistance to schools that require help. The lack of research in this area is due to lack of university participation and lack of federal funding.

MacKinnon, D.W. *In Search of Human Effectiveness*. Buffalo, NY: The Creative Education Foundation; and Great Neck, NY: Creative Synergetic Associates, 1978. Chapter III: "What Do We Mean by Talent?" 21-26.

"Talent" as used by the Greeks, in the New Testament, and by Chaucer refers to both non-intellective and intellective factors. More recent definitions refer to talent as a "special and unitary aptitude." The author defines talent as "a veritable complex of attitudes, developed abilities, special skills, abstract knowledge and technical know-how as well as complicated motivational structure of the personality."

Newland, T.E. *The Gifted in Socioeducational Perspective*. Englewood Cliffs, NJ: Prentice-Hall, 1976. 406pp.

This textbook emphasizes both educational factors (philosophy and practice) and social factors. A socially based definition of giftedness is favored, and on the basis of a research study, it is argued that an IQ in the lower range of 120 to 125 is necessary to fulfill society's needs for persons in major contributive roles. "Gifted" should be reserved for children with conceptualization capacity, and "talent" for children with other capacities. A third group, the "skillful," would include those who make social contributions in ways that do not involve superior cognitive capacity.

In discussing the confusion about the relationship between creativity and giftedness, the authors point to the following problems: (1) Technically untrained people assume a relationship between giftedness and creative behavior. (2) People hold oversimplified and unjustified expectations about the information yielded by intelligence tests. (3) Some of the problems are tempered by Guilford's contributions. (4) There is "growing social unrest" about testing, and about intelligence testing in particular. (5) Dissatisfaction exists with the "intellectual effectiveness and relevance of contemporary education." (6) There is an uncritical equation between the psychologist's "divergent thinking" and the educator's "creative thinking."

Stein, M.I. "Creativity in Genesis." *Journal of Creative Behavior* 17 (1983): 1-8.

Because the words "creativity" and "creative" are used with such abandon, the author goes back to the Book of Genesis to learn how these words are used. He reports that in the Hebrew there is one word, *baràh*, which is used exclusively for God's creative activities; it means to create *ex nihilo*. When human creative activities are referred to, words like *asàh* and *yatzàr* (which are also used for God's activities) are used. This means that people use that which exists in combination with other already existing things or transform that which exists into something new. People do not create *ex nihilo*.

In closing, the author cautions the reader to remember that the material cited comes from the first two chapters of Genesis. If we persist in using terms like "creative" for every modification and inconsequential change, then we should keep in mind that only nine short chapters later (after the material cited), in Chapter 11, there is the story of the Tower of Babel.

IDENTIFICATION

Baker, M. "Teacher Creativity and Its Relationship to the Recognition of Student Creativity." *Creative Child & Adult Quarterly* 3 (1978): 106-115.

Twenty-six teachers were divided into two groups of more and less creative teachers using the Torrance Tests of Creative Thinking. The two groups then rated 705 students on creativity. No significant differences in ratings were obtained from the two groups of teachers. Both more and less creative teachers tended to overrate students who were relatively close to their own creative abilities. The teachers were conservative in their judgments, rating low creative students higher and high creative students lower than they tested.

Ciha, T.E.; Harris, R.; Hoffman, C.; and Potter, M.W. "Parents as
    Identifiers of Giftedness, Ignored but Accurate." *Gifted Child
    Quarterly* 18 (1974): 191-195.

    Can parents' judgments be used as screening devices for identify-
ing the gifted before they enter school? Teachers and parents of
465 kindergarten children participated in this study, representing
various socioeconomic and minority groups. Fifty-eight children
scored an IQ of 132 and above on the Slosson Intelligence Test and
were regarded as gifted. Both parents and teachers rated the
children on giftedness; parents also rated their children on traits.
Parents correctly identified 67% of the children as gifted (by the
test measure) and teachers identified 22%. Although parents over-
estimate their children's giftedness, the authors recommend using
them for initial screening for kindergarten children.

Foster, W. "The Unfinished Task: An Overview of Procedures Used to
    Identify Gifted and Talented Youth." In Colangelo, N., and Zaffrann,
    R.T. (Eds.). *New Voices in Counseling the Gifted*. Dubuque, IA:
    Kendall/Hunt, 1979. 63-75.

    The identification problem is primarily a problem in measurement,
with emphasis on reliability and validity. Work on measuring
giftedness is reviewed and a three-phase process (screening, verification, and placement) is recommended for the identification of
the gifted.

Foster, W. "Leadership: A Conceptual Framework for Recognizing and
    Educating." *Gifted Child Quarterly* 25 (1981): 15-25.

    From the gifted point of view, leadership may stem from above
average ability, task commitment and creativity. Together these
form a g-factor which could be basic to all eminent performance.
In discussing leadership from a leadership point of view, the
author reviews four models: the great person model, the small group
dynamics model, the nonleader view of leadership found in attribu-
tion theory, and the social role perspective. These four viewpoints
need to be integrated to yield useful information for the gifted
and talented area.

Fox, L.H. "Identification of the Academically Gifted." *American
    Psychologist* 36 (1981): 1103-1111.

    The criteria for identifying the gifted discussed here are: scores
on general intelligence tests, creativity tests, teacher recommendations, and scores on standardized achievement tests. The author is
part of Stanley's group at Johns Hopkins University and prefers to
identify students by test scores on specific subject matter (e.g.,
mathematics) followed up by a testing program which includes diagnostic testing, clinical methods, and evaluation of a student's
products. This approach has identified more academically gifted
students among the disadvantaged than other programs.
    In her review of the field, the author points out that definitions
of giftedness vary widely, are poorly defined, and differ in the

number of areas included and the degree of excellence required. The academically talented should be identified in a two-stage process: (1) screening--which includes tests and recommendations from various sources and (2) placement--to be done by experts using diagnostic testing, difficult tests, interviews, and evaluations of products at science fairs, essays, poems, and short stories. For both screening and placement, it is best to err on the side of leniency. Programs using the two-stage process include The Gifted and Talented Education Project (GATE) in the Baltimore City Public Schools and the school system in Flint, Michigan.

Hagen, E. *Identification of the Gifted*. New York: Teachers College, Columbia University, 1980. 50pp.

Attempts to differentiate between *gifted* and *talented* have not resulted in much clarification. Ultimately, the criterion for giftedness is what the child will do as an adult and not what the child does in school. The problem, then, is to determine what indicators of superior achievement in the adult can be appraised in children. The literature on adult creativity does not help much in this regard.

It is important to remember, when identifying a child as creative, that one is making a predictive statement. As such statements are not absolutely accurate; it is important to make repeated evaluations of the child. To identify the potentially gifted child, it is important to (1) define what is meant by potentially gifted in one's own school; (2) decide which indicators of potential giftedness will be accepted; (3) decide on sources of information for each indicator; (4) decide which instruments will be used to gather information; and (5) establish a system for combining and weighing different kinds of information as a decision is made about a child.

Predictions should not be made for more than one year as longer predictions are less reliable than shorter ones. Assessment of giftedness should involve both quantitative and qualitative factors concerning abilities, achievements, and other characteristics. Assessments involve human value judgments and should not be made mechanically.

Kough, J., and De Haan, R.F. *Teacher's Guidance Handbook*. Vol. 1: *Identifying Children with Special Needs*. Chicago, IL: Science Research Associates, 1955.

Various procedures and observational techniques are presented to aid teachers and others in the nomination of gifted and talented children for school programs. Others (e.g., Crabbe, 1977, p. 57) have drawn upon this source. Four basic principles are common to all procedures: each child should receive equal consideration on each behavioral characteristic considered, each child should be observed in a variety of situations, each child should be compared with other children, and raters should be aware of their biases. All data should be checked against and supplemented by the use of cumulative records, standardized tests, informal tests, and other situations.

Lawless, R.F. *Programs for Gifted/Talented/Creative Children (for
    Little or No Money)*. Buffalo, NY: D.O.K. Publishers, 1977. 7-34.

Test scores are good for identifying only a small number of gifted
children. Teachers and other school personnel are fallible but
their observations are important and should be noted using forms
such as the Atwater Scale and the Renzulli and Hartman Scale for
Rating Behavioral Characteristics of Superior Students. Students
missed by teachers can be picked up either by parents' nominations
or self-nomination.

Following a case study model, the author recommends presenting
all of the data collected on a child to a committee of 6-8 persons
(including teachers, parents, specialists, counselors, school psychologists, and principals) who then decide on how to weight the
different data and to plan the child's educational program. Various
forms are suggested to help in this endeavor.

Martinson, R.A. "Children with Superior Cognitive Abilities." In
    Dunn, L.M. (Ed.). *Exceptional Children in the Schools: Special
    Education in Transition*. 2nd ed. New York: Holt, Rinehart and
    Winston, 1973. 189-241.

This chapter discusses various procedures for identifying gifted/
talented students and their characteristics. Also discussed are
educational plans and programs, special educational groupings, early
school admission and acceleration, provisions for gifted/talented
in different countries, and possible future developments.

Perrone, P.A.; Karshner, W.W.; and Male, R.A. "Identification and
    Talented Students." In Colangelo, N., and Zaffrann, R.T. (Eds.).
    New Voices in Counseling the Gifted. Dubuque, IA: Kendall/Hunt,
    1979. 76-88.

The Guidance Institute for Talented Students at the University of
Wisconsin works with six talent categories: (1) convergent thinking
and behavior; (2) divergent/creative thinking and behavior; (3) goal
related thinking and behavior; (4) social skills and behavior;
(5) physical skills and behavior; and (6) affective thinking and
behavior. These categories are regarded as "structural in nature";
gifts in different areas (music, mathematics, drama, etc.) can
manifest themselves in one or more talent structures. For each of
the six talent categories, ten behaviors, from simple to complex,
are presented. The identification instrument used at the Guidance
Institute is also presented.

Richert, E.S., with Alvino, J.J., and McDonnel, R.C. *National Report
    on Identification: Assessment and Recommendations for Comprehensive
    Identification of Gifted and Talented Youth*. Sewell, NJ: Educationa
    Improvement Center--South, 1982. 451pp. Paper. (Two chapters are
    annotated here: Chapter 4--"Definition and Conception of Giftedness,
    83-127, and Chapter 8--"Three Stages of Identification: A Step-by-
    Step Approach," 235-298. See Chapter 12 for an annotation of the
    section on the uses of tests and questionnaires for identification
    purposes.)

Attempts to clarify the issues involved in defining giftedness are discussed. Significant definitions are integrated into two broad categories: (1) internal--those definitions which involve assumptions about innate capacities and include intellectual ability, creativity, multiple talents or aptitudes, and personality traits, and (2) external--those definitions which involve characteristics that occur independently of innate characteristics. The latter develop through formal education/training, socio-economic factors, opportunity/chance, social utility/historical values, and original contributions/cultural standards.

There are five definitions of giftedness prevalent in the U.S.: exceptional intellectual ability, multiple intellectual abilities, creativity, multiple talents, and the federally legislated definition as contained in the Marland Report. Three stages are set forth for identification. The first of these is (1) Nomination in which unbiased tests are used to find a large group of potentially gifted and talented students. Care should be taken not to screen out disadvantaged students. The pool of talented and gifted students should be about 20% to 30% of the school population and it should contain economically or culturally disadvantaged students in the same proportion as they are in the school population. (2) Assessment allows students' abilities to be matched with available programs. (3) Evaluation allows for a review of decisions and mid-course corrections so that the best matches are made.

Throughout the book, discussions are presented in detail; they include forms, diagrams, and other aids to explain the kinds of information that needs to be obtained and how to obtain it.

Robinson, H.B.; Roedell, W.C.; and Jackson, N.E. "Early Identification and Intervention." In Passow, A.H. (Ed.). *The Gifted and the Talented: Their Education and Development. The Seventy-eighth Yearbook of the National Society for the Study of Education.* Chicago, IL: University of Chicago Press, 1979. 138-154.

The authors discuss the work of the Child Development Research Group at the University of Washington which has engaged in a longitudinal study of intellectually advanced young children. A preschool program is provided for some of the children and a counseling service is provided for the parents. The authors say that intellectually advanced children do not develop equally under all conditions; the group is quite heterogeneous in both intellectual and nonintellectual characteristics. Among the various points made about identification, the authors say: (1) Identification programs should be so designed as to allow a child to manifest his/her abilities. Intellectually advanced children may behave like average children unless they are presented with challenges. (2) Inconsistency in performance has to be allowed for. (3) The most comprehensive battery of tests may not provide all the information one should have about a child. One should therefore also have a parents' report.

In looking to future questions that need to be answered, the authors point to the importance of learning more about "the long-term implications of various types of intellectual precocity." More information is also needed about the similarities and differences in thinking and problem-solving strategies in intellectually advanced and intellectually average children.

Tannenbaum, A.J. *Gifted Children: Psychological and Educational Perspectives.* New York: Macmillan, 1983. Specifically, Chapter 19,
   "Identifying the Gifted." 342-371.

   A review of the evidence on identification effectiveness is presented as is a review of the value of various sources for identification data. Identification is regarded as "far from an exact
science." Its exactitude varies with the student's age, special
abilities, and membership in a subcultural group.
   The author's process of identification consists of three stages--
screening, selection, and differentiation. For screening, school
performance data is used as well as instruments which focus on far-
fetched indicators. Children are put in real or simulated educational environments to show what they can do before being selected.
In the differentiation stage, identification is made through the
curriculum itself. "In the last analysis, identification of the
gifted is related not only to systematic observation and intelligent
interpretation of test data, but to the development of educational
opportunities that facilitate self-identification."

Torrance, E.P. "Differences Are Not Deficits." *Teachers College
   Record* 75 (1974): 471-487.

   This article contains the Checklist of Creative Positives which
can be used when teachers and others observe children in a variety
of activities. It does not depend on the use of tests and requires
a minimum of training. On the basis of observations, behaviors can
be encouraged and trained or the children who manifest such behaviors can be selected for gifted programs.
   Among the behaviors noted are: expressing feelings and emotion;
improvising with commonplace materials; being articulate in role
playing and storytelling; enjoying one's ability in visual arts,
creative movement, dance, dramatics, music, rhythm, etc.; expressive
speech; flexibility and fluency in nonverbal media; participation
in and enjoyment of small group activities and problem-solving activities; responsiveness to concrete material and kinesthetic stimuli;
expressiveness through gestures and body language; humor; richness
of ideas; originality in problem-solving; problem-centeredness;
emotional responsiveness; and "quickness of warm-up."

Torrance, E.P. "Some Creative Dimensions to the Issues of Identification." In Gallagher, J.J., et al. *Issues in Gifted Education.* Ventura, CA: Ventura County Superintendent of Schools, 1979. 1-26.

   Identification of talented and gifted children should be a "dynamic
creative process." Standardized tests for identification purposes
should be avoided and responsive environments developed in which
children can initiate activities and in which their creative potentialities can be manifest. A model for studying and predicting behavior is presented which contains three components: skills, abilities, and motivations. Research data in support of the model are
also presented.
   A history of creativity tests is provided although the author
does not believe that identification of the gifted and talented
should be limited to these tests. Even with his own creativity

tests, the author says he believed from the start "that creative behavior requires more than creative thinking abilities."

Rationale and validity data are presented for the Torrance Tests of Creative Thinking. To measure motivation there are two scales: the Creative Motivation Scale and the What Kind of Person Are You?, both developed by the author. For a measure that relates to hemispheric dominance, the author presents his Your Style of Learning and Thinking. Other tests reported on are: Sounds and Images and Thinking Creatively in Action and Movement.

Chapter 4

CHARACTERISTICS, PART 1:
LIFE HISTORY

A CAUTION

--Parloff; Datta; Kleman; and Handlon, 1968

PIONEERING STUDIES OF ADULT CREATIVITY

--Goertzel, V., and Goertzel, M.G., 1962
--Roe, 1952

OMNIBUS STUDIES

Anastasi and Schaefer

--Anastasi and Schaefer, 1969
--Schaefer and Anastasi, 1968
--Schaefer, 1969
--Schaefer, 1972

Stanley's Study of Mathematically Precocious Youth

--Benbow and Stanley, 1980

Owens' Biographical Inventory

--Payne and Halpin, 1974

Taylor and Ellison's Biographical Inventory

--James; Ellison; and Fox, 1974
--Taylor and Ellison, 1967

Familial Characteristics

--Albert, 1980
--Aldous, 1973
--Bee; Barnard; Eyres; Gray; Hammond; Spietz;
    Snyder; and Clark, 1982
--Heilbrun, 1971
--McClelland and Pilon, 1983

A CAUTION--
On the Application of the Characteristics of
Creative Adults to Potentially Creative Adolescents

Parloff, M.B.; Datta, L.; Klemen, L.; and Handlon, J.H. "Personality Characteristics which Differentiate Creative Male Adolescents and Adults." *Journal of Personality* 36 (1968): 528-552.

The adult sample in this study consisted of the mathematicians, research scientists, writers, and architects who had been studied at the Institute for Personality Assessment and Research at Berkeley. There were 200 of them with 101 classified as "more creative" and 99 as "less creative." The mean age of the former was 47.7 years and of the latter, 45.5.

The adolescent sample came from the male entrants in the 22nd and 24th Annual Science Talent Search conducted by Westinghouse. Two hundred sixty-six were classified as "more creative" and 672 as "less creative." The criterion was the judges' evaluations of submitted products. There were no differences between the two groups. Their average age was 17.7 and they had an average grade-point average of 3.7. On the Science Aptitude Test they scored 50.03 and on the SAT-Verbal 681.5. Socioeconomic status rated according to the Redlich scale was 2.19 and 62.5% were first-born or only children.

The California Personality Inventory was administered to all groups. Factor analysis of the data indicated that the same factor structure was obtained for the adult and adolescent samples. Four factors were obtained: Disciplined Effectiveness, Assertive Self-Assurance, Adaptive Autonomy, and Humanitarian Conscience.

The more creative adults and adolescents were similarly differentiated from their lesser creative colleagues by having greater Assertive Self-Assurance and Adaptive Autonomy. On Disciplined Effectiveness, adult creatives had lower scores than their controls although higher scores were characteristic of the creative adolescents. No differentiating characteristics for the adult or adolescent sample were found for the Humanitarian Conscience factor. Using a discriminant function analysis, 64% of the adult sample and 66% of the adolescent sample were correctly identified. For the adult sample, prediction varied among the vocations. More creative writers, mathematicians, and architects were discriminated in 71% of the cases while the research scientists were correctly identified in 43%. For the less creative groups, accuracy of identification ranged from 79% for the architects to 57% for the writers and research scientists.

In the adolescent group, 64% of the more creative and 61% of the less creative were correctly identified. These data for sub-groups among the adolescents indicates that correct identification in the more creative group ranged from 75% for mathematicians, biochemists, and nonscientists to 50% for chemists and engineers. Less creative

individuals were correctly identified in 75% of the mathematicians
to 50% of the biochemists. "In brief, although the personality
factor mean differences between the more and less creative groups
are statistically significant, the extent of the overlap in means
permits misclassification in about one-third of the total cases."
    Finally, the authors used the combination of personality charac-
teristics which best discriminated among the adults, applied it to
adolescents and found only chance relationships. "It appears therefore that the identification of the more and less creative adolescent is better achieved by use of personality characteristics derived
from the adolescent than by characteristics from the adult sample."
Personality characteristics differentiating between more and less
creative adults cannot be applied without modification to identifying
the potentially creative adolescent.

                    PIONEERING STUDIES OF ADULT CREATIVITY

Goertzel, V., and Goertzel, M.G. *Cradles of Eminence*. Boston, MA:
    Little, Brown & Co., 1962. 362pp.

    This book surveys "the emotional and intellectual climate in which
eminent people of the twentieth century were reared." Some included
here are eminently wicked and some are eminently good. The authors
follow the dictionary sense of eminent to mean: "standing high in
comparison with others." People born in the U.S. were included if
there were at least two books about them in the biography section
of the Montclair, N.J., Public Library. People born outside of the
U.S. were included if at least one book appeared. Only those who
lived in the twentieth century were included. Once a person met
the criteria, works about him/her could be read that were found any-
where. People were excluded if biographies were written about them
because of their inherited positions: kings, queens, princes, etc.
    The following are some summary statements of the findings based
on the 400 persons who met the authors' criteria: 1. Most of them
were not born in the great metropolitan areas but drifted into them.
2. "In almost all of the homes there is a love for learning in one
or both parents, often accompanied by a physical exuberance and a
persistent drive toward goals. Fewer than ten percent of the parents
failed to show a strong love for learning." 3. About half of the
parents held very strong opinions about a controversial subject and
were set apart in their own time. These were the parents of nearly
all of the statesmen, humanitarians, and reformers. 4. None of the
20 poets was the son or daughter of a poet. 5. The majority of
writers and poets came from families where they witnessed tense
psychological dramas involving their parents. 6. "Nearly half the
fathers were subject to traumatic vicissitudes in their business or
professional careers." 7. Twenty-five percent of the mothers were
described as "dominating" but very few of the fathers were so
described. 8. "Wealth is much more frequent than is abject poverty.... Three hundred and fifty-eight families (some wealthy) can be
classified as representing the business or professional classes."
9. Nevertheless, over one-fourth of the sample showed such problems
as blindness, deafness, being crippled, sickly, homely, undersized,

overweight, had a speech defect. In many of these cases, compensation for handicaps may have been a factor in the drive to achieve. 10. A history of accident-proneness is found in explorers and adventurers. 11. Domineering or overpossessive mothers produced dictators, military men, or poets. 12. Fourteen had stepmothers. 13. The homes of the subjects were free of mental illness that required hospitalization. 14. Children were tutored by professionals or by their parents. 15. Secondary school was disliked and prestige college was accepted best. 16. Three-fifths of the subjects were dissatisfied with their schools and schoolteachers and four-fifths showed exceptional talent.

These results are compared with more recent studies, including the work of MacKinnon, Torrance, Getzels and Jackson, etc. Among the authors' closing remarks there is the following: "The parents of the Four Hundred had strong intellectual and physical drives, were open to new experiences and kept their own love for learning intact even in old age. Today's parents of gifted children are subject to stronger pressure to have the child conform to mediocrity than were the parents of the Four Hundred."

Roe, A. *The Making of a Scientist*. New York: Dodd, Mead, 1952. 244pp.

There is no completely differentiating factor between scientists and non-scientists or between various fields of science, although certain patterns do emerge. Some of these are listed below. (1) There are often professional fathers and intellectual values in the home. If learning for its own sake was not stressed in the home, then the subject had a close relationship with someone else, usually a teacher, who held such values. (2) They all developed early independence and intense private interests which, except for the social scientists, were shared with few others. (3) They read widely and enjoyed school and studying. (4) Early interests differentiated the groups: physical scientists engaged in tinkering or devising gadgets, biologists were interested in natural history, and social scientists contemplated literary careers. (5) Social scientists and theoretical physicists were higher in verbal than non-verbal abilities, experimental physicists were the reverse, and anthropologists were low in mathematical ability. (6) Biologists relied heavily on rational controls while the other two groups tended to be uncritical. Physicists were not interested in people, avoided interpersonal relationships, and were often anxious. Social scientists were concerned with human relationships. (7) Research provided all subjects with a way of accomplishing, on their own, something that really mattered to them. They were capable of a great deal of work and high concentration and got a lot of satisfaction from their work.

Some of the educational implications include the following. Students should know aspects of themselves and aspects of living other than purely intellectual ones so that they do not look to professions for satisfactions that they cannot supply. "Driveness" can be of value in mastering a field but it is a hindrance when it leads to refusal to face other problems in one's profession or life. Investigation should be encouraged to satisfy curiosity; this is negated by classroom authoritarianism. On the other hand, it is the

responsibility of the home to help the child achieve the internal
discipline necessary for maturity and social living. A placid life
and life without obstacles results in postponement of full personal
responsibility. Last, the author discusses the possibility of individual action or group action without authoritarian direction in
diverse situations.

Roe, A. "Early Differentiation of Interests." In Taylor, C.W. (Ed.).
*The Second (1957) Research Conference on the Identification of
Creative Scientific Talent.* Salt Lake City: University of Utah
Press, 1958. 58–108.

Two hypotheses are suggested: (1) Differences in home experience
are correlated with differences in basic orientation toward people.
Overdemanding and overprotective environments lead to basic orientation toward people, often in a defensive or narcissistic way.
Neglect in the home environment leads to orientation to ideas or
things. (2) These life orientations determine a person's later interests. Orientation toward people may result in interest in social
work, clinical psychology, etc. The narcissistic element leads to
science and technology. In a group exposed to an environment of
acceptance, aptitudes will have a more important relation to future
interest since the child has more freedom and is often actively
encouraged to demonstrate them.
    Creativity will be defensive in people from overprotective or
overdemanding homes. The author found physical scientists to have
a freedom and ease of working in marked contrast to artists and,
to a lesser extent, social scientists.

OMNIBUS STUDIES

Anastasi and Schaefer

Anastasi, A., and Schaefer, C.E. "Biographical Correlates of Artistic
and Literary Creativity in Adolescent Girls." *Journal of Applied
Psychology* 53 (1969): 267–273.

    All procedures in this study were the same as those reported by
the authors in their other studies of their biographical inventory.
The main difference is that the subjects are adolescent girls and
the fields are artistic and literary creativity.
    The results indicated the following points. 1. The means of both
creative groups are significantly higher than those obtained from
corresponding control groups. 2. Point-biserial correlations between biographical inventory scores and a dichotomous criterion of
creativity was .34 for the art group and .55 for the control group.
3. A final questionnaire consisting of 40 items for artistic creativity and 82 items for literary creativity was developed. 4. Characteristic of the creative students in both fields was a "*pervasive
and continuing* interest in their chosen field and absorption in its
pursuit." 5. Creatives had more "unusual experiences" in their

backgrounds than did controls. They daydreamed about unusual things, had unusual collections, had imaginary companions, had eidetic imagery, and reported that their fathers used unusual discipline. "One could speculate that the prevalence of atypical experiences in their daily life may contribute to the low level of conformity and conventionality generally found to characterize creative persons at all ages." 6. Although both creatives and controls came from intellectually superior homes, significantly more fathers attended college, graduate school, or professional school than was true of the control groups. More controls reported that no musical instrument was played in the family and more of the creatives reported having two or more collections. 7. When parental influence was considered, the majority of the items referred to the father's influence rather than the mother's. In the study of the high school boys, the reverse was true. "If such results truly indicate a greater influence of the opposite sex parent on creative children, they may help to explain the finding that in their attitudes, interests, and problem-solving styles creative individuals show more traits of the opposite sex than do controls and generally conform less closely to sex stereotypes." 8. The creative-writing key has twice as many items as the creative-art key. The extra items indicate strong intellectual and cultural orientation and breadth of interest in the student and in the home from which she comes. 9. The correlates of creativity in this study of girls is very similar to that found for boys, with the possible exception of reversal of role model and the greater influence of opposite-sex parent on creative offspring. 10. Items that cut across both sex and field of interest are "continuity and pervasiveness of interest in chosen field; prevalence of unusual, novel, and diverse experiences; and educational superiority of familial background."

Suggestions for Further Reading

There are numerous references in this and the other articles by the same authors on biographical factors and tests as predictors of creativity or as differentiators between more and less creative individuals. These are only a sample.

Dauw, D.C. "Life Experiences of Original Thinkers and Good Elaborators." *Exceptional Children* 32 (1966): 433–440.

Domino, G. "Maternal Personality Correlates of Sons' Creativity." *Journal of Consulting and Clinical Psychology* 33 (1969): 180–183.

Dreyer, A., and Wells, M. "Parental Values, Parental Control, and Creativity in Young Children." *Journal of Marriage and the Family* 28 (1966): 83–88.

Freeberg, N.E. "The Biographical Information Blank as a Predictor of Student Achievement." *Psychological Reports* 20 (1967): 911–925.

Henry, E.R. "Conference on the Use of Biographical Data in Psychology." *American Psychologist* 21 (1966): 247–249.

Smith, W.J.; Albright, L.E.; Glennon, J.R.; and Owens, W.A. "The Prediction of Research Competence and Creativity from Personal History." *Journal of Applied Psychology* 45 (1961): 59–62.

Taylor, C.W.; Ellison, R.L.; and Tucker, M.F. *Biographical Information and the Prediction of Multiple Criteria of Success in Science.*
Greensboro, NC: Richardson Foundation, 1966.

Schaefer, C.E., and Anastasi, A. "A Biographical Inventory for
Identifying Creativity in Adolescent Boys." *Journal of Applied
Psychology* 52 (1968): 42-48.

The purpose of this study was to develop and cross-validate a
biographical inventory for identifying creativity in high school
boys in artistic and scientific fields.

Four hundred male students from six high schools in metropolitan
New York participated in the study. There were 188 seniors, 144
juniors, and 68 sophomores. Socioeconomically all of the subjects
were superior for the geographical area from which they came.
Schools were regarded as offering opportunity for creative achievement. Four criterion groups were established: creative and control
artistic and creative and control scientific. Creatives were selected by teacher nomination and a score above a cutoff on Guilford's
Alternate Uses and Consequences Tests. Control subjects were said
by the same teachers not to have produced any creative products and
were below the Guilford cutoff score. The artistic boys were involved in graphic art and literary expression while the scientific
groups included the sciences and mathematics. Subjects (creative
and control) were matched for school attended, class, and grade-point
average. No differences were found in census tract data as a measure
of socioeconomic differences. Subjects were tested after school
hours and paid.

A biographical inventory of 165 questions was developed on the
basis of research reported in the literature. The questions were
grouped into five sections: physical characteristics, family history,
educational history, leisure-time activities, and miscellaneous.
Questions "dealt with objective facts regarding present or past activities and experiences, some called for expressions of preference
and others concerned anticipated plans and goals." Responses were
given to multiple choice, checklist items, and open-ended questions.
Groups of subjects were split up and the inventory was cross-
validated.

In both artistic and scientific groups, the creative subjects
scored significantly higher than the controls. The key developed
for the artistic group contains 140 items and 60 items are contained
in the scientific key. The following results are based on the items
in the final keys.

1. The creative subjects in the artistic area were more clearly
differentiated from their controls than were the subjects creative
in the scientific areas.

2. The creative scientific student "resembles the academically
superior student more closely than does" the student creative in
the arts.

3. "While creative students in both artistic and scientific fields
can be significantly differentiated from academically equated controls by means of a biographical inventory, this study strongly suggests that the former can be more readily differentiated than the
latter."

4. Family background was academically superior in the families of the creative students whose parents provided role models of interest in the student's field.

5. It was also found that "the creative student himself manifests a *strong intellectual and 'cultural' orientation*."

6. Creatives were also characterized as having a "*pervasive and continuing enthusiasm*" for their chosen field.

7. Creatives had broad interests.

8. Creatives had stronger drives to novelty and diversity.

9. The creatives in the arts came from environments of greater diversity than was true of the creatives in science.

"In conclusion, creative students in artistic and scientific fields do share important common features in experiential background and personal traits, but they also exhibit notable differences in both respects. Consequently, any investigation of creativity that fails to consider area of creative achievement may produce a blurred or distorted picture of the creative person. Although the distinction between scientific and artistic creativity is undoubtedly a major one, further breakdown of artistic creativity into literary production and graphic art might be fruitfully explored in further research."

Schaefer, C.E. "The Prediction of Creative Achievement from a Bio-graphical Inventory." *Educational and Psychological Measurement* 29 (1969): 431-437.

This study investigated "the validity of a biographical inventory in combination with other instruments in the prediction of creative achievement at the high school level." (The study was one of con-current validity rather than predictive validity.)

Eight hundred students (male and female) from 10 high schools in the metropolitan New York area participated in the study. The schools were selected because they had programs for creative achieve-ment. The subjects were predominantly seniors (434), but juniors (272) and sophomores (94) were also included. The students consti-tuted eight criterion groups of 100 students each, according to a three-fold system of classification: achievement (creative or con-trol), field of achievement (artistic or scientific), and sex. Creative achievement was assessed by a combination of teachers' evaluations and creativity test scores (they scored above a cutoff point in Guilford's Alternate Uses and Consequences tests). Control subjects were nominated by the same teachers and scored below the cutoff on the Guilford tests. Creative and control students in each field were matched for school attended, grade level, classes in which they were enrolled, and grade-point average. Subjects were paid to participate in the testing after school hours.

A 165-item Biographical Inventory was constructed for this study, based on the research literature. The items were grouped according to five sections: "physical characteristics, family history, educa-tional history, leisure-time activities and miscellaneous." Ques-tions dealt with objective facts about past and present activities and experiences, preferences, anticipated plans, and goals. Separate scoring keys were developed for each of the specialty areas. In addition, for the biographical material criterion, groups were divided into two groups of 50 each. One group was used to develop the scoring key and the other was used for cross-validation purposes. In addition to the Biographical Inventory, the following additional tests were administered: Barron-Welsh Art Scale, the Gough Adjective Check List, and the Franck Drawing Completion Test.

For 21 scales, directional hypotheses were advanced and 18 showed criterion group differences as predicted. "Furthermore, the BI (Biographical Inventory) was one of the most effective instruments in differentiating creative from control subjects across all four fields of achievement." Multiple regression analyses were also calculated and the biographical inventory was "the only instrument to be included in the four optimal test batteries." The BI was best in differentiating adolescent creativity for both sexes across fields.

The relationship of the biographical inventory to creativity is consistent with Taylor's conclusion, "that the biographical inventory is the most valid instrument for the prediction of creativity against an outside criterion." Other studies have also found that biographical inventories are the best single predictors of complex criteria. Biograpical data, as good predictors of future behavior, are consistent with the idea that the past is the best predictor of the future.

Suggestions for Further Reading

Brenner, M.H. "Use of High School Data to Predict Work Performance." *Journal of Applied Psychology* 52 (1968): 29-30.

Henry, E.R. "Conference on the Use of Biographical Data in Psychology." *American Psychologist* 21 (1966): 247-249.

Holland, J.C., and Nicholls, R.C. "Prediction of Academic and Extracurricular Achievement in College." *Journal of Educational Psychology* 55 (1964): 55-65.

Schaefer, C.E. "Predictive Validity of the Biographical Inventory Creativity: Five-year Follow-up Study." *Psychological Reports* 30 (1972): 471-476.

This is a report of a five-year follow-up study of students in New York high schools that the author and his associates have reported on in other studies, in which they investigated the concurrent validity of a biographical questionnaire. In part, this report is a report of the predictive validity of the Biographical Inventory Creativity (BIC). It is also a study of the predictive validity of the early criterion measures.

Students were selected for the study on the basis of teacher nomination, one or more creative products, and a score above a cutoff on Guilford's Alternate Uses and Consequences tests. The control group was nominated by the same teachers as having no observable evidence of creative accomplishment and they scored below the cutoff on the two Guilford tests.

When the original data were collected, there were, among the 800 students, 434 seniors, 272 juniors, and 94 sophomores. The data reported here were collected five years later, but no information is provided as to what the subjects were doing or how many in each of the previously mentioned classes responded to the questionnaire for follow-up data. Of the locatable subjects, about 50 to 60% responded so that there were 390 subjects in the follow-up. These

are regarded as representative of the initial group of 800 subjects.
There were eight groups of subjects: creative art, writing boys;
control art, writing boys; creative math-science boys; control math-
science boys; creative art, girls; control art, girls; creative
writing girls; and control writing, girls.

Follow-up data were collected by means of the Independent Activities Questionnaire (IAQ) developed by Klein (1967) which is a self-
report questionnaire collecting information about creative accomplishments in art and design, writing, mathematics, and science.
Evidence indicates that this questionnaire was answered honestly
with verifiable information.

Results indicated that the means of the creative groups were
higher than the means of their respective control groups, except
for boys in the math-science field. The variability was also greater
and hence, data were analyzed in terms of median splits and chi-
squares. The results indicated "that the creative groups consistently scored significantly higher than their respective control groups
on the scales directly related to their previous fields of achievement." The art-writing field proved to be most predictable.

The data are regarded as consistent with other studies in the
literature (Holland, 1964; Roberts, 1965) which report that the
best predictors of creative achievements in college and on the job
are measures of previous achievements.

Another finding of this study is that creative students continue
to utilize their energy in the same fields in which they excelled
in high school. "Thus, creative behavior does not tend to become
more generalized with increasing age; rather it seems to be directed
toward a specific field at an early age and this field of concentration is stable over time."

Suggestions for Further Reading

Dellos, M., and Gaier, E.C. "Identification of Creativity: The
Individual." *Psychological Bulletin* 73 (1970): 55-73.

Holland, J.C. "The Assessment and Prediction of the Creative Performance of High-aptitude Youth." In Taylor, C.W. (Ed.). *Widening
Horizons in Creativity.* New York: Wiley, 1964. 293-315.

Kagan, J., and Moss, H.A. *Birth to Maturity: A Study in Psychological Development.* New York: Wiley, 1962.

Klein, S.P. *A Description of the Independent Activities Questionnaire.* Princeton: Educational Testing Service, 1967. (Res.
Monogr. Rm-67-14.)

Nichols, R.C., and Holland, J.C. "Prediction of the First Year
College Performance of High Aptitude Students." *Psychological
Monographs* 77, No. 570 (1963).

Roberts, R.J. "Prediction of College Performance of Superior Students." *National Merit Scholarship Corporation Research Reports*
1, No. 5 (1965).

Stanley's Study of Mathematically
Precocious Youth

Benbow, C.P., and Stanley, J.C. "Intellectually Talented Students:
Family Profiles." *Gifted Child Quarterly* 24 (1980): 119-122.

Five hundred and seven gifted boys and 366 gifted girls between
11 and 12 years of age who matched or outscored children four years
older, filled out extensive questionnaires when they took part in
the 1976 Talent Search for the Study of Mathematically Precocious
Youth. Among the results were: the families of the gifted were,
in general, larger (3.01 children for boys and 3.25 for girls) than
the national average of 1.7. The girls came from larger families
than did the boys and their sibling position was lower than that of
the boys. No significant correlations were found between SAT scores
and birth order or number of siblings in the family.

Parents were living and well educated. The father's educational
level correlated higher with children's ability than did the mother's
educational level. SAT-Math scores for both sexes correlated more
highly with parents' educational levels, father's occupational level,
and father's occupational status than they did with the subjects'
SAT-Verbal scores.

Owens' Biographical Inventory

Payne, D.A., and Halpin, W.G. "Use of a Factored Biographical Inventory to Identify Differentially Gifted Adolescents." *Psychological
Reports* 35 (1974): 1195-1204.

The biographical questionnaire in this study was the one developed
by Owens (1969) in which the subjects were 173 males and 209 females
who were high school students participating in the 1972 Georgia
Governor's Honors Program (an 8-week summer program for the academically and artistically gifted and talented). The students were
gifted in different areas: art, drama, foreign language, English,
math, music, science, and social science. The questionnaire had been
factored.

The data for the girls indicated that they were significantly
different from each other, according to the areas they represented,
in terms of the following factors: social leadership, academic
achievement, scientific-artistic interests, cultural-literary interests, and maladjustment. The data for the boys indicated that
the life history factors that differentiated them according to their
areas of interest were: intellectualism, social introversion, positive academic attitude, and sibling friction.

The authors also analyzed the data to determine which of the
factors differentiated the artistically and academically talented
males and females from their counterparts who had average ability.
The results of this analysis indicated that, for the males, the
following factors differentiated both the artistically and academically talented from the average: intellectualism, socioeconomic
status, sibling friction, and social desirability. In addition, for
the artistically talented, the following factors also differentiated
them from the average: positive academic attitude and athletic in-

terest. The following factors also differentiated the academically
talented boys from the average boys: academic achievement, social
introversion, scientific interest, and religious activity.
   Similar analyses were undertaken to investigate which of the factors differentiated the artistically and academically talented girls
from the girls who were average. The following factors differentiated both the academically and artistically talented girls from
the average girls: social leadership, academic achievement, cultural-
literary interests, scientific-artistic interest, socioeconomic
status, athletic participation, and maladjustment. The factors that
differentiated only the artistically talented from the average were:
maternal warmth, popularity with the opposite sex, and being "Daddy's
girl." The factors that differentiated the girls who were academically talented from the average girls were: parental control and
positive academic attitude.

Taylor and Ellison's Biographical Inventory

James, L.R.; Ellison, R.L.; and Fox, D.G. "Prediction of Artistic
   Performance from Biographical Data." *Journal of Applied Psychology*
   59 (1974): 84-86.

   Some items were selected from and others were adapted from the
Taylor and Ellison biographical inventory that was used for predicting scientific and engineering performance. There were 200 general
biographical items such as "developmental history, parents and
family life, extracurricular activities, etc." and biographical
items specific to the arts such as "number of hours devoted to daily
practice, artistic accomplishments, special schools attended, etc."
   The inventory was administered to an art sample of 501 subjects
from various art schools and 312 subjects in non-art areas from two
urban high schools. No attempt was made to match the art and non-
art samples on various biographical data. "However, the only practical difference between the two samples was a significantly higher
proportion of females in the art sample (.61 vs. .41)."
   Multiple criteria were obtained for the art subjects, including
rating scale data, behavioral data, and creativity checklist data.
These were completed by teachers. There were also self-report data
on number of awards and grade point average in major art areas.
   Significant cross validities were obtained against the art vs.
non-art criterion and multiple art criteria (art sample only),
within and across artistic areas. "A tentative conclusion was that
different biographical inventory scoring keys should be employed
to predict an art versus nonart criterion and performance criteria
in the arts; however, predictive rather than concurrent validation
studies are required for more conclusive evidence."

Taylor, C.W., and Ellison, R.L. "Biographical Predictors of Scientific
   Performance." *Science* 155 (1967): 1075-1079.

   In view of the fact that so many studies of biographical factors
refer to this study, which is based on adults, it is referenced here
despite the fact that it does not apply directly to children.
   A large number of studies are summarized in this article on the

use of a biographical inventory developed by the authors. In their
final summary statement they say, "The biographical approach to the
identification of scientific talent has shown significant results
in a variety of situations which included laboratories, fields of
specialization, and age groups." There is much work to be done
which includes validating the biographical approach in different
organizational settings and in different fields of work, etc.

Familial Characteristics

Albert, R.S. "Family Position and the Attainment of Eminence: A
    Study of Special Family Positions and Special Family Experiences."
    Gifted Child Quarterly 24 (1980): 87-95.

It is hypothesized that gifted children hold a special position in
the family which, together with family events (unexpected death or
separation), can help prepare them for particular careers. Subjects
included U.S. presidents, British prime ministers, Nobel Prize
winning scientists, and non-eminent persons in Britain and the U.S.
Autobiographies, biographies and empirical works were studied.
    Sample findings include the following. More scientists than
politicians were only sons or daughters. Death in the family played
a larger role in the lives of future politicians. Birth order is
rejected as the basis for establishing a child's rank in the family.
Special position is a recommended substitute to refer to the family's
recognition of the child's talent and uniqueness.

Aldous, J. "Family Background Factors and Originality in Children."
    Gifted Child Quarterly 17 (1973): 183-192.

Using selected Torrance tests as measures of originality with
third grade boys and girls, the author hypothesized that boys will
do better than girls; middle class children better than lower class
children, children from small families better than children from
large families, and children whose classmates are of a different
socioeconomic background will do better than those whose classmates
have the same background.
    The results included the following observations. Boys were not
more original than girls (perhaps because the girls were still too
young to have learned passive sex roles). Middle class children
scored higher than working class children. The mother's employment
was not related to children's scores except where her job was of
higher prestige than the father's and then the child's originality
score was lower than that of the comparison group. Children from
smaller families, especially those with one or two children, scored
higher than children from larger families. Data on school composition did not support the marginal man theory. Ordinal position,
by itself, did not relate to originality. But, there was an interaction between ordinal position and sex. Boys who were oldest
scored higher than those who were not. Girls who were only children
also had higher scores than girls who were middle, oldest, and
youngest children. The scores for the last three groups were much
the same.

Additional analysis using IQ scores (Lorge-Thorndike and California Mental Maturity Scale) yielded no significant differences from
the above results. The one exception was that the lower originality
finding for children from the larger family was not supported. When
the father's occupation was included as a control variable, less
originality was found only with blue collar children.

Bee, H.L.; Barnard, K.E.; Eyres, S.J.; Gray, C.A.; Hammond, M.A.;
Spietz, A.L.; Snyder, C.; and Clark, B. "Prediction of IQ and Language Skill from Perinatal Status, Child Performance, Family Characteristics, and Mother-Infant Interaction." *Child Development* 53
(1982): 1134-1156.

After a thorough review of infant and child development studies,
the authors point out some important differences between their
study and those reviewed. In this study, the child's status at
birth, and several times thereafter, plus a study of the quality of
the environment allowed the investigators to say something about
the relative value in child development studies of information
about the individual and the environment. Because of its design,
this study says something about the predictive value of "general
demographic or 'ecological' family characteristics." Finally, this
study says something about the differences in the predictive equa-
tions for mothers who differ in level of education.

For this study, data were gathered from 193 (with some attrition
over time) healthy working class and middle class primiparous mothers
and their infants. The 4-year longitudinal study investigated the
value of several variables for the prediction of intellectual factors
and language outcome during the preschool years. In their summary,
the authors report their results as follows: "(1) Measures of perinatal or infant physical status were extremely weak predictors of
4 year IQ or language. (2) Assessments of child performance were
poor predictors prior to 24 months, but excellent predictors from
24 months on. (3) Assessments of mother-infant interaction and
general environmental quality were among the best predictors at each
age tested, and were as good as measures of child performance at
24 and 36 months in predicting IQ and language. (4) Measures of
family ecology (level of stress, social support, maternal education)
and parent perception of the child, especially when assessed at
birth, were strongly related to child IQ and language within a low-
education subsample, but not among mothers with more than high
school education. Patterns of prediction were similar for 48 month
IQ and 36 month receptive language; predictions were notably weaker
for 36 month expressive language."

Heilbrun, A.B. "Maternal Child Rearing and Creativity in Sons."
Journal of Genetic Psychology 119 (1971): 175-179.

It is hypothesized in this study that the male child who perceives
the mother as high on control but low on nurturance will be low on
creativity. A male who has experienced such a child rearing technique has been found to be "especially susceptible to influence by
external evaluative cues and limited in his ability to influence
his own behavior."

To gather data on the control variable, the Parent Attitude Research Instrument (PARI) was utilized (Heilbrun, 1966; Schaefer, 1961; Schaefer and Bell, 1958). For measures of perceived maternal nurturance, the Parent-Child Interaction Rating Scale (Heilbrun, 1964, 1970) was used. The subjects, with an average age of 18.9, were volunteers from undergraduate classes at Emory University. Ninety-six males volunteered; 41 participated in the first study and 54 in the second.

The measure of creativity was the empirically derived scale by Smith and Schaefer (1969). In Study I, the subject described himself with the Adjective Check List administered under standard conditions. In Study II, the subject described himself as others viewed him. Cutoff scores were established for control and nurturance and the populations were divided according to high and low on both variables. The hypothesis was supported in the study.

Suggestions for Further Reading

Heilbrun, A.B. "Parent Model Attributes, Nurturance Reinforcement and Consistency of Behavior in Adolescents." *Child Development* 35 (1964): 151-167.

————. "Perceived Maternal Child Rearing and the Effects of Vicarious and Direct Reinforcement upon Later-Adolescent Males." *Child Development* 41 (1970): 253-262.

Heilbrun, A.B.; Orr, H.K.; and Harrell, S.N. "Patterns of Parental Child Rearing and Subsequent Vulnerability to Cognitive Disturbance." *Journal of Consulting Psychology* 30 (1966): 51-59.

Schaefer, E.S. "Converging Conceptual Models for Maternal Behavior and for Child Behavior." In Glidewill, J.C. (Ed.). *Parental Attitudes and Child Behavior*. Springfield, IL: Thomas, 1961. 124-146.

Schaefer, E.S., and Bell, R.Q. "Development of a Parental Attitude Research Instrument." *Child Development* 29 (1958): 339-361.

Smith, J.M., and Schaefer, C.E. "Development of a Creativity Scale for the Adjective Check List." *Psychological Reports* 25 (1969): 87-92.

McClelland, D.C., and Pilon, D.A. "Sources of Adult Motives in Patterns of Parent Behavior in Early Childhood." *Journal of Personality and Social Psychology* 44 (1983): 564-574.

This is a longitudinal study of ratings obtained from mothers on their child-rearing practices in 1951, when their children were 5 years old. Social motive scores were obtained from 78 of the children 26-27 years later. The social motive scores for need achievement, need power, and need affiliation (or intimacy) were based on stories written to Thematic Apperception Test (TAT)-like pictures. Need achievement was found to be related to scheduling of feeding and severity of toilet training; need power was related to permissiveness for sexual and aggressive behaviors (but not for other behaviors). No child-rearing practices were associated with need affiliation. The findings related "to attitudes or behaviors involving specific practices at certain periods in a child's life as being critical for motive development, as basic-personality theorists have argued."

The early learning cited above accounts for, at most, 10-30% of the variance in adult motive scores. Later experiences in life and school are also important for differences in need achievement and need power. The authors also suggest that the reason they found relationships between child-rearing variables and person character-istics, in contrast to many studies which did not, may be "because our adult social-motive scores are more generic person characteris-tics that are less influenced by situational demands and response sets than the behaviors sampled in previous studies."

Chapter 5

CHARACTERISTICS, PART 2:
GENDER, BRAIN, METAMORPHIC COMPETENCE

GENDER

--Callahan, 1979
--Fox, 1975
--Helson, 1971
--Kogan, 1972
--Leder, 1981
--Lee and Karnes, 1983
--Schaefer, 1970
--Stanley and Benbow, 1982

MASCULINITY/FEMININITY

--Milgram; Yitzhak; and Milgram, 1977
--Suter and Domino, 1975
--Urbina; Harrison; Schaefer; and Anastasi, 1970
--Walberg, 1969

BRAIN DOMINANCE

--Gowan, 1978
--Martindale and Hasenfus, 1978
--Martindale, 1975
--Reynolds, 1981
--Reynolds and Torrance, 1978
--Robinson, 1982
--Torrance and Reynolds, 1978

METAPHORIC COMPETENCE

--Gardner and Winner, 1978
--Gardner; Winner; Bechhofer; and Wolf, 1978

GENDER

Callahan, C. "The Gifted and Talented Woman." In Passow, A.H. (Ed.). *The Gifted and the Talented: Their Education and Development*. *The Seventy-eighth Yearbook of the National Society for the Study of Education*. Chicago, IL: University of Chicago Press, 1979. 401-423.

The latter part of this chapter is devoted to a consideration of the research findings on the similarities and differences between males and females on a series of psychological variables. The lack of gender differences on the Stanford-Binet may be accounted for by the fact that the test was constructed to minimize sex differences. Other research indicates that (1) There is no difference in how males and females learn. (2) Up to age 10 or 11, boys and girls do equally well on measures of verbal performance. (3) After 11 years of age, girls do better than boys on measures of verbal performance in both simple and complex measures. (4) Until 9-13 years of age, there are no differences in quantitative ability; after that, boys do better. (5) Differences in quantitative ability are accompanied by differences in scientific achievement. (6) On spatial ability tests, boys start to do better at the beginning of adolescence and this increases through high school. (7) "No difference is found in the problem-solving tasks of response inhibition or problem restructuring." (8) On tests of concept mastery and reasoning and measures of nonverbal creativity, no differences are found. But after age seven, girls are better on measures of verbal creativity. "Thus it appears that the only areas where boys in the general population seem clearly and consistently superior to girls are visual-spatial ability and achievement in mathematics and science. Further, these differences are only apparent after the onset of adolescence."

If women are to fulfill their potential it is important that they develop a strong locus of control and "gain confidence in their own ability to control their fates." To avoid being labelled as abnormal and possibly to avoid the risk of rejection, women have been oriented to conformity and thus one finds greater homogeneity in the data obtained from women in various studies than one obtains from males.

Among the personality characteristics that differentiate the successful gifted female from her less successful peers are: "psychological mindedness, intellectual efficiency, tolerance, conscientiousness, flexibility, independence and autonomy, narcissism, modesty, originality, exactitude and aloofness." A comparison of successful female psychologists with male psychologists shows that the women are higher on "intelligence, superego strength, and unconventionality. These findings would seem to indicate that gifted women must have much more distinct personalities and inner strength in order to succeed."

Among the family and background variables that affect the development of the personality of the gifted and talented girl, the author cites: identification with father or masculine model, sibling order, and number of brothers. For a study of differences in values, the author points to a study of male and female students in math and science in which gifted females were found to score higher than normal females on the theoretical, political, and economic values. Nevertheless, they are still lower than males on these values and higher than males on the social, aesthetic, and religious values.

There are cultural barriers to the gifted female and "the studies examining teacher behavior, organizational reward systems, test bias, and social biases suggest that many cultural handicaps for the gifted woman" exist. Administrative programing has not paid sufficient attention to sex differences and there has been insufficient attention to models, sex of instructor, timing of enrichment, etc. The author concludes with the plea that special consideration be given to the counseling needs of gifted women. "Test biases should be identified, occupational counseling needs to be broadened, and counselors need to be sensitized to the needs of gifted females."

Fox, L.H. "Mathematically Precocious: Male or Female?" In Miley, J.F., et al. *Promising Practices: Teaching the Disadvantaged Gifted*. Ventura, CA: Ventura County Superintendent of Schools, 1975. 30–38.

This paper summarizes some of the differences obtained between male and female students in the Johns Hopkins University Study of Mathematically Precocious Youth (SMPY). The author reports that in the various contests conducted by the program, using a "difficult pre-college level test of mathematical reasoning ability," the boys were found to test at least 35 points higher than the girls. This occurs as early as grades seven and eight. Whether the differences are due to biological factors, cultural factors, or both is not clear.

The author also provides some descriptive information about the high scoring boys and the girls. High scoring boys (SAT-Math = 660 or more) "had stronger orientations towards investigative careers in mathematics and science and greater theoretical value orientations than did their less mathematically precocious males and female peers." Girls "are far less likely than boys, particularly the most mathematically talented boys, to seek out special experiences related to mathematics and science. Girls tend to have values and interests of a more social than theoretical nature."

The author concludes that there are two directions in which future education can go. "First we could concentrate upon boys all efforts to find and foster high level achievement and talent in mathematics, since they are easier to find and to work with. This first direction sounds very much like what, perhaps unintentionally, is occurring in most schools today. The second direction would be to concentrate our efforts to identify talented young women as well as young men, but also modify or restructure our instructional strategies for girls to optimize their chances for high level achievement. The long-term benefits of this second approach could have some quite gratifying results."

Suggestions for Further Reading

Astin, H.S. "Sex Differences in Mathematical Precocity." In Stanley, J.C.; Keating, D.P.; and Fox, L.H. (Eds.). *Mathematical*

Talent: Discovery, Description, and Development. Baltimore, MD:
Johns Hopkins University Press, 1974.

Fox, L.H. "Values and Career Interests of Mathematically Precocious
Youth." Paper presented at Annual Meeting of American Psychological Association, Montreal, Quebec, Canada, 1973.

Fox, L.H., and Denham, S.A. "Values and Career Interests of Mathematically and Scientifically Precocious Youth." In Stanley, J.C.;
Keating, D.P.; and Fox, L.H. (Eds.). *Mathematical Talent: Discovery, Description, and Development*. Baltimore, MD: Johns Hopkins
University Press, 1974.

Helson, R. "Women Mathematicians and the Creative Personality."
Journal of Consulting and Clinical Psychology 36 (1971): 210-220.

This paper is based on 45 women mathematicians of an estimated
300 in the U.S. when the study was undertaken. Eighteen of the
group are "virtually all creative women mathematicians in the United
States." The criterion was ratings by experts in the field of
specialization on a 7-point scale, with a rating of 4.0 indicating
that the subject was about as creative as the author of an average
research paper in a journal of mathematics. The women in this study
were "clearly more creative" than authors of such average papers.
A wide variety of procedures were administered to this group, a
process consistent with other studies at IPAR (Institute for Personality Assessment and Research) at the University of California
in Berkeley.

The most characteristic traits of the creative were "(a) rebellious
independence, narcissism, introversion, and a rejection of outside
influence; (b) strong symbolic interests and a marked ability to
find self-expression and self-gratification in directed research
activity; (c) flexibility, or lack of constriction, both in general
attitudes and in mathematical work." In elaborating on this last
point, the author adds, "That the creative women sought and to a
considerable degree attained an integration and simplification of
life, despite obstacles, would appear to be one of the important
findings of the study."

Turning to the personal histories, the author found that her
subjects grew up in homes where learning and culture were valued.
Many grew up outside of the U.S. and at least one parent was European
Hence, they may have avoided the anti-intellectual climate in the
U.S.

Relationships of the Creative (Cr) and Control (Cn) groups with
their parents are compared and some of the findings follow. 1. Cn
fathers are described as warm in 50% of the cases and their typical
occupation was that of business man or skilled worker. The Cr
fathers were professionals and seldom warm people. 2. Cn mothers
were as well educated as Cn fathers and daughters identified with
them. Cr women came from families where the parents were not of
the same intellectual status. If they did not come from large families, there was no brother. Cr women identified more with the father
than the mother. 3. Cn women yield the following picture: "In some
cases, a shy, intelligent girl found that mathematics as a subject
in which she could excel, and the standard of her family--sometimes
the rather narrow standards of the immigrant trying to make good--

encouraged her to pursue scholastic excellence in a conventional
way. In other cases, the child seemed concerned to defend herself
against impulse, and to use mathematics for this purpose. There
were, of course, other patterns which attained less statistical
prominence." By contrast, the Cr women are described as "coping
with her problems (by) sublimation and a search for autonomy in fantasy rather than repressive techniques.... One forms the picture of
a very intelligent child who was attracted by the father's intellectual status, felt alienated from her mother, adopted her father's
attitudes toward work and achievement but received relatively little
attention or affection from him. Isolated from both parents, she
developed the strategy of making herself autonomous by nurturing,
gratifying and 'growing' herself in symbolic activity."

Comparing the development of the female creative mathematician
with the male creative mathematician, the author says: "Most boys,
of course, undergo estrangement from the mother as a part of acquiring a masculine identity. This estrangement, termed independen-
dence, is eased by considerable social support, and the main ob-
stacle to the development of a creative personality in men seems to
be that what the mother represents will be devalued and repressed
too much, so that pleasure in imaginative play or attention to
feeling is rejected as feminine. Thus one finds among the men
mathematicians that the mother is described with more respect and
warmth by the creative men than by the comparison Ss. In a sense,
it would seem that respect for the mother encourages a cathexis of
symbolic activity in the boy, whereas a lack of respect may engender
it in the girl."

The three sets of traits which were presented as most characteristic of women also appear as characteristics of the creative person
generally, although they are more clear in creative women mathematicians than they are in men mathematicians who are also creative.
The author says, drawing on her work with Crutchfield (Helson and
Crutchfield, 1970a, 1970b), that "Among the creative men some were
original, flexible, ambitious, but essentially conventional individuals." A conventional woman would not be able to develop the concentration necessary to develop a new symbolic structure.

Kogan, N. "Creativity and Sex Differences." *Journal of Creative
   Behavior* 6 (1973): 1-13.

Generally speaking, sex differences have not been found in measures
of divergent thinking, ideational fluency, associative productivity,
originality, uniqueness, spontaneous flexibility, etc. This is true
despite the fact that the concurrent and predictive validity of the
divergent-thinking tests is not yet established. Nevertheless,
divergent thinking accounts for some "negligible portion of the
variance" of talented persons' activities and accomplishments. No
differences have been reported in the productivity of female Ph.D.'s
when compared to male Ph.D.'s.

However, "Ideational fluency and uniqueness, for example, do not
intercorrelate with other variables in the same direction and/or
degree in male and female samples. Further, males and females are
differentially affected by the kinds of testing or experimental
contexts employed to assess or alter levels of divergent thinking."
For males, the author argues that ideational fluency and uniqueness

are determined largely by internal cognitive factors, whereas external
situational influences have an effect on females' responses. The
author concludes: "To the extent that women are highly sensitized
to the social context in which they are working, the possibility of
being distracted from strictly cognitive involvements is high. It
appears that men are more capable of screening out the interpersonal
context, and hence can pursue their work in a more single-minded,
persistent, and nondistractible fashion."

Leder, G. "Fear of Success: Mathematics Performance and Career Choice."
In Kramer, A.H., et al. (Eds.). *Gifted Children: Challenging Their
Potential--New Perspectives and Alternatives*. New York: Trillium
Press, 1981. 165-177.

The purpose of this study was to investigate the relationship
between Horner's concept of the fear of success and sex differences
in performance in mathematics. Twenty girls and 30 boys in the
8th grade of a special program for able students in schools in the
metropolitan areas of Melbourne and Victoria, Australia, participated in the study. The students came from two different schools.

The following procedures were administered to the students: a
measure of the fear of success, a mathematics performance measure,
and questionnaires in which students were asked about their future
course and career intentions and "if and why they thought there
were fewer women than men in careers in science and mathematics."

The results were:

1. No differences were found in the mean fear of success scores
of the students in either school and there was no interaction
between school and sex. The data for male and female students in
both schools were therefore combined.

2. Eighty percent of the girls and 83.3% of the boys thought that
the study of mathematics was important for their future plans.

3. Fifty percent of the girls and 60% of the boys intended to
take as many mathematics courses as they could in high school.

4. Eighty percent of the girls and 83.3% of the boys thought that
mathematical competence was becoming important for most professional
careers.

5. Girls rated careers involving knowledge of literature and arts
significantly higher than did boys. Boys, on the other hand, rated
careers which involved a knowledge of mathematics, the physical
universe, and physical science significantly higher than girls.
Boys also tended to rate careers involving a knowledge of business
practices higher than girls. There were no sex differences on
careers involving a knowledge of human behavior or careers involving
a knowledge of law and political philosophy.

6. Twenty percent of the girls and 53.3% of the boys said they
intended to pursue a career in mathematics or a scientific field.

7. Girls showed a significantly higher fear of success than did
boys.

8. Girls with a strong preference for a male-preferred area had
a lower fear of success score than those with a strong preference
for a career in a field preferred by females. The difference was
not significant.

9. "Overall, little support was found for Horner's contention that
girls who opt for 'male careers' are lower in FS (fear of success)

than girls who opt for more traditional 'female' careers."

10. For the girls, but not for the boys, there was a negative correlation between fear of success and mathematics performance.

In conclusion, the author says, "Some support was found for the effect of social pressures on career choice and for the lower performance in mathematics of girls particularly aware of such social pressures. Further research in this area seems indicated. In particular, a longitudinal study of the long term effects of able students of FS seems appropriate."

Lee, L.A., and Karnes, F.A. "Attitude of the Gifted Toward Academic Subjects." *Journal for the Education of the Gifted* 6 (1983): 80-85.

This study is based on a summer residential program with 58 female and 68 male students who had IQs of 120 or above. They were asked to respond to a questionnaire which contained statements about four academic areas in the upper elementary and junior high school curriculum. The subjects were students in grades 4 through 7. Female students had a more positive attitude to reading than male students, and the latter had a more positive attitude to science than did the former. Mathematics showed no gender differences and no significant attitudinal differences were found across grade levels.

Schaefer, C.E. "A Psychological Study of 10 Exceptionally Creative Adolescent Girls." *Exceptional Child* 36 (1970): 431-441.

The girls in this study were part of a larger study of 200 creative girls who attended high schools that offered special programs for creative achievements. The girls were nominated by their teachers as having produced a creative work (story, poem, painting) and because they scored above a cutoff point on Guilford's Alternate Uses and Consequences Tests. The study from which the girls came is described at length in Anastasi and Schaefer, 1969.

For purposes of the present study, teachers and department heads were asked for girls who had given evidence of "exceptionally creative" work. The girls were 16 and 17 years of age and in the process of completing their senior year at five high schools in the New York metropolitan area. Among them were 9 Caucasians and 1 Oriental. Four of the girls came from divorced homes or homes in which one parent had died.

The author summarizes the results as follows:

1. The girls had shown evidence of their creative work in elementary school and early childhood.

2. They persevered in their creative activities, practicing their skills repeatedly and getting reinforcement from teachers and parents.

3. They had various role models (parents, siblings, teachers, and friends) to emulate.

4. Parents were of advanced age, high educational level, and had interests in cultural and intellectual pursuits.

5. They identified more with their fathers than with their mothers but were emotionally independent of both.

6. They read at an early age and remained avid readers.

7. Although they had difficulty with mathematics, they achieved a

high level of academic success with little effort. Their favorite subjects in elementary and high school were art and writing.

8. They had outstanding teachers.

9. They were active in extracurricular activities that gave them opportunity for creative expression and they took positions of leadership in these activities.

10. The girls were thinking of careers in art or writing and hoped for high achievements in these fields.

11. They had creative hobbies which they had begun in early childhood.

12. They preferred one or two close friends rather than a wide circle of acquaintances.

13. They were given to fantasy and "reported several unusual mental phenomena, including imaginary companions, synaesthesia, and déjà vu experiences."

14. Their self-concepts included characteristics usually associated with creativity: "openness to change and impulse expression, imagination, curiosity, aggressiveness, autonomy, and emotional sensitivity."

15. Projective test data yielded evidence for unresolved conflicts about femininity and autonomy.

Stanley, J.C., and Benbow, C.P. "Huge Sex Ratios at Upper End." *American Psychologist* 37 (1982): 972.

Based on experiences in the 8 talent searches thus far in the Study of Mathematically Precocious Youth under Stanley's direction at Johns Hopkins University, the authors report a disproportionate number of boys compared to girls. Searches to date have involved 34,000 students between 11 and 13 years of age. Boys and girls are matched on in-grade mathematics tests and the better motivated girls enter the talent searches. Nevertheless, boy and girl ratios on the SAT-Math test are: "2:1 at -500, 5:1 at -600, and 17:1 at -700 (Benbow and Stanley, 1980, 1981; cf. Fox, 1976). The ratio is climbing, for in a recent survey, there were 61 boys and 0 girls who scored at least 700 on SAT-Math.

This comment was written in response to a paper by Hyde (1981). The authors' concluding comment is: "Thus, despite Hyde's guarded optimism, we view the situation as grave where mathematical reasoning ability of the level needed to obtain a Ph.D. degree in the mathematical sciences, physics, or engineering with distinction from a top-flight university is concerned. It seems to us that much research into causes and remedies is sorely needed, rather than further efforts at trying to minimize the magnitude of the sex differences."

Suggestions for Further Reading

Benbow, C.P., and Stanley, J.C. "Sex Differences in Mathematical Ability: Fact or Artifact?" *Science* 210 (1980): 1262-1264.

————. "Mathematical Ability: Is Sex a Factor?" *Science* 212 (1981): 118-119.

Fox, L.H. "Sex Differences in Mathematical Precocity: Bridging the Gap." In Keating, D.P. (Ed.). *Intellectual Talent: Research and Development*. Baltimore, MD: Johns Hopkins University Press, 1976.

Hyde, J.S. "How Large Are Cognitive Gender Differences? A Meta-analysis Using w^2 and d." *American Psychologist* 36 (1981): 892-901.

MASCULINITY/FEMININITY

Milgram, R.A.; Yitzhak, V.; and Milgram, N. "Creative Activity and Sex-Role Identity in Elementary School Children." *Perceptual and Motor Skills* 45 (1977): 371-376.

This study, conducted in Israel, focused on the relationship between sex-role characteristics and creative activity in elementary school boys and girls. The prediction was: "a high over-all level of creative activity across different areas would be associated with high scores on both masculine and feminine scales."

Eighty boys and 56 girls participated in the study. They ranged in age from 9 to 12 and were in grades 4 to 6 in the Haifa area. The children were candidates for admission to special programs conducted for talented children. All had IQs of 120 or above as measured by an Israeli group intelligence test that consists of four subareas: vocabulary, sentence completion, oddities, and arithmetic.

The criterion measure was a self-report one which consisted of eight activity areas: music, science, art, social leadership, writing drama, sports, and dance. For each area there was a series of accomplishments in ascending order. A single score was obtained. The students also were given four subtests of the Wallach and Kogan battery which consisted of alternate uses, pattern meanings, similarities, and line meanings. These were scored for ideational fluency and overall number of responses. An overall score for all subjects was obtained.

To measure sex-role identity, the Bem Sex-role Inventory was used. Boys scored higher on the masculine part of this scale and girls scored higher on the feminine part as was expected. Unexpectedly, the masculine and feminine scales correlated .48 for the boys and .55 for the girls (both significant). In college student samples, these scales are reported as being uncorrelated.

The results lead the authors to conclude that: "The present study supports the position that cross-sex-typing or the simultaneous endorsement of masculine and feminine sex-role characteristics confers an advantage on children making such endorsements. Children high on both scales tend to engage in a wide variety of nonacademic creative activities, while the participation of sex-typed children is restricted to activities conventionally associated with their own sex only." Androgyny (in which there is a balance of male and femal scores) did not correlate with creative performance.

Suter, B., and Domino, G. "Masculinity-Femininity in Creative College Women." *Journal of Personality Assessment* 30 (1975): 414-420.

Since femininity is apparently related to creativity in males, the current study was undertaken to examine the relationship between masculinity and creativity in women. The literature indicates that the father is the more important role model for creative women than control women (Domino, 1969; Helson, 1966, 1967; Schaefer, 1970). Also, creative women have difficulty in adjusting to the culturally expected feminine sex role in adolescence (Helson, 1967; Schaefer, 1970). Helson (1966) did not find statistically significant differences between high creative and low creative college females on

the feminine scale of the California Psychological Inventory (CPI)
and the masculinity-femininity scales of the MMPI, nor were there
differences found on scales related to masculinity. But the high
creative women were rated more masculine than the low creative group.
On the other hand, Littlejohn (1967) compared ninth-grade high and
low creative females and found that the high creatives scored significantly higher in the masculine direction on the female scale of
the CPI and the masculine-femininity scales of the MMPI.

From a pool of 400 college female subjects who ranged in age from
18 to 22, the authors selected two subgroups of 45. The high creative group were those who scored at the 75th percentile and above on
college norms on the Remote Associates Test (Mednick & Mednick,
1967) and Schaefer's (1970) Biographical Inventory. The low creative
group scored below the 25th percentile on these tests. The two
groups were equal in verbal aptitude (SAT scores) and both averaged
about 19.6 in age.

The following tests were administered: The California Psychological
Inventory Femininity Scale, the masculinity-femininity scale of the
MMPI, the Franck Drawing Completion Test (Franck and Rosen, 1949),
the Webster Scales of Masculinity-Femininity (Webster, 1956) and the
Gough Adjective Check List (Gough and Heilbrun, 1965). The Webster
Scale measures: (a) conventionality--preference for conventional
female roles, (b) passivity--lack of aggressiveness, dominance,
etc., and (c) feminine sensitivity--emotionality, fantasy, introspec-
tion, neurotic trends, and esthetic interests. The Adjective Check
List was administered under three sets on instructions. In the first,
the subjects were asked to describe themselves. In the second, they
were asked to describe males as they are described in everyday con-
versation. In the third, they were asked to do the same for women.

The results of the study indicated that no differences were found
with the femininity scale of the CPI, the masculinity-femininity
scales of the MMPI, the Franck Test, or the conventionality and sensitivity scales of the Webster Scales. Significant differences were
found on the passivity scale of the Webster (the high creatives were
less passive) and on the ratio measure established for the Adjective
Check List, with the high creatives describing themselves as more
masculine.

Suggestions for Further Reading

Domino, G. "Maternal Correlates of Sons' Creativity." *Journal of
Consulting and Clinical Psychology* 33 (1969): 180-183.

Franck, K., and Rosen, E. "A Projective Test of Masculinity-Femininity." *Journal of Consulting Psychology* 13 (1949): 247-256.

Gough, E.G., and Heilbrun, A.B., Jr. *The Adjective Check List
Manual.* Palo Alto, CA: Consulting Psychologists Press, 1965.

Helson, R. "Personality of Women with Imaginative and Artistic Interests: The Role of Masculinity, Originality and Other Characteristics in Their Creativity." *Journal of Personality* 34 (1966):
1-35.

Helson, R. "Personality Characteristics and Developmental History
of Creative College Women." *Genetic Psychology Monographs* 76
(1967): 205-226.

Schaefer, C.E. "A Physiological Study of 10 Exceptionally Creative Adolescent Girls." *Exceptional Children* 43 (1970): 431-441.

Webster, H. "Personality Developments During the College Years: Some Quantitative Results." *Journal of Social Issues* 12 (1956): 29-43.

Urbina, S.; Harrison, J.B.; Schaefer, C.E.; and Anastasi, A. "Relationship Between Masculinity-Femininity and Creativity as Measured by the Franck Drawing Completion Test." *Psychological Reports* 26 (1970): 799-804.

This study tested the hypothesis that creative subjects would share more of the characteristics of the opposite sex than would noncreative subjects. To gather the necessary data, the Franck Drawing Completion Test was used. This test consists of a series of 36 incomplete line drawings which are to be completed by the subject as he/she wishes. "Completions are scored principally on the basis of certain formal categories, such as closing the stimulus versus leaving it open, expanding from the stimulus outward versus elaborating within its area, making the stimulus sharper versus making it blunter. Some content categories are also utilized most of which are based on Freudian symbol theory." Only the first 12 drawings of the test were used in the study.

Subjects were selected from the Schaefer and Anastasi (1968) and Anastasi and Schaefer (1969) studies. In each of the four sex-creativity groups, there were 60 subjects.

The results indicated that there was a significant difference in the scores obtained for girls and boys. There was no statistical difference between the creative and noncreative subjects nor was there a significant interaction between creativity and sex. No differences were found for field of work when differences were tested for sex of subjects.

In discussing why the main hypothesis, that creative individuals would have opposite characteristics, was not supported, the authors say: "The overlapping of masculine and feminine traits that is found more often in creative persons than in noncreative persons probably occurs only in those traits conducive to creativity. There seems to be no foundation for the assumption that overlap occurs in *all* masculine and feminine traits, and particularly not in those measured by the Franck Drawing Completion Test (FDCT)."

Walberg, H.J. "Physics, Femininity, and Creativity." *Developmental Psychology* 1 (1969): 47-54.

Data obtained from subsamples of 705 girls, who were taking a new high school physics course, were compared with similar data obtained from 1,369 boys on 58 cognitive, attitudinal, and behavioral measures. Girls were higher than boys on verbal aptitude (but not on quantitative and spatial abilities), "social values and interpersonal needs, cautiousness especially about science experiences, and aesthetic (rather than theoretical) valuations." Such characteristics may lead to greater success in high school, but they will not be effective and will even penalize women who might seek eminence in later scientific careers.

Suggestions for Further Reading

Bing, E. "Effect of Childrearing Practices on the Development of Differential Cognitive Abilities." *Child Development* 34 (1963): 631-648.

Maccoby, E.E. (Ed.). *The Development of Sex Differences*. Stanford, CA: Stanford University Press, 1966.

Walberg, H.J. "Dimensions of Interests in Boys and Girls Studying Physics." *Science Education* 45 (1967): 320-326.

BRAIN DOMINANCE

Gowan, J.C. "Incubation, Energy and Creativity." *Journal of Mental Imagery* 2 (1978): 23-32.

The left hemisphere is concerned with convergent thinking and the right with divergent thinking. "Right hemisphere imagery is the vehicle through which incubation produces creativity.... The function of the left hemisphere appears to be to prepare an alphanumeric matrix so that the image can be intellectually negotiated with others."

Martindale, C., and Hasenfus, N. "EEG Differences as a Function of Creativity, Stage of the Creative Process, and Effort to Be Original." *Biological Psychology* 6 (1978): 157-167.

The authors present two experiments designed to study the relationships between creativity and EEG alpha. Twelve subjects (5 male and 7 female), who were students in a creative writing course at the University of Maine, were paid to participate in the first experiment. Since there were no sex differences in the results, the data are combined for both groups. The creativity criterion was the rating the subjects received from two instructors for themes they wrote in their creative writing class.

The first experiment focused on the possible differentiation between the inspirational stage of the creative process and the elaboration stage. Data for each of the two stages were obtained after the experimenters asked their subjects to construct a story about the following: "A man meets a woman and asks her out on a date." Subjects were instructed to be as original as possible. The subjects were given three minutes to think about their stories and five minutes to write them. The three-minute thinking period was regarded as the inspirational phase and the five-minute writing period, as the elaborational phase. Brain wave (EEG) data were gathered during resting periods, inspirational and elaborational periods, all with the subjects keeping their eyes open.

The results were that the high creative group had a higher mean alpha index during the inspiration stage and a higher mean alpha index during the elaborational phase than did the less creative subjects. The interesting finding for the authors was that highly creative subjects had a low level of arousal during the inspiration phase as compared to the elaboration stage. The highly creative subjects had significantly higher alpha during the inspirational

stage than during the elaborational stage. The two indices were
the same for the less creative subjects. Furthermore, the highly
creative subjects had higher alpha indices during the inspiration
steps (relative to the elaboration stage) than did the less creative
subjects. The results of the second experiment indicated similar
effects. In addition, the results were found to be specific to
creative subjects only when they were instructed to be original.
No consistent relationships were found between creativity and basal
EEG alpha.

There are other comments by the authors that should be noted.
Cortical arousal is related to the biphasic creative process that
has been elaborated by psychoanalysts such as Kris (1952) as well
as Blum (1961) and Martindale (1971). These works suggested "that
secondary process cognition accompanies medium levels of cortical
arousal while primary process thought accompanies either high or
low levels of cortical arousal. If this is the case, regression
from secondary process to primary process thought must entail variation in level of cortical arousal.... It seems likely that the
primary process state characterizing creative inspiration would be
accompanied by low rather than high arousal. If this were the case,
then we could translate Kris' hypothesis to the physiological level:
The creative process involves an initial inspirational stage carried
out at a low level of cortical arousal followed by a subsequent
elaborational stage entailing high arousal. It should be the case
that this pattern would be more typical of creative individuals
than of those who are not creative."

The authors also point out that previous research (Martindale and
Armstrong, 1974; and Martindale and Hines, 1975) indicated that
high creative subjects are not as good at controlling alpha wave
production during biofeedback as less creative subjects. The high
creatives are good at control for a few seconds and then lose control. "These results suggest that the alpha enhancement effect durin
the inspirational phase is probably not due to purposeful self-
control but is a more automatic process."

Suggestions for Further Reading

Martindale, C. "Degeneration, Disinhibition, and Genius." *Journal
of the History of the Behavioral Sciences* 7 (1971): 177-182.

Martindale, C., and Armstrong, J. "The Relationship of Creativity
to Cortical Activation and Its Operant Control." *Journal of Geneti
Psychology* 124 (1974): 311-320.

Martindale, C., and Hines, D. "Creativity and Cortical Activation
During Creative, Intellectual and EEG Feedback Tasks." *Biological
Psychology* 3 (1975): 91-100.

Martindale, C. "What Makes Creative People Different." *Psychology
Today* 9 (1975): 44-42.

Highly creative people exhibit an increase in alpha waves from
both hemispheres of the brain during a creative task. Subjects low
in creativity show a decrease in alpha waves and an increase in
beta waves in the left hemisphere during a creative task. These particular subjects also exhibit a greater ability to concentrate.

Reynolds, C.R. "The Neuropsychological Basis of Intelligence." In Hynds, G.W., and Obrzut, J.E. (Eds.). *Neuropsychological Assessment of the School-aged Child: Issues and Procedures*. New York: Grune & Stratton, 1981.

This chapter looks briefly at the problem of handedness and cerebral dominance as they have been believed to relate to the cognitive functioning of children. A number of major neuropsychological theories of intelligence and the cognitive processes of the brain are presented, including Halstead's, Luria's, Das', etc. "Finally, an attempt is made to reconcile the Luria-Das model with current research on hemispheric specialization."

The author makes some distinctions between biological and psychological intelligence. "The notion of biological and psychological intelligence briefly described here is relatively new and remains to be elaborated elsewhere in the future." Among the ways in which biological intelligence and psychological intelligence differ is that biological intelligence represents the "general physiological efficiency of the brain." Psychological intelligence, on the other hand, "is the principal determinant of an individual's level of function, and psychological intelligence is the principal determinant of an individual's method of performing intelligent functions."

The theories of Halstead, Luria, and Das et al., are theories of psychological intelligence; further work with them will enhance our understanding of how the brain carries out higher order thinking. The mechanisms of biological intelligence are "in a primitive state and will likely as not fall to the neurophysiologist and behavioral neurochemist for resolution." Further work with hemisphericity "should lead to a rich investigation of early learning in school and school-related subjects. The reconceptualization of dominance may open a whole new era of research in quest for the aptitude x treatment interaction."

Reynolds, C.R., and Torrance, E.P. "Perceived Changes in Styles of Learning and Thinking (Hemisphericity) Through Direct and Indirect Training." *Journal of Creative Behavior* 12 (1978): 247-252.

The purpose of this study was to investigate whether it is possible to modify thinking and learning styles (hemisphericity) in short-term (6 to 12 weeks), intensive training programs. One program involved direct training in a specific style that was right brain oriented. The other involved indirect training in which subjects were exposed to various styles and experiences. It was hypothesized that when training was in a specific style then that training, if it were effective, should produce a shift toward that style. On the other hand, when subjects were exposed to various styles and experiences, the shift should be to "a more integrated style, promoting cerebral complementarity (interhemispheric cooperation)."

There were two groups in this study. Group 1 consisted of 200 gifted and talented high school students who were involved in the 1977 Career Awareness Component of the Georgia Governor's Honors Program. These students were involved in indirect training. They had been selected for outstanding achievement in various areas: visual arts, music, science, social science, mathematics, industrial

design, etc. Complete pre-test and post-test data were available
on 192 of the 200 participants. Group 2 was composed of 68 graduate
students from different fields, who were involved in a course on
creative thinking. They were the group involved in direct training
for right hemisphere dominance.

Group 1 students spent two hours each day for six weeks working
in their special areas of interest. The remainder of their time was
spent in a variety of interdisciplinary activities: career education, current problems, futurism, and special interest groups.
There were also experiences in field training, research, etc.
"There were deliberate and systematic attempts to help students see
clear relationships among information from different disciplines
and between information in their own discipline and their future
careers...."

Group 2 had lectures and readings in their creative thinking
class. In addition, they had extensive and intensive training in
creative problem solving which involved brainstorming, imaging, etc.
"Emphases were clear on the specialized functions of the right
cerebral hemisphere. The class met four hours each week for 11
weeks and each person engaged in a variety of creative experiences
outside of class as part of the course requirements."

The questionnaire, Your Style of Learning and Thinking, was administered to both Groups 1 and 2 during the first day of their
respective experiences and during the last week for post-test
measures. According to their scores, students were classified as:
"Right (utilizing those styles most closely associated with right
cerebral hemisphere function), Left (utilizing those styles most
closely associated with left cerebral function), Integrated (utilizing styles showing primarily cerebral complementarity in information processing), or Mixed (showing no clear preference for any of
the other styles, tending to show right preference for some tasks,
left for others, and integrated for yet other problems)."

Both hypotheses were confirmed. Group 1 students who had diverse
learning and thinking experiences showed the greatest increase in
the direction of the integrated category. There was a slight increase in the number of students falling into the Mixed category.
Group 2, trained specifically in creative thinking procedures which
were right brain dominant, showed significant increase in the number
of persons classified as right brain dominant. Decreases, of course,
occurred in the three other categories.

The authors drew the following conclusions:

1. It is possible to modify a person's style of thinking and
learning.

2. It is likely that the direction can be controlled.

3. If this work continues with the same results, it may be possible to train individuals to shift their style as demanded by the
problems that confront them.

4. This would have implications for various fields: creative
problem solving, special education, learning disabilities, etc.

5. One does not know how long the changes reported here will
last.

6. More research is necessary on longitudinal effects and the
meaning of the Mixed category.

7. There is a need for replication with more typical groups since
the two groups studied here were not very typical.

Suggestions for Further Reading

Bever, T.G., and Chiarello, R.S. "Cerebral Dominance in Musicians and Non-musicians." *Science* 186 (1974): 537-539.

Gazzaniga, M.S. *The Bisected Brain.* New York: Appleton-Century-Crofts, 1970.

Kinsbournes, M. "The Ontogeny of Cerebral Dominance." In Aaronson, D., and Reiber, D. (Eds.). *Developmental Psycholinguistics and Communication Disorders.* New York: New York Academy of Sciences, 1975.

Krueger, T.H. *Visual Imagery in Problem Solving and Scientific Creativity.* Derby, CT: Seal Press, 1976.

Samples, R.E. "Are You Teaching Only One Side of the Brain?" *Learning* 3 (1975): 24-30.

Robinson, D.N. "Cerebral Plurality and the Unity of Self." *American Psychologist* 37 (1982): 904-910.

This is a discussion of old and new literature on the relationship of "self," "self-identity," "personal identity" and "split-brain" data. Of special relevance to this book is the caution implicit in the following statement about "split-brain" research. "Each year seems to bring a number of qualifications of claims about these patients (with surgical 'deconnection' of the cerebral hemispheres), and it is therefore too early to say which of the empirical claims might be taken as final. Nevertheless, the evidence is quite consistent in pointing to some form of psychological 'deconnection' as a corollary of commissural sectioning."

Torrance, E.P., and Reynolds, C.R. "Images of the Future of Gifted Adolescents: Effects of Alienation and Specialized Cerebral Functioning." *Gifted Child Quarterly* 22 (1978): 431-445.

The purpose here is to try to understand the relationships between alienation and styles of learning on images of the future among a group of gifted adolescents. The subjects were 200 gifted and talented students in the 1977 Career Awareness Component of the Georgia Governor's Honors Program. These students were selected on the basis of outstanding achievement in a variety of areas: music, science, visual arts, mathematics, French, etc. The students were given the Allen Adolescent Alienation Index (1973), and Your Style of Learning and Thinking. At the end of the 6 week summer program, students were asked to write an essay in which they would describe, among other things, what they had accomplished at the end of their careers.

The results indicated that alienation scores were generally quite low, and lower than those obtained by high school students generally. Nevertheless, a high and low alienation group was selected and their responses on several variables were studied. None of the differences were significant at the .05 level. Some trends in the findings are discussed and illustrated with the essays that the students had written. Data on the styles of learning and thinking questionnaire were used to classify the students as right, left, and integrated

dominance. Their essays were analyzed and the results revealed the
following. Integrated and right brain dominant individuals showed
more satisfaction with their projected future careers, their perception of self changed, their perception of the world changed,
they showed commitment to working for a better world, they showed
an awareness of future problems and proposed future solutions, and
they perceived themselves as creative problem solving people. With
a fair degree of consistency, the right hemisphere group excelled
over the integrated group. Statistically, chi squares were obtained
for: unconventional careers, the effects of life and culture, the
use of the environment to meet human needs, educational problems,
optimism about the future, and strategy of resolving conflicts.

In concluding the paper, the authors state: "We hope that some of
you share our excitement in these emerging insights concerning the
development of images of the future of gifted students and educational
methodologists for enlarging, enriching, and making more accurate
our images of the future. The challenge is great."

METAPHORIC COMPETENCE

Gardner, H., and Winner, E. "The Development of Metaphoric Competence:
   Implications for Humanistic Disciplines." *Critical Inquiry* 5 (1978):
   123-141.

This paper summarizes some of the authors' research on metaphoric
comprehension and metaphoric production. With regard to the former,
results in progress or tentative findings suggest: 1. Children in-
terpret metaphors in a concrete manner until middle childhood.
Only after about 10 years of age do children demonstrate a consistent ability to understand metaphor. 2. Children are better able
to decode metaphors if they are presented in context rather than
in isolation. 3. With regard to metaphoric production, it was
found, consistent with the "child-as-poet" position, that preschool
children (3 and 4 year olds) did better than college students and
significantly better than children of 7 or 11 in the production of
appropriate metaphors. They also produced more inappropriate metaphors. "Indeed, their performance reflected an insensitivity to
(or a willingness to disregard or cut across) conventional boundaries
of experience and language.... They lacked the 'blue-pencilling'
and 'decentering' capacity to reject those metaphors which, while
appealing to them, would not make sense to other individuals."
4. It is conceivable that objects and actions may be organized
differently in the mind of the child than in older subjects. It
is possible that physiognomic and synesthetic factors are operative
in the mind of the child. Children seem to be able to respond to
the expressive features of objects. If that is all they can do,
then they cannot be considered metaphorically competent. "But if,
as appears to be the case, children have available to them both
this mode of organization and the more typical superordinate taxo-
nomic classes, then their early language can justifiably be termed
metaphoric." Other hypotheses are also entertained. 5. In discussing the finding that preschoolers are better at metaphoric
production than children in middle childhood who are literal (they

do not produce metaphors on request and they tend to produce literal or narrational paraphrases of metaphors), the authors suggest that this may be culturally motivated but it may also be a necessary stage in the production of metaphors. 6. Research was also conducted with brain dominance as a variable. The left brain, as is known, is dominant for language and, therefore, individuals with injury to that side of the brain (left-hemisphere or aphasic subjects) should lose their metaphoric capabilities while those with injury to the right side of the brain (right-hemispheric patients) should retain theirs. But the converse should be true if one accepts more recent brain dominance work which indicates that the right side of the brain is involved in artistic, intuitive, and affective matters and the left side of the brain is involved in abstract and logical thought. Using tasks requiring nonverbal matching behavior on the part of the subject or a verbal paraphrase, they found: (a) Left-hemisphere patients with language difficulties had trouble paraphrasing metaphors. Right-hemisphere patients had difficulty but did paraphrase appropriately. (b) The picture condition led to unexpected results. Left-hemisphere aphasic subjects made the correct match while right-hemisphere patients selected the literal match. On the basis of these data, the authors say "metaphoric competence is not of a single piece. It is possible to be metaphorically competent in one modality or with one type of stimulus while appearing relatively incompetent (or primitive) when the same metaphor is presented in another modality or when another modality of response is required." Thus the authors suggest: "Our brain-damaged patients offer evidence for the existence of one neural 'center' housing knowledge of linguistic features and a second 'center' which judges the situational appropriateness of linguistic figures."

Gardner, H.; Winner, E.; Bechhofer, R.; and Wolf, D. "The Development of Figurative Language." In Nelson, K. (Ed.). *Children's Language.* Vol. 1. New York: Gardner Press, 1978. 1-38.

This chapter contains a review of the history and research on figurative (non-literal) language, which includes metaphors, jokes, proverbs, stories, etc. The chapter contains sections on metaphoric production and metaphoric understanding.

A tentative model of non-literal word use during early childhood consists of the following stages: "(1) The emergence of metaphoric object substitutions: 18 months. (2) The emergence of enactively-based, post-referential speech: 18-24 months. (3) The emergence of perceptually-based, post-referential speech: 24-36 months. (4) The acquisition of appropriate syntactic constructions: 36-50 months." A model of metamorphic development is also presented as follows: 1. Children in preschool years are actively involved in metaphoric productions; some metaphors are appropriate and others are not. These children cannot grasp "the potency and aptness of what they have fashioned, and they display little awareness of cultural rules governing the production of figures of speech." They are limited by the egocentricism and their inability to "blue-pencil" inappropriate metaphors. They cannot paraphrase or appreciate the metaphors of others. With manageable tasks, they perform better than might be expected; "This performance may signal a kind of intuitive understanding of the processes whereby domains are mapped onto one another,

which may contribute to later, more sophisticated forms of metaphoric understanding."

2. Children in early primary years have an increasing awareness
of dictionary definitions and they show literal use of words in
their speech. "Subsequent 'self-conscious' or 'mature' metaphor
may only be able to emerge against a background of literal mastery."
Apparently, development of metaphor usage depends on appreciating
what words usually mean and how they are organized.

3. A discovery (or re-discovery) of the use of metaphor takes
place in preadolescent years. By 10 or 11, children are able to
offer appropriate paraphrases and metaphors.

4. With the attainment of formal logical operations in adolescence
metaphoric capacity becomes possible. "The child's cognitive and
linguistic capacities have now advanced to the point where he can
classify objects in a variety of ways, reflect upon language as an
object, and deal not only with the given objects of the present,
but also with a universe of possibilities.... Such intellectual
growth is reflected in metaphoric tasks."

Suggestions for Further Reading

Billow, R.A. "Cognitive Developmental Study of Metaphor Comprehen-
    sion." *Developmental Psychology* 11 (1975): 415-423.

Burt, H.R. "An Investigation of Grade Five Students' Reading
    Understanding of Similes." Masters thesis, University of Alberta,
    1971.

Kogan, N. "Metaphoric Thinking in Children. Developmental and
    Individual-Difference Aspects." Paper presented at Society for
    Research in Child Development, Denver, CO, April 1975.

————. "Sensitivity to Visual Metaphor." Paper presented at the
    International Congress of Psychology, Paris, July 1976.

Malgady, R.G. "Figurative Language Development and Academic
    Achievement." Unpublished paper, State University of New York at
    Brockport, 1976.

Winner, E.; Krauss, B.; and Gardner, H. "Children's Capacity to
    Perceive Metaphoric Relationships." Unpublished paper, Harvard
    University, 1975.

Chapter 6

CHARACTERISTICS, PART 3:
INTELLIGENCE AND/OR CREATIVITY

HISTORY

--Kreuter, 1962
--Seagoe, 1972
--Sellin and Birch, 1980

TERMAN

--Terman, 1925
--Terman, 1917
--Cox, 1926
--Burks; Jensen; and Terman, 1930
--Terman and Oden, 1947
--Terman, 1954a
--Terman, 1954b
--Terman and Oden, 1959
--Oden, 1968
--Sears, 1979

Critique

--Tannenbaum, 1983
--Jacobs, 1970

Additional Studies of the Gifted

--Bridges, 1973
--Durr, 1964
--Haggard, 1957

The Extremely Gifted

--Feldman, 1979
--Hollingworth, 1926
--Hollingworth, 1942
--Lorge and Hollingworth, 1936

The Gifted Underachiever

--Whitmore, 1980

IQ Myths

--Bane and Jencks, 1976

Heredity/Environment--Race Differences

--Block and Dworkin, 1976
--Jones, 1984
--MacKenzie, 1984
--Vernon, 1979

BURT

--Burt, 1975

GUILFORD

--Guilford, 1967
--Guilford, 1970 and 1977
--Guilford, 1972
--Guilford, 1975

Validation Studies

--Harrington; Block, J.; and
   Block, J.H., 1983

Critique

--Nicholls, 1972
--Richards, 1976
--Guilford, 1976
--Harvey and Seeley, 1984
--Piechowski and Colangèlo,
   1984
--Tannenbaum, 1983a
--Tannenbaum, 1983b
--Vernon, P.E.; Adamson; and
   Vernon, D.F., 1977
--Wallach and Kogan, 1965

Sternberg

--Sternberg, 1977
--Davidson and Sternberg,
   1984

Evaluation of Guilford's Tests

--Richert; Alvino; and Mc-
   Donnel, 1982a
--Richert; Alvino; and Mc-
   Donnel, 1982b
--Richert; Alvino; and Mc-
   Donnel, 1982c

GETZELS AND JACKSON

--Getzels and Jackson, 1962
--Getzels, 1979 (Getzels and
   Csikszentmihalyi, 1976)

Critique

--Tannenbaum, 1983
--Vernon, P.E.; Adamson; and
   Vernon, D.F., 1977
--Wallach and Kogan, 1965

TORRANCE

--Torrance, 1962
--Torrance and Aliotti, 1969
--Torrance, 1969
--Torrance, 1965
--Torrance, 1972
--Torrance, 1971
--Torrance, 1982
--Houtz; Rosenfield; and Tenten-
   baum, 1978
--Rieger, 1983

Critique

--Haddon and Lytton, 1968
--Haddon and Lytton, 1971
--Tannenbaum, 1983
--Vernon, P.E.; Adamson; and
   Vernon, D.F., 1977
--Wallach and Kogan, 1965

Evaluation of Tests

--Richert; Alvino; and Mc-
   Donnel, 1982a
--Richert; Alvino; and Mc-
   Donnel, 1982b
--Buros, 1972
--Wallach, 1971

WALLACH AND KOGAN

--Wallach and Kogan, 1965

Validation Studies

--Rotter; Langland; and
   Berger, 1971
--Hattie, 1980
--Wallbrown; Wallbrown; and
   Wherry, 1975

Critique

--Cronbach, 1968
--Vernon, P.E.; Adamson;
   and Vernon, D.F., 1977
--Tannenbaum, 1983

GENERAL CRITIQUES

--Tannenbaum, 1983
--Vernon, P.E.; Adamson; and
   Vernon, D.F., 1977
--Wallach and Kogan, 1965

NEEDED RESEARCH

--Treffinger and Poggio, 1972

HISTORY

Kreuter, G. "The Vanishing Genius: Lewis Terman and the Stanford
Study." *History of Education Quarterly* 2 (1962): 6-18.

From the beginning Terman felt that the intelligence test could
find the person of genius. He did not believe that parents and educators were sufficiently aware of the geniuses in their midst and
he was critical of American educational methods that did not take
children's needs into account. His bias in favor of hereditary
factors was fundamental to his work and was evident in his doctoral
dissertation, "Genius and Stupidity," in which he concluded that
there was a gulf between the capacities of the gifted child and the
"dunce" which could not be accounted for in environmental terms.

At the time of his first volume, Terman believed that "only good
would come from the man of genius," environment could not create
genius but inhibit it, educational methods were inadequate for training superior students, and ethnic and racial differences existed.
Even when he found that a disproportionate number of his gifted
children had fathers who were in the professions, Terman cited this
as evidence of the children's superior heredity.

At the time of the second volume, it was found that the students
did not fulfill their achievements, and a new emphasis appeared in
Terman's writing. Failure to rise did not mean that true achievement was trivial. The gifted, he believed, had made heroic sacrifices, had shown uncommon judgment in their daily lives, had shown
many acts of kindness, and had discharged their social and civic
responsibilities conscientiously. In the second follow-up study,
eugenic recommendations were dropped and by 1947, "dunce" and "genius"
were no longer used. The interactions between heredity and environment were now regarded as complex; personality factors were now important, and the zeitgeist was more important than the intelligence
test in determining accomplishment.

When, by the 1955 report, Terman's results indicated that there
was a lack of evidence that people of modest achievements were any
less able intellectually than those who reached high places, Terman
was not discouraged and did not want it to be otherwise. He argued
that one could take solace in the fact that some of the small jobs
in society, as well as the larger ones, were being carried out by
gifted people.

According to the author, Terman did not change his ideas in three
important respects: his attitude toward growth and development, the
importance he assigned to "adjustment," and "his commitment to the
existing values of American society."

Terman kept his political and economic ideas out of his published
writings. But; the author thinks it is a limitation of Terman's
work that "it never decided how the gifted should connect *themselves*
with life, or what the social value of genius might be."

Suggestions for Further Reading

Fancher, R.E. *The Intelligence Men: Makers of the IQ Controversy.*
New York: Norton, 1985.

Seagoe, M.V. "Terman and the Gifted." *Elementary School Principal*
51 (1972): 76-78.

This article contains some biographical material about Terman.
He began a 2-year teacher training course in 1892 when he was 15
at the Danville, Indiana, Normal School. At Indiana University he
began research on giftedness and, as a result of his thesis, was
nominated for a fellowship at Clark University in educational psychology under G. Stanley Hall. He attended Hall's seminar and one
of his classmates was Gesell. Hall did not approve of Terman's interest in "precocity" in mental tests and therefore Terman switched
to Stanford.

To study giftedness Terman developed an instrument with a variety
of tasks, some of which were included in the Stanford-Binet. His
doctoral dissertation, dated 1906, involved a comparison of "brilliant" and "stupid" boys in a variety of tasks.

Terman had had tuberculosis so that the worry about his health
and finances were quite a problem to him in graduate school; when
he graduated he went to California because of his health. For one
year, he was a high school principal. The next three years found
him teaching courses in educational psychology at the Los Angeles
Normal School where he was friendly with Gesell and where he undertook a health program of his own.

In 1910, Terman was asked to join the State Department of Education at Stanford University as a specialist in child growth and
health. "There he developed courses, participated in school surveys, wrote books on school health, and stimulated graduate work
on individual differences."

He started a revision of the 1905 and 1906 Binet scales, publishing the Stanford Revision of the Binet in 1916 which was dedicated
to Binet. Within a year of publication of this work, Terman became
a national figure.

During World War I, Terman worked on the Army Alpha and Army Beta
and became friends with Yerkes and Boring. After the war, when he
returned to Stanford, Terman edited the Measurement and Adjustment
Series. He then spent time standardizing the National Intelligence
Tests, the Terman Group Tests of Mental Ability and the Stanford
Achievement Test. He was elected president of the American Psychological Association in 1922. He got involved in the nature-nurture
controversy with people like William C. Bagley and Walter Lippman.
In 1923, Terman was appointed Chairman of the Department of Psychology
at Stanford. He built it up; among the people he attracted were
three who were later to become presidents of the American Psychological Association.

In 1920 he started his work on the gifted. With regard to education, Terman advocated one to three years of acceleration. The
gifted child should spend at least part of the time in a group to
work on abstractions and develop independence. Specially trained
teachers should provide enrichment. The child "should meet a minimum
of drill, routine, and structuring and a maximum of problem solving,
initiative and independent planning." Counseling should be avail-

able and used as needed. "Education but education with a distinctively different emphasis, is the key to their full productivity
and to society's subsequent gain."

Sellin, D.F., and Birch, J.W. *Educating Gifted and Talented Learners.*
Rockville, MD: Aspen Systems Corporation, 1980. 359pp. (Especially
"The Historical Context," 10-16.)

The authors cite Gowan's (1977) history of interest in gifted and
talented people, noting especially his idea that this interest was
stimulated by: "(1) regard for the dignity of the individual person,
(2) curiosity about the unfolding of human development, and (3) concern for the nurture of the unusual or unique." Following Gowan,
they also divide history into Pre-Terman, The Terman Era, and Post-
Terman.

The authors point out that the gifted child movement has its
roots in the late 19th century and early 20th century in the works
of such psychologists as Hall, Dewey, Cattell, and Terman. "Their
orientation was toward the individual. Each person was, to them, a
unique mind and soul, worthy and precious, and capable of positive
development. Thus all exceptional persons are valued, including the
gifted and talented." Recent persons in the same tradition include
Rogers, Hollingworth, and Torrance.

The measurement of individual differences was the next step.
Mathematics and psychology were combined by people such as: Kuhlmann,
Thorndike, Guilford, Burt, and Binet. Measurement led to exploration
in the area of development by later people such as Piaget and Erikson.
Development is viewed as a unity "made up of affective, cognitive,
and psychomotor domains."

"The contributions of this era are: (1) a picture of human development as the continuing expanding of new skills; (2) a view that human
nature can be understood, balanced against a modest affirmation that
much remains to be understood; (3) concern for the unusual as a basis
for understanding the usual; and (4) esteem for the dignity of the
person. This epoch created the context for Terman's contributions."

The next period was the Terman period, and it was made possible
by the work of Binet and Simon with their first measure of intelligence in 1908. A key concept in that work was the concept of the
Mental Age. A few years later, Stern developed the concept of the
IQ. He "recognized that the mental age gave a useful indication of
a child's present mental status or amount or stage of intellectual
development. He conceived of an added dimension of mental measurement, however, that would be derived by dividing a child's mental
age at a given time by the child's chronological age at the same
time. The resulting quotient (MA/CA=IQ), if stable over time, would
give information as to the rate of the child's mental development.
These indicators of the stage of mental development (MA) and the
rate of mental development (IQ) triggered a burst of mental measurement activity." The concept of MA made standardization possible
and norm referenced tests were added to teachers' own tests or criterion referenced tests.

Terman saw the possibilities of applying measurement techniques
to all children, including the gifted, to verify "stages of human
development, the initiation of long-range studies." Terman joined
Stanford in 1910 and adapted, revised, and standardized the Binet-

Simon Scale on 905 children from the ages of 5 to 14. Longitudinal studies were begun in 1921.

In the Post-Terman era the following works were published: Schwrimmer's work on *Great Musicians as Children* in 1930; Leta Hollingworth's 1926 book on children with IQs above 180, and Paul Witty's 1930 longitudinal look at 100 gifted children. Guilford published his Structure of Intellect. Pegnator and Birch established the utility of effectiveness and efficiency as research constructs which enabled them to compare identification procedures. Getzels and Jackson and Torrance studied creativity. Gallagher and Aschner and Meeker studied the applicability of Guilford's work to curricular design. Passow and Goldberg's work on gifted underachievement during this period pointed to the importance of basic skills and the child's need to identify with supportive teachers. Pressey and Stanley emphasized naturalness and appropriateness of acceleration and the "role of the mentor and an atmosphere of furtherance."

From this historical survey the authors learn that the attitudes of the society toward the gifted and the talented affect the form and quality of education provided them. Education does not homogenize students; it increases individual differences and the same education is not appropriate for all. "Advocacy on behalf of the gifted and talented person is a part of advocacy for all those with marked individual differences."

TERMAN

Terman, L. *Mental and Physical Traits of a Thousand Gifted Children.* In Terman, L. (Ed.). *Genetic Studies of Genius.* Vol. 1. Stanford, CA: Stanford University Press, 1925. 648pp.

Data were collected on over 1400 children. Most of the report is based on a typical group of 643 children, for whom most extensive data were available, and a second group of 309, with less extensive data. Control data for 600 to 800 unselected children were also obtained. The children were from the California public school system and mostly from large urban centers.

The purpose of the study was to show "in what traits and to what extent, a representative group of intellectually superior children differs from a group of unselected normal children."

Students in the study were selected by teacher nominations, siblings of those already selected, casual information, accident, etc. These pupils were studied with the National Intelligence Scale B, Form I. Those who scored at the 90th percentile (in some cases as low as the 80th percentile) were studied with an abbreviated form of the Stanford-Binet. One was used for those who had foreign parents and another for those with non-foreign parents. Students who scored an IQ of 125 or more (120 if older) were then given the complete Stanford-Binet. On the complete Stanford-Binet, the younger pupils (below 11) who obtained an IQ of 140 and older pupils (13.5 to 14) who had an IQ of 132 were retained for the complete study.

All of the above were procedures for grades 3 to 8; variations in it occurred for grades 1 and 2. It is assumed that 80% to 90% of qualified pupils were covered.

Available for each child in the intensive study were data from intelligence tests, achievement tests, an information test, a knowledge test, an interest blank, a reading record, a list of traits filled out by parents, a list of traits filled out by teachers, ratings of the home, medical measurements, anthropometric measurements, and tests of character and personality. The results follow.

Demographic

1. Boys were more numerous than girls (ascribed to differential death rate of embryos).
2. Data of racial origin, based on comparison with population of concerned cities indicate "a 100% excess of Jewish blood; a 25% excess of parents who are of native parentage; a probable excess of Scotch ancestry; a very great deficiency of Latin and Negro ancestry."

Family and Home

3. Half of the parents were from cities of 10,000 or more; grandparents slightly more were of rural origin.
4. About a third of the fathers were professionals; 50% were semiprofessional and business men; and the remainder were skilled, semiskilled, and unskilled.
5. Social class was highly correlated with intelligence.
6. Mean family income $4,705 with standard deviation of $3,805.
7. Home ratings on Whittier Scale yielded a mean score above that of unselected school population.
8. About 16% of the boys and 2% of the girls were involved in paid work outside the home at some time.
9. Parents were divorced in 5.2% of the cases and in 1.9% separated; both figures were lower than in the general California population.
10. Parents completed twice as many school grades (twelve) as the average adult.
11. One fourth of the subjects had at least one parent who was a college graduate and 17% of the parents held a college degree.
12. Books in home libraries ranged from 0-6,000 with a median of 202 and a mean of 328.
13. There was "considerable indirect evidence that the heredity of gifted subjects is much superior to that of the average individual."
14. The number of families with two children in the group was more than 1,200 times that of chance expectancy.
15. About one quarter of the members of the Hall of Fame were related to the subjects.
16. Forty-four known relatives had been listed in *Who's Who*, and 58 other relatives were considered eminent.
17. One family has 34 known relatives listed in *Cyclopedia of American Biography* or in *Who's Who*.
18. Parents and grandparents held responsible posts in great numbers.
19. The proportion of miscarriages and infant mortality in families of gifted was extremely low.
20. Ages of the parents at the time of the gifted child's birth (father = 33.6; mother = 29.0) was slightly lower than those reported by Cattell for parents of American men of science.

21. Birth weight was about three fourths of a pound in excess of norm.

22. Nineteen percent of the male births and 12% of the female births had been instrument deliveries.

23. The proportion of those who had been breast fed was considerabl higher than for the general population, and was higher for cases above 160 IQs than for the entire group.

24. The age of learning to walk and talk was lower than for normal children.

25. About half as many gifted as control children were reported as having frequent headaches.

26. "General weakness" was reported 30% less frequently.

27. More than half of the gifted group had had tonsillectomies. In contrast, about a quarter of the control group had had tonsillectomies.

28. Mouth breathing was reported less frequently for the gifted than for the control group.

29. Defective hearing was reported about two and one half times more often for the control group than for the gifted.

30. Defective vision was reported about a quarter more often for gifted.

31. Frequency of colds was equal.

32. Onset of puberty was somewhat earlier among gifted than control girls; a similar result occurred among boys but there was a smaller number among them above 12.

33. Nervousness was reported in 13.3% of the gifted and 16.1% of the controls.

34. Stuttering was reported in 2.6% of the gifted and 3.4% of the controls.

35. Preponderance of first-born gifted occurred in families of two or more.

36. Forty-two of the fathers and 13 of the mothers were deceased.

37. Small proportions of both fathers and mothers had one or more chronic illness; the figures were probably less than for corresponding ages in the general population.

38. Longevity of grandfathers was greater than expected.

39. Record of insanity was reported in 0.4% of parents and .3% of grandparents, and 37 other relatives. Few other cases of hereditary defect reported.

Physical Characteristics

40. The gifted were physically superior to comparison groups in height, weight, and breathing standards. They surpassed American norms in the forementioned and California standards in height and weight.

41. Physical traits of girls were more variable than those of boys.

42. The majority were mesocephalic.

43. The correlations between all physical traits were positive and high.

44. Medical examinations of 591 found them physically superior to unselected children of the same age.

School History

45. Most entered school at 6.25 years.

46. Eighty-five percent accelerated, not one retarded. Average acceleration was 14%. Eighty-two percent were said to deserve more promotion.

47. Mean chronological age and mean mental age differed by 2.8 years in first grade and by nearly five years in the fifth grade.

48. As a rule, teachers said gifted children were doing work of superior quality; the superiority was greatest in "thought" subjects.

49. Two and a half times as many gifted as control children were rated as "very even" in mental ability, but twice as many of the gifted were rated as "very uneven."

50. By the age of 8, the gifted, on the average, had attended two different schools and by the age of 11, the average was 3.

51. The average number of days absent from school was 12.

52. Only 1% were reported by parents as disliking school.

53. Schools reported less than half as many gifted children displayed an undesirable attitude toward school.

54. More than half learned to read before starting school, most with little or no formal education.

55. Roughly 70% of the parents had let the child set his/her own pace; 20% had encouraged a rapid program; and 10% had held them back.

56. On the average, the gifted child spent two hours of homework per week on school lessons.

57. More than half of the group had private lessons in special subjects and spent 6.5 hours per week on them.

58. Indications of superior ability in arithmetic were reported by parents of half the group; similarly, for a third in music; and for dramatics, drawing, or painting, it was somewhat less.

59. Eight percent of the parents reported never having observed signs of superior intelligence in their children; for others, intellectual superiority was first noted at about 3.5 years.

60. Nothing had been found that led Terman to conclude that the attainments of his gifted children were, in any considerable degree, "the product of artificial stimulation or forced culture."

Achievement Test Data

61. Very great superiority of the gifted over the unselected children on the Stanford Achievement Test.

62. Average gifted child mastered subject matter 40% above his/her chronological age, but he/she was held back to a grade that was only 14% beyond the norm for his/her age.

63. Superiority of gifted was most marked in general information, language usage, and reading. Least marked in history and civics.

64. For a given age, no correlation existed between educational accomplishment and the number of terms the gifted child had attended school.

65. The intelligence level of the gifted was higher than their achievement scores.

66. Gifted children were interested in abstract subjects and less interested in "practical" ones than unselected children.

67. Subject preference of gifted boys and gifted girls were more alike than those of control boys and control girls.

68. Gifted boys resembled control boys in subject preference far more than gifted girls resembled control girls.

69. Gifted children more frequently than controls rated as "very

easy" subjects such as literature, grammar, debating, and ancient history.

70. The controls rated as "very easy" far oftener than the gifted, subjects such as sewing, drawing, painting, general science, singing, folk dancing, and penmanship.

71. Gifted boys found shop work easy more often than did control boys.

72. Control girls found arithmetic easy somewhat oftener than did gifted girls.

73. Gifted girls showed a high correlation with gifted boys in subjects found easy, but no resemblance to control girls.

74. One and three quarters times as many gifted as control children had collections; twice as many had collections of a scientific nature.

Occupational Interests

75. On the Barr scales, gifted preferred higher rated occupations than did controls.

76. Among the gifted there was less distance between the occupational ambitions of the child and his/her father's occupational status than among the controls.

77. "Gifted children have more enthusiasms than average children, and their interests appear to be in general no less wholesome."

Play Interests

78. Gifted children had measurably greater interest in activities requiring thinking, and ones that were mildly social and quiet; they indicated slightly less interest in competitive games than controls.

79. Gifted boys scored slightly higher in a masculinity rating of activity interests than did control boys at all ages except 13; gifted girls did not differ consistently from control girls.

80. Gifted children scored higher on maturity of activity interests than controls.

81. The sociability of activities was lower for gifted than controls.

82. Gifted children played alone slightly more; they more often preferred older playmates; they showed less sex preference in choice of playmates; and the girls showed far less sex preference than boys.

83. Gifted children were usually sought as companions to the same extent as control children.

84. Little difference was found between control and gifted children in the extent to which they were teased by others or cried when they could not have their way.

85. "However, somewhat more gifted than control are said to be regarded by other children as 'queer' or 'different.'"

86. Gifted boys were more frequently said to have play interests that were not normal than was true among control boys, and the reverse was true for the girls.

87. Many gifted children had imaginary playmates but no comparable data were available for controls.

88. Teachers reported that 88% of gifted and 34% of control children read more than the average child.

89. Gifted children, according to our lists, read over a wider range and read more science, history, biography, travel, folk tales,

informational fiction, poetry, and drama, and a lower proportion of adventure, mystery, and emotional fiction. In both gifted and control groups, boys showed a wider range than girls.

90. Gifted children scored decisively higher than control children in intellectual and social interests, and did not differ materially in activity interests.

Personality Characteristics

91. In tests of "character" gifted children scored higher than control group.

92. Gifted girls scored higher than gifted boys.

93. In trait ratings by parents and teacher, gifted children excelled in: intellectual, volitional, emotional, moral, physical, and social traits. Controls were rated higher on mechanical ingenuity.

94. A two-year follow-up study revealed "that the gifted children have not lost in educational or general ability, and that gains have far outbalanced losses with respect to such traits as social adaptability and breadth of interests."

95. "The gifted are not free from faults and at least one out of five has more than the average child of the general population. Perhaps one out of twenty presents a more or less serious problem in one or another respect."

Teachers and Teaching

96. Although Terman's work does not focus on pedagogical problems Terman observes, "The present neglect of superior talent is sufficiently indicated by the inability of teachers to recognize it. One of the most astonishing facts brought out in this investigation is that one's best chance of identifying the brightest child in a classroom is to examine the birth records and select the youngest, rather than to take the one rated as brightest by the teacher."

Predicting Future

97. Prediction of the future is profitless. To expect a majority to achieve eminence is unwarranted. Eminence is a poor measure of success and is a product of chance combinations of personal merit and environmental factors.

98. Although the group studied is superior, it is not like the group of adult geniuses studied by Galton and others. A child in the gifted group had to rate as high as the first in two hundred, but in Galton's study, the subject ranked as the first in four thousand.

Terman, L.M. "The Intelligence Quotient of Francis Galton in Childhood." *American Journal of Psychology* 28 (1917): 209-215.

Based on descriptions of Galton's knowledge between 3 and 8 years of age, it is estimated that Galton's IQ in childhood was not far from 200. This is the basis for estimating the IQs of eminent men used by Cox in *The Early Mental Traits of Three Hundred Geniuses*.

Cox, C.M. *The Early Mental Traits of Three Hundred Geniuses*. In Terman, L.M. (Ed.). *Genetic Studies of Geniuses*. Vol. II. Stanford, CA: Stanford University Press, 1926. 842pp.

This book is based on eminent persons who lived between 1450 and 1850 and who were above the rank of 510 in Cattell's list. The list included writers, statesmen and politicians, scientists, soldiers, religious leaders, philosophers, artists, musicians, and revolutionary statesmen.

Pertinent results include the following:

1. The true IQs of the group averaged above 160; many were above 180, and few were below 140. (Estimates were made on the basis of achievements to age 17 and to age 26.) "It should be emphasized that the task set was not to estimate what the childhood IQ of a given subject was, *but the IQ that would most reasonably account for the recorded facts.*"

2. Basing data on a selected sample intended to be representative of the group studied, Cox found that "the reported influence of *current events, or movements, and of travel,* although evidence is but slight; the reported influence of *home, home training and discipline, breadth of home interests, community and education* is considerable; and the reported *amount of education of reading,* whether literary or scientific, approaches the highest possible score."

3. In a study of the group's interests, it was found "that factors other than intellectual make for eminence, and that greater *social* or *activity interest* may offset a lesser interest in intellectual matters."

Conclusions

"1. *Youths who achieve eminence have, in general, (a) a heredity above the average and (b) superior advantages in early environment....* Eminence is not a function of either heredity or environment alone."

"2. *Youths who achieve eminence are distinguished in childhood by behavior which indicates an unusually high IQ.... The extraordinary genius who achieves the highest eminence is also the gifted individual whom intelligence tests may discover in childhood....*"

"3. That all equally intelligent children do not as adults achieve equal eminence is in part accounted for by our last conclusion: *youths who achieve eminence are characterized not only by high intellectual traits, but also by persistence of nature and effort, confidence in their abilities, and great strength or force of character....* The appearance in childhood of a combination of the highest degree of general ability, special talent, seriousness of purpose, and indomitable persistence may well be greeted as indicating a capacity for adult achievement of the highest rank."

Burks, B.S.; Jensen, D.W.; and Terman, L.M. *The Promise of Youth: Follow-up Studies of a Thousand Gifted Children.* In Terman, L.M. (Ed.). *Genetic Studies of Genius.* Vol. III. Stanford, CA: Stanford University Press, 1930. 508pp.

This follow-up was written 8 years after Vol. I of the *Genetic Studies of Genius.* Terman summarizes that:

1. The gifted children came predominantly from families "of decidedly superior intellectual endowment and of slightly superior physical endowment."

2. During the last two generations, the fecundity of these families has decreased greatly.

3. The average IQ of the siblings of children with IQs above 140 is approximately 123.

4. As a group, the intellectually gifted are slightly superior to other children in health and physique and tend to remain so.

5. As a group, children who are gifted are not intellectually one-sided, emotionally unstable, lacking in sociability or social adaptability, nor do they possess other types of maladjustments.

6. "Indeed, in practically every personality and character trait such children average much better than the general school population."

7. As a group, the children in the study are normal or superior in social intelligence ratings, social interests, and play activity.

8. The gifted boys are similar to other boys of corresponding age in masculinity and femininity. Gifted girls deviate significantly from the norm in the direction of masculinity.

9. In terms of measured character traits, the gifted child is on a par with the unselected child of 13 or 14.

10. In traits rated by teachers, gifted children show their superiority to the average most in intellectual and volitional qualities and least in physical and social characteristics.

11. The average gifted child is accelerated 14% of his age in school progress; but, as measured by achievement tests, he/she is accelerated by 40% of his/her age.

12. No correlation was found between achievement tests and the number of years the gifted have attended school by the age of 10.

13. Gifted boys "maintain or almost maintain their relative superiority to the common run in intelligence, at least through the period of adolescence."

14. "Girls somewhat more often than boys show a drop in IQ as adolescence is approached, or soon thereafter."

15. Achievement in high school and college continues in line with the IQ originally found in 1921-22.

16. The gifted children practically never fail high school subjects.

17. Three-quarters of the grades obtained by high school girls and almost half of those obtained by boys are A's.

18. Gifted children in their senior year in high school score above the 90th percentile of all high school seniors in a high school content examination.

19. College is attended by 90% of the gifted boys and 80% of the gifted girls. Most of them graduate.

20. The children who graduate from high-grade universities earn Phi Beta Kappa or other honors about three times as frequently as do other graduates.

In his summary, Terman says, "It is to be hoped that the superstitions so commonly accepted relative to intellectually superior children have been permanently swept away by the factual data these studies have presented. It is simply not true that such children are especially prone to be puny, over-specialized in their abilities and interests, emotionally unstable, socially unadaptable, psychotic, and morally undependable; nor is it true they usually deteriorate to the level of mediocrity as adult life is approached."

Terman, L.M., and Oden, M.H. *The Gifted Child Grows Up.* In Terman, L.M. (Ed.). *Genetic Studies of Genius.* Vol. IV. Stanford, CA: Stanford University Press, 1947. 448pp.

This is a follow-up study of Vol. I of *Genetic Studies of Genius* after 25 years. Data were obtained from 97.7% of the 1,467 living subjects concerning the following: general information, personality and temperament, present marriage (test of marital happiness), strong vocational interest blank, Concept Mastery Test, and supplementary information (from parents or close relatives). Stanford-Binet test data were obtained from 364 children and the following data were obtained from a good number of the spouses: Concept Mastery Test, Test of Marital Happiness, and Test of Marital Aptitude. Data were obtained for the period 1940-1945 on military and nonmilitary service, education since 1940, occupation and income for 1941-1944 inclusive, publications, general physical and mental health, marital history, offspring, etc. The results included the following:

1. Deaths indicated a lower mortality rate than in the general population for the same age group. Suicides and accidental deaths had the same sex ratio among the gifted as among the general population. But, there was a markedly greater frequency among the males in both groups.

2. Low incidence of ill health was reported (by self-ratings). Height was considerably above the average by about 1.5 inches for males and 1 inch for females.

3. In terms of mental health, only 4% reported serious maladjustment for any period in their lives to date and 1.3% reported actual psychosis. For all kinds of maladjustment and serious problems, a large proportion indicated marked improvement or complete recovery.

4. Decrease of 9 or 10 points in IQ over the 25-year period may be accounted for by maturational changes, environmental factors, and school training. The net difference, not explained by errors of measurement and differences in functions measured, may be less than five IQ points.

5. Gifted people had achieved records in college extracurricular activities that were definitely superior to the average for college students. Nearly two-thirds reported active avocational interests; over one-third had three or more avocational interests.

6. There was a correlation between childhood IQ and both the probability of graduating from college and the probability of an "A" average in college. The amount of schooling more closely related to scores on the 1940 Concept Mastery Test than to childhood IQ; this was probably due to the fact that schooling would influence scores on the Concept Mastery Test.

7. There was a relationship between the amount of education that gifted subjects obtained and the amount of education completed by their parents. The figures for the whole gifted group on both college entrance and college graduation were about eight times what it was for the general population in California. They graduated from college, on the average, one year younger than did the average college graduate in California.

8. Occupationally, both college and non-college graduates, among the gifted, held positions of responsibiliry to a greater extent than did college graduates in general. Their unemployment record was better than those of California men and college graduates in general. Earned income was higher than that of college graduates of corresponding age. Earned income was related to amount of education.

9. The Strong vocational test was a valuable aid in education and

vocational guidance of the gifted. Few were successful in their
occupations who scored low in the occupations on the test.

10. By self-report, this group excelled the general population
in voting regularly. Professionals rated themselves more liberal
in political and social views than did the others. Those who earned
more than $350 a month were more conservative. College graduates
did not differ from non-graduates in political attitudes. Increased
radicalism and an increase in nervous symptoms and mental maladjustment were associated.

11. Incidence of marriage and age of marriage was the same as for
the general population. But for college graduates, the incidence
was markedly higher and the age at marriage lower than for college
graduates in general. This was particularly true of women. By
1945, 84% of both men and women were or had been married. By 1945,
14.5% of the men and 12.7% of the women had been divorced or separated.
No correlation was found between divorce rate and childhood IQ.
Divorce rate was half as high among college graduates as among non-
graduates in the study. The average intelligence of the spouses was
equal to that of the average college graduate. The large majority
of the spouses had been to college, and the large majority of husbands were in higher status occupational groups.

12. The mean IQ of the 384 children was 127.7 and corresponds to
Galton's law of filial regression. Low incidence of feeble-minded-
ness or borderline mentality among offspring. The proportion of
children with IQs of 150 or higher was 28 times as great as for the
unselected children on whom the test was standardized.

13. The gifted person was just as normal in sexual adjustment
as the control group. Both groups had the same degree of marital
happiness or unhappiness.

14. Gifted husbands averaged lower on the test of marital aptitude
than the husbands of gifted wives; gifted wives were about equal to
wives of gifted husbands. The man appears to be handicapped by
superior intelligence for marriage.

15. Married and unmarried men in the group differed significantly
from each other on the marital aptitude test. Among the women
in similar groups the means were almost the same.

16. Influence of school acceleration in causing social maladjustment had been exaggerated. Nevertheless, the majority of those who
had been accelerated and those who had not, stressed the disadvantages of acceleration more than the advantages.

17. Subjects who had IQs of 170 or above were compared with the
gifted group as a whole; no significant differences were found for
either sex on age at walking, talking, puberty, or marriage. No
differences were found in health, in divorce rate, or in fertility.
Mental adjustment ratings were the same except that a smaller proportion of the women were rated as satisfactory in the high group as
in the low group. Men in the high IQ group achieved higher occupational status.

18. Numerous comparisons were made between the groups ranked the
highest fifth and the lowest fifth concerning success, i.e., the
extent to which a subject made use of his/her superior intellectual
ability. The greatest contrast between the two groups was in drive
to achieve and in all-around social adjustment. In the gifted group,
success was associated with stability rather than instability.

19. Among the gifted, 42.5% were in the armed forces and this was

a larger percentage than for all males in the country aged 18 to 44.
Those rejected were probably less than the national average. Seventy
percent of those in the Army and 75% of those in the Navy became
non-commissioned officers. Half of the army men had the rank of
captain or higher and 45% in the Navy held the rank of lieutenant
or better. Seventy men received ninety citations. Twenty-one were
killed.

20. Half of the men and more than half of the women were in one
or another of the professions. This was nine times the proportion
of all employed adults for the men.

21. Sixteen percent of the total gifted group and 25% of those
who completed college received Phi Beta Kappa or Sigma Xi. Seventy-
three of the subjects had the Ph.D. or an equivalent degree. Seventeen were still working on their doctorates. Of those who completed
college, 20% held one or more undergraduate scholarships. One hundred five subjects (7.6%) had one or more graduate fellowships and
114 (8.2%) had one or more graduate assistantships.

22. Earned income was higher for the gifted than for the general
population.

23. By 1945, when the group was close to 35 years of age, the
group had published 90 books or monographs and approximately 1,500
articles. The group had more than one hundred patents but nearly
half went to two men.

24. There was no one in the group who showed the promise of
equaling Shakespeare, Goethe, Tolstoy, etc. and this may be attributed to the fact that "such eminence in a given field is usually
possible only at a given stage of cultural progress and can never
be closely paralleled in a different era. For one thing, science
and scholarship are growing so highly specialized that eminence is
becoming progressively more difficult to attain." Furthermore, much
depends on "chance and circumstance," and "Fame ... is a poor
measure of creative genius."

Terman, L.M. "Scientists and Nonscientists in a Group of 800 Gifted
   Men." *Psychological Monographs* LXVIII (1954a): 44pp.

This is a study of the material collected to 1951 on those people
who did or did not become scientists. The following subgroups were
established: physical science research; engineering; medical-
biological, physical or biological science (non-research); social
science; lawyers; humanities; and non-college.

Although no one in the science group compares to Roe's scientists,
Terman says that "their total contribution to science is many times
the amount that could be expected from the same number of men picked
at random in the general population."

Many differences between scientists and non-scientists are presented. These include:

1. The family backgrounds of the medical-biological and physical
science researchers appeared, on the whole, to be most favorable.
Engineers and non-researchers in the physical-biological area had
the least favorable backgrounds. The social scientists, lawyers,
and humanists were intermediate.

2. It is almost unanimous that "early ability or interest in
science is far more common among children who later become physical

scientists, engineers, or biologists than among those who enter non-scientific fields."

3. In masculinity of interests, the science groups ranked high and the non-science groups low.

4. Non-science groups scored better than science groups on a majority of 18 variables related directly or indirectly to social adjustment. Lawyers and social scientists were most consistently high, and physical-scientist researchers and engineers most consistently low.

Almost 200 variables which did not yield significant differences between groups are listed in an appendix. Many of these variables resemble those which did differentiate between the two groups in this study. Hence, caution is recommended by the author in evaluating the results.

Terman, L.M. "The Discovery and Encouragement of Exceptional Talent." *American Psychologist* 9 (1954b): 221-230.

Terman begins this, the first annual Walter Van Dyke Bingham memorial lecture, with a summary of his research findings on children with IQs of 140 or higher. He notes that they are superior to unselected children in health, physique, and social adjustment; markedly superior in moral attitudes; and vastly superior in mastery of school subjects. All of this refutes the general belief that the gifted are one-sided. The superiority continues to appear in studies at mid-life proving "beyond question that tests of 'general intelligence,' given as early as six, eight, or ten years, tell a great deal about the ability to achieve either presently or 30 years hence. Such tests do not, however, enable us to predict what direction the achievement will take, and least of all do they tell us what personality factors or what accidents of fortune will affect the fruition of exceptional ability."

The final body of data considered by Terman concerns the 150 most and 150 least successful men in his gifted group. Here, the "most spectacular differences between the two groups came from three sets of ratings, made in 1940, on a dozen personality traits. Each man rated himself on all traits, was rated on them by his wife if he had a wife, and by a parent if a parent was still living. Although the three sets of ratings were made independently, they agreed unanimously on the four traits in which the A (most successful) and C (least successful) groups differed most widely. These were 'persistence in the accomplishment of ends,' 'integration toward goals, as contrasted with drifting,' 'self confidence,' and 'freedom from inferiority feelings.'" These data are consistent with those obtained by Cox in her study.

Terman concludes, "In our gifted group success is associated with stability rather than instability, with absence rather than with presence of disturbing conflicts—in short, with well-balanced temperament and with freedom from excessive frustrations."

Terman, L.M., and Oden, M.H. *The Gifted Group at Mid-Life: Thirty-five Years' Follow-up of the Superior Child.* In Terman, L.M. (Ed.). *Genetic Studies of Genius.* Vol. V. Stanford, CA: Stanford University Press, 1959. 187pp.

Data obtained in this thirty-five year follow-up reveal the following:

1. There was "a small but fairly consistent sex difference in the direction of more maladjustment among gifted women than among the men of our group." Among the women, there was a slightly larger percentage who required hospitalization for a mental disorder than was true among the men. For suicide, the pattern agrees with that obtained for the general population--more men commit suicide than women and the sex difference in rate is less for the gifted than for the population as a whole. Among the gifted, the rate is less than twice as high for men as for women, while for the country, as a whole, the suicide rate for males is three to four times that for females.

2. Ten men and 3 women were considered alcoholics. (The problem in evaluating the seriousness of these numbers is affected by the small numbers involved.)

3. Seventeen men (2.0%) and 11 women (11.7%) have been or were known to be homosexuals.

4. None of the women had been in prison and none in reform school (two had been arrested for vagrancy). Their record in this regard was better than the men's. Among the men, three had records of juvenile delinquency and spent time in juvenile reformatories. One subject had a prison sentence for forgery. (All four were later married and employed and responsible citizens.) Three other boys were brought before a Juvenile Court for behavior difficulties and released to their parents' custody.

5. Considerably more women than men discontinued their schooling below the college graduate level.

6. A study of the relationship of intelligence test scores to general adjustment is not consistent. For the childhood Binet IQ, maladjustment among women is highest at the highest IQs and no difference is found for the men. In the Concept Mastery Test, the sex difference is in the other direction.

7. Analysis of the retest data on the Concept Mastery Test for the gifted and their spouses ("also intellectually superior on the average though less highly selected than the gifted) give strong evidence that intelligence of the type tested by the Concept Mastery Test continues to increase at least through 50 years of age."

8. Although of superior college material, more than 10% of the men and more than 15% of the women did not enter college, and 30% did not graduate. Financial problems, lack of parental encouragement, and lack of recognition of the student's abilities by the high school are some of the factors discussed.

9. Although the study was not concerned with school practices, a study was made of acceleration; the results were in favor of those rapidly promoted. "It was concluded that children of IQ 135 or higher should be promoted sufficiently to permit college entrance by the age of seventeen at latest, and that a majority in this group would be better off to enter at sixteen. Acceleration to this extent is especially desirable for those who plan to complete two or more years of graduate study in preparation for a professional career."

10. In the area of occupations, the versatility of the group is most evident. "The men range in occupations from semiskilled labor to top-ranking university administrators, famed scientists, literary

figures, high level officers and executives in business. The group
is pretty well concentrated on the upper rungs of the vocational
ladder with none at the bottom and only a few on the lower steps."

11. As far as women are concerned, it is pointed out that fewer
than half are employed outside the home. "... A number of women
have reached high levels of achievement. As a group, however, the
accomplishments of the gifted women do not compare with those of
the men. This is not surprising since it follows the cultural pattern to which most of the gifted women as well as women in general
have succumbed. Not only may job success interfere with marriage
success, but more women who do seek a career outside the home have
to break through many more barriers and overcome many more obstacles
than do men on the road to success. Although the gifted women
equalled or excelled the men in school achievement from the first
grade through college, after school days were over the great majority
ceased to compete with the men in the world's work."

12. The breadth and versatility of interests differentiated this
group in their childhood and youth. At this point, in mid-life,
more than four-fifths said they had two or more avocational interests
and more than fifty percent said they had three or more interests.
While there are no norms to make any comparison with the general
population, "the data indicate a considerable breadth and diversity
of interests." The authors also say, "many of the special abilities
that had been evidenced by the subjects in their youth found expression in hobbies and avocations at mid-life. Talent in creative
writing, art, dramatics, and music was especially noteworthy."

13. Reading interests were wide, covering both fiction and non-
fiction.

14. Membership in one or more clubs or organizations, chiefly
professional or business and social, were reported by four-fifths
of the men and two-thirds of the women. The group also manifested
interest in and responsibility for community and civic welfare
organizations.

15. The men reported a slightly higher proportion of membership
in their churches but less than two-fifths of the men and more than
one-half of the women feel moderately or strongly inclined toward
religion.

16. Politically, the men and women in the group consider themselves close to the center on a continuum ranging from radicalism
to conservatism. On a nine-point scale both males and females are
slightly to the right of the mid-point. More than half the men and
a bit more than half the women say they are Republicans. They
"usually" or "always" vote.

17. From 1940 to 1950, the group became less radical and more conservative. Several held important elective offices and several
had appointments to responsible positions in federal and state
governments.

18. In the last chapter, the authors pull things together and say:
"The follow-up for three and one-half decades has shown that the
superior child, with few exceptions, becomes the able adult, superior
in nearly every aspect to the generality. But, as in childhood,
this superiority is not equally great in all areas."

19. There are a number of other specific points that should be
noted. "The data indicate that not only do the mentally superior
hold their own but that they actually increase in intellectual
stature as measured by the Concept Mastery Test."

20. "The record points to the conclusion that capacity to achieve far beyond the average can be detected early in life through tests of general intelligence."

21. Intelligence tests, "do not, however, enable us to predict what direction the achievement will take, and least of all do they tell us what personality factors or what accidents of fortune will affect the fruition of exceptional ability."

22. Looking at the specific achievements of the women, the authors report: "That 7 women [are] listed in *American Men of Science*, 2 in Directory of American Scholars, and 2 in *Who's Who in America*, all before reaching the age of 43, is certainly many times the expectation from a random group of around 700 women. Publications of the gifted women include 5 novels; 5 volumes of poetry and some 70 poems that have appeared in both literary and popular journals; 32 technical, professional, or scholarly books; around 50 short stories; 4 plays; more than 150 essays, critiques, and articles; and more than 200 scientific papers. At least 5 patents have been taken out by gifted women. These figures do not include the writings of reporters and editors, nor a variety of miscellaneous contributions."

23. The authors point out that a number of the men have made substantial contributions to the physical, biological, and social science Seventy are listed in *American Men of Science*--39 in physical sciences, 22 in biological sciences, and 9 in social sciences. Three were elected to the National Academy of Sciences. Ten of the men appear in the *Directory of American Scholars* and 31 men appear in *Who's Who in America*. The men, as a group, published nearly 2000 scientific and technical papers and articles and some 60 books and monographs in science, literature, art, and humanities. Patents were granted to 230. They wrote 33 novels, about 375 short stories, novelettes, and plays; 60 or more essays, critiques, or sketches and 265 miscellaneous articles.

24. "Although not more than three or possibly four men (again women are not included) could be consideredd failures in relation to the rest of the group, there are 80 or 90 men whose vocational achievements fall considerably short of the standard set by the group as a whole."

The authors also comment about areas in which there was no outstanding accomplishment. They say "There are, however, a few fields, all dependent on special talent, in which there has been a lack of outstanding accomplishment. These are the fine arts, music, and, to a lesser extent, literature. The group has produced no great musical composer and no great creative artist. Several possessing superior talent in music or art are heading university departments in these fields and have produced some excellent original work, but none seems likely to achieve a truly great piece of creative work. There are a number of competent and highly successful writers among the subjects but not more than three or four with a high order of literary creativity. Perhaps it is not surprising, in view of the relatively small size of our group, that no great creative genius in the arts has appeared, for such genius is indeed rare. In any case these are the only major fields in which the achievement of our group is limited."

In the last section, entitled "Some Comments on Success," the authors say that "the criterion used in this study reflects both the present-day social ideology and an avowed bias in favor of achievement that calls for the use of intelligence. It is concerned with vocational accomplishment rather than with the attainment of personal happiness. And the record shows that the gifted subjects, in overwhelming numbers, have fulfilled the promise of their youth in their later life achievements."

The concluding remarks are: "We would agree with the subjects that vocational achievement is not the only--perhaps not even the most important--aspect of life success.... Even failure to rise above the lowest rungs of the occupational ladder does not necessarily mean that success in the truest sense has been trivial. There may have been heroic sacrifices, uncommon judgment in handling the little things of daily life, countless acts of kindness, loyal friendships won, and conscientious discharge of social and civic responsibilities. If we sometimes get discouraged at the rate society progresses, we might take comfort in the thought that some of the small jobs, as well as the larger ones, are being done by gifted people."

Oden, M.H. "The Fulfillment of Promise: 40-year Follow-up of the Terman Gifted Group." *Genetic Psychology Monographs* 77 (1968): 9-93.

The 40-year follow-up of the Terman group is divided into two parts. The first part contains follow-up data collected by mail questionnaire from 664 men and 524 women. For some questions, there are replies or information for more than that number. (Only 26 subjects--10 men and 16 women have been lost track of completely.) The median age of the subjects at the time of filling out the questionnaire was 49.6 years for the men and 49.0 years for the women. Approximately 80% were born between 1905-1914.

In the first part, the summary of the data obtained with a four-page questionnaire yields the following:

1. The evidence indicates that "with few exceptions the superior child becomes the superior adult." Data collected in 1940 and 1950 with the Concept Mastery Test indicates that the subjects maintained their intellectual superiority.

2. The mortality rate is lower than that of the general white population of similar age.

3. Physical health is good or very good.

4. Serious mental illness and personality problems are not more, and possibly less, than for the general population. And, "crime is practically nonexistent."

5. Among the men, there are approximately 87% who are either professionals or in higher business and semiprofessional levels. The superior vocational record of the men is also reflected in their many publications, patents, recognitions, honors, etc.

6. The women were less interested in vocational careers and 42% of them were employed full-time (three-fifths of them doubled as housewives). In first place was teaching and in second place was secretarial and related office work. Those who did go into professions did exceedingly well. Being a housewife was quite satisfying to the women but few of the housewives limit themselves to their homes--they are usually involved in community welfare and civic betterment. The men also participate in such work.

7. The men and the women vote "always" or "usually." On the
average, they consider themselves "about midway between 'extremely
radical' and 'extremely conservative'" in political and social attitudes. The men, more frequently than the women, consider themselves to be right of center. Both men and women became more conservative from 1940 to 1960. This may be a function of age and/or
socioeconomic factors.

8. "Two-thirds of the men and almost as large a proportion of the
women consider that they have lived up to their intellectual abilities fully or reasonably well." Education and occupational status
are related to the extent to which subjects believe their intellectual abilities have been realized. Very successful men are more
likely to express satisfaction with their accomplishments. If a
woman is employed full-time she is more likely to express satisfaction with having lived up to her abilities than if she is a housewife.

9. Eighty percent of the men and 84% of the women say they get
greatest satisfaction from "'work itself.'" "'Marriage'" and
"'children'" are in second and third place. Only when the data are
computed for married couples is marriage a bit above work.

10. "Now after 40 years of careful investigation there can be no
doubt that for the overwhelming majority of subjects the promise of
youth has been more than fulfilled. The Terman study has shown that
the great majority of gifted children do indeed live up to their
abilities."

The second part of the study is devoted to the correlates of
vocational success. Two judges evaluated the achievements of 750
men up to 1960, forming two groups of 100 men. One group was regarded as more successful vocationally than the other.

1. Few family background characteristics differentiated between
the two groups. Among those that did were the superior socioeconomic status of the parents and the stability of the home (as reflec
ted in the divorce rate which was lower in the successful group).

2. The parents of the more successful group encouraged them to
develop initiative and independence, to succeed in school, and to
go to college.

3. In their youth and early childhood, the more successful group
was more interested in school success, leadership, and in having
friends. The more successful group also reported above average
energy, "vocational planning at an earlier age, and greater satisfaction in their work."

4. Ratings on traits by parents and teachers in 1922, all favored
the more successful group although the difference was statistically
significant only for volitional traits. In 1928, when the subjects
were in their adolescence, the more successful group rated higher
not only on volitional traits but also on intellectual traits and,
to a somewhat lesser degree, on moral and social traits.

5. There is little difference in the early scholastic records of
the two groups. But the more successful ones were more accelerated
so that they completed the eighth grade and high school at younger
ages. It was in high school that the differences began to appear.
The more successful group got higher grades and also participated
more in extracurricular activities. Thus, more of the more successful group graduated from college than was true of the less successfu
group. The more successful group "was younger at receiving their

degrees, earned better grades, won more honors, and more often held positions of leadership in college activities."

6. In the early years, the more successful group had more interest in collections, liked school better, and were more tractable in discipline.

7. Ratings on personality traits by parents and wives in 1940, when the men were close to 30 years of age, indicated that the more successful group was rated higher on "self-confidence, perseverance, and integration toward goals." The more successful group suffered less from feelings of inadequacy although this datum was less marked than the others. Field workers' ratings also differentiated in favor of the more successful group on "appearance, attractiveness, poise, attentiveness, curiosity and originality."

8. Both the more and less successful groups maintained their intellectual superiority over time. When there was a difference in later life, it could be accounted for by education which was in favor of the more successful group.

9. During adulthood, several variables which had not stood out in earlier periods began to be significant. These include health and general adjustment. The physical condition of the more successful group was "good or very good" and in terms of adjustment, the less successful group was more prone to difficulties in social and emotional adjustment. Related to their poorer adjustment may be the fact that, in the less successful group, there were more single men and those who did marry more frequently divorced.

10. In 1960, when the average age of the group was 50, the difference between the groups was manifest in "self-ratings on ambition for excellence in work, recognition for accomplishments, and vocational advancement in all of which" the more successful group surpassed the less successful group.

The concluding comment is: "In any case one must conclude, as was done in the 1940 study of success that intellect and achievement are far from perfectly correlated, and that emotional stability and a composite of the personality traits that generate a drive to achieve are also necessary for outstanding achievement among intellectually gifted men."

Sears, P.S. "The Terman Genetic Studies of Genius, 1922-1972." In Passow, A.H. (Ed.). *The Gifted and the Talented: Their Education and Development. The Seventy-eighth Yearbook of the National Society for the Study of Education.* Part I. Chicago: University of Chicago Press, 1979. 75-96.

The bulk of this chapter refers to the use made of data collected in 1972 by Robert Sears and Lee Cronbach, who served as Terman's scientific executors. Before presenting this data, note should be taken of several comments made in reference to Terman and/or his work prior to the discussion of the 1972 data.

1. Gifted and unselected groups were not random samples of the American population. All the gifted and most of the unselected came from California and chiefly from urban centers.

2. "Not surprisingly, but unhappily for those who wish to untangle the effects of heredity and environment on child IQ, the parents of the gifted were better educated than the general population."

3. In terms of ethnic origin, there were fewer Negro parents and fewer parents of Mexican origin but twice as many of Jewish origin compared to the general population. Chinese children were not sampled since at the time of the study these children were attending special schools.

4. "Terman was meticulous in reporting deviations (from general population norms with regard to ethnicity for example) from a normative group, although he occasionally got carried away in his generalizations by his own group differences than for examination of the fifty-year development of a group of IQ-talented, environmentally advantaged children."

5. Terman was concerned that the myths about the gifted ("'early ripe, early rot'") would be harmful to them. His data found these myths to be false. The folk tales were disproved in terms of averages, "but for an individual child in either the gifted or unselected group, the IQ was often not a strong predictor of other qualities."

6. There is still much data for sub-sample analyses and longitudinal study on such matters as social, intellectual, and personality development.

7. The promise of confidentiality is meticulously kept, with access to materials limited to professional staff.

Since 1972, there have been various studies that utilized the research data. Results are summarized here and references may be found in Sears' chapter.

1. Life cycle satisfactions--Both male and female subjects were asked about areas in which they sought and experienced life satisfaction. "Early judgments, made retrospectively, of the importance of occupation as a goal in life, show the expected sex difference, with men ascribing greater importance to it." Working women were as satisfied with their job situation as were the men.

A study of employment and retirement was also undertaken. In 1972, the men were in their early sixties. Time for mandatory or voluntary retirement was approaching. It was noted that there was a steady decrease in fully employed men from 97% at ages 51-55 to 60% at ages 61-65. A number of predictors of work persistence were found. Those who continued their full-time employment were better educated, had higher occupational status, had been more successful in their careers from ages 30 to 50. They described themselves as more ambitious than others and income was not found to be a significant predictor of satisfaction. A path analysis of life history variables from 1940 to 1972 that predicted occupational satisfaction in 1972 indicated that high satisfaction in 1972 could be predicted from the fact that, at an average age of 30, they had high self-ratings on persistence and had stated that the current occupation had been deliberately chosen. "In the next two decades a liking for the work chosen, reported superior health, a belief that potential had been lived up to, and a self-rating of having higher ambition than other men were also predictive. Interestingly enough, there was no predictive value from such objective measures of success as occupational status, income or education."

Work pattern satisfaction was also studied for women. A naive theory was wrong which predicted that married women with children and income-producing work who lived on a higher than average income would report higher satisfaction. It was found that many of the

women would have chosen a career, or a career except when raising a
family, rather than the homemaker or work-for-income-only work
pattern. For women, the early predictors of work pattern satisfaction were the status of the occupation; higher status jobs led to
more satisfaction. Those who rated high on work pattern satisfaction not only rated occupational success high but also their success
in family life and cultural activity. Self-rating of ambition made
in 1960 was also predictive.

2. Family life: Marriage, divorce, children--For the men, intact
marriages, as compared to divorces, were significantly predicted
in their self-ratings on affectionate relations with and attachments
to parents, especially the mother. Scores on Terman's Marital
Happiness Test predicted unbroken marriages in 1972 with data obtained in 1940. An older age at marriage and a positive rating on
mental health by the research staff also predicted stable marriages.

For the women, comparisons were made between women who were currently married in 1972 (not necessarily a first marriage), women
who were currently divorced and women who had always been single.
The married women felt their parents' marriages had been happier
than was the case with the other two groups. Their educational
level was lower because it was interrupted by marriage and children.
Their husbands were well educated and often held professional and/or
managerial positions and their incomes were high.

To predict family life satisfaction for the men, a path analysis
included positive weights for the Marital Happiness Test and favorable
attitudes toward the parents, especially toward the father. A large
amount of income work by the wife had a negative effect on the hus-
band's family life satisfaction. Whether this was cause or effect
is not known.

It was also found that by 1972, 27% of the women had been divorced
from their first husbands (a little higher than for the generality)
and 21% of the men had a history of divorce or separation. The
income of the men reduced the probability of marriage and the income of the women raised the probability of divorce and reduced the
women's likelihood of remarrying.

3. School investments in gifted children: Home and school--This
was a study conducted by an economist who was interested in whether
there were payoffs for special education for the gifted. It was
found that the mother's education (assuming that mothers spent more
time educating young children than fathers) was significantly related to IQ, while the father's was not. This suggested that home
investments rather than wholly genetic factors underlie the relationship.

Neither preschool instruction nor family income predicted later
level of education by age 29 and 39. The subject's education depended on parents' education and family size. Boys' education also
depended on IQ, with greater opportunities existing for bright boys
to get higher education than for bright girls.

There was a relationship between years of school and lifetime
earning patterns. The men who had greater "intensity" of earlier
schooling (acceleration in school and possibly more intense personal
involvement) had higher lifetime earning possibly because they entered the work force earlier than the peer group. The greatest
differential was during the early years when their earnings rose
at a more rapid rate.

With regard to special instruction at home or school acceleration, it was found that with the former, the quality of time inputs by parents was associated with higher IQ and special instruction had more of an impact than generalized time inputs. The mother's education (but not the father's) had a much larger effect on IQ. These effects were stronger in the first-born than on later-born children. For acceleration, it was found that 67% of the students were accelerated in elementary school and in high school, 74% of the boys and 84% of the girls were accelerated. These data, the author suggests, have to be dealt with cautiously because of sampling characteristics. Thus, while acceleration may have meant early entrance into the work force for the Terman group, it may or may not hold true for non-Terman groups.

4. Prediction of possible suicide--Shneidman used the Terman study to find evidence for or prodromal cues for suicide in the sample. He was presented with 30 case folders and was not told whether the men were dead or alive. In fact, five had committed suicide, ten men had died of natural causes, and fifteen were in fact still living. Shneidman then ranked the 30 cases for probability of suicide. The five actual cases were ranked 1, 2, 4, 5 and 6 and the predictive signals were found as early as age thirty, although the files as presented said the men were 50. "It was clear that suicidal men had carried the seeds of their self-destruction for many years and that somewhere along the line they had failed to find compensating support from their outer world."

5. Studies under way--There is a study of the cranial measurements of the gifted which will be compared with measurements obtained from a normative sample in the same decade. Twenty-six records of subjects with IQs of 180 and above have been selected and compared with equally high IQ subjects studied by Hollingworth. Another comparison sample will be 26 individuals who are gifted in the Terman group, but who have IQs below 180. Finally, the group is moving to later maturity and, thus, there will be opportunities to study gerontologically related questions.

Critique

Tannenbaum, A.J. *Gifted Children: Psychological and Educational Perspectives*. New York: Macmillan, 1983. Specifically, the section titled "Criticisms of the Terman Studies," 114-115.

Citing different studies, the author points out that the Stanford-Binet is primarily related to academic school subjects and that it ignores such matters as motivation and imagination. Consequently, the children in Terman's study who were successful later in life were successful in fields that were school related. This is a restrictive point of view when considering all of the fields which do not depend on academic aptitude. Also, if cross-sectional data were collected and compared with longitudinal data, it might have been possible to study differences between high IQ people who were different from each other depending on whether they became 40 years of age in 1950, 1970, or 1980.

To the above, Tannenbaum adds that, despite the criticisms of Terman's work, it would be wrong to deny the importance of his data for the study of the relationship of intellectual abilities to giftedness. It would, however, also be an error to assume that individuals need an IQ of 135 to fulfill themselves in various lines of human endeavor. "The cut-off point for IQ is undoubtedly not fixed for the many forms of excellence that are known and appreciated, but it is easy to imagine that at least above-average general ability is necessary for those whom our society values highly."

Jacobs, J.C. "Are We Being Misled by Fifty Years of Research on Our Gifted Children?" *Gifted Child Quarterly* 14 (1970): 120-123.

Ever since Terman's studies, people have relied on similar research methods and have come up with similar results; the gifted are superior to the non-gifted and schools cannot harm the gifted who continue to improve no matter what. In criticizing Terman's work, the author argues that his sampling method was at fault. Terman relied on teachers' nominations and additional screening by a group intelligence test followed by an individual intelligence test. From other research cited, it is known that when teachers nominate the gifted, they miss half of the gifted children. Also, the gifted are not high scorers on group intelligence tests.

The author's own research has shown that while previous studies claimed that they were about gifted children in general or about all gifted children, it would be more appropriate to say that they were about children who possessed qualities which allowed teachers to recognize them as gifted. Those who possessed abilities which caused teachers not to recognize them were not even considered. The results of the studies therefore apply only to those gifted who share attributes with children studied: those which caused them to be recognized by their teachers as gifted. The characteristics found do not apply to all gifted children. Studies of children not recognized as gifted revealed negative growth trends (manifested in loss of measured intellectual ability) while those selected on the basis of teachers' selections indicated positive growth trends.

Additional Studies of the Gifted

Bridges, S. *Problems of the Gifted Child: IQ-150.* New York: Crane, Russak & Co., 1973.

The author, a member of the Schools Council Working Party on Gifted Children in England, has taught children in Scotland, England, Kenya, and Nigeria. Education of the gifted needs to be a cooperative venture of education authorities, teachers, parents, and the children themselves. Among the difficulties in this field, the author mentions: the definition of creativity; the identification of creativity; and the attitudes of educational authorities, parents, teachers, and the children themselves.

The gifted children with whom the author had contact had the following characteristics: they were modest about their abilities, the work was too easy for them, and they became bored and felt that this was normal in life and in school. Their attitudes need to be changed as do those of adults.

Durr, W.K. *The Gifted Student*. New York: Oxford University Press, 1964. 296pp.

This textbook covers a range of topics including the definition and identification of giftedness, school and curricular programs, motivation, guidance, the administration of a gifted program, and chapters on teachers of the gifted, parents, and the community.

The chapter on characteristics of the gifted contains a table (p. 43) which is a compilation of the most significant research on a special sub-group among the intellectually gifted. This is that group of underachiever-students who test high but who do not excell. Some of the characteristics of this group are considered under four different headings, including: family background and relationships, personal adjustment, school, and social adjustment.

Haggard, E. "Socialization, Personality and Academic Achievement in Gifted Children." *Social School Review* 65 (1957): 388-414.

The purpose here was to study the development of gifted children in the University of Chicago Laboratory School who came from advantaged homes. These children, it was assumed, would channel their energies to high achievement if the socialization process went smoothly. Low achievement would result when difficulties occurred in the socialization process. Assuming that hereditary factors were constant, then children showing different patterns of achievement would have different personality characteristics.

Forty-five children at the University of Chicago Laboratory School were studied with a variety of procedures over a five-year period as they progressed from grades 3 to 8. The results were: (1) High achievers in the third grade were sensitive to the socialization process. (2) They regarded their parents as overprotective, pressuring for achievement, and lacking in emotional warmth. (3) By seventh grade, these high achieving students regarded all adults with antagonism. (4) Nevertheless, they got along better with parents, teachers, and peers than low achieving students. (5) By grade seven, they showed an increase in their level of anxiety and a decrease in their originality and creativeness. (6) Children similar in level or pattern of achievement were similar in a variety of personality and other non-intellectual characteristics. (8) In the educational setting of the University of Chicago Laboratory School, other children exhibited strong pressures on their peers to achieve academically. (9) Non-intellectual as well as intellectual factors need to be considered in predicting academic success. (10) To produce clear thinkers, it is necessary to help children develop into emotionally healthy individuals who are also trained to master intellectual tasks.

The Extremely Gifted

Feldman, D. "The Mysterious Case of Extreme Giftedness." In Passow, A.H. (Ed.). *The Gifted and the Talented: Their Education and Development. The Seventy-eighth Yearbook of the National Society for the Study of Education*. Chicago: University of Chicago Press, 1979. 335-351.

Terman believed that an IQ of approximately 135 was necessary for remarkable achievement in any field. Although Terman's subjects did turn in some remarkable achievements, they were not geniuses. "Only in 1954, did Terman realize that the label 'genius' could not be justifiably applied to his subjects." Because of the area that Terman and his group concentrated on, there is little if any work on children of extreme giftedness. There are, in fact, only two: one by Hollingworth (1942), which is a case study of children of IQ 180+, and another study by a Swiss of nine child prodigies who were studied with tests and interviews (Baumgarten, 1930). The aim of this chapter is to focus on these children and to describe a study conducted at Tufts University that is oriented to a better understanding of extreme giftedness.

The author uses Piaget's framework which has been extended to incorporate child prodigies. The difference between the Piagetian approach and the IQ-based view is that the latter, "locates the cause of phenomenal achievement primarily *within the child*. Prodigious achievement is better conceptualized as a remarkable *coincidence*. The coincidence consists of a human organism with a set of powerful predispositions or qualities that interact in a human environment over a segment of time during which it becomes possible for that individual to express the potential he possesses." There were three subjects under the age of ten at the time of the study. Two of them were chess players and one was involved in musical composition. These children were observed when they were taking their lessons, while they gave recitals and concerts, and while they competed in tournaments. Their families and teachers were interviewed to provide information on the educational phase of the children's development. The other concern of the study was the psychological characteristics of the children.

The most salient characteristic of the children is the *passion* with which they pursue their work. The author concludes by saying, "Early prodigious achievement thus is related to creativity if in no other way than because precocious mastery provides more time and more opportunity for an individual to reach the limits of his craft, to confront the unknowns, to go beyond the frontiers of the discipline he has mastered. But one thing is clear. No matter how remarkable are the feats of child prodigies, these feats are not achieved without intensive, prolonged, *educational* assistance."

Hollingworth, L.S. *Gifted Children: Their Nature and Nurture*. New York: Macmillan, 1926. 374pp.

Although much work on deviates has been supported from a humanitarian point of view, the author believes that problems which had been regarded as stemming from education and economics are "essentially problems of biological heredity and variation." The recency of information about the gifted is reflected in the fact that the author says that all that is known about the gifted was learned in the 10 years previous to the publication of the book.

Genius, according to the author, is a "wonderful capacity for mental performance" and talent is "remarkable ability" which "falls short" of the "superlative." The author discusses Galton's contributions and points out that for him, ability follows the same general laws of frequency as stature and weight. In reviewing the histories

of gifted individuals, the author points out that their play interests were often quite unusual and often solitary play is described.
The author's historical review not only includes the characteristics of eminent individuals, as indicated above, but it also contains material on the development of mental testing. The author
points out that while studies of eminence were going on among adults,
there was the growth of the child-study movement in Germany, Switzer-
land, and France which emphasized that the child was not a minia-
ture adult. At the same time, the mental test movement was developing. The interest in mental testing goes back at least as far as
Plato who, in *The Republic*, speculated about ways of identifying
the intellectually gifted so that they could be educated to be
leaders in his Utopian state. Plato was especially concerned that
they should be identified when they were children.

Essentially the book, published in 1926, pulls together what is
known about giftedness to that date. There is a hereditary bias
involved in the approach to giftedness with the limit to one's
ability being set by one's endowment. Hollingworth agrees with
Cattell, "that what a person can do depends on his congenital
equipment; but we must also agree that we do not, from studies of
eminent adults, know how far what he actually *does do* depends on
his environment." The gifted are tall and physically heavy, well
nourished, have larger heads than a group of unselected children,
and are stronger and swifter than the unselected. Parents, as well
as teachers, are not good judges of the gifted. A conspicuous symptom
of superior intelligence is an early interest in reading. While the
gifted are rated above average in character traits by others, they
are usually underestimated in this regard by their parents and by
themselves. They are above average in emotional stability and they
walk and talk earlier than unselected children. As to birth order,
Terman found a disproportionate number of first born as did Cattell
in his study of men of science. In Hollingworth's study of children
with IQs above 135, more than half were first born (including 18 only
children). Special talents are independent of intelligence. The
book contains case studies of children with IQs of 180 and above,
as well as chapters on curriculum and the social and economic implications of work in this field.

Hollingworth, L.S. *Children Above 180 IQ Stanford-Binet. Origin and
Development.* Yonkers-on-Hudson, NY: World Book Co., 1942.

Prior to the Stanford revision of the Binet, 19 cases were reported in the literature of children with IQs of 180 and above.
This is a report of 12 additional cases after the Stanford revision.

Thirteen of the parents were Jewish, nine were British, two were
German, and two were French. Remote ancestors were successful and
in professions. No cases of mental deficiency were found. While in
some cases, families were found who were in economic distress, in
general, the economic status of the families was moderate. In ten
out of twelve cases, the fathers were in professions and mothers
were employed in a variety of areas. All but two fathers were high
school graduates; five went beyond high school and had been in
business or trade school and four were college graduates. All but
two of the mothers were high school graduates and five held college
degrees. The median age of the fathers at their child's birth was

31 and for the mothers, it was 28.5. Five of the subjects were
only children, five were oldest. Thus 10 out of the 12 subjects
were first born. IQ of siblings was invariably about 130 but not
as high as 180. Of the 19 cases in the literature, 12 were girls
and 7 were boys; with the added 12 cases in this study, there are a
total of 31 cases with 16 girls and 15 boys.

The median age at walking was 14 months (about average for children
in general) and the median age of talking was 14 months (considerably earlier than the norm). The average age for the first tooth
was between the 6th and 7th month. Median age for learning to read
was 3 years. All but one of the 10 cases for whom height is reported, exceed the norms. Six were heavier than their peers and
health was generally good for the group.

Turning to educational history, the author reports that the
children had problems in school from the beginning. If their problems were handled well, they became a benefit to society and if they
were handled poorly, the results could be negative. Later in school,
there were different degrees of adaptation ranging from opposition
and truancy through indifference and, at the positive extreme, rapt
and enthusiastic preoccupation with study and work. The best ad-
justments occurred where parents, teachers, and principals identified
giftedness right away, where educational guidance was sought, and
where the children were helped in other ways. The easiest adjust-
ments occurred when the children were in groups of similar children.

One-third of the highly intelligent children showed "notable signs
of creativeness." Intelligence in some instances was directed in
"wholly conventional channels" and such children showed no creativity. As adults, these children did not regress to mediocrity
but retained their initial distinguished status. Thus, the subjects'
highly superior status at 7 or 9 years of age was highly predictive
of their status on the Army Alpha at or near 16 to 19 years of age.

Although Terman used an IQ of 140 for genius, Hollingworth believed that, at this level, one is far from genius. An IQ of 160
leads one to expect mildly noteworthy accomplishments. Five children
who were in their mature years stood out from their contemporaries.
None of those with IQs of 140, 150, or 160 had, at maturity, the
honors and prizes won by those with IQs of 180 at maturity. Those
with 190 IQs go through the ceiling of intelligence tests. The
term genius, according to Hollingworth, should be applied to IQs
at or near 180.

Another study by Hollingworth in this book contained 36 boys and
19 girls (average age of 18 years and 6 months) with IQs ranging from
135-190. All but four of them were Jewish. Their personality
characteristics, as revealed on the Bernreuter test, indicated that
they were "less neurotic, more self-sufficient, and less submissive
as a group, than are the populations with which they are comparable...." The more intelligent the child, the more he/she is likely
to become involved in "puzzling difficulties." These children are
taller, heavier, stronger, and healthier than children in general.
They may suffer from feelings of inferiority in size and strength
because they are accelerated in school and they compare themselves
with others who are older than they. Their self-confidence may be
impaired because they are not selected for leadership by friends.
If they are not challenged, their work falls below capacity and they
become idle and get involved in daydreaming. They never learn that

others are different than they are and they tend to become isolated.
The optimum IQ for gaining the confidence of others and for becoming
a leader ranges between 125-155. Those with IQs of 170 are too
intelligent to be understood by people in general. These children
are not socially annoying and they are superior in emotional stability and control. Hollingworth discusses other special problems of
these children in various areas, such as: problems of work, problems
of adjustment to classmates, problems of play (with special attention to the problems of the gifted girl in this regard), problems
of conformity, etc. As children, the gifted are at the mercy of
those who do not understand them as well as they should, though with
maturity, the gifted child can take care of himself/herself. This
book then concludes with a chapter on "The Elementary Schooling of
Very Bright Children" and a last chapter that concerns itself with
"general principles and implications."

Lorge, I., and Hollingworth, L.S. "Adult Status of Highly Intelligent
Children." *Journal of Genetic Psychology* XLIX (1936): 215-226.

Twenty-one persons who scored 130 or higher on the Stanford Binet
when they were 7-9 years old were restudied when they were 20-25
years old. Those with IQs of 180 or above in childhood stood out
from their peers in adulthood. None of those with IQs of 140, 150,
or 160 approached the achievements of those who had IQs of 180 in
childhood. Those with IQs of 160 had "mildly noteworthy achievements." The term genius should be reserved for those with IQs of 180

The Gifted Underachiever

Whitmore, J.R. *Giftedness, Conflict and Underachievement.* Boston:
Allyn and Bacon, 1980. 462pp.

The author presents a thorough history of the field but, for this
section, we will concentrate on her summary of the history of work
with underachievers. The first serious study of gifted underachiever
was done in 1940 by Agnes Conklin who studied the failures of 62
children with IQs from 130 to 163. Conklin argued that some "'factor
of competence'" was more important to adjustment than intelligence.
In 1942, Musselman concerned himself with why 297 gifted high school
students with superior intelligence frequently failed or did mediocre
work. He suggested that attention be paid to the students' drive
for achievement and that the schools make better provisions for such
students.
In 1947, Terman and Oden published their work on the 150 most and
the 150 least successful subjects in their study and found that "the
high achievers had significantly more drive to achieve and were more
socially adjusted. The authors concluded that superior success
appeared to be associated with stability and the absence of disturbing conflicts rather than with instability and emotional tensions."
There was little research on the gifted underachiever until the
late fifties when studies of underachievers became quite popular.
In a review by Gallagher and Rogge (1966) cited by Whitmore, it was
said, "the descriptive portrait of the gifted underachiever is clear,

but how he got that way or what can be done about it is not." Since there was so much information already available, it was also suggested in this review that work comparing achievers and underachievers had "reached a point of diminishing returns." Underachievers had low self-concepts and poor adjustment patterns. The homes of the children were implicated. The studies reviewed had frequently suggested counseling but evaluations of treatment had not been encouraging.

There has been relatively little work on gifted underachievers since the middle sixties. In the late seventies, interest in the problem was revived. One such study with which the author was affiliated was conducted at the Cupertino Union Elementary School District and was designed to identify children in kindergarten and the first grade who might be gifted. Focus was on a group of underachievers of 140+ IQs who were not working up to their intellectual level. On the basis of her work, the author established three major groups of underachieving students: "(1) the aggressive, (2) the withdrawn, and (3) the erratic, less predictable child who vacillates between aggression and withdrawal." Because teachers focused on "problem behaviors," the high IQ students frequently went unnoticed. The aggressive male students were very disruptive in the classroom; the most difficult to identify were the withdrawn and the erratic. The erratic children had psychomotor-perceptual problems or were suffering from "mild cerebral dysfunction." Looking at them differently, what the author calls seeing them in terms of etiological factors, four types are evident which reflect "the source of their learning or achievement problems and were useful in determining individual treatment programs." The classifications were: "(1) Learning Disabled, (2) Behaviorally Disordered or Emotionally Disturbed, (3) Neurologically Handicapped or Minimally Brain Damaged, and (4) Paralyzed Perfectionists."

The author presents what she regards as the characteristics and conditions that create vulnerable children: (1) Perfectionism, (2) Supersensitivity, (3) Deficit social skills, (4) Social isolation, (5) Unrealistic expectations, and (6) Lack of appropriate educational provisions. The school can contribute positively in the following ways: (1) The curriculum, (2) The instructional style and philosophy of the teacher, and (3) The social climate of the classroom. A central concept in the author's thinking involves self-perception and the student's self-esteem which reflects the student's concept of self-worth. At Cupertino, attention centered on trying to get the underachiever to change self-perceptions and attitudes to school. The program was student-centered; the major elements were: "(a) the individualization and personalization of the teaching-learning process; (b) the pupil-teacher partnership in learning; (c) the support of a responsive peer group; and (d) an atmosphere of freedom to express, experiment and explore without threat of failure or rejection. Parents make a significant contribution to the program through their participation in monthly parents meetings and conferences with the teacher and child." The author presents detailed steps for organizing the special class, a chapter on strategies for modifying self-perceptions and building self-esteem, and strategies for building social skills and for modifying classroom behavior. Material for evaluation is also presented.

The author reports finding "exemplary high achievers, mediocre achievers with healthy self-concepts and budding ambition, and continuing chronic underachievers who have not demonstrated their intellectual abilities with any regularity in school." A surprising finding was that a disproportionate number were planning to enter music or drama. They may have chosen the arts because of their success in these fields and "the lack of appropriate academic motivation and rewarding curricula." As the author says, some of the graduates from the program regard themselves as "academically lazy."

Further research and experimentation are necessary to identify high and low achievers and the culturally different gifted. These students have to be studied and school programs have to be developed for them. Many groups have to work together on this, including school boards, taxpayers, state departments of education, and federal funding agencies. "If, at last, the commitment is firm and the support is steady, America may salvage and fully develop its most valuable natural resources: the potential leaders of tomorrow."

IQ Myths

Bane, M.J., and Jencks, C. "Five Myths About Your IQ." In Block, N.J., and Dworkin, G. (Eds.). *The IQ Controversy*. New York: Random House, Pantheon Books, 1976.

To help clear the air about IQ and achievement tests, the authors first summarize the best available evidence and then turn to a discussion of myths about IQ. The evidence they cite is as follows: (1) "IQ tests measure only one rather limited variety of intelligence, namely, the kind that schools (and psychologists) value...." (2) "The poor are seldom poor because they have low IQ scores, low reading scores, low arithmetic scores, or bad genes. They are poor because they either cannot work, cannot find adequately paying jobs, or cannot keep such jobs. This has very little to do with their test scores." (3) Test results depend on heredity as much as they do on genes. (4) "While differences in the environments that children grow up in explain much of the variation in their test scores, differences in their school experiences appear to play a relatively minor role." (5) "If school quality has a modest effect on adult test scores, and if test scores then have a modest effect on economic success, school reforms aimed at teaching basic cognitive skills are likely to have miniscule effects on students' future earning power."

These five conclusions, say the authors, contradict the accepted myths about IQ which include (italics in original): (1) *"IQ tests are the best measure of human intelligence."* (2) *"The poor are poor because they have low IQs. Those with high IQs end up in well-paid jobs."* (3) *"Your IQ is overwhelmingly determined by your genetic endowment."* (4) *"The main reason black children and poor white children have low IQ scores is that they have 'bad' genes."* (5) *"Improving the quality of the schools will go a long way toward wiping out differences in IQ and school achievement and, therefore, in children's life chances."*

Heredity/Environment--Race Differences

Block, N.J., and Dworkin, G. (Eds.). *The IQ Controversy: Critical Readings*. New York: Pantheon Books, Random House, 1976. 557pp.

The controversy is whether or not intelligence has a substantial genetic component. The issue started with Galton's *Hereditary Genius* (1869), when the hereditary point of view was first presented, and returned to center stage 100 years later with Jensen's "How Much Can We Boost IQ and Scholastic Achievement" in the *Harvard Educational Review* (1969).

Because the controversy is current, the authors present a collection of articles reflecting all sides of the issue. There are four parts to this work. Part I contains papers which provide a retrospective glance at the debate over IQ testing in the 1920s and concludes with a more recent article on the same subject. In Part II, the controversy concerning the genetic component is presented. In Part III, the implication of the possible genetic component is considered for various issues of social and educational policy. In Part IV, the editors have the last word.

Jones, L.V. "White-Black Achievement Differences." *American Psychologist* 39 (1984): 1207-1213.

To examine differences in white-black achievement over approximately the last 15 years, the author evaluates data collected by the National Assessment of Educational Progress and the College Entrance Examination Board which provides data on the SAT (Scholastic Achievement Test). Data for reading were evaluated on the basis of data collected in 1971, 1975, and 1980 for ages 9, 13, and 17. At each age, white-black differences declined. Specifically, the average white-black difference of 20% for students born in 1953 is reduced to 10% for those born in 1970. The improvement of the black students did not occur at the expense of improvement of the white students.

Analysis of SAT-Verbal scores from 1965 to 1983 revealed that "average SAT-V scores for white students declined by 8 score points, but average scores for black students increased by 7 score points." Turning to math scores provided by the National Assessment of Educational Progress for ages 9, 13, and 17 with data collected in 1973, 1978, and 1982, the author reports that "we see a consistent decline in the average difference between whites and blacks at each age and considerably higher relative levels of average performance in mathematics for black children born since 1965 than for black children born earlier." White-black differences also declined in SAT math scores. Average SAT-M scores for white students declined by 9 score points over an eight-year period while the average for black students increased by 15 score points. Thus, "we may safely conclude that the gap between white and black average verbal and quantitative achievement levels for elementary and secondary students has appreciably narrowed over the 1970s. Similar analyses of NAEP data for other subjects--writing, science, and social studies--support the same conclusions in those areas...."

The gap between white-black achievement differences is "incontrovertible" but this result cannot "with confidence" be attributed "to educational or social programs that were initiated with this as their goal. It is possible that the trend reflects long-term effects of school desegregation." Another contributing factor is that black students may be recognizing the available career opportunities that result from educational achievement.

"For many academic subjects, including mathematics, average achievement scores for black students remain substantially lower than the average score for whites. There is good reason, then, to attend to one of the eight recommendations of the Education Commission of the States' Task Force, 'Serve better those students who are now unserved or underserved,' that is, 'increase participation by women and minority students in courses such as mathematics and science that are related to careers in which these groups are underrepresented."

MacKenzie, B. "Explaining Race Differences in IQ: The Logic, the Methodology, and the Evidence." *American Psychologist* 39 (1984): 1214-1233.

The "hereditarian fallacy" in work on race differences in IQ is based on "the evidence for high within-race heritability for IQ and the failure of various environmental explanations to account completely for mean racial differences." Neither of these two bases is directly relevant to the issues involved in racial differences in this area. Studies based "on jointly genetic/environmental designs" that control for genetic and environmental factors are needed in this area. Information available from such designs supports "an environmental over a genetic account, although the evidence is not presently sufficient and gives little insight into what the relevant environmental differences might be." To get at environmental differences may mean that we should not focus on the usual "heredity versus environment" type of questions but "on the detailed causal influences on the development of intellectual level generally."

Vernon, P.E. *Intelligence: Heredity and Environment.* San Francisco, CA: W.H. Freeman, 1979. 374pp.

The author summarizes the major studies that show environmental and genetic effects on intelligence "to show that the gap between them is much smaller than is generally believed." There have been problems with investigations on both sides. "Earlier writers have probably exaggerated the degree of heritability of intelligence, and more recent workers have scaled down their estimates. Contrariwise, the advocates of environmentalism have often failed to provide adequate scientific proof for the malleability of children's traits and abilities by the environment in which they are reared, or to recognize that rather limited effects can be brought about by environmental changes."

The author presents thirty items of evidence and indicates whether they favor environmental or genetic factors. He finds that there are "almost as many environmentally favorable as genetically favorable items, though the environmental tend to be less convincing than the genetic because of difficulties in identifying and measuring the crucial environmental variables."

He concludes "that there is no clear verdict in either direction. Genetic and environmental factors are always both involved, and their relative variance cannot as yet, be quantified. It is doubtful, though, whether the proof or disproof of a strong hereditary component would make much practical difference to social, political, and educational policies. Such proof should not imply any discrimination against members of lower scoring racial-ethnic groups." Education needs to be more diversified to provide better learning environments for children with different gene patterns. Various kinds of "alternative" schools and "individualized instruction" programs have worked well in this regard.

Intelligence tests are used best for diagnostic purposes. In talking about creativity and divergent thinking, the author makes the following comments: (1) Guilford criticized ability tests and achievement tests because they were in multiple-choice form and therefore put a premium on convergent thinking. Other types of tests encouraged a wide variety of responses. "Guilford's criticism fitted in with a general indictment of the American educational system for favoring conventionality and conformity to the teacher's instruction and the textbook, and for discouraging students with ideas of their own, who might become the creative scientists and artists of the next generation." (2) The extent to which tests of creativity correlate with intelligence depends on the heterogeneity of the sample studied. It appears that the data on this relationship would yield evidence of nonlinear regression. Above an IQ of 115, divergent scores are more and more independent of convergent performance. (3) Although unusual types of tests may measure different things than conventional tests measure, they do not necessarily measure creativity. (4) Interesting differences have been reported between high-divergers and high-convergers in the areas of personality, leisure time pursuits, composition writing, etc. (5) "The creativity of outstanding artists and scientists is probably more a matter of personality and motivation than just of certain 'styles' of thinking." (6) Divergent thinking scores are unreliable over time and hence it is unlikely that they will reveal any strong genetic component. (7) "... Divergent thinking ability (as a possible indicator of creativity) has received much attention, probably more than it deserves."

BURT

Burt, C. *The Gifted Child*. New York: Wiley, 1975.

This book was published posthumously. The author's hereditary orientation and the fact that he was censured by the British Psychological Association for his work on twins are well known. The early chapters of this book present the basis in evolutionary theory and evolutionary findings for regarding intelligence as genetically based. These same early chapters also trace the study of intelligence from the Greeks to the present time.

Much of the confusion about intelligence stems from the fact that its lay meanings are incongruent with its technical meaning which can be traced back to Spencer. In the lay world, the term intelligence has a rather broad meaning whereas in psychology, the word was originally adopted as a convenient shorthand name for the well-defined concept of inborn, general, cognitive capacity. Tests of intelligence were not selected because they measured specific abilities prized by Western communities but because, as the statistical evidence showed, out of the whole range of cognitive abilities, they furnished high correlations with the general cognitive factor.

With regard to creativity, Burt argues that "whatever may be its precise psychological nature, its proportionate contribution, if we may trust the figures obtained in the various factorial studies, is only one-third that of 'general intelligence.'" He also believes that "Creativity *without* general intelligence produces nothing of interest or value." (p. 165)

Burt differentiates two levels of giftedness. One group consists of the moderately gifted with IQ's below 150 (although not stated, it may be as low as 140 or a bit less) and the highly gifted who are above that level. (This is the group that Galton calls "genius"). A highly gifted child may be as much ahead of the majority of moderately gifted children as these are ahead of the average child. There are too few of the highly gifted for generalizations but Burt suggests that within this group, maladjustments tend to increase in severity and number with increase in intelligence.

In line with this last statement, Burt observes that Terman may have underestimated the frequency of neurotic behavior and problems in the gifted because he initially selected subjects for his study on the basis of teachers' nominations. Nevertheless, Terman observed that neurotic behavior was especially frequent among the brightest. In general, gifted children differ from average children in: intellectual, volitional, physical, emotional, moral, and social characteristics, in roughly descending order. The differences are greatest in intellectual and least in moral and social characteristics. The order varies somewhat in different studies.

Several of Burt's findings that are not unlike those reported by Terman were:

1. Compared to the average child, the gifted child is "taller, stronger, and healthier."

2. Generally, the gifted child is free from "abnormality of whatever kinds; physical, intellectual, emotional and nervous."

3. They are generally gifted all around until they begin to specialize.

4. "They show a much greater fund of common sense, originality and intellectual curiosity than others of their own age."

5. In most respects, they are "more mature; they work harder; they are more scrupulous, conscientious and truthful; they readily take the lead; and unless disheartened by repeated frustration, display greater self-confidence and finer social qualities."

6. "The defects that a few occasionally exhibit are usually traceable to the specific conditions under which they have developed, and especially to the fact that their exceptional abilities have been overlooked or their needs inadequately met." (p. 172)

In the next to the last chapter of his book, Burt considers the later life of the gifted and selects for presentation Terman's

follow-up studies. In this regard, Burt selects for special note
the fact that, in Terman's study of the 150 most successful and the
150 least successful of his subjects, differences in their lives
were observable and predicted by their parents and teachers. Burt
discusses why the gifted do not go to college, mentioning financial
need, lack of interest, the attraction of full-time jobs, and, with
the women, early marriage. He also gives reasons why they drop out
of college; these include: inadequate work habits, lack of appropriate motivation, loss of interest in the subject matter, and dissatisfaction with the quality of teaching or the type of counseling
provided.

Burt differentiates between potential ability and realized ability.
He believes that environmental factors are needed to help fulfill
an individual's potentialities although genetic factors limit what
the environment can do. Thus, Burt says, "Educational and social
writers frequently assure us that the conditions provided by the
ideal home or school can and should 'stimulate mental growth.' But
the phrase contains a fallacious metaphor. It implies the old-
fashioned notion that the effects of exercise and training tend to
become generalized or transferred. Transfer, however, is effective
only in very restricted and specialized ways. No doubt, in the absence of propitious conditions in the environment, the child's
potentialities will not be realized to the fullest. But it is
equally possible that his genetic potentialities may themselves be
severely limited." (p. 186)

Better ways are needed to identify the gifted. Intelligence should
not be the sole criterion; special abilities and disabilities, temperament, and character should be noted as well. Emphasis should be
on selection and should include information from formal tests and
observations inside and outside of class. Selection should occur at
the earliest possible age.

The last chapter deals with Burt's ideas about education for the
gifted. Some of the points he makes are: acceleration may meet part
of the gifted child's needs, but they are far from adequate; special
subjects for the gifted can be started early; educational programs
have to vary with the age of the child--at the early ages, an adequately trained teacher is appropriate but later, specialists from
industry and the professions may be necessary; teaching machines are
suited to older children but one must not forget that it is not the
machine so much as the teaching program that is important; better
outlets for creativity are critical; records should be kept on the
development of the gifted child who should be systematically studied
so that he/she receives appropriate educational training; and a
special type of residential school might also be helpful.

In concluding his book, Burt states that there are two misconcep-
tions that lead to the neglect of the gifted. (1) Teachers under-
rate abilities; they may know that these students are intelligent
but they do not know how intelligent they are. (2) The number of
gifted children in the population is underestimated; "the number of
those with IQs of over 140 is nearly four times as great as current
estimates would suggest." (p. 207)

Guilford, J.P. *The Nature of Human Intelligence*. New York: McGraw-
Hill, 1967.

   This is the basic text which opposes the traditional way (for example, the Stanford-Binet test) of obtaining a single IQ score. It
posits the importance of obtaining measures of different factors
which constitute the structure of intellect. This book also provides the stimulus for the creativity-intelligence controversy.
The author presents the historical background for his work, the
rationale for factor analysis (especially for the kind of factor
analysis that the author uses), the reasons he differs with other
factor analysts, the kinds of factors he considers to be part of his
structure of intellect, and much more. What follows are some of the
main points.

   There is no one answer to the question: what is a psychological
factor? Guilford suggests the following: when the results of several
psychological tests are intercorrelated at a certain desired level
("desired" and therefore indicating some of the subjectivity involved in this procedure), then it is said that they share something
in common called a factor. This is an underlying, latent variable
along which individuals differ. The test scales along which they
differ are called manifest variables. The test and the test scores
can be observed but the factor cannot be observed. The factor that
is measured is understood by looking at the test items, how the test
intercorrelates with other tests, how it fits in with the theory of
human behavior, and the like. Factors come about because of heredity
and environmental conditions. Practice can affect test scores but
the effect of practice is seen primarily in the factor being measured

   There are different approaches to factor analysis and Guilford has
disagreements with each of them. For example, Guilford differs with
the father of factor analysis, Spearman, who argued that there was a
universal factor *g* and a factor that was specific to the test called
s. A test in the intellectual area has only one common factor and
a unique specific component. Guilford argues that Spearman had to
agree, eventually, that correlations between tests had to be accounted
for by a *g* or group factor. Guilford also argues that any genuine
zero correlation between pairs of intellectual tests can disprove
the existence of a universal *g* factor. Hierarchical model factors,
as reflected in the works of Burt and Vernon, are also considered.
These involve group factors. Guilford has various technical objec-
tions to these approaches but on the practical level, he argues that
the group factors change with the test batteries used.

   When Guilford started his own work of organizing intellectual factors into a system, some 40 factors were known. Later, it was
learned that there were a possible 120 factors of which 98 are known
to date. For these factors there are tests. In organizing the factors, Guilford made use of the morphological cube that the astronomer
Zwicky developed. Each side of the cube provides information on
one of three categories: content, operations, and products. The
Content category refers to the kind of information an individual
works with; it is composed of the Figural, Symbolic, Semantic, and Behavioral. Operation refers to what the individual does with the information or content with which he/she is presented; the specific

categories are: Cognition, Memory, Divergent Production, and Convergent Production. Products refers to the form that the information
takes as it is processed and classified; the categories are: Units,
Classes, Relations, Systems, Transformations, and Implication.

Guilford, J.P. "Creativity: Retrospect and Prospect." *Journal of
Creative Behavior* 4 (1970). Also in Parnes, S.J.; Noller, R.B.; and
Biondi, A.M. *Guide to Creative Action*. New York: Scribner's and
Sons, 1977. 137-145.

In 1950 the author presented his views on creativity as his
presidential address before the American Psychological Association.
In this paper the author comments on several major developments in
the field since that time. He covers the following topics. He discusses the work of several important research centers like his own
Aptitudes Research Project at the University of California; the Institute for Personality Assessment and Research (IPAR) at Berkeley;
Torrance's institutes, first at the University of Minnesota and now
at the University of Georgia; and Getzel's and Jackson's work at the
University of Chicago. He also comments on Calvin Taylor's work and
the work of the Creative Education Foundation, the Creative Problem-
solving Institute, the *Journal of Creative Behavior*, Joe MacPherson's
work, and the work of the Richardson Foundation (now the Center for
Creative Leadership) in Greensboro, North Carolina.

The author regards creativity in education as one of the most important developments since his 1950 paper. With regard to creativity
he points out that it is not one thing, but takes many forms. The
divergent production factor has been well accepted by the field but
it has to be remembered that divergent production is not one ability.
There are actually 24 such abilities and, at the time of the paper,
23 had already been demonstrated. It is important to note that
divergent production operations are not the only ones making significant contributions to creativity. In testing for creativity
one should be careful with the testing conditions. Fluency of thinking, which occurs among the divergent-production factors, has received a good deal of attention. But transformation has not. Four
of the transformation factors intersect with the divergent-production
factors but 16 of them lie outside the divergent-production area.
Scientists and creative non-scientists rated transformation higher
than divergent-production abilities in interviews. Evaluation has
also been neglected in studies of creativity.

Turning to education, Guilford says that students should get practice in all abilities covered by his SI. The learner should also
be apprised of his SI abilities as measured by test data. Provision
should be made for individual instruction to take account of individual differences in abilities and parents should be taught how
to teach the abilities. New strategies for thinking should also be
developed and taught.

There is a shortage of ingenuity in the solution of social problems. The youth of our country should be taught how to develop
solutions to these problems and that the resort to violence is a
failure to be creative. Teachers of youth should also see to it that
motivation is intrinsic and not extrinsic. Our times are trouble-
some. But with the overhaul of higher education there is hope.
Colleges that focus on and devote "themselves to creative education

can, and probably will, serve significant roles" in the solution of
society's problems.

In this paper Guilford also brings the reader up to date on the
number of known factors in his Structure of Intellect model. There
are 98 known factors distributed as follows: Cognition, 24; Memory,
18; Divergent production, 23; Convergent production, 15; and Evaluation, 18.

Guilford, J.P. "Intellect and the Gifted." *The Gifted Child Quarterly* 16 (1972): 175-184, 239-243.

This paper is a non-technical summary of the author's point of
view as presented in his 1967 book. The following points are made:
Intelligence includes creativity and is broader than creativity.
The evidence is decidedly against Spearman's point of view that
there is a *g* factor in a non-pathological population. There may be
a number of broad underlying abilities for some of the 15 categories
like memory ability, semantic ability, or for transformation. There
are likely to be less broad categories for other abilities like
visual memory, behavioral divergent production, and symbolic cognition. Higher-order intellectual factors do exist but current
orthodox factor-analytic procedures for demonstrating them are not
acceptable to the author. When two basic factors are correlated
because they have tests in common, it may be because there were not
adequate controls used so that there would be only one ability per
test. The SI model is not a means of classifying tests. The model
is regarded by the author as descriptive of both tests and abilities.

Guilford, J.P. "Varieties of Creative Giftedness, Their Measurement
and Development." *The Gifted Child Quarterly* 19 (1975): 107-121.

New material on the author's Creativity Tests for Children is
presented here as well as a sharpening of several other points made
in other articles. Some of Guilford's observations are listed below.

1. Problem solving requires a minimum of creative thinking. "The
problem solver must take one or more novel steps in his mental functioning, and novelty is the sine qua non of creativity."

2. Gifted children have the potential for becoming effective problem solvers but promise may not be fulfilled "either for lack of
immediate need, motivation, or development of skills in creative
thinking. We can educate those children either with or without the
cultivation of such talents; they will ordinarily not blossom to
full extent on their own."

3. To understand creative thinking, it was suggested, in the 1950s,
to apply the four concepts of fluency, flexibility, originality, and
elaboration. Later work indicated that there were divisions in each
of the concepts. The purpose of this paper is to clarify the different kinds of fluency.

4. The Creativity Tests for Children are revisions of the adult
tests and while they are aimed at grade four to six, they could
still be used with adults. These are tests for divergent production
abilities, restricted to the two content areas of visual-figural
and semantic; these are thought of as the most important areas in
the educational process. There are a total of 11 tests and it takes

ten minutes to administer each test. Scoring guides are provided.
"No test is scored for more than one Structure of Intelligence (SI)
ability. The intercorrelations are thus kept very low (averaging
about .25), which means a relatively low degree of redundancy and a
high degree of information regarding intraindividual differences."

5. "The unique importance of Divergent Production (DP) functions
for creative thinking has been generally emphasized, but perhaps
equally important is the category of transformation abilities. Not
all the transformation abilities reside in the DP category. They
are to be found in all the operation categories, and, of course, in
all the content categories. While there are 30 DP abilities in the
SI model as described earlier (six products times five operations),
there are almost as many (25) in the transformation category (five
operations times five contents)."

6. The best research evidence that SI abilities are involved in
education for creative problem solving comes from studies by Parnes
and Noller (1972, 1973) where they used nearly 40 SI abilities in a
study of an experimental group and a control group. The former had
gone through a creative studies program at the New York State University College at Buffalo. The control group had applied for the
program but was not accepted. There were about 150 subjects in each
group.

The results indicated that, while both the experimental and control groups were about the same at the beginning, there were numerous
gains in the experimental group at the end of the training.

7. If one wants students who get high grades, then the best thing
to do is to select gifted students on the basis of scores on the
Stanford-Binet. This test places undue emphasis on cognition and
memory as one might expect in traditional education. In terms of
contents, it is heavy with semantic information with little attention
paid to visual-figural information, and no attention paid to audi-
tory-figural or behavioral information. For products, the Stanford-
Binet overemphasizes units and systems and classes receive no attention. "The Wechsler scales, and others, take small steps toward
redressing some of these imbalances, in their inclusions of more
nonverbal tests, but they all fall short of covering some of the
more important aspects of potential for problem solving."

8. IQ scales need to be supplemented. "It could even be suggested
that IQ tests could be replaced by semantic-divergent-production
tests in the selection of the gifted, because of the one-way relation
between the two kinds of measurement...."

9. For appropriate guidance of the gifted child, one should know
the child's profile of SI abilities.

10. SI abilities can be introduced into practice in curricula;
examinations; special exercises like the Parnes' workbook for adults;
and the Meeker, Sexton, and Richardson exercises for children.

Validation Studies

Harrington, D.M.; Block, J.; and Block, J.H. "Predicting Creativity
in Preadolescence from Divergent Thinking in Early Childhood."
Personality and Social Psychology 45 (1983): 609-632.

Two divergent thinking measures, Instances and Unusual Uses, were

administered to 75 middle class children who were 4 and 5 years old.
Six and seven years later, when these children were preadolescents,
their creativity was evaluated by their sixth grade teachers. These
creativity evaluations were free of halo effects and showed discriminant and construct validity. A score of the earlier responses,
which was based on imagination and sensitivity to task constraints,
correlated .45 with the criterion and was significant beyond the
.001 level. The composite high quality score accounted for 14% of
the variance beyond that which would be accounted for by sex, conventionally measured intelligence, and divergent thinking fluency.

As a measure of the construct validity, the authors used the
California Child Q-Sort developed by Block and Block. Eight of these
items correlated .40 or more with the criterion and from them we
learn that the children were described as: resourceful in initiating
activities; interesting and arresting; using and responding to
reason; having unusual thought processes; appearing to have high
intellectual capacity; curious and exploring; having an active
fantasy life; and the negative correlation, tending to become rigidly
repetitive or immobilized under stress.

While the correlations with characteristics that one would relate
to creativity were obtained as just reported, there were no significant correlations with behavior which would have been considered
socially desirable like: "is helpful and cooperative," "is eager to
please," "is protective of others," "is vital, energetic, lively,"
"is cheerful," "is calm and relaxed, easy going." "In short, the
teachers appear to have discriminated well between creativity and
other socially desirable characteristics."

The authors conclude that there is reason to be optimistic about
the possibility of tracing the roots of mature creativity into early
childhood since the results reported here are congruent with the
results that adults report about their childhood.

Schubert, D.S.P. "Intelligence as Necessary but not Sufficient for
   Creativity." *Journal of Genetic Psychology* 122 (1973): 45-47.

Intelligence scores on the Army General Classification Test were
correlated with scores on the Creative Imagination Test for two
groups of men differing on intelligence test scores. One group
(N=35) had scores of 111 or higher on the AGCT and 40 scored 89 or
lower. The correlation for the high intelligence group was .01 (not
significant) and .44 (p < .01) for the less intelligent group. The
correlations were not significantly different from each other.

Intelligence sets upper limits on possible creativity. Considered
as a capacity, it may allow the development of an ability without
insuring its development.

The data are congruent with suggestions that creativity and intelligence become more similar as the range of intelligence is
lowered. The data are also consistent with Guilford's triangular
scatterplot diagram of the intelligence-creativity relationship.
The data also extend the database for the relationship between intelligence and creativity to include both verbal and quantitative
abilities. The author notes that in some studies, only verbal estimates of intelligence were included. The author also notes that
"Other factors, including personality, probably are related to the
expression of creativity for a given intelligence level." (p. 47)

Zegas, J. "A Validation Study of Tests from the Divergent Production Plane of the Guilford Structure-of-Intellect Model." *Journal of Creative Behavior* 10 (1976): 170-177 and 188.

To investigate the criterion validation for the divergent production tests, the criterion was successful performance in a field of study where it was expected that creativity was involved, e.g., English, music, or art. It was hypothesized that persons who chose the aforementioned fields as a major field of study would perform differently than others on a group of divergent production tests. Art majors were expected to do better than a general population on tests related to divergent production of figural products; music majors would do better on divergent production of symbolic products, and English majors would do better on divergent production of semantic products.

The subjects were 106 persons--33 males and 73 females between 17 and 55 years of age. All were college undergraduates. Thirty-two were in English, 20 in music, 19 in art and 35 represented the general population. The results indicated that the hypothesis was supported and the author believes that construct validity for the tests was achieved.

Critique

Nicholls, J.G. "Creativity in the Person Who Will Never Produce Anything Original and Useful: The Concept of Creativity as a Normally Distributed Trait." *American Psychologist* 27 (1972): 717-727.

To assume that creativity is normally distributed is unnecessary "and difficult to sustain." "The use of divergent thinking tests as measures of creativity has, by leading to research on divergent thinking which is conceived and interpreted in the context of creativity, impaired our understanding of this process." Among the basic points made in this paper are the following:

1. To make certain that a trait of creativity has the same meaning for normal persons as for eminent creators, the important characteristics have to be isolated among the eminent creators and then it has to be shown that they are positively related in unselected samples.

2. On a theoretical level, ideational productivity (divergent thinking) may be regarded as related to creative achievement.

3. When one obtains measures of divergent thinking under gamelike conditions, as did Wallach and Kogan, then intelligence and creative thinking are regarded as unrelated. "However, if creativity measures are unrelated to intelligence, this suggests that the capacity for original, culturally meaningful achievement is unrelated to intelligence."

4. On the basis of research evidence, "it is concluded that approaches to creativity anchored to products are preferable to the trait-based approach." Research indicates that "the concept of creativity as a normally distributed trait is not well supported by the available evidence. And even if it were better supported, its restricted and variable relevance to creative workers of different types, in different fields, and at different times would have to be

acknowledged. As the concept is not necessary for the study of creativity in people in general, approaches anchored to achievement criteria seem preferable."

5. Tests of divergent thinking should not be called creativity tests. "Intelligence tests do not exhaust the meaning of intelligence, but they are valuable predictors of many aspects of intelligent behavior. A parallel claim cannot be made for divergent thinking creativity tests."

Richards, R.L. "A Comparison of Selected Guilford and Wallach-Kogan Creative Thinking Tests in Conjunction with Measures of Intelligence." *Journal of Creative Behavior* 10 (1976): 151-164.

Since Guilford and Wallach-Kogan support different conceptions of creative ability, the author undertook this study in which some of the tests developed by both authors (those tests requiring verbal responses from the same sample) were used together. The Guilford and Wallach-Kogan tests differ in content, administration, and scoring. Guilford's tests have a greater variety of items and are scored for fluency, flexibility, originality, and elaboration. The Wallach-Kogan tests are scored only for fluency and originality.

The Guilford tests are administered under strict time conditions while the Wallach-Kogan tests are untimed and administered under relaxed conditions. The Guilford tests have been administered to many different kinds of populations while the Wallach-Kogan tests have been used with college students and school children and, thus, may suffer from restricted range. Guilford's tests are less reliable but they normalize distributions, unlike the Wallach-Kogan tests, which may affect linear relationships.

The research included, as mentioned above, tests from both Guilford's and the Wallach-Kogan battery. These timed tests were administered to 483 naval recruits during their first weeks of training. The study found that there were fewer differences between the two sets of tests than one might have expected from the researchers' theoretical positions. Another major finding supported the Wallach-Kogan argument favoring a unitary and independent dimension for creativity.

As part of their conclusion, the authors say: "An interpretation of the present scatters leave the creativity-intelligence distinction less clear--for Guilford and Wallach-Kogan measures alike--while, on the other hand, providing a basis for drawing further distinctions between creativity variables."

Guilford, J.P. "Aptitude for Creative Thinking: One or Many?" *Journal of Creative Behavior* 10 (1976): 165-169.

This paper was written in response to Richards' (1976) paper. The following points are made: (1) The higher correlations in the Richards paper may stem from the overlap in the tests used, which would make the correlations spuriously higher. (2) Guilford compares the data from Richards' study and several of his own. The average correlation in the Richards study was .47, while in his study it was .30. These differences may be accounted for by differences in motivation. Since divergent thinking tests are speeded, they

are more likely to be affected by motivation. Also, since the subjects, Navy enlistees, were told that their scores would not be revealed to the Navy, some may have been more relaxed than others.
Guilford believes that more of his results are motivation-free.

In conclusion Guilford says, "we must tolerate the idea of higher-
order factors, each of broader generality.... But because of the
limited sizes of correlations between tests of different first-order
abilities, the influences of those broader abilities are evidently
quite restricted." Also, creative aptitude is inadequately revealed
if one limits oneself solely to divergent-production abilities.
One also needs to involve operations categories other than production. "Abilities for dealing with transformations are probably as
important as those for divergent production, and they are found in
other operational categories, also."

Lastly, "both intelligence and creative aptitude, which is an important part of intelligence, are multivariate. In either case we
must avoid the fallacy of believing that one word means just one
thing. The goal of simplicity is definitely appealing, but pursuit
of it can get in the way of understanding."

Harvey, S., and Seeley, K.R. "An Investigation of the Relationships
Among Intellectual and Creative Abilities, Extracurricular Activi-
ties, Achievement and Giftedness in a Delinquent Population." *Gifted
Child Quarterly* 28 (1984): 73-79.

There is a lack of information about giftedness in antisocial
youth which this study of 114 delinquents in Colorado addresses.
The conclusions of this study are: (1) Although it is difficult to
locate all the gifted youth in a delinquent population, "it is clear
that quite a sizable number of those students have clear and identifiable high potential." (2) Their gifts are not clearly indicated
by school records or family situations. (3) Creative and athletic
abilities may not be indicated in their records. (4) The gifted
in the delinquent group differed from their normal counterparts "in
that they had very high abilities in the area of fluid intelligence
and, in most cases, did less well on the achievement test in relation
to these high fluid abilities." This fluid ability is hard to
identify and to program for. (5) The fluid ability may color their
learning styles; if so, their delinquency could be deflected if one
could identify their appropriate learning style. (6) An unexpected
finding was that "a creative energy factor [was] isolated in this
study, it was also determined that this factor had direct loadings
from both intellectual and divergent production abilities. This
finding has implications for both the assessment and development of
creativity."

Piechowski, M.M., and Colangelo, N. "Developmental Potential of the
Gifted." *Gifted Child Quarterly* 28 (1984): 80-88.

To make up for the shortcomings of the psychometric approach with
gifted students, the authors present a model of developmental potential which has five dimensions or modes of mental functioning.
These include: psychomotor overexcitability, sensual overexcitability,
intellectual overexcitability, imaginational overexcitability, and

emotional overexcitability. These were tested in an Overexcitability
Questionnaire (QEQ) administered to gifted adolescents in Iowa. The
results indicated that two intellective variables (imaginational and
emotional) were identified in the gifted as was one broadly intellective variable (intellectual overexcitability). No age trends were
indicated. "The three variables ... are viewed here as critical
contributors to the creative power and productivity of gifted people.

Tannenbaum, A.J. *Gifted Children: Psychological and Educational Perspectives.* New York: Macmillan, 1983a. 125-130.

The author cites evidence from a number of sources that are critical of Guilford's model. They are as follows:
1. A study by Carroll argued that the statistical techniques used
by Guilford did not provide opportunity to reject hypotheses.
2. Horn and Knapp supported the Carroll study and argued that
while the model may have heuristic value, it may not have much empirical support. The hypotheses in the Guilford model are confirmed
in 93% of the tests. "They charge that Guilford used similar arbitrary procedures to force solutions in support of his Structure of
Intellect paradigm, when in fact, such an approach makes it possible
to promulgate an arbitrary theory about factor structures."
3. McNemar says that Guilford's work has fractionated the material
into "'more and more factors of less and less importance' [which]
may reflect nothing more than some special sign of 'scatterbrained-
ness.'"
4. The Guilford factors still have to be tested for concurrent and
predictive validity. It may be that none of the factors correlates
with a single line of activity any more than does a measure of
general intelligence. But Guilford never intended to compete with
the IQ. "He attempted to show mental functioning as represented by
an aggregate of special competencies that can be discerned and
described." Thus, the factors can provide some good guidance for
educators as few of the abilities in Guilford's Structure are
covered in any curriculum.

Suggestions for Further Reading

Carroll, J.B. "Review of the Nature of Human Intelligence by J.P.
Guilford." *American Educational Research Journal* 73 (1968):
105-112.

Horn, J.L., and Knapp, J.R. "On the Subjective Character of the
Empirical Base of Guilford's Structure-of-Intellect Model."
Psychological Bulletin 80 (1973): 33-43.

McNemar, Q. "Lost: Our Intelligence--Why?" *American Psychologist*
19 (1964): 871-882.

Tannenbaum, A.J. *Gifted Children: Psychological and Educational Perspectives.* New York: Macmillan, 1983b. 271-273.

Material cited in this section makes the following points.
1. A study by Rekdal (1979) is cited to indicate that there has
been an increase in biographical and personality questionnaires to
locate creative adults. But, for children, the increase has been on

tests derived from performance measures such as those developed by Guilford and his associates.

2. For Guilford to call his tests, tests of creativity, they should intercorrelate at an appropriate high level. But Wallach has presented evidence to show that the intercorrelations in the battery are low.

3. At best, the available data suggest "a weak second-order or group factor that may be labelled 'creativity.'" It is perhaps wrong to say that the tests measure a unitary phenomenon as there may be "several kinds of discrete creative functions."

4. Concurrent validity rather than predictive validity for the total battery rather than single sub-tests is primarily reported.

5. The reasons that the battery has difficulty with validity include the following: (a) The questions do not have face validity; questions on divergent thinking do not reflect what may be involved in creativity. (b) The reliability of the tests are low, as Guilford himself said. This reflects the instability that individuals have with performing creatively and this would affect the predictive validity of the battery. (c) The tests may be measuring unrelated abilities and, hence, the tests would vary in validity across different areas. (d) The tests are limited to cognitive functions although nonintellective factors may be equally important in creative functioning. (e) It may be so difficult to evaluate the creativity of any human accomplishment that it may be impossible to work with the validity of any instrument in this field.

Suggestions for Further Reading

Rekdal, C.K. "Genius, Creativity, and Eminence." *Gifted Child Quarterly* 23 (1979): 837-854.

Wallach, M.A. "Creativity." In Mussen, P.H. (Ed.). *Carmichael's Manual of Child Psychology.* Vol. 1. New York: John Wiley and Sons, 1970. 1211-1272.

Vernon, P.E.; Adamson, G.; and Vernon, D.F. *The Psychology and Education of Gifted Children.* Boulder, CO: Westview Press, 1977. 216pp.

Commenting on Guilford's work, the authors write that the Guilford model seems to be too elaborate to be very practical. The tests required to gather data on all 120 factors could never be administered to any individual or group. But Guilford's factors do help in differentiating different kinds of talent. In this regard Vernon et al. cite an unsuccessful study by Hills (1955) which tried to show that mathematicians had a particular pattern or profile.

Guilford's convergent-divergent distinction appears to be related to a dimension of reality vs. fantasy that Vernon has found in his own work, but the distinction "is quite inadequate as a criterion of creativity." Guilford was not the first to investigate divergent thinking tests. Binet had used inkblots as a measure of "fluency of imagination" and Burt (1926) had used a Consequences test as a measure of creative thinking for his battery for vocational guidance. In the 1940s Thurstone used fluency tests as well. Nevertheless, little progress was made in this area until Guilford and others came along.

Suggestions for Further Reading

Burt, C.L., et al. *A Study in Vocational Guidance.* Industrial Health Research Board Report, No. 33, [1926].

Hills, J.R. *The Relationship Between Certain Factor-Analyzed Abilities and Success in College Mathematics.* Reports from the Psychological Laboratory, No. 15. University of Southern California, 1955.

Thurstone, L.L. *Primary Mental Abilities.* Psychometric Monographs, No. 1. Chicago: Chicago University Press, 1938.

Wallach, M.A., and Kogan, N. *Modes of Thinking in Young Children: A Study of the Creativity-Intelligence Distinction.* New York: Holt, Rinehart and Winston, 1965. 357pp. Specifically pp. 9-13.

In their critique of Guilford's work, the authors cite an analysis of data presented by Thorndike which was based on correlations between factors. They say that Thorndike reported that, in one of the studies of Guilford's group, the average correlation among the six general intelligence indicators was .43. Among the divergent thinking factors, it was .27. The average intercorrelation between the intelligence and the divergent thinking factors was .24. "These relative magnitudes suggest that most of what the divergent thinking measures have in common is the variance they share with the measure of general intelligence." According to Wallach and Kogan, Thorndike says that associational fluency and word fluency, which are regarded as divergent thinking factors, were more highly correlated with "conventional intelligence measures than with the remaining divergent thinking measures."

For Guilford, fluency involves rapid generation of ideas and, as one might expect because of their orientation to the timing factor, Wallach and Kogan are critical of this approach. In their discussion of another analysis presented by Thorndike, the authors say, "The present considerations suggest little warrant for conceptualizing a general cognitive dimension of creativity that is like the concept of general intelligence but exists apart from the latter."

STERNBERG

Sternberg, R.J. *Intelligence: Information Processing and Analogical Reasoning.* Hillsdale, NJ: Lawrence Erlbaum Associates, 1977.

This book has three goals: (1) to specify a componential theory of intelligence, (2) to outline a method for studying this theory called componential analysis, and (3) to present the beginning of a theory of intelligence in the form of a componential theory of analogical reasoning. The introductory material contains a good deal of background information for readers interested in various approaches to factor analysis. Principles of factor analysis are considered and the author takes the position that factor analysis can serve as a source of hypotheses about intelligence as well as a means of arguing in favor of one theory of intelligence over another. While in the different theoretical approaches the unit of analysis is a factor, there is not much consensus among factor analysts as to what a factor is. Some, like Burt and Vernon, take descriptive views of factors while Guilford takes a causal view. For Guilford, a factor is a "latent variable" along which individuals differ. It is an intervening variable for Guilford and is very much like drive and habit which are inferred from observed data.

A brief description of the steps in factor analysis is provided which includes: selection of tests (the range of tests should be broad but not so broad as to blur the results), selection of subjects (this should involve a broad representative sample), administration of tests, and scoring and computing basic statistics. This presentation is followed by a discussion of the procedures of factor analysis and the kinds of decisions that are involved in these procedures. Among the latter are: the choice of method of factor analysis, the number of factors wanted, the type of rotation used, etc.

Of particular note in this book is the author's survey of factor theories of intelligence--Spearman's Two-factor Theory, Thomson's Theory of Bonds, Holzinger's Bi-Factor Theory, Thurstone's Multiple Factor Theory, Guilford's Structure-of-Intellect, and Burt's and Vernon's Hierarchical Models.

The author has a number of comments about Guilford's approach (in addition to the one mentioned previously). When discussing the criteria involved in factor rotation, Sternberg says that Guilford's criteria are most lenient and that the large number of factors that Guilford comes up with is due both to this lenience in rotation and to the large number of tests used. Guilford, compared to other factor theorists, used the largest number and most diverse sampling of tests. This combination results in a "finer discrimination in patterns of individual differences," and an increase in "the number of reliable factors." In discussing Guilford's position on method and criteria for rotation in factor analysis, Sternberg says that "Guilford ... rotated his factors according to a subjective procedure in which the criterion was minimization of the discrepancy between the observed and the predicted pattern of factors. That rotation was used which best supported Guilford's theory."

Sternberg discusses the misuses of factor analysis as well as its statistical and psychological limitations. With regard to the latter, Sternberg says, "factor analysis provides no way to discover or explicate the processes that in combination constitute intelligent behavior." He also says, "the components of intelligence are intra-individual--they exist within individual subjects. Factor analysis, however, is generally inter-individual--it analyzes patterns of individual differences across subjects ... while certain modes of factor analysis could be used intra-individually, it has not been shown that they could discover underlying components of intelligence."

The author succinctly states, "Factor analysis is not a direct means toward the discovery of the basic underlying components of mental ability. Unfortunately, this has been one of the most common purposes for which factor analysis has been used." Although some think that factor analysis "fails to provide techniques for discovering constellations of mental operations," Sternberg believes that his approach does. His technique of "componential analysis" is used "to identify the component mental operations underlying a series of related information-processing tasks and to discover the

organization of these component operations in terms of their relations both to each other and to higher-order constellations of mental
abilities.... From an information-processing viewpoint, componential analysis may be viewed as a set of procedures for discovering
the identity and organization of elementary information processes."
The component, the unit of analysis in Sternberg's procedures, "is
an elementary information process that operates upon internal repre-
sentations of objects or symbols." "The component may translate a
sensory input into a conceptual representation, transform one conceptual representation into another, or translate a conceptual
representation into a motor output."

For Sternberg, there have been disagreements among theorists of
intelligence over three main issues: (1) the correct definition of
intelligence which the author regards as irresoluble; (2) the determination of the unit of intelligence, for which the author offers
his concept of the "component"; and (3) how to partition the chosen
unit, which the author says can be resolved through experimental
work within the framework of componential analysis. For the author,
"Intelligence is defined in terms of: (1) the existence of components; (2) the utilities of rules of combining components; (3) the
utilities of modes for executing components; (4) the utilities of
orders for executing component values; (5) the component values.
Higher utility refers to lower overall solution time and lower
overall error rate."

Davidson, J.E., and Sternberg, R.J. "The Role of Insight in Intellectual Giftedness." *Gifted Child Quarterly* 28 (1984): 58-64.

The typical view of intelligence, which regards IQ as unidimension-
al, "typically leads to the conclusion that exceptional intelligence,
as represented by intellectual giftedness and retardation, are opposite ends of a single scale. In some quantitative sense, this may
be true, but the attributes that best distinguish the intellectually
gifted are probably not the same as those that best distinguish the
retarded. Rather, the gifted are probably above average, but not
necessarily exceptional, in those attributes that distinguish the
retarded from the normal. At exceptional levels of intellectual
talent, qualitatively different attributes start to matter contrarily
to those that distinguish normal from retarded performance." While
Sternberg's previous work emphasized the relationship between intellectual giftedness and componential skills, the current work
focuses on the processes involved in insightful thinking, which is
another example of the information-processing point of view regarding
intelligence.

The importance of insightful thinking is discussed and several
studies are presented in which gifted students are found to be superior to non-gifted students. Studies regarding the effectiveness
of training in this area are also presented.

Evaluation of Guilford's Tests

Richert, E.S., with Alvino, J.J., and McDonnel, R.C. *National Report
on Identification: Assessment and Recommendations for Comprehensive*

Identification of Gifted and Talented Youth. Sewell, NJ: Educational Improvement Center-South, 1982a. 339.

This is the conference evaluation of Guilford's Creativity Tests
for Children. The test is designed to be administered to grades 4
and up and to individuals or to groups. The entire test battery
requires 100 minutes and no special training is required to administer the test battery.

The test norms are based on 1300 children from four California
districts and one in Florida. Split-half reliabilities range from
.42 to .97 with most clustering around .0 and .80. For validity
data, the report states that the Guilford tests correlate -.06 to
.35 with the Torrance Tests of Creative Thinking. The report states
that the test battery is designed to measure divergent production
although the semantic tests are not recommended for those students
with limited knowledge of English or for disadvantaged populations.
The test is also regarded as providing information for the Assessment
stage of the identification process. The words "Validity: limited"
appear as a caution.

Richert, E.S., with Alvino, J.J., and McDonnel, R.C. *National Report
on Identification: Assessment and Recommendations for Comprehensive
Identification of Gifted and Talented Youth.* Sewell, NJ: Educational
Improvement Center-South, 1982b. 378.

This screening form consists of 12 tests from the Structure-of-
Intellect (SOI) Learning Abilities Test which is also considered
in this book. The screening form is designed to measure "Creativity,
visual and auditory memory, visual perception and convergent production" in grades 1-6 and 7 and 8 combined. The standardization
group consisted of 1,560 students on each of the tests. There is
no information provided in the Manual on reliability and validity
(according to this report). A profile can be obtained for each of
the twelve test scores and, according to this report, the information
can be useful in the Assessment stage of the identification process.

Richert, E.S., with Alvino, J.J., and McDonnel, R.C. *National Report
on Identification: Assessment and Recommendations for Comprehensive
Identification of Gifted and Talented Youth.* Sewell, NJ: Educational
Improvement Center-South, 1982c. 379.

This test consists of 26 Structure-of-Intellect (SOI) abilities
based on Guilford's Structure of Intellect and which relate to
learning the school curriculum. The factors relate to "reading,
arithmetic, creativity, cognition, memory, evaluation, convergent
production, and divergent production." Normative data are provided
by grades 1-6 and 7 and 8 combined. The number of subjects in the
standardization populations ranged from 132 to 1,560. The tests
are untimed and no special training is necessary for administering
the tests. No data are reported for reliability or validity.

Students who score three years above grade level in an ability
are regarded as gifted. "It can be useful in diagnosis of spatial
and verbal abilities, in connection with academic abilities and in
program planning." According to this report, this test has been

extensively researched with minority populations although no reliability and validity data are provided. As a caution, the tests are
not recommended for students with English-language deficiencies.

GETZELS AND JACKSON

Getzels, J.W., and Jackson, P.W. *Creativity and Intelligence: Ex-
plorations with Gifted Students.* New York: Wiley, 1962.

The IQ has been the main and often the sole criterion of giftedness. But the IQ can be criticized for various reasons and therefore the authors decided to use other conceptions of giftedness, as
well as high IQ, in the study of children. The authors concentrated
their energies on two categories of children. The first consisted
of those children who varied in terms of cognitive excellence and
the second consisted of those who varied in terms of psychosocial
excellence. In the cognitive category there were two subgroups of
children. One was high in intelligence but not as high in creativit
The second subgroup was high in creativity but not as high in intelligence. For the study of psychosocial excellence there were
also two subgroups. One was a group high in morality but not high
in psychological adjustment. The other was high in psychological
adjustment but not high in morality. Because the impact of this
study in the field was felt primarily on the relationship between
creativity and intelligence, the material presented here is limited
to this area.

Each group in the creativity/intelligence research was studied
in terms of their behavior in school: how well they did in tests of
scholastic achievement, how they were perceived by their teachers,
and the meaning they attached to their educational experiences.
The authors also investigated the character of the group's value
orientations, their career goals, their fantasies and imaginative
productions. Data were also gathered on the students' home environments.

The subjects in the study were students in a private midwestern
school. All students from the sixth grade through the senior year
of high school (292 boys and 241 girls) participated in the study
that yielded some 40 test scores collected over 20 hours during a
period of several weeks. In addition to data collected from the stu
dents, data were also collected from school records, parental questionnaires, and parental interviews. Relatively complete data were
available from 245 boys and 204 girls. From this population experimental groups were selected.

The experimental groups were: The high creativity group, which
consisted of 15 boys and 11 girls who had scored in the top 20%
on the creativity instruments used for the same age and sex but
below the top 20% in IQ. The high intelligence group scored in the
top 20% among their age and sex peers for intelligence but below
the top 20% on the creativity measures. In this group there was a
total of 17 boys and 11 girls. There was no study of the group
that scored high on creativity and high on intelligence.

The school the students attended was in Chicago. It kept good
records and provided good cooperation; these advantages were regarde

as overriding the atypicality of the student population. The students came from middle class and upper middle class families and many of their parents were affiliated with a large university as faculty, staff, or graduate students. Others, not affiliated with the university, were employed in professions, management, and white collar positions. Many parents held college degrees and a sizable number held advanced degrees. Few of the parents were in semi-skilled and unskilled occupations.

Admission to the school the students attended was based on past academic performance, entrance test scores, and interviews with the child and parents. The average IQ of the children on admission was 132, with a standard deviation of 15.

Intelligence test data were available from the school office. For each student there was a score available on the Binet, the Henmon-Nelson, or some other intelligence test (about a dozen had WISC scores). To make the intelligence test scores comparable, they were converted by regression analysis to comparable Binet scores.

For the authors, creativity is a cognitive ability for which information can be obtained on paper-and-pencil tests. Creative thinking, they believe, is to be found to some degree in all persons, children as well as adults, in all fields of endeavor. Their orientation also emphasizes the fact that they are interested in "creative potential."

The creativity tests involved the ability "to deal inventively" with material that was verbal and numerical and involved spatial relationships. Scores on these tests did not depend on single correct responses (as in most intelligence tests) but "on the number, novelty, and variety of adaptive responses to a given stimulus task."

The following tests were used to gather data on creativity: Word Association Test, in which subjects write as many meanings as they can think of for the stimulus words. Uses Test, in which subjects are presented with five common objects (bricks, pencils, paper clips, toothpicks, and sheets of paper) and are asked to write as many different uses as they can for each object. Hidden Shapes (Gottschaldt Figures), in which the subject is presented with 18 simple figures, each of which is followed by four complex figures. The subject's task is to recognize that complex figure in which the simple figure occurs. Fables Test, in which students are presented with four fables whose last lines are missing. Students are asked to supply a moralistic, a humorous, and a sad ending for each fable. Make-up Problems Test, in which students are presented with four complex paragraphs that contain many numerical statements about buying a house, building a swimming pool, etc. For each paragraph the students are to use the available information to make up mathematical problems that can be solved with the information contained in the paragraphs.

The authors present a table of intercorrelations between the creativity tests and the IQ tests. They say, "Noteworthy in the table are the relatively low correlations between IQ and performance on tests requiring the indicated creative thinking abilities."

Results of the study are presented in terms of three major categories: The subjects as students, as individuals, and as family members. Some of the findings in each of the three categories follow.

As students, the high IQ and the high creative samples scored significantly higher than the total population in scholastic achievement test scores but not significantly different from each other.
The authors say, "Indeed, despite the 23-point difference in mean
IQ between the high Creatives and the high IQs, the achievement
scores of the two groups are equally superior to the achievement
scores of the school population as a whole." On two measures of
motivation for achievement the two experimental groups did not differ from each other or from the total student population. Thus,
one cannot ascribe the apparent overachievement of the high creatives to motivational differences alone. When teachers were asked
to rate the extent to which they liked having the students in class,
it was found that teachers preferred the high IQ students over the
average student but the high creativity students were not so preferred, even though the scholastic performances of the high creatives and high IQs were the same.

Turning to the data on the students as individuals, it was found
that the high creatives and the high IQs agreed as to what they
thought made for adult success and they also agreed as to what they
thought teachers approved. Nevertheless, they disagreed as to what
qualities they preferred for themselves. High IQ students were
success oriented; the characteristics they valued in themselves and
the characteristics they believed made for success were quite close.
But for the high creativity students the relationship between the
characteristics they valued in themselves and those they believed
made for success as adults were "virtually nil." Thus, the high
creatives were not regarded as success oriented.

High IQ students were moderately teacher oriented; the characteristics they liked for themselves and the characteristics they thought
teachers liked were closely related. But no such relationship was
found for the high creatives. The high creatives appeared to value
qualities which they felt their teachers valued least. With regard
to fantasies, analysis of the students' stories revealed that "The
high creative adolescents were significantly higher than the high
IQ adolescents in stimulus-free themes, unexpected endings, humor,
incongruities, and playfulness, and showed a marked tendency toward
more violence in their stories." In their drawings done for the
assigned title "Playing Tag in the School Yard," the high creatives
were more stimulus free, more fanciful, and more humorous than their
high IQ classmates and they also tended to express more aggression
and violence. Finally, with regard to their career aspirations,
high creatives were "diffuse" in their occupational goals and they
appeared to be willing to deal with a greater range of career possibilities. As to quality of career goal, the high creativity students were "eccentric" in that they were more willing to deal with
career risks and to take greater liberties with adult standards of
success.

As for the data on the students as family members, it was found
that the parents of the high IQ child had a higher educational level
than the parents of the high creativity child. The former also had
more specialized training than the latter. A larger proportion of
the high creative fathers were in academic or educational occupations. And, although more of the high IQ mothers had more professional training, more of them were exclusively housewives. Thus,
the mothers of the high IQ children had more time to devote to their

children than did the mothers of the high creatives. The former were regarded as being "more vigilant about the 'correct' upbringing of their children" than were the mothers of the more creative children. The ages of the mothers of the two groups of children and the fathers of the two groups were similar. There were, however, greater differences of age between the parents of the high IQ children than between the parents of the high creative children. The mothers of the high IQ children also seemed to give more evidence of financial insecurity in their own early lives than was true of the mothers of the high creatives. The homes of the high IQ children had more magazines than was true of the homes of the more creatives. "Suffice it to say that the greater number of mass media journals and children's magazines tends to support three of our general impressions about the high IQ homes: greater conformity to conventional standards, greater child-centeredness, and greater implicit if not explicit pressure for the child to do well scholastically." More of the mothers of the high IQ children found more than one unfavorable quality in their children. It appeared as if these mothers were constantly on the lookout for things to improve in their children. Although the high IQ mothers were more critical of their children and of the school their children attended, they expressed "fewer misgivings and uncertainties" than did the high creative mothers about their child-training practices.

When asked about the friends they would like their children to have, the high IQ mothers spoke of external characteristics like good manners, good family, etc., and the high creative mothers spoke of internal characteristics like values, openness, etc. The authors say, "the overall impression of the high IQ family is that it is one in which individual divergence is limited and risks minimized, and the overall impression of the high creativity family is that individual divergence is permitted and risks are accepted."

Getzels, J.W. "From Art Student to Fine Artist: Potential, Problem Finding, and Performance." In Passow, A.H. (Ed.). *The Gifted and the Talented: Their Education and Development. The Seventy-eighth Yearbook of the National Society for the Study of Education.* Chicago: University of Chicago Press, 1979. 372-387. The book version is: Getzels, J., and Csikszentmihalyi, M. *The Creative Vision: A Longitudinal Study of Problem Finding in Art.* New York: John Wiley & Sons, 1976.

The subjects in this study were students at one of the most selective degree-granting art schools in the nation. The author compares these students with other students of the same age and sex on a series of psychological measures. On two speed and power tests of intelligence, the students were within college norms. Differences were found, however, in favor of the art students on a test of spatial visualization and on a test of aesthetic perception and taste. Differences were also found in the Allport-Vernon-Lindzey Study of Values and Cattell's Sixteen Personality Factors Questionnaire (16 PF). "On three of the values and six of the personality factors, the male and female art students differed from the norms in the same direction. That is, they had higher aesthetic and lower economic and social values, and they were more aloof, introspective, alienated, imaginative, self-sufficient, and experimental in outlook.

These nine characteristics seemed to be a consistent dispositional
pattern of both the male and the female art students." The women
were also more dominant than women their age and the men were more
sensitive than men their age. The author talks of the women's
dominance as reflecting masculinity and the male sensitivity as
reflecting femininity.

The second matter discussed by the author are differences between
the four sub-groups of students: fine art, advertising art, industrial art, and art education. There were no differences on the cognitive tests but there were differences on the personality and
value tests. The fine art students had higher aesthetic and lower
economic values, the advertising and industrial art students had
higher economic and lower aesthetic values, and the art education
students had lower economic and aesthetic values but higher social
values. On the Cattell 16 PF Test, the fine art students were significantly different from at least one of the other groups on
sociability, super-ego strength, sensitivity, imaginativeness,
shrewdness, and self-sentiment. Thus, "Personality dispositions
and values affect how the young persons will choose to apply their
graphic talent. Those who value social goals will tend to use
their talent in a teaching capacity; those who value material and
worldly goals will tend to use their talent in the more remunerative
and conventional advertising and industrial capacities. Students
who are characterized by the highest aesthetic values and imaginative
dispositions will have the courage--or be driven by their values and
dispositions--to risk specialization in fine art, where creativity
is more encouraged for its own sake, but where material and social
rewards are unpredictable and rare."

Relationships were studied between the tests and measures of
artistic achievement in the school. "There are systematic relationships between the perceptual, value, and personality characteristics
of art students and their achievement in art school--relationships,
however, that vary by sex of the student and by field of specialization."

To get at problem finding, the authors developed a procedure especially for this investigation. At the art school, a studio was
developed that contained two tables, an easel, drawing board, paper,
and a variety of dry media. From various classrooms, 31 male fine
art students were asked to compose a still-life problem on the
second table, using as many objects as they wanted, and then to
make a drawing of the still life. Thirty-one fine arts students
worked on the problem with observers taking notes. Three major
variables stood out: the number of objects handled; what was done
with the objects (some students picked them up and went to the table
to draw while others studied the objects); the uniqueness of the
objects selected.

The thirty-one artist students were rank-ordered on the basis of
a composite score based on the three aforementioned variables.
The drawings produced by the students were then evaluated by artist-
critics and the problem-solving composite was then correlated with
variables in the criterion. A correlation of .28 (not significant)
was obtained with craftsmanship; a correlation of .54 (significant
at the .005 level) was obtained with originality; and a correlation
of .40 was obtained with aesthetic value (significant at the .025
level).

The study also concerned itself with the social and personal context of becoming a fine artist. Among the various factors discussed
were a number of relationships between family background characteristics, as related to success, and failure after school. Successful
artists came from families of higher socioeconomic backgrounds
where the father had a higher education and the mother was employed
outside the home. Differences were also found in sibling order;
13 or 81% of the subjects who were successful were eldest sons but
only 5 or 33% of the unsuccessful artists were eldest sons. Fifty
percent of the unsuccessful artists were middle sons while none of
the successful group was.

Overall grade point average was not related to subsequent status
but, when grades were divided between studio courses and academic
courses, it was found that the successful artists got the best
grades in the studio courses. Good grades in academic courses were
related to failure rather than success as an artist. Teachers'
ratings in originality and artistic potential during the first year
of school were also related to success. "The last result is surprising. Correlations with the success criterion and the problem
finding composite was .30 (significant at the .05 level); when this
was added to the other two ratings--ratings of the actual drawing
and ratings obtained from an interview--the correlation was raised
to .41 (significant at the .01 level)."

Critique

Tannenbaum, A.J. *Gifted Children: Psychological and Educational Per-*
spectives. New York: Macmillan, 1983. 283-288.

The author's review of the Getzels-Jackson study contains the
following comments:

1. In a study by Hudson in England, it was found that creativity
tests and IQ scores were associated with various personality differences. Boys who specialized in history and English were strong
on the open-ended (divergent thinking) tests and relatively weak on
IQ. Those majoring in the physical sciences showed the opposite
effect. Students who majored in the classics, modern languages, and
ecology were distributed between the two extremes.

2. Torrance and his coworkers undertook some 15 partial replications of the Getzels and Jackson study. They found similar results
only where students were taught in a way in which they had a chance
to use their creative thinking abilities or where the average IQ
for the school was high. "Furthermore, the creative pupils 'over-
achieved' in the sense that their education quotients were considerably higher than were their intelligence quotients."

3. Torrance and Wu report a 22-year follow-up study of elementary
pupils who were divided according to their IQ and creativity test
scores. The high creative groups had better quality career images
than the high IQ/low creativity groups. The low IQ/high creative
group scored higher than the other groups on creative style of life.
Thus Torrance believes that some of the children he calls gifted
sometimes "fall short of being identified as gifted even though they
equal or excel over those who qualify on the basis of IQ alone."

4. Other replications do not find creativity and IQ measures
equally valid in distinguishing high from low scholastic achievers.
    5. Questions were also raised about whether intelligence and crea-
tivity measures were indeed independent. This group included the
studies by Marsh, Thorndike, and Wallach. The last paper argued that
the small discrepancy between inter-individual and intra-individual
correlations could have been eliminated if the intelligence test
data had been collected at the same time as the creativity test data.
    6. A sampling problem was also raised in a study by Hasan and
Butcher which argued that even the low IQs averaged an IQ of 127,
which put them at the 95th percentile in terms of test norms. Only
in such a biased sample, it was argued, is it possible to distinguish creative from intelligent children. In an unselected sample
it was expected that the measures of convergent and divergent thinking scores would overlap. Other studies confirm the Getzels and
Jackson results.
    7. Since the Getzels and Jackson studies are more frequently
replicated with high IQ populations than with randomly selected
groups, there may be an IQ threshold in the relationships between
IQ and creativity (low above the threshold and high below the
threshold). In reviewing relevant data, Tannenbaum says, "It would
therefore seem from these studies that creativity tests do not add
much to IQ in identifying superior scholastic potential."
    8. In a report of the findings of Edwards and Tyler (1965), Tannen-
baum quotes from the study as follows: "the *generalizability* of the
Getzels and Jackson and the Torrance findings about the relationship
of creativity scores to academic achievement is limited. They apparently do not apply to all kinds of students, all kinds of
schools, and all kinds of intelligence creativity tests."

Suggestions for Further Reading

Edwards, M.P., and Tyler, L.E. "Intelligence, Creativity, and
    Achievement in a Non-selective Public Junior High School." *Journal
    of Educational Psychology* 56 (1965): 96–99.

Flescher, I. "Anxiety and Achievement of Intellectually Gifted and
    Creatively Gifted Children." *Journal of Psychology* 56 (1963):
    251–268.

Hasan, P., and Butcher, H.J. "Creativity and Intelligence: A Partial
    Replication with Scottish Children of Getzels and Jackson's Study."
    British Journal of Psychology 57 (1966): 129–135.

Hudson, L. "Intelligence, Divergence, and Potential Originality."
    Nature 196 (1962): 601–602.

Marsh, R.W. "Statistical Re-analysis of Getzels and Jackson's
    Data." *British Journal of Educational Psychology* 34 (1964): 91–
    93.

Thorndike, R.L. "The Measurement of Creativity." *Teachers College
    Record* 64 (1963): 422–424.

Torrance, E.P. *Education and the Creative Potential.* Minneapolis:
    University of Minnesota Press, 1963.

Torrance, E.P., and Wu, T. "A Comparative Longitudinal Study of the
    Adult Creative Achievements of Elementary School Children Identi-
    fied as Highly Intelligent and as Highly Creative." *Creative
    Child and Adult Quarterly* 6 (1980): 71–76.

Wallach, M.A. "Creativity." In Mussen, P.H. (Ed.). Carmichael's
    Manual of Child Psychology. Vol. 1. New York: John Wiley and
    Sons, 1970. 1211-1272.

Vernon, P.E.; Adamson, G.; and Vernon, D.F. The Psychology and Educa-
    tion of Gifted Children. Boulder, CO: Westview Press, 1977. 216pp.

   This study comments on several aspects of the Getzels and Jackson
study. Vernon et al. claim that Getzels and Jackson used miscellaneous tests and they "intercorrelated with one another no higher
than they did with intelligence tests." Hence, they do not stand
as independent tests of an independent variable. They also say
that the evidence seems to be that the degree of relationship between intelligence and divergent thinking tests vary as a function
of the age and ability of the children tested, the kinds of tests
used and the conditions of testing. "Thus the statement commonly
made, on the basis of Getzels and Jackson (1962) results, that intelligence tests fail to discover 70 percent of creative students
is definitely misleading."

Wallach, M.A., and Kogan, N. Modes of Thinking in Young Children:
    A Study of the Creativity-Intelligence Distinction. New York: Holt,
    Rinehart and Winston, 1965. 357pp.

   In their critique of the Getzels and Jackson study, the authors
make the following points:
   1. One can question the degree to which the creativity tests are
independent of intelligence. The five creativity tests correlated
significantly with IQ for the boys beyond the .05 level. Among the
five creativity tests used with the girls, four of the five correlated
significantly (beyond the .05 level). Moreover, two of the five
correlations for the boys were "substantial" (.38 and .37) and,
similarly, two of the five correlations for the girls were substantial since they correlated .39 and .37 with intelligence.
   2. The creativity tests correlate no more strongly with each
other than they do with intelligence. This holds for both boys and
girls. Therefore, there is no evidence here to support the notion
that there is a single, unified dimension of general intelligence
or g.
   3. Because of the evidence of the nature of the intercorrelations
among the creativity tests and their relationships with intelligence, it was improper for Getzels and Jackson to sum the five creativity measures "as if these measures possessed something in common
that was distinct from what they also shared in common with general
intelligence."
   4. The authors review the creativity tests used by Getzels and
Jackson, saying that what these tests "have in common is the fact
that they co-vary with individual differences in general intelligence, an inference far different from the one which Getzels and
Jackson draw."
   5. The authors cite a study by Thorndike which supports their
point of view. They quote from Thorndike as follows: "It is of
some interest to extract a first factor from this table of correlations and compare the factor loadings of the several tests.... The

factor loadings are all fairly modest and the loading for the conventional intelligence falls about midway among the 'creativity' tests (1963).' That is to say, no warrant exists in these data for designating a psychological attribute of creativity from general intelligence." This conclusion is also supported by a factor analysis of the Getzels and Jackson data by Marsh (1964).

Other studies that followed designs similar to Getzels and Jackson, but with different tests and procedures, are also presented by Wallach and Kogan and all duly criticized.

Suggestions for Further Reading

Marsh, R.W. "A Statistical Re-analysis of Getzels and Jackson's Data." *British Journal of Educational Psychology* 34 (1964): 91-93.

Thorndike, R.L. "Some Methodological Issues in the Study of Creativity." In *Proceedings of the 1962 Invitational Conference on Testing Problems*. Princeton, NJ: Educational Testing Service, 1963. 40-54.

TORRANCE

Torrance, E.P. *Guiding Creative Talent*. Englewood Cliffs, NJ: Prentice-Hall, 1962. Chapters 2 and 3.

This is one of several background sources recommended in the Manual for the Torrance Tests of Creative Thinking. This summary of the recommended chapters in *Guiding Creative Talent* relates to the Minnesota Tests of Creative Thinking, a forerunner of the Torrance Tests of Creative Thinking. References to the other sources and a reference to the manual are presented below. Another citation in this book refers to Torrance's *Rewarding Creative Behavior*.

Chapter 2 presents a history of the work done in the assessment of creativity and the definitions which have guided the author's research. In reviewing the history, Torrance points out that one of the reasons that much of the early work did not catch on "lies in the failure of researchers to deal adequately with the difficult problems of criteria and validity." These aspects finally received due attention at the University of Utah conferences on the identification of creative scientific talent (Taylor, 1956, 1958, 1959).

Chapter 3 focuses on the development of the Minnesota tests and the research and data obtained with them. Torrance's work began in this area in 1958 at the Bureau of Educational Research at the University of Minnesota. At the beginning, alternate forms of Guilford-type tests were developed as well as new ones. "The tasks developed were constructed on the basis of analyses of reported experiences of eminent scientific discoverers, inventors, and creative writers. An attempt was made to construct tasks which would be models of the creative process, each requiring several types of thinking. This approach represents a departure from that of Guilford and his associates. Perhaps the greatest divergence is from Guilford's insistence that predictor measures should represent single factors (C.W. Taylor, 1959). The Bureau's program has been to develop complex tasks presumed to involve the creative process and then to examine the products for evidences of various types of thinking, or, to use Guilford's term factors. A calculated attempt has also been made to develop tasks which will grip the interest of the subject and which will permit him to 'regress in the service of the ego' which appears to be important in creative thinking (Schafer, 1958)." Thus, over a three-year period, some 25 tasks were developed. "All call for the production of divergent solutions, multiple possibilities, and some types of thinking involved theoretically in creative behavior." A number of validity studies are reported.

1. Wallace (1960) studied sales productivity and the amount of customer service among 61 saleswomen who were in the upper and lower thirds of their departments. Using various tests of Torrance's, as well as different variables, it was found that the high producers scored higher than the low producers on the tests. Those who were low in both variables (customer service and sales production) were much lower than the other groups in creative ability. The Ask-and-Guess Test produced a total score which differentiated the high and low sales producers in the noncreative departments from those in the creative departments.

2. A study was carried out by the Bureau in which the criterion was creativity in industrial design as decided upon by college faculty. There were 10 creatives and 12 noncreatives; using scores on several of the tests, it was found that the creatives scored significantly higher than the noncreatives.

3. Students were divided in terms of their scores on Torrance's tests and one student from each of the five levels was selected to constitute the group of five. The group's task was to initiate ideas and to demonstrate them with toys. There were group pressures to restrict ideas from the most creative members but 68% "managed to initiate a larger number of ideas than any other member of the group.... Those who produced the most ideas on the test also tended to produce the most ideas in his group task." No such linear trend was evident when IQ scores were used.

4. Using sociometric data of nominations for different criteria (e.g., "Who in your class comes up with the most ideas?") and factor analyzing these data, it was found that children tended to perceive individuals as having good ideas if they maintained a good "batting average" of "good ideas" to "wild, silly, or incorrect" ideas. Thus, the individuals with a moderate number of good ideas and no low quality ideas would be more likely to be nominated as having good ideas than one with a large number of good ideas along with a sizeable number of low quality ideas. Those students who starred on the criterion of good ideas were compared with those who received no choices on this variable. It was found that the former had significantly higher scores on the tests than did the latter.

In a separate study, those students who received the highest creativity score in each class were matched with a classmate of the same sex and IQ. It was found that the former "were more frequently chosen than their matched classmates on the 'wild ideas' and 'naughty ideas' criteria. Teachers nominated them more frequently as talkative and as having 'wild' ideas. The most creative boys apparently had a far greater impact on their classmates than did the most creative girls.

5. Data are presented from 8 partial replications of the Getzels and Jackson study. Five were at the elementary school level, one at

the high school level, and two at the graduate level. The results
were: (a) On the measures of intelligence, the highly intelligent
group is significantly higher than the high creativity group.
Nevertheless, the highly creative groups are still very high in
intelligence. (b) A study of the degree of overlap between the
groups identified as gifted revealed that "In most of the groups
studied, about 70 percent of the most creatives would have been
eliminated if a 'gifted' group was being selected on the basis of
the intelligence test or Miller Analogies." There were exceptions
in two schools where the highly intelligent also tended to be the
highly creative. This, Torrance says, may be due to the distribution of talent in these schools or to the intelligence measures
used. In one case, it was the California Mental Maturity Test and
the other was the Lorge-Thorndike Test. (c) The measures of creative thinking and IQ correlate no more than one would expect. The
highest correlation was .32 and that was obtained between the
measures of creative thinking and the Otis Quick-Scoring Test of
Intelligence. (d) With regard to achievement, the differences between the two groups is so small that it could occur by chance.
Thus, in only two of eight situations do Torrance's data contradict
the Getzels and Jackson data. (e) In terms of areas where the
achievement occurs, the author reports, "it will be observed that
there is a fairly general tendency for the highly creative groups to
do better on reading and language skills than on work-study and
arithmetic skills."

6. In conclusion, since only in some schools do highly creative
students learn as much as highly intelligent ones, the question
remains whether anything can be said about the conditions under which
this would occur. To answer this question Torrance suggests: (a) In
some situations, students are taught to learn creatively so that
these abilities become important to them. (b) One might look to
the distribution of abilities to find a "threshold" when a higher IQ
does not make much of a difference. The figure might be set at an
IQ of 120 although most children with such scores would not get into
gifted programs. (c) The data may be related to different kinds of
achievements for which different measures need to be developed.

In summary, the results just presented are cited as "indirect
evidence of the validity of the tests of creative thinking." It is
hoped that "more adequate evidence" will be provided in the future.

Suggestions for Further Reading

Schafer, R. "Regression in the Service of the Ego." In Lindzey, G.
    (Ed.). *Assessment of Human Motives*. New York: Rinehart and Co.,
    1958. 119-148.

Taylor, C.W. (Ed.). *The 1955 University of Utah Research Conference
    on the Identification of Creative Scientific Talent*. Salt Lake
    City: University of Utah Press, 1956.

————. *The 1957 University of Utah Research Conference on the
    Identification of Creative Scientific Talent*. Salt Lake City:
    University of Utah Press, 1958.

————. *The 1959 University of Utah Research Conference on the
    Identification of Creative Scientific Talent*. Salt Lake City:
    University of Utah Press, 1959.

Wallace, H. "Tests of Creative Thinking and Sales Performance in a Large Department Store." In Torrance, E.P. (Ed.). *Creativity: Second Minnesota Conference on Gifted Children*. Minneapolis: Center for Continuation Study, University of Minnesota, 1960.

The following are the references for the Manual for the Torrance Tests of Creative Thinking and for the various background sources listed in the manual.

Torrance, E.P. "Examples and Rationales of Test Tasks for Assessing Creative Abilities." *Journal of Creative Behavior* 2 (1968): 165-178.

————. *Guiding Creative Talent*. Englewood Cliffs, NJ: Prentice-Hall, 1962. Chapters 2, 3, Appendix.

————. "Minnesota Studies of Creative Behavior: National and International Extensions." *Journal of Creative Behavior* 1 (1967): 137-154.

————. *Rewarding Creative Behavior: Experiments in Classroom Creativity*. Englewood Cliffs, NJ: Prentice-Hall, 1965. Chapter 3 and Appendix A.

————. "Scientific Views of Creativity and Factors Affecting Its Growth." *Daedalus* 94 (Summer 1965): 663-681.

————. *Torrance Tests of Creative Thinking: Directions Manual and Scoring Guide*. (For Figural and Verbal tests separately--1974 Revisions.) Bensenville, IL: Scholastic Testing Service, 1974.

Torrance, E.P., and Aliotti, N.C. "Sex Differences in Levels of Performance and Test-Retest Reliability on the Torrance Tests of Creative Thinking Ability." *Journal of Creative Behavior* 3 (1969): 52-57.

Few sex differences have been found below the fourth grade level in the U.S. After the fourth grade, girls excel over boys on all verbal tests and on elaboration in figural tests. Boys do better than girls on figural originality. This is in keeping with the findings that boys are aware of their sex identification in the first grade but not during the second, third, and early fourth grade, which covers the period of latency. Fifth grade children are aware of their sexual identification which their behavior on the tests reflects.

When the question is raised, whether the obtained sex differences are biological or sociocultural, the authors reason from data collected in India that the differences are sociocultural. A study is presented of fifth grade boys and girls. The fifth grade was selected because sex identifications appear at this grade level and differences in creative functioning should be obtained. The results indicated that girls do better than boys on all verbal tests. With figural tests, the boys do better than girls on flexibility and originality but the girls do better on elaboration. With regard to test-retest reliability one week apart, the boys show greater stability than the girls, especially on the figural tests. Test-retest reliability is "reasonably satisfactory, somewhat more satisfactory for the verbal than the figural measures and somewhat more satisfactory for boys than for girls."

The fact that girls do better on the verbal forms of the test is attributed to the fact that verbal development is stressed more for boys than for girls. Girls do better on figural elaboration because women in our society are expected to make things fancy and to work on details. Boys are expected to be freer and, therefore, do better on originality. Thus, differences in gender on the tests can be attributed to differences in the cultural treatment of boys and girls and to the ways in which children identify with the sex roles of their society.

The authors suggest that an interesting study for the future would be the investigation of how sex role identification affects creative functioning. Interesting questions include, "Do girls with strong female identification perform better on verbal tasks and on figural elaboration than do girls with weak female identification? Do boys with strong male identification perform better than boys with weak male identification on the originality measures?"

Torrance, E.P. "Prediction of Adult Creative Achievement Among High School Seniors." *Gifted Child Quarterly* 13 (1969): 223-239.

The material covered in this section summarizes the results obtained in a follow-up study, conducted in 1966, of 69 (33 male and 36 female) University of Minnesota High School seniors who had taken the Torrance Tests of Creative Thinking in 1959. The mean IQ of these tests, both on the Lorge-Thorndike Intelligence Tests and the Stanford-Binet, was 121. Only two students had IQs below 100.

In the follow-up study, the students (many of whom were still in graduate school or in the armed forces) responded to a checklist of creative achievements including: poems, stories, songs written and/or published; books written and/or published; changes in philosophy of life; original suggestions in work situation; grants received; patentable devices, inventions, etc. An index of quality of achievement was obtained from five judges (all advanced students of creativity), as well as an index of quantity and an index of originality The data were available for 46 of the original 69 students. Interscorer reliability was high. The results claimed that intelligence correlated significantly with the quality score only. Originality and flexibility correlated with three criteria: quality of creative achievements, quantity of creative achievements, and creativeness of aspirations. Fluency correlated with the first two, while elaboration only with the second. High school achievement and peer nominations creativity criteria while in school did not correlate at all.

The author concludes that "The evidence arising form this study strongly supports the suggestion that measures of thinking ability be given consideration in selecting high school seniors with the greatest promise for creative achievement. In this study, those who scored highest on the measure of originality as high school seniors had not only amassed an extraordinary record of creative achievement in literature, science, music and art, but they had laid strong foundations for future creative achievement. They were well on their way to attaining their doctorates in some of the most distinguished universities in the world."

Torrance, E.P. *Rewarding Creative Behavior: Experiments in Classroom Creativity.* Englewood Cliffs, NJ: Prentice-Hall, 1965.

Chapter 3 contains a brief survey of the history of attempts to measure creativity as well as a statement of the problems involved in measuring creativity and the author's attempts to deal with these problems while he was at the University of Minnesota. Appendix A contains descriptions of the instruments and the behaviors studied.

Torrance, E.P. "Predictive Validity of the Torrance Tests of Creative Thinking." *Journal of Creative Behavior* 6 (1972): 236-252.

This paper contains major short-range and long-range predictive validity studies of the Torrance Tests of Creative Thinking. It also contains the report of a 12-year follow-up study with high school students that was begun in 1959.

A list of nine short-range studies, ranging from one week to nine months, is presented. It includes an array of subjects, including: gifted 4th graders, 2-6 graders, 5-6 graders, ages 9 to 12, high school business teachers, graduate students in educational psychology, high school students, and elementary school teachers. The numbers of teachers in the groups ranged from 12 to 125. The kind of creative behavior predicted included: humor and fantasy, creative ideas about science toys and uses, originality of imaginative stories, differential response to curriculum tasks, provocative classroom questions, subject matter tests of productive thinking, creative classroom behavior, creative questions in science, and teaching success in inner-city schools.

In these validity studies, Torrance has not included studies in which grades and achievement scores on multiple-choice school achievement tests have been used. While the results of some of these studies have been positive and others have been negative, Torrance regards them as irrelevant since they do not call upon creative abilities. Work which is based on a misconception of the tests is also regarded as irrelevant; one such work is discussed.

Five long-range prediction studies are presented in tabular form and discussed. The samples of subjects included here are: junior elementary education majors, 12th graders, 7th graders, 2-4 graders, 7-12 graders. The number of students in these studies ranged from 16 to 236 and the number of years for the studies ranged from 5 to 12. The kinds of predicted creative behavior included: creative teaching behavior; ratings of creativity of highest achievement, quantity of creative achievements; creativeness of aspirations; creative achievement out of school; achievements in creative arts and science; and quality of creative achievements. The predictive correlations in these studies ranged from .46 to .62 (all significant at better than the .01 level).

The major long-term prediction study reported in this paper involved the Torrance Tests of Creative Thinking which was begun in 1959. The participants were the entire enrollment of the University of Minnesota High School (including grades 7-12). The majority of these students came from professional and business families although there was also a large number of students from a less affluent neighborhood which lacked a school building. The mean IQ of the

total group on the Lorge-Thorndike Test was 118 and the mean percentile rank on the Iowa Tests of Educational Development was 84 on
national norms.

The tests for this group consisted of: Ask Questions, Guess
Causes, Guess Consequences, Product Improvement, Unusual Use of an
Improved Product, Unusual Use of a Common Object, and Circles. In
1959, the tests were scored according to the guide available at that
time; later, in 1961, they were rescored for originality according
to the newer guide.

For the criterion for creative achievements, an index was developed based on the following: "Poems, stories, songs written;
Poems, stories, songs published; Books written; Books published;
Radio and television scripts or performances; Original research
designs developed; Philosophy of life changed; In-service training
for co-workers created; Original changes in work situation suggested;
Research grants received; Scientific papers published in professional
journals; Business enterprises initiated; Patentable devices invented;
Literary awards or prizes received for creative writing, musical
composition, art, etc." (This is a revised list. From a previously accepted list, the following were dropped: "subscribed to professional magazine or journal, learned a new language, gave a public
speech, took up a new hobby, changed religious affiliation, elected
or appointed to a student office, joined professional club or organization.")

Three criterion measures were used: (1) For a measure of quantity
of creative achievements, the number of creative achievements listed
or checked by the student was indicated. (2) Five judges used a
10-point rating scale to rate the level of creativeness reflected in
three of the most creative achievements listed by the student.
(3) A similar measure was obtained for the creativeness of aspirations listed by the students. These are the aspirations that the
subjects had for the future, assuming that they had the necessary
talent, training, and opportunity.

Only the 12-year follow-up will be presented here, although the
earlier seven-year follow-up is also presented in the article.
Because there are many similarities between the two studies, anyone
interested in comparing them should read the original article. The
results of the 12-year follow-up indicate the following: (1) In combining the scores on the creativity test battery to predict the combined creativity criteria, a correlation of .51 was obtained for the
total sample. However, the creative achievements of the women were
less predictable than the achievements of the men. (2) Data for the
relationships between the creativity criteria and the creativity
test variables, as well as the IQ scores for the Lorge-Thorndike
Tests, are presented in tabular form for both males and females
separately. These data indicate that, for both men and women, the
creativity tests all correlate significantly with the criteria for
males and females separately. For males, the correlations range
from .27 to .45 and for females, they range from .25 to .41.
(3) The correlations are a "shade lower" for the women than they are
for the men. (4) The IQ scores are found to correlate significantly
with the creativity criteria for the males. (5) For the females,
the IQ scores correlate lower (as was the case with the creativity
scores) with the criteria. Thus, the only non-significant correlation appears in the relationship between IQ and the Quantity cri-

terion for females. The only correlation that was significant at
the .05 level (rather than the .01 level as in all the other instances) was the relationship between IQ and future aspiration for
the females. (6) Thus, the creativity measures did better in predicting the women's creativity scores than did the IQ measures.
But, the IQ measures and the creativity measures did equally well
in predicting the criteria for the males.

Torrance then raises the question of how well one of the variables,
originality, predicted the criterion when calculating the relationships for each grade level. The first time the study was undertaken,
there were students from grades 7-12 so that when criterion data
were collected twelve years later, the 7th graders were 25 years
old and the 12th graders were 31. The results of this analysis
indicate that the correlations between "originality" and the three
creativity criteria (quantity, quality, and aspiration) for the 9th,
10th, 11th, and 12th graders are significant and at about the same
level for the total population. The poorer success in predictions
for the 7th and 8th graders could be attributed to a variety of
factors. Perhaps the 7th graders were in some kind of a slump in
their creative functioning as they had done less well on the creativity tests in the 7th than in the 6th grade. Of greater importance might be the fact that a large proportion of the 7th and 8th
graders were either in military service or in college. Many of them
had undergone a period of rebellion or exploration and had only recently begun "an achievement orientation to life."

Torrance concludes that these results, for a fairly advantaged
group of high school students who had had the opportunity to develop
their creative abilities, indicate that the creativity tests can
predict "real-life adult creative achievements." It is doubtful
that such favorable results would be found for a population severely
limited in opportunity and/or freedom." It is to be expected that
the differences between the more and less creative subjects will
widen as more time elapses.

Torrance, E.P. "Are the Torrance Tests of Creative Thinking Biased
Against or in Favor of 'Disadvantaged' Groups?" *Gifted Child Quarterly* 15 (1971): 75-80.

Early experience showed that economically deprived, black, and
other minority group children did as well on Torrance's tests as
children from other groups. Continued studies on racial and socioeconomic groups by others, which Torrance cites, have maintained
and supported the early findings. The author raises the question
of whether the tests will predict the achievements of adults from
their performances as children. Basically, Torrance says that the
tests do predict for advantaged groups but will only predict for
disadvantaged groups if there is some "powerful intervention."

Torrance, E.P. "Misperceptions about Creativity in Gifted Education:
Removing the Limits on Learning." In Kaplan, S.N., et al. *Curricula
for the Gifted: Selected Proceedings of the First International Conference on Curricula for the Gifted*. Ventura, CA: Ventura County
Superintendent of Schools, March 1982. 59-74.

with Guilford's presidential address to the American Psychological Association in 1950, for there has been research in Western countries in this area since the late 1880s and earlier in some Eastern cultures. 2. There is no academic or artistic content in teaching materials designed for creative thinking and problem-solving. Torrance advocates teaching creativity techniques with course content. 3. It is not true that creativity research has been concerned almost exclusively with divergent thinking, for researchers have long said that divergent thinking is not all there is to creativity. 4. Some may believe that creative thinking is a rational process while others say that creative thinking is something wild and unstructured, involving even psychic abilities. Torrance says that great persistence and discipline are involved in creativity although it goes beyond the rational. 5. It is a misperception that the drop in SAT scores is related to the teaching of creativity in education. There is nothing in research studies to support this. Moreover, there is a study which shows that training in creative dramatics increases reading comprehension more than instruction in remedial reading. 6. It is not true that practice skills and creativity are antithetical; no one would deny the importance of drill and practice. 7. The claim that creativity tests have no validity is denied by Torrance who presents many studies to support his position. 8. Another misperception is that the longer the time period for which one tries to predict behavior, the less accurate are the predictions. Torrance says that, while this may be true for some tests, it is not true for his tests of creativity. 9. It is inappropriate to use creativity test scores for screening in special gifted programs. Torrance presents research evidence to indicate that creatively gifted students who fall short of the IQ screening criterion for giftedness (an IQ of 130 or higher) achieve just as well as those who pass this IQ criterion. 10. Torrance presents research data to refute the misperception that black and other disadvantaged children who are identified as creatively gifted are not really gifted.

   Torrance concludes this paper by saying how important it is to remove the limits on learning. "Serious limits have been placed on gifted education through our identification methods. In general, our search for giftedness has been too passive, too white, and too middle class. We have been too obsessed by a single concept of giftedness and have been too slow in adopting a multi-criteria approach to identification. Such an approach must be accompanied by multi-talents teaching, the application of multiple evaluation criteria to educational outcomes, more open-ended educational experiences self-directed learning, and instructional methods providing opportunities for the use of modality, thinking, and learning style strengths. If the curriculum is truly future-oriented, many unnecessary restraints on learning will vanish. More curricular attention must be given to helping students enlarge, enrich, and sharpen their images of the future."

Houtz, J.; Rosenfield, S.; and Tetenbaum, T. "Creative Thinking in
   Gifted Elementary School Children." *Gifted Child Quarterly* 22
   (1978): 513-519.

   This study posits that if children demonstrated strengths and weaknesses across a wide range of tasks rather than consistently high

performance, then there would be a need for creativity training.
Two hundred and thirty-three subjects in grades 2 to 6 at the Hunter
College Elementary School participated in this study.

A 7-point creative problem-solving model was utilized which tested
the following characteristics: (1) sensitivity to problems, (2) preparation activities, (3) analysis of problem elements, (4) reorganization of problem elements, (5) idea generation, (6) foreseeing consequences, and (7) evaluation of ideas. Tests for the above tasks
were selected from Torrance's and others' tests. Achievement test
data and other pertinent test information were also available.

The results revealed that: (1) Creative thinking task performance
reached a plateau from the fourth grade on. (2) Growth on problem-
solving tasks continued through the sixth grade. (3) Individual
variations in task performance were obtained. Children showed
strengths and weaknesses, the range of which was greater in the
higher grades. (4) There is a need for training in creativity and
problem-solving skills for the gifted. (5) Achievement is more
closely related to a high tolerance for ambiguity. Self-esteem is
more critical in problem-solving situations. (6) If one has superior
intellectual ability, it does not guarantee that one will have
superior creativity or problem-solving ability.

Rieger, M.P. "Life Patterns and Coping Strategies in High and Low
Creative Women." *Journal for the Education of the Gifted* 6 (1983):
98-110.

The predictive validity of the Torrance Tests of Creative Thinking
was investigated in a 21-year follow-up study by the author. Data
were first collected when the women were in grades 3-5. Those women
(N=42) whose scores fell above the median were called high creatives
and those whose scores fell below the median were called low creatives (N=41). Twenty-one years later, questionnaires were sent to
the women to obtain data on marital status, educational and career
history, sources of support and domestic coping strategies, long-
range goals, and satisfaction with life. Measures of high school
and post-high school achievements were also obtained. The latter
served as the criterion and included: "quantity of high school creative achievements; quantity of post-high school creative achievements;
quantity of self-actualizing, publicly unrecognized creative activities; quality of creative achievements; and creativeness of aspirations for the future."

Using a composite creativity index to predict the combined creativity criteria, a canonical correlation of .69 was obtained. Thus,
the high creatives are regarded as fulfilling their potentials to
a greater extent than is true of the low creatives. Other items
that differentiated the high creatives from the low creatives were
that they had a stronger sense of personal independence and they
were more likely to be unmarried (never married, or divorced), to
marry at a later age, to have fewer children, and to have more education. Career commitment, although intense among the lows, was
particularly so among the highs. The highs focused on both career
responsibilities and family while lows focused on one or the other.
The highs also opted for more egalitarian and less sex-typed roles
in their domestic lives.

The results presented here are regarded as providing stronger
support for the Torrance tests than a related study of high school
students (Torrance, 1972). For the women in the high school study,
the canonical correlation was .46 while in this study, the correlation was .69.

Suggestions for Further Reading

Torrance, E.P. "Creative Young Women in Today's World." *Exceptional Children* 38 (1972): 597-603.

Critique

Haddon, F.A., and Lytton, H. "Teaching Approach and the Development
of Divergent Thinking Abilities in Primary Schools." *British Journal
of Educational Psychology* 38 (1968): 171-180.

In the introduction to this paper the authors make the following
points: (1) There is strong evidence that those who score high on
tests of divergent thinking "will be particularly fertile in creative original production in their own life situation." (2) There
is little evidence that those who score high on convergent thinking
will lack creativity. (3) "The best way of looking at this question
probably is to regard high scores on divergent thinking as an indication of lack of anxiety about non-conformist responses, a necessary
but not a sufficient condition for creative work. To avoid undue
claims, we have used the term 'divergent thinking' rather than
'creativity' throughout." (4) Divergent thinking abilities can be
distinguished from convergent abilities. (5) Divergent thinking
abilities may provide some new insights into cognitive functioning.
(6) Tests of divergent thinking may supplement the usual intelligence
tests. (7) Tests of divergent thinking may provide information as
to "the type rather than the level of future performance." (8) This
model of cognitive abilities implies that divergent and convergent
thinking are complementary aspects or different styles of intellectual functioning.

From this introduction, they then proceed with their hypotheses.
Their interest is in the effects of particular school situations on
divergent thinking and they cite a number of studies. For their
own study, the authors selected two kinds of schools. One is the
"Formal or traditional school which places emphasis upon convergent
thinking and authoritative learning and the Informal or progressive
school, where the emphasis is upon self-initiated learning and creative activities." Another is an informal school "in which children
move freely, both within the classroom and in the school generally.
Particularly noticeable is the freedom of access to the libraries
and the extent to which children work in them unsupervised. The
Formal schools are not unfriendly but one senses a tighter rein and
a firmer directive. Class work is more in evidence." Two hundred
and eleven pupils, 11 to 12 years of age, of all ability levels but
matched for verbal reasoning quotient (as a measure of intelligence)
and socioeconomic background participated in this study.

It was predicted that divergent thinking scores (measured by Torrance's Minnesota Tests of Creative Thinking) would be higher for
the children from the Informal schools because this type of school

was thought to encourage the development of personality traits associated with divergency. This prediction was fulfilled.

Another hypothesis that was studied was the relationship between
intelligence and divergent thinking. It was predicted that the correlation between the two would decrease as the intelligence of each
sub-group rose. However, it should be noted that the correlation
between intelligence and divergent thinking was higher in the Informal schools because they apparently encouraged the development
of both sets of abilities.

Other hypotheses related test scores to the students' sociometric
status. It was hypothesized that the very values of the school
would affect how the high intelligence and high divergent thinking
pupil would be accepted. The results essentially supported Getzels
and Jackson. Relationship between intelligence and sociometric choice
was positive and negative for the relationship between intelligence
and divergent thinking. In one school, the relationships were reversed.

In their concluding paragraph, the authors point to the importance
of the teacher's approach. They say, "it would seem that it is
based on the teacher's confidence in the child's ability to think
adventurously and in new directions, which in turn, will determine
the child's estimation of himself and of his abilities. If the
teacher can enter into the child's thinking, if she is prepared to
let work develop in unexpected directions according to the child's
needs and interests, if she can find and express genuine pleasure
in the child's efforts, then self-initiated learning can be developed.
It is in this climate that divergent thinking abilities are seen to
flourish."

Haddon, F.A., and Lytton, H. "Primary Education and Divergent Thinking Abilities--Four Years." *British Journal of Education* 41 (1971):
136-147.

This study is a follow-up of the Haddon and Lytton (1968) study.
One hundred and fifty-one of the 211 children were traced and the
battery of divergent thinking tests administered in 1968 were re-
administered together with some other tests and questionnaires.
At the time of this testing, the children were close to completing
their four years of secondary schooling. The results included the
following: (1) Much of the variance in the divergent scores, particularly the verbal ones, was accounted for by the intelligence measure.
(2) There was also an effect attributed to the primary school attended. Children from the informal schools still had the higher
divergent thinking scores. (3) The effect that was obtained could
not be attributed to the secondary school. (4) The measure of intelligence was a better predictor of scores on the verbal divergent
tests at 15 than the verbal divergent thinking tests predicted.
The intelligence test measure was only marginally inferior as a predictor of the total divergent thinking score. (5) Comparison of
test scores at 11 and 15 showed an increase in divergent thinking
scores over time. "Overall the divergent tests behaved like measures
of cognitive abilities which are both fairly stable in relative
ranking and show reasonable development in raw scores." (6) There
is a relationship between socioeconomic status and divergent thinking scores. (7) There was no significant relationship between

divergent thinking and course or career choices. The difference
between this finding and that reported by Hudson (1966) that divergent thinkers would gravitate to art subjects and convergent thinkers
to science subjects was not sustained. This might be accounted for
by the fact that in Hudson's study, pupils were classified as
"divergers" or "convergers" depending on the relative standings
both pupils had on the tests. In this study, divergers and convergers were defined in terms of the level of their ability. While
these findings are not directly counter to Hudson's, they suggest
that Hudson's findings should not be interpreted simplistically.

The use of teacher ratings as an external criterion with the divergent thinking tests yielded a correlation of .286, "and so there
is some validation of the tests as measuring qualities recognised
as creativity by teachers of English." No such correlations were
obtained with the Torrance Interest Blank. The data reported here
do not bear out the Wallach and Wing (1969) data which were collected on college students.

Insofar as personality is concerned, no correlation was found
between divergent thinking and personality data. "There was, in
fact, no evidence that high performers on the DTA tests were perceived by their teachers to be·in any way different in personality
from other pupils, nor was there any suggestion that high divergent
ability is associated with an anti-authority stand."

In concluding their paper the authors say, "If ... the primary
school is a formative influence in the development of divergent
abilities, and if, as we have demonstrated in this research, this
development is sufficiently permanent to be measurable after four
years of secondary schooling, then the role of the primary school
in determining pupils' abilities at later stages of education takes
on increasing importance."

Tannenbaum, A.J. *Gifted Children: Psychological and Educational Perspectives.* New York: Macmillan, 1983. 273-277.

The author's review of the Torrance battery makes the following
points.

1. A study of the interrelatedness among the subtests (discriminant validity) found an average correlation of .77 which is high
among the scores on fluency, flexibility, and originality. Elaboration appears to be unrelated to the other measures.

2. The intercorrelations for trait consistency, the extent to
which fluency correlates with fluency on each of the subtests, are
fairly low.

3. Another study by Torrance that is discussed focuses on the
predictive value of the battery. On the basis of this study,
Torrance reported that his tests were equal to or better than intelligence measures in forecasting later achievements. Moreover,
it was reported that the Torrance tests' predictive validity improved as the subjects mature. Tannenbaum commented that this may
occur because, as the individual matures he/she becomes more differentiated. Tannenbaum also notes that the creativity tests and the
other predictors were better in predicting achievements in writing,
science, medicine, and leadership than in music, visual arts, business, and industry.

4. Two other studies with contradictory results are cited. One study was a reanalysis of the data obtained by the first. Cropley combined the scores from six of the tests into one score, and from four criterion measures he also combined the criteria and found rather high correlations between the two. However, Jordan reanalyzed the findings and came up with contradictory results. He found errors in Cropley's procedure for determining the predictive validity of the tests.

5. Tannenbaum takes note of Torrance's follow-up study and reports that this is one study with consistently positive results. However, careful and thorough replications are recommended.

6. Torrance cites several studies to show that there is no bias in favor of racial or socioeconomic factors in his work. Tannenbaum's comment is: "It is hard to imagine any test of creative performance, let alone potential, in which the results are entirely unaffected by hereditary factors or by forces in the environment that are so prominent in determining racial or socioeconomic status.... What else is there to account for human variability? Torrance does not specify these factors, but he implies that, while they are potent enough to account for individual differences in test performance, they do not discriminate against racial and socioeconomic groups and thus preserve the bias-free nature of the measures."

Suggestions for Further Reading

Cicirelli, V.G. "Form of the Relationship Between Creativity, IQ, and Academic Achievement." *Journal of Educational Psychology* 56 (1965): 303-308.

Crockenberg, S. "Creativity Tests: A Boon or Boondoggle for Education?" *Review of Educational Research* 42 (1972): 27-45.

Cropley, A.J. "Creativity and Intelligence." *British Journal of Educational Psychology* 36 (1966): 259-266.

Jordan, L.A. "Use of Canonical Analysis in Cropley's 'A Five-Year Longitudinal Study of the Validity of Creativity Tests.'" *Developmental Psychology* 11 (1975): 1-3.

Torrance, E.P. "Creativity Research in Education: Still Alive." In Taylor, I.A., and Getzels, J.W. (Eds.). *Perspectives in Creativity*. Chicago: Aldine Publishing Company, 1975. 278-296.

―――. "Predicting the Creativity of Elementary School Children (1958-80)--and the Teacher Who 'Made a Difference.'" *Gifted Child Quarterly* 25 (1981): 55-61.

Vernon, P.E.; Adamson, G.; and Vernon, D.F. *The Psychology and Education of Gifted Children*. Boulder, CO: Westview Press, 1977. 216pp.

The four variables for which the Torrance Tests are scored "intercorrelate so highly that there seems little point in trying to distinguish them."

Wallach, M.A., and Kogan, N. *Modes of Thinking in Young Children: A Study of the Creativity-Intelligence Distinction*. New York: Holt,

Rinehart and Winston, 1965. 357pp.

In their critique of Torrance's work, the authors make several
points. A report by Torrance and Gowan is cited as reporting that
the verbal and nonverbal creativity measures do not correlate
highly, indeed they are low and "appear largely independent." Thus,
from Wallach and Kogan's point of view, there are two kinds of creativity. Then the authors cite data from the Wechsler Intelligence
Scale for Children in which verbal and performance data are correlated. "In contrast, the Torrance group reports that verbal and
performance indices of 'creativity' are largely independent. Here
is evidence, then, to the effect that the creativity domain as defined by the Torrance group does not possess the kind of generality
characteristic of the intelligence domain. In the light of such
information, it becomes a rather serious distortion for the Torrance
group continually to treat 'creativity' as if it were the same *type*
of psychological concept as 'intelligence.' On the evidence they
describe, the creativity concept already breaks down into two relatively independent forms, one visual, the other verbal."

In other studies cited, Wallach and Kogan say that a composite
score was used as a measure of creativity and these related to an
IQ measure from which age has been partialled out. But age has not
been partialled out of the creativity measures. Under such conditions, when intelligence and creativity are related with data for
which there is a reasonably extensive age range, the degree of relationship between creativity and intelligence will be underestimated.
Studies of the Torrance tests are not presented so that it is impossible to determine to what extent they intercorrelate with each
other and with intelligence. But, since the tests are very much
the same as those in the Getzels and Jackson study, it would appear
that the tests are not really independent of intelligence.

Evaluation of Tests

Richert, E.S., with Alvino, J.J., and McDonnel, R.C. *National Report
on Identification: Assessment and Recommendations for Comprehensive
Identification of Gifted and Talented Youth.* Sewell, NJ: Educational
Improvement Center-South, 1982a. 391.

The Torrance Tests of Creative Thinking (1966) is designed for the
range of grades from kindergarten through graduate school. The test
takes 45 minutes and no special training is needed to administer it.
It is individually administered in kindergarten through the third
grade and then it can be group administered for grades four through
graduate school.

The test measures creativity "by assessing fluency, flexibility,
originality, and elaboration." The tests are verbal and involve
the use of words in the following activities: "Asking, guessing
causes, guessing consequences, product improvement, unusual uses,
and unusual questions." Normative data provided for each subtest
concern fluency, flexibility, originality, and elaboration. The standardization group consisted of 13,663 students from kindergarten
through graduate school on both forms of the test in schools throughout the U.S.

Interscorer reliability data are provided as are data for the reliability of the alternate forms and test-retest reliability. Validity data are provided for content, construct, and concurrent and predictive validities. Scoring is subjective and information contained here may have to be supplemented by information from other tests. The Verbal Test is not recommended for students with linguistic problems or language deficiencies.

Richert, E.S., with Alvino, J.J., and McDonnel, R.C. *National Report on Identification: Assessment and Recommendations for Comprehensive Identification of Gifted and Talented Youth.* Sewell, NJ: Educational Improvement Center-South, 1982b. 390. Figural Test.

The Figural Test of the Torrance Tests of Creative Thinking (1966) is a group administered test designed for students in the range from kindergarten through graduate school. It requires 30 minutes but no special training for administration except a thorough understanding of creativity and the test.

The tests "measure creativity by assessing fluency, flexibility, originality, and elaboration." Creative thinking is measured by "picture construction, picture completion, and parallel lines." There are two forms of the test and normative data are provided for grades ranging from kindergarten through graduate school on fluency, flexibility, originality, and elaboration. The standardization consisted of 19,111 students throughout the U.S.

Interscorer reliability is reported, as is alternative form reliability and test-retest reliability. Content, construct, concurrent, and predictive validities are reported. Scoring tends to be subjective "and users need to be aware of those aspects of creativity not being measured in order to supplement information from the tests." As cautions, this report points out that reliability and validity are limited and this test "assesses creativity only for figural interpretation of fluency, flexibility, originality and elaboration."

Buros, O.K. *The Seventh Mental Measurements Yearbook.* Highland Park, NJ: The Gryphon Press, 1972. 831–842.

A number of persons reviewed the Torrance Tests of Creative Thinking, Research Edition, 1966, and their comments are included below. The reviews have been published in various sources; to find these sources one should consult the yearbook. Statements about the characteristics of the test (e.g., the variables measured, etc.) are not presented unless the reviewer has a specific comment to make about the characteristic.

L.L. Baird writes that the test manual says that the tests attempt to assess various activities in terms of Guilford's divergent thinking factors. He further writes that, "no evidence is provided for any relation with Guilford's model, and no effort is made to seek logical connections with Guilford's work. (No correlations of the Torrance Test of Creative Thinking (TTCT) with the Guilford battery are reported.) In general the tests seem to be derived from Torrance's long thinking about creativity and tend to be eclectic, rather than based on a systematic theory of creativity.... Some of the rationales given for the scales are rather vague and discursive.

The relation between a scale score and the interpretation provided for the score in some cases seems to be based more on the rationale for the scale than on the evidence provided for it."

In discussing the reliability and validity, the author says, with regard to the former, that the scales have adequate reliability and, with regard to the latter, that the test measures behaviors that are congruent with the literature on creativity. The interpretation of test scores, when they are based on restricted samples, tend to be, and have to be, tentative. "The interpretations provided for the scale scores are clear, but seem to go beyond the evidence presented in the manual." The scales are supposed to measure independent traits but the evidence available suggests, "that there is a great deal of overlap in the scales."

In summary, the reviewer says that the TTCT is useful for future research and that work with it has already made a significant contribution to the creativity literature. "However, without better norms, studies of predictive validity, and anchoring of the test to real-life creative behavior, the TTCT should probably be used for assessing of an individual's creative potential with only great caution. If the author and publisher could make these changes ... the test could be a powerful and useful tool for research and practice, thus joining Torrance's other significant contributions to our understanding of creativity."

R.L. Thorndike believes that since the scores for fluency, flexibility, and originality are all obtained from the same data, they are going to be intercorrelated. He presents evidence in support of this. "Thus, the evidence of consistently different meaning for the fluency, flexibility, and originality scores is almost vanishingly small." Hence, the author wonders whether it is wise to use separate scores for each of the variables or whether a single score on each form of the test would be adequate. Perhaps future research with the tests will make it possible to collect the necessary data to determine whether the tests "merit their somewhat ambitious title."

M.A. Wallach believes it is more parsimonious to assume that correlation of test scores on fluency with peer judgment of fluency may be attributed to general intelligence alone. Similarly, the relationships between the TTCT and academic achievement can be related, not to creativity, but to general intelligence. "In sum, we have been able to find little evidence in support of an interpretation of the Torrance tests that would construe them as 'creative thinking' rather than simply as 'thinking.'" The Torrance battery may serve as a substitute for a general intelligence test. The title may therefore be misleading because the creativity label would create false expectations. "Furthermore, the Torrance materials for assessing fluency may represent an approach that has the potential for defining a considerably different kind of talent than is caught in the net of the general intelligence concept, but this would constitute a very different kind of emphasis than the Torrance battery provides."

J.L. Holland writes that the TTCT has useful reliability and validity for research purposes. The tests need to be linked to other tests of originality and to criteria of social relevance to "become powerful and valuable tools for research and practice."

R. Hoepfner believes that the intercorrelation of the variables indicate that there is overlap and nonindependence of test scores. The 8 possible scores obtained do not cover the universe of all abilities involved in creative thinking. The predictive validity of the tests is in line with other tests and it is low. Because creative thinking as measured by the tests may be affected by personality and motivational factors, the stability of the scores may be affected and hence reliabilities are variable. Perhaps major improvements that are promised will be fulfilled "so that the revision may offer theoretical, scientific, and practical values not yet incorporated into this bold venture into the mystery of creativity."

Wallach, M.A. *The Intelligence/Creativity Distinction.* New York: General Learning Press, 1971. 1-32.

The author presents the theoretical rationale for the Wallach and Kogan (1965) study which focused on the importance of permissive conditions for obtaining the lack of relationship between ideational fluency and intelligence. Evidence is first presented in support of the lack of relationship, but when additional evidence is surveyed, the author (p. 14) says, "contrary to the original Wallach-Kogan interpretation, a permissive context for assessing ideational fluency is not necessary to demonstrate its independence from intelligence." There is the qualifier that the lack of relationship between ideational fluency and intelligence may hold from "around the middle to the upper end of the distribution" of intelligence.

Turning to the relationship between ideational fluency and creativity in real life, the author draws upon his other study with Wing (Wallach and Wing, 1969) in which ideational fluency predicted "a range of talented accomplishments in the nonacademic environment. Intelligence, while predicting academic forms of achievement did not predict these other kinds of attainments. Since the latter seem to denote activities, some of which should qualify as what we mean by manifestations of creativity, evidence has been provided suggesting that ideational fluency—as distinct from intelligence—does play a role in creativity." The author is then quick to add that "This role—while present to a statistically significant degree—is nevertheless a small one. Presence or absence of creative attainments depends on many other considerations besides ideational fluency."

In the course of the paper, the author is critical of attempts to learn about creativity by studying "noncriterial correlates of ideational fluency" and of trying to learn about creativity by studying ways to encourage ideational fluency.

The author concludes with the following: "We may conclude, then, that within the upper part of the intellective skills range intelligence test scores and grades on standard academic subject matter are not effective signs as to who will manifest the strongest creative attainments in nonacademic contexts. Empirical documentation of this relative unpredictability of creativity criteria from intellective skills data suggests that a separation between these two realms genuinely exists."

WALLACH AND KOGAN

Wallach, M.A., and Kogan, N. *Modes of Thinking in Young Children: A Study of the Creativity-Intelligence Distinction.* New York: Holt, Rinehart and Winston, 1965. 357pp.

In the first chapter of this book, the authors review and severely criticize other studies in this area, specifically, Guilford, Getzels and Jackson, and Torrance. Many of their criticisms of these other works have been presented elsewhere, where these other studies are considered. The authors write: "The measures that have been construed as indicators of creativity are not indicators of some single psychological dimension parallel to and distinct from the dimension of intelligence defined by conventional intelligence test indices. On the basis of this evidence, then, there is questionable warrant for proposing the very conceptualization which most researchers have proposed: that creativity is not intelligence, and that individual differences in creativity possess the same degree of psychological pervasiveness as individual differences in general intelligence. This is a rather discouraging conclusion to have to draw."

To try to rectify the problem, the authors decided to undertake a new try at conceptual analysis and to develop appropriate measurement techniques. Their analysis of the work done in the creativity area led them to the following conclusions: (1) "We are suggesting, then, that if we arrange a situation in such a manner that only appropriate associations are provided by the individual, greater creativity should be indicated by the ability to produce more associations and to produce more that are unique." Their approach is quite associative and very much influenced by Mednick's theory and the Remote Associates Test (RAT). But they do not go all the way with Mednick for they believe that the RAT involves convergent thinking and also that the approach is too artificial in placing the experimenter, who knows the one correct answer, in an omniscient state. (2) Again influenced by Mednick and others who showed the effects of time on the nature of associative responses produced, the authors opt for obtaining responses in a relaxed game-like atmosphere rather than a test atmosphere.

The subjects were fifth grade children of 10 to 11 years of age in an elementary school. They were middle class with more than half of them coming from families where the father was a business manager, executive, sales representative, or accountant. There were others whose fathers were professionals. Some 6% came from upper-level blue collar occupations. In sum, the children came from professional and managerial backgrounds, they were Protestant and white, and in a New England school. There were 151: 70 boys and 81 girls.

Two women in their early twenties collected the data over a 6 to 7 week period. Care was taken to have the administration and the teachers avoid any reference to tests to facilitate the development of a game-like atmosphere. During the first two weeks, the experimenters gathered observational data on the children. The children became accustomed to the experimenters which reinforced the atmosphere that the experimenters tried to develop.

Some seventeen procedures were administered. Three subtests of the Wechsler Intelligence Scale for Children were administered close to the end of the testing schedule: Vocabulary, Picture Arrangement, and Block Design. These were selected primarily because they correlated so well with the total intelligence score. In addition, the experiment included the School and College Ability Tests to provide measures of verbal and quantitative aptitude. The Sequential Tests of Educational Progress was also used for its indices of academic achievement. In total, there were 10 indices of general intelligence covering verbal, visual, and quantitative skills which are consistent with the usual measures of "intelligence," "aptitude," and "academic achievement."

To collect the creativity data (with scores for number and uniqueness of responses) five tests were used: Instances, Alternate Uses, Similarities, Pattern Meanings, and Line Meanings. They also included verbal and visual materials. The tests were administered in a relaxed atmosphere and the subjects were encouraged to take their time.

The results indicated that the 10 creativity tests for the 151 children were intercorrelated. Forty-three of the 45 intercorrelations are beyond the .05 level and 41 of the 45 are beyond the .01 level. Similarly, the intelligence measures are intercorrelated with 43 of the 45 coefficients significant beyond the .05 level and 38 of the 45 beyond the .01 level. The correlation between intelligence and creativity tests was .09. Thus, the creativity factors intercorrelate but are independent of the intelligence dimension. The data for boys and girls are similar to the data for the total population. Four groups of children were then established: (1) High in both creativity and intelligence. (2) High in creativity but low in intelligence. (3) Low in both creativity and intelligence. (4) High in intelligence and low in creativity.

Many results are presented and the reader has to consult the book to learn about them all. For the behavior in the school environment, the authors report that, with respect to the data obtained from the girls, there is an interaction between intelligence and creativity. It makes a difference whether creativity is located in a context of high or low intelligence. Hence, the authors question whether Getzels and Jackson were wise in selecting groups that had only maximum differences in intelligence and creativity. "Our results unequivocally demonstrate that such generalizations are unwarranted, at least in a female population." For boys, only the intelligence variable exerts an influence on the behavior ratings.

To convey something of the flavor of the behavioral data with the girls, here are some selections from the authors' summary. The high creative and high intelligence girls are highest in self-confidence and least oriented to self-deprecation. They are sought out by others and seek others out, too. They are highest in attention span, concentration, and interest in academic work. The high creative but low intelligence group are least confident and least assured. They are least able to concentrate and maintain attention. These girls are high on disruptive attention seeking. The low intelligence, low creativity group are better off than the previous group, socially, as they are more confident and assured. They apparently compensate for their poor academic performance by social activity.

The high intelligence and low creativity group, just as the high-high group of girls, is confident and assured. They are sought as

companions but do not seek others. A girl in this group is least
likely to seek attention in a disruptive way and is hesitant about
expressing opinions. This girl is also strongly oriented to academic
achievement but aloof in her social behavior.

Case studies are also presented. The analyses are collated and
some of the characteristics referred to are as follows: High creativity and high intelligence allow internalized control and freedom.
High creativity and low intelligence create unworthy and inadequate
feelings. Low creativity and high intelligence includes the children
who are "addicted" to school achievement. Low intelligence and low
creativity includes those children who are quite defensive and who
either adapt through social activity, regress passively, or have
psychosomatic symptoms.

The implications of the findings for education are discussed and
the authors conclude by saying, "It seems reasonable to expect that
if one were to make an accurate assessment of children's creativity
and intelligence status and if one were to apply environmental aids
appropriate to the child's mode of thinking, many children could
conceivably be moved toward higher levels of cognitive functioning."

In addition to presenting data on the behavior of the students in
the school environment, data are also presented on the students'
categorizing and conceptualizing behavior, sensitivity to physiognomic properties, anxiety, and defensiveness.

Validation Studies

Rotter, D.M.; Langland, L.; and Berger, D. "The Validity of Tests
  of Creative Thinking in Seven-Year-Old Children." *Gifted Child
  Quarterly* 15 (1971): 273-278.

This is a study of the predictive validity of some of the Wallach
and Kogan tests. The subjects were 61 second graders in two public
elementary schools in California. There were 23 boys and 38 girls
with a mean age of 7.9 years. One boy was Spanish-American and one
was black; otherwise, all the others were from lower to upper middle
class homes. Using the California Mental Maturity Test, the average
IQ was 119.7 with a range from 81 to 143.

Two of the Wallach and Kogan tests were used. One was based on
verbal cues (Alternate Uses and Instances) and the other was based
on visual cues (Pattern Meanings and Line Meanings). These were
adapted in some ways so that, for example, the creativity tests were
scored for number of associations and not for uniqueness of response.
There were no sex differences in IQ or creativity or activity
measures. The results also indicated that there was no relationship
between the creativity and the intelligence indices.

The creativity test and the IQ test data were correlated with
items checked on a 100-item checklist of creative activities very
similar to the checklist developed by Torrance. With this measure,
the results indicated that none of the IQ measures correlated with
the creative activities but creative ability, or resourcefulness in
generating ideas, did show a strong relationship to a number of
non-academic accomplishments in different areas. In some cases the
Wallach-Wing data were supported and in some, they were not.

Hattie, J. "Should Creativity Tests be Administered under Testlike
Conditions?" *Journal of Educational Psychology* 72 (1980): 87-98.

   This study was designed to compare three conditions of test administration: gamelike testing, conventional testing, and testing
conditions on two consecutive days. Gamelike conditions were selected because of the Wallach-Kogan results and repeated tests were
based on Maltzman's research which indicated the value of repeated
presentation of stimulus words in a free association situation.
   All the children were sixth grade pupils in New Zealand. Twenty-
eight boys and twenty-eight girls participated in the untimed game-
like test; another group of 28 boys and 28 girls randomly selected
from a larger group were selected for the two types of conventional
test situations.
   The following subtests were selected from Torrance's and Wallach
and Kogan's battery of tests: Instances, Circles, Product Improvement, Unusual Uses, and Pattern Meaning. It required 90 hours to
administer the tests under gamelike conditions.
   The results were: (1) No significant differences were obtained in
social class, age, and intelligence across conditions. (2) The
subjects in the gamelike situation were significantly less fluent
than the subjects in the testlike group. (3) Responses on the
second day were more unusual. (4) The two-day test session stimulated
more responses. (5) Time limits did not inhibit unique responses.
(6) A gamelike method of testing, because it requires so much time,
is not feasible for classroom testing. (7) The two-day procedure
is too dissimilar from normal conditions to make it useful.
(8) Other conditions, such as establishing better rapport between
examiner and student, might be of value. (9) Conventional testlike
conditions seem to be the best choice.

Wallbrown, F.H.; Wallbrown, J.D.; and Wherry, R.J. "The Construct
Validity of the Wallach-Kogan Test for Inner-City Children." *Journal
of General Psychology* 92 (1975): 83-96.

   The Wallach-Kogan creativity test was administered to 73 students
(45 girls and 28 boys) who attended grades 3 and 4 in an inner-city
parochial school in Columbus, Ohio. The results supported Wallach
and Kogan's theoretical formulations. Creativity and intelligence
measures were found to be independent. The creativity factors that
held together were: general, visual, and verbal creativity, plus a
weak methods factor for crayon drawing. The factors that held together for intelligence were: a relatively strong *g* factor and four
primary factors which include verbal precision, freedom from dis-
tractability, perceptual organization, and quasi-specific. The factor
analysis was obtained with the Wherry-Wherry hierarchical factor
solution. The authors disagree with Cronbach (see p. 188).

Suggestions for Further Reading

   Wherry, R.J. "Hierarchical Factors Solutions Without Rotation."
   Psychometrika 24 (1959): 45-51.

   Wherry, R.J., and Wherry, R.J., Jr. "WHEWH Program." In Wherry,
   R.J. (Ed.). *Psychology Department Computer Programs.* Columbus,
   OH: Department of Psychology, The Ohio State University, 1969.

Ward, W.C. "Creativity in Young Children." *Child Development* 39
    (1968): 737-754.

As demonstrated by Wallach and Kogan, one of the conditions that
the relationship between IQ measures and creativity test measures
is the context in which the testing occurs. This study was undertaken to learn whether similar results would be obtained with kindergarten children and with children 7 and 8 years of age. Creativity
measures were the same as those used by Kogan and Wallach, except
that items were selected specifically for younger children.
    Results indicated that a clear creativity-intelligence separation
appeared in 7- and 8-year-old boys, thus replicating Wallach and
Kogan's results for older children. With kindergarten, the results
were ambiguous. "The two creativity procedures, whose content Guilford (1956) would label 'semantic' showed correlations similar to
those found in older children: high positive relations among uniqueness and fluency measures, and moderate negative relations with IQ;
but they had generally nonsignificant correlations with measures
derived from the test with figural content. For boys, the figural
test also showed positive correlations with IQ, significant for the
measure of unique responses." The author suggests that a unitary
creativity dimension is present in kindergarten children but that
it is not measured by the figural test at this age.

Critique

Cronbach, L.J. "Intelligence? Creativity? A Parsimonious Reinter-
    pretation of the Wallach-Kogan Data." *American Educational Research
    Journal* 5 (1968): 491-511.

Studies in the field have been appropriately criticized for "inadequate designs, inadequate analysis and reporting, and a tendency to
cling to preconceptions." The Wallach-Kogan (WK) study has several
positive characteristics. It starts with a good critique of earlier
studies; it has a battery of tests that are interrelated but, at the
same time, are independent of conventional measures of intelligence;
and it contains interesting characteristics of the subjects involved.
    However, results that are presented as significant or near-sig-
nificant are "peculiarly inconsistent." WK did not use the most
advisable statistical procedures for analyzing their data. Specifically, they treated the data for each sex separately before checking
to see whether there was an interaction between the results obtained
and the subjects' sex. Their technique essentially cut the degrees
of freedom in half and limits the power of the study. "Moreover,
it leads one to draw different conclusions about boys and girls
where perhaps no difference exists." Cronbach therefore undertook
an analysis of the data to learn which of the results could be supported or rejected with the new statistical analyses. Furthermore,
Cronbach argues that the results of his analysis should take prece-
dence over other suggestions that one undertake the WK type of study
at different age levels. If the data do not hold up under the new
analysis then it would not be wise to pursue further work. On the
other hand, if the new analysis proved to support the WK analyses
and report of the results, then there would be specific leads and
specific directions to follow.

WK followed an appropriate approach in trying to open up a new field; they tried a number of variables, in every possible way, to suggest hypotheses. While this is appropriate in opening up a field, "it is not a way to arrive at safe conclusions." The author writes, "I would like to see a more conservative standard applied when a study is given the dignity of book-length presentation, advertised to a general audience, and accompanied by a discussion of 'implications and applications for education.'"

The author says that he has been guided by several considerations. (1) Variables should be given neutral names and questionable connotations should be avoided. (2) Simple conclusions rather than complex conclusions should be accepted wherever the data are accounted by the former. (3) No relation where the data indicate a probability of less than .05 should be interpreted. (4) There is a preference here for emphasizing the strength and character of relationships. (5) The full power of the data should be used. Each of these points is discussed fully. This is followed by the technical data for the regression analysis that is used. This analysis results in the conclusion "*that there is no persuasive evidence in this study of different relations in the boy and girl populations.*"

In concluding his paper, Cronbach says that his evaluation of the WK study indicates areas of agreement and areas of disagreement but he feels that the areas of disagreement come closer to the truth than do the data of the original investigators. Two brief concluding paragraphs follow. "Our study shows--as do critiques of earlier studies that Wallach and Kogan offer--that there are many pitfalls in their study of creativity. Investigators must be unusually painstaking and self-critical in analyzing their data if they are not to make a premature commitment to attractive but questionable hypotheses." "While the WK study performs a service in reminding us of the emotional stresses present in some high-achieving children, the study does not seem to shed light on 'creativity' and 'intelligence.' An attempt to draw out implications and applications is premature."

Vernon, P.E.; Adamson, G.; and Vernon, D.F. *The Psychology and Education of Gifted Children.* Boulder, CO: Westview Press, 1977. 216pp.

In commenting on the Wallach and Kogan study Vernon cites the Cronbach paper to point out that the statistical technique used by Wallach and Kogan was statistically inefficient and that a multiple regression technique should have been used.

Tannenbaum, A.J. *Gifted Children: Psychological and Educational Perspectives.* New York: Macmillan, 1983. 277-280.

The author's review of the Wallach and Kogan battery contains the following points:

1. Two studies by Hattie are cited that are critical of the administration conditions. In an earlier study by Hattie a question is raised about testing under untimed and gamelike conditions. Hattie, in a later study, compared gamelike conditions, conventional test conditions, and test conditions on two consecutive days and came to the conclusion that conventional test conditions produced the best results.

2. Studies seem to suggest that the test scores correlate better with concurrent than with predictive accomplishments.

3. The Wallach and Wing study showed that test scores correlated with out-of-classroom activities, but SAT scores did not. However, "it may be difficult to justify some of the extracurricular experien as necessarily 'creative.'"

4. A study by Rotter, Langland, and Berger, working with 7-year-old children, had results that were similar to those reported by Wallach and Wing although they did not show the same results for relationships with the physical sciences, arts, and crafts.

5. Two other studies by Wallbrown and Huelsman and Bartlett and Davis also reported good results with concurrent validity. Studies of predictive validity by Kogan and Pankove reflect equivocal results according to Tannenbaum. He recommends replication and says, "to say that an instrument's predictive validity has not been disproven conclusively is a long way from confirming that it is valid. The burden of proof is with the test constructor, and subsequent research should supply further support of data. These conditions remain yet to be met consistently in research on creativity."

6. In a study by Cropley, carried out with Australian university students, it was found that the Wallach-Kogan tests intercorrelated highly among themselves but low with IQ. However, when the intercorrelational matrix was factor analyzed, it was found that there was one general factor on which both the intelligence and the creativity tests loaded highly. Cropley doubted whether the creativity tests and the intelligence tests were really measuring different things.

7. Tannenbaum reviews two studies by Welsh who conducted a study similar to that conducted by Wallach and Kogan. This study worked with adolescents. The clusters of nonintellective traits revealed in this study, based on combinations of creativity and IQ tests, were the same as that revealed by Wallach and Kogan. To account for the nonintellective data, it is argued that there are two personality dimensions that could account for the data. One of these is "Intellectence" in which individual interests range from concrete to abstract. Intellectence is related to performance on IQ measures The other dimension is "Origence" and it is associated with scores on creativity tests.

A study by Hitt and Stock with engineers and scientists also revealed personality differences. In commenting on these studies, Tannenbaum says that they may "suggest that perhaps measures of creativity *do* help us to understand how people function, primarily with respect to their personal habits, attitudes, values and life styles rather than special aptitudes.... In the aggregate, these investigations show that people are different from each other, depending on how they perform on tests of creativity, and they may vary more predictably in their belief systems and the behavior codes than in their abilities to solve or find problems. The question remains, however: Does so-called 'creativity' reveal potential for original thinking or clues to the Origence dimension of personality?

Suggestions for Further Reading

Bartlett, M.M., and Davis, G.A. "Do the Wallach and Kogan Tests Predict Real Creative Behavior?" *Perceptual and Motor Skills* 39 (1974): 730.

Cropley, A.J. "Creativity and Intelligence." *British Journal of Educational Psychology* 36 (1966): 259-266.

Hattie, J.A. "Conditions for Administering Creativity Tests." *Psychological Bulletin* 84 (1977): 1249-1260.

————. "Should Creativity Tests Be Administered Under Test-like Conditions?" *Journal of Educational Psychology* 72 (1980): 87-98.

Hitt, W.D., and Stock, J.R. "The Relation Between Psychological Characteristics and Creative Behavior." *Psychological Record* 15 (1965): 133-140.

Kogan, N., and Pankove, E. "Creative Ability Over a Five-Year Span." *Child Development* 43 (1972): 427-442.

————. "Long-term Predictive Validity of Divergent Thinking Tests: Some Negative Evidence." *Journal of Educational Psychology* 66 (1974): 802-810.

Rotter, D.M.; Langland, L.; and Berger, D. "The Validity of Tests of Creative Thinking in Seven-Year-Old Children." *Gifted Child Quarterly* 15 (1971): 273-278.

Wallach, M.A., and Wing, C.W., Jr. *The Talented Student: A Validation of the Creativity-Intelligence Distinction.* New York: Holt, Rinehart and Winston, 1969.

Wallbrown, F.H., and Huelsman, C.B., Jr. "The Validity of the Wallach-Kogan Creativity Operations for Inner-City Children in Two Areas of Visual Arts." *Journal of Personality* 43 (1975): 109-126.

Welsh, G.S. *Creativity and Intelligence: A Personality Approach.* Chapel Hill: Institute for Research in Social Science, University of North Carolina at Chapel Hill, 1975.

————. "Personality Correlates of Intelligence and Creativity in Gifted Adolescents." In Stanley, J.C.; George, W.C.; and Solano, C.H. *The Gifted and the Creative: A Fifty-Year Perspective.* Baltimore, MD: Johns Hopkins University Press, 1977. 75-112.

GENERAL CRITIQUES

Tannenbaum, A.J. "Problems in Assessing Creativity." *Gifted Children: Psychological and Educational Perspectives.* New York: Macmillan, 1983. Chapter 14.

After a systematic review of the evidence on tested creativity, Tannenbaum summarizes the state of affairs as follows:

1. It is not certain that divergent thinking tests pick up characteristics that other tests are said to overlook. Studies like those of Getzels and Jackson do not provide consistent results. In correlational studies, some studies support and others do not support the finding that creativity test scores and achievement are independent when IQ is partialled out. There appears to be such a relationship when divergent thinking processes are characteristic of educational programs and achievement criteria.

2. Creativity test scores and IQ scores, when correlated, vary
from near zero correlations to correlations that are somewhat positive and significant. A hypothesis suggested by McNemar to account
for these findings, which suggests that there would be a high range
of creativity scores at the high IQ extremes but a narrower range
at average and below-average IQ levels, has not yet been substan-
tiated.

3. Correlations between IQ and different kinds of divergent thinking variables are quite diverse. Citing a study by Wallach, Tannenbaum points out that ideational fluency is more independent of
general intelligence than other divergent thinking skills such as
word fluency, flexibility, or originality.

4. There is work which favors the argument that creativity and
intelligence are separate entities. Other studies argue that the
two are only partly distinguishable from each other. For the argument that they overlap entirely, there is no evidence. The concluding sentence is based on a citation from Thorndike which argues
that such abilities as divergent thinking or creative thinking
probably do exist which are "unrelated to thought processes measured
by conventional intelligence tests."

Vernon, P.E.; Adamson, G.; and Vernon, D.F. *The Psychology and Edu-*
cation of Gifted Children. Boulder, CO: Westview Press, 1977.
85-98.

The following comments were culled from Chapter 6 which is devoted
to a discussion of divergent thinking tests. One set of points are
made with regard to the scoring of the divergent thinking tests.
The first of these is that it is tedious and time-consuming to score
the divergent thinking tests. Consequently, the tests are not likely
to be applied to large numbers of subjects. In some instances, it
is not merely a matter of counting the subject's responses as it is
not always clear what a response is.

Another point is that the decision as to what constitutes a rare
response is frequently a subjective decision. Rare responses seem
to be bizarre responses on occasion and investigators in this area
have argued that such responses turn out to be appropriate if one
asks the child about them. This, according to these authors, involves subjective judgments. (Apparently it is unavoidable and
even Vernon has used a procedure in which rarity of response is
taken into account.) With regard to this point, the authors also
say that it is undesirable to take another psychologist's list of
responses, for it would not be suitable for other subjects such as
those in England or Canada. It is suggested that a psychologist
wanting to use this procedure should develop his/her own list of
responses.

Turning to the conditions of administration and instructions used,
the authors feel that these contribute to the unreliability of the
divergent thinking tests. A child's performance on the test are
affected by "the conditions of testing, the way the instructions are
phrased, and the frame of mind of the testees." According to the
authors, Torrance administers his tests, as he does convergent
thinking tests, with time limits and with the instruction: "to think
of as many ideas as you can ... that no one else will think of."
Wallach and Kogan administer the tests in a gamelike atmosphere. A

report is then given of a study by Vernon which compared results obtained with gamelike and normal testlike conditions with 8th grade students. It was found that the gamelike conditions produced more responses of higher quality. But test conditions, say the authors, cannot be standardized. It is impossible to keep permissiveness from deteriorating into bedlam.

Further evidence for the effects of instructions on subjects' responses comes from a study by Hudson in which more responses were found when subjects were asked to give responses as if they were bohemian artists or even a "pedantic Scottish engineer." Thus, fluency and unconventionality can vary according to the subjects' set and to how they conceive their task. This weakness should not be exaggerated and the instructions and general approach should be kept constant, with minor variations ignored as in Binet testing.

The last point on this score is that test-retest reliability with the divergent thinking tests are lower than they are with the convergent thinking tests when retests occur over long periods. In this regard, a study by Haddon and Lytton is cited with a .62 correlation over long periods. However, the later scores were predicted as accurately by a verbal intelligence test as by the first-occasion divergent tests. Thus, the authors say that one does not know whether the lack of reliability is due to changes in creative abilities and divergent thinking with growth, or to what extent the obtained variations may be due to variations in testing conditions or attitudes.

The next major area considered is factorial consistency in the different tests used. The authors open with the general statement that the evidence is "extraordinarily contradictory." The variations, they say, may be attributed to the following:

1. Different divergent thinking tests are used by different investigators; Getzels and Jackson used a miscellany of tests while Wallach and Kogan emphasized tests with oral responses.

2. Conditions of administration and the manner in which these conditions affect the responses differ.

3. The subjects used in different studies are quite heterogeneous. In a study by Hasan and Butcher (1966) with a group of Scottish students who were 12 years old, a correlation of .74 between IQ and divergent thinking tests was obtained, indicating that there was little difference between the two.

4. The subjects' ability level differs. It has been suggested that, above an IQ of 120, intelligence and divergent thinking are independent but that below, they are related. This "threshold hypothesis" is not conclusive although the authors consider it plausible.

5. Divergent and convergent thinking factors "are distinctive" but "overlap." In this regard, studies by Cropley (1966) and Vernon are cited. There is no set figure as to the degree of overlap since it will vary with the age and ability of the children, the kinds of tests used, and the conditions of testing. It is likely that, for children who are given the Binet and oral divergent thinking tests, the correlation is a lot higher than under other conditions. For this reason the authors say that the statement often made on the basis of the Getzels and Jackson study, that intelligence tests fail to discover 70% of creative students, "is definitely misleading."

6. Psychologists who write about divergent thinking tests and call

them creativity tests are making a claim which is not justified.
Just because these tests involve unusual responses, they do not
necessarily measure that which is shown by the creative artist or
scientist or even the child who produces something constructive.

7. When scores on divergent thinking do correlate with a criterion,
the results may be a function of the fact that it is the verbal
intelligence component that is responsible for the correlation and
not the divergent thinking component. Since it is easier to get a
measure of intelligence, it would not be wise to use a measure of
divergent thinking. Wallach and Kogan and Getzels and Jackson
tried to overcome this by contrasting high divergent and high convergent children. But, as in the analysis of the Wallach and Kogan
data, Cronbach showed that their procedures were statistically inefficient and that a multiple regression analysis should have been
used.

In the same context, it should be pointed out that Torrance and
Yamamoto found that children rated as showing curiosity or as having
original ideas scored high on divergent thinking tests, and the
same was obtained for children rated by their peers as having "wild
and fantastic ideas." But other studies yield correlations of less
than .3 and even lower when intelligence is held constant.

8. Studies of the relationships between divergent thinking tests
and school achievement yield "somewhat contradictory results." This
may be because there is no consistent difference between school subjects and, possibly, because the difference in relevance of divergent
thinking for different subjects is not consistent and depends on
how a subject is taught. In this regard, the authors cited Haddon
and Lytton (1966) who found that progressive English primary schools
that emphasized self-initiated learning had higher divergent thinking
scores than schools, matched with the other schools for IQ, that
were more conventional and formal. The differences persisted for
four years (Haddon and Lytton, 1971). But, Lytton and Cotton (1969)
did not confirm the finding that the type of teaching in the secondary school affected performance on divergent thinking tests.

Another study in this context was by Dewing who found a correlation of .39 between divergent thinking scores and a criterion based
on teachers' and peers' ratings when IQ was held constant. Vernon
also found fairly good correlations in a similar study. However,
in this study, when IQ was constant, the correlations dropped and
Vernon did not think it worthwhile to have administered the divergent
thinking tests. The authors also call attention to the fact that
the correlations cited are for concurrent validity studies and not
for long-term predictive studies in which correlations would drop.

9. In the study just cited, Vernon did not find that children who
were high in divergent thinking were disliked by their teachers.
For example, the girls were high in sociometric popularity and the
boys conformed to adult standards rather than expressing rebellious
or independent opinions. The authors also point out that Torrance
and Lytton suggested that high divergent thinkers are more popular
in those schools where there is a positive value placed on creative
learning.

10. Considering validity studies with students who were somewhat
older and looking at studies with adults that used divergent thinking
tests, the authors say, "the evidence is very patchy." There are
studies which report relationships by Shapiro, Torrance, Drevdahl,

and Elliott, "yet no-one seems to have sufficient faith in the test to advocate their regular application in selecting creativity-talented workers. Presumably most psychologists are put off by the difficulties of standardized administration and scoring."

Another idea in this context, that has also not been followed up, stems from the work of Cropley and Hudson who reported that divergent thinking tests in a follow-up study showed no agreement with first-year academic performance but were more predictive of achievements in the third and fourth years. This may be related to the fact that, during the first year, the courses and the examinations were factual and rigid while later courses welcomed more originality on the part of the students.

11. Hudson argues, and the authors agree, that divergent thinking should not be identified with creativity but rather, that convergent and divergent thinking should be regarded as cognitive styles. This is based on Hudson's results, from his study in English secondary schools and universities, in which he found that divergers specialize in art subjects and convergers, in science subjects. The authors of this book point out that, in other countries, where specialization in arts and science are postponed, one does not find the same association between divergent-convergent scores and specializations. The data are also confounded with sex differences. Relevant here is Ausubel's critical comment: "Creativity is one of the vaguest, most ambitious, and most confused terms in psychology today.... Scores on measures of divergent thinking are indeterminably contaminated by such factors as fluency and glibness, uninhibited self-expression, impulsivity, and deficient self-critical ability."

12. While divergent thinking tests do not tell us much about adult abilities, they do tell us about adult interests. In this regard, the Wallach and Wing study is cited. This study found that SAT correlated with grades and not with activities like music, science, and leadership. Divergent thinking tests better predicted visual arts, writing, science, and student leadership but did not do too well in social service, music, and drama. There are other predictive studies by Torrance which are very promising for the predictive validity of the divergent thinking tests. In Canada, a study by Maslany (1973) did not find that divergent thinking tests contributed significantly to the prediction of either academic or non-academic accomplishments.

The authors then draw the following conclusions: "In general, then, divergent thinking tests are disappointing. They do elicit some kind of 'imagination', and are related to certain personality traits and interests, but too inconsistently to be of much practical value." In answer to the question, "Why?," the authors offer the following suggestions: (1) Unlike the convergent thinking tasks, the divergent thinking tasks do not provide the subjects with a clear task. (2) The divergent thinking tasks are superficial and people do not try to do their best on them. Also, people do not work with the same dedication and emotional involvement on the divergent thinking tasks as they would on real tasks. (3) Those who may be regarded as "creativity testers" assume that all manifestations of creativity involve the same kind of verbal fluency and unconventionality. Factors involved in scientific work may be quite different than factors involved in literary work.

With all of the above in mind, the authors say that divergent thinking tests may be all right for identifying students for gifted programs. Students who do well on these tests but who might be overlooked by teachers are likely to come to the fore. Torrance's test may be of help in this regard. However, the authors feel that "a better collection of subtests could be put together, and the psychologist who wants to use them should prepare his own local list of common and unusual responses, rather than relying on lists from a somewhat different cultural group."

Suggestions for Further Reading

Ausubel, D.P. *Educational Psychology: A Cognitive View*. New York: Holt, Rinehart and Winston, 1968.

Cronbach, L.J. "Intelligence? Creativity? A Parsimonious Reinterpretation of the Wallach-Kogan Data." *American Educational Research Journal* 5 (1968): 491-511.

Cropley, A.J. "Creativity and Intelligence." *British Journal of Educational Psychology* 36 (1966): 259-266.

————. "Divergent Thinking and Science Specialists." *Nature* 215 (1967): 671-672.

Dewing, K. "The Reliability and Validity of Selected Tests of Creative Thinking in a Sample of Seventh Grade West Australian Children." *British Journal of Educational Psychology* 40 (1970): 35-42.

Drevdahl, J.E. "Factors of Importance for Creativity." *Journal of Clinical Psychology* 12 (1956): 21-26.

Elliott, J.M. "Measuring Creative Ability in Public Relations and Advertising Work." In Taylor, C.W. (Ed.). *Widening Horizons in Creativity*. New York: John Wiley, 1964. 396-400.

Haddon, E.A., and Lytton, H. "Primary Education and Divergent Thinking Abilities—Four Years On." *British Journal of Educational Psychology* 41 (1971): 136-147.

————. "Teaching Approach and the Development of Divergent Thinking Abilities in Primary Schools." *British Journal of Educational Psychology* 38 (1968): 171-180.

Hasan, P., and Butcher, H.K. "A Partial Replication with Scottish Children of Getzels and Jackson's Study." *British Journal of Psychology* 57 (1966): 129-135.

Hudson, L. *Contrary Imaginations*. London: Methuen, 1966.

————. *Frames of Mind*. London: Methuen, 1968.

Lytton, H. *Creativity and Education*. London: Routledge and Kegan Paul, 1971.

Lytton, H., and Cotton, A.C. "Divergent Thinking Abilities in Secondary Schools." *British Journal of Educational Psychology* 39 (1969): 183-190.

Thurstone, L.L. *Primary Mental Abilities*. Chicago: University of Chicago Press, Psychometric Monographs, No. 1, 1938.

Torrance, E.P. "Curiosity of Gifted Children. Performance on Timed and Untimed Tests of Creativity." *Gifted Child Quarterly* 13 (1969a): 155-158.

————. "Long Range Prediction Studies and International Applications of the Torrance Tests of Creative Thinking." *Proceedings XVII Congress, International Association of Applied Psychology.* Liège, 1971.

————. "Prediction of Adult Creative Achievement from High School Seniors." *Gifted Child Quarterly* 13 (1969b): 223-229.

————. *Rewarding Creative Behavior.* Englewood Cliffs, NJ: Prentice-Hall, 1965.

Vernon, P.E. "Effects of Administration and Scoring on Divergent Thinking Tests." *British Journal of Educational Psychology* (1971): 241-257.

————. "The Validity of Divergent Thinking Tests." *Alberta Journal of Educational Research* 18 (1972): 249-258.

Wallach, M.A., and Wing, C.W. *The Talented Student: A Validation of the Creativity-Intelligence Distinction.* New York: Holt, Rinehart and Winston, 1969.

Yamamoto, K. "Relationships Between Creative Thinking Abilities of Teachers and Achievement and Adjustment of Pupils." *Journal of Experimental Education* 32 (1963): 3-25.

Wallach, M.A., and Kogan, N. *Modes of Thinking in Young Children: A Study of the Creativity-Intelligence Distinction.* New York: Holt, Rinehart and Winston, 1965.

The authors summarize their critique of Getzels-Jackson, Torrance, and Guilford as follows. They say that measures that have been presented as measures of creativity do not indicate that they are part of a "single psychological dimension parallel to and distinct from the dimension of general intelligence defined by conventional intelligence test indices." They also write that, "on the basis of this evidence, then, there is questionable warrant for proposing the very conceptualization which most researchers have proposed: that creativity is not intelligence, and that individual differences in creativity possess the same degree of psychological pervasiveness as individual differences in general intelligence. This is a rather discouraging conclusion to have to draw."

The authors are also critical of the context in which the tests are administered. They say, "Three generalizations can be made when we consider the situational context for the various 'creativity' procedures in the studies reviewed earlier in this chapter. First, the authors invariably refer to their procedures as 'tests'; second, these procedures are group-administered to large numbers of students in a classroom setting; third, these procedures are timed and the time limits are relatively brief, or temporal constraint is implied through the use of the group administration arrangement. In short, the features of temporal freedom and a nontest context, which our analysis suggests are important if something akin to creativity is to be assessed, are conspicuous by their absence." In their own research, the authors prefer "freedom from time pressure and a gamelike rather than examination or test setting."

NEEDED RESEARCH

Treffinger, D.J., and Poggio, J.P. "Needed Research on the Measurement of Creativity." *Journal of Creative Behavior* 6 (1972): 236-252.

This paper addresses itself to the major issues in three categories that require further work and research; validity, reliability, and usability. In the category of validity, the authors point to 5 deficiencies. (1) More theoretical work and the integration and evaluation of the research work has to be done. (2) There need to be both conceptual definitions and operational definitions. (3) There needs to be more work on both new and more appropriate external criteria of creativity. Associated with this is a need for more work on the validity and reliability of existing criteria. (4) There is a need for multivariate studies of creativity. (5) "There are needs for longitudinal studies, well-controlled experimental studies, replications, and for developmental and cross-cultural studies."

In discussing reliability, they point out that: (1) New ways have to be sought for measures of reliability and there has to be "emphasis on the specification of 'error' components." (2) When one employs traditional measures of stability of tests, one must consider whether creativity is a stable trait and concern oneself with the best measures for determining the proper interval for assessing reliability. In addition, there has to be work on the effects of motivation, mood, and situational variables on the reliability of test scores. (3) When using alternate forms of tests, one should pay attention to the selections of the proper tests. Creativity tasks may not be "discrete 'items'" and hence the scores derived from various tasks may neither be "additive, nor meet many fundamental assumptions involved in the traditional determination of reliability indices."

With regard to usability, the authors say: (1) The effects in variations in test administration and conditions of work on creativity tests have to be studied better and better understood. (2) Criteria must be established for studying such factors as "originality and 'imagination.'" (3) Research on creativity measures should provide data on interscorer correlations and comparisons of means and variances among and between scorers and test norms should also be provided. (4) Where norms are presented, they should be presented with extensive supporting data on the normative groups and the tasks involved.

The authors conclude their paper with the following statement: "These problems are very complex, and may not soon be resolved. It seems necessary to recognize them, however, and to take into account such problems in the interpretation of research in which 'creativity' measures are used. It would also be of significant value to researchers in the psychological study of creativity if support were increased for research in these areas."

Chapter 7

CHARACTERISTICS, PART 4:
PERSONALITY AND OTHER FACTORS

GENERAL

--Callahan, 1981
--Davis and Rimm, 1979
--Howell, 1979
--Hunt and Ranhawa, 1980

PERSONALITY AND COGNITIVE FACTORS IN TRANSACTION

--Berman; Evyatar; and Globerson, 1981
--Smith and Carlsson, 1980
--Smith and Carlsson, 1983
--Soueif and El-Sayed, 1970

SELF-CONCEPT

--American Association for Gifted Children, 1978
--Bohrnstedt and Felson, 1983
--Dean, 1977
--Ross and Parker, 1980
--Schaefer, 1969
--Schaefer, 1972
--Schaefer, 1973
--Tidwell, 1980

PSYCHOLOGICAL DIFFICULTIES

--Impellizzeri; Farrell; and Melville, 1976
--Isaacs, 1979
--Samuels, 1981

ATTITUDES TO GIFTEDNESS

--Ford, 1978
--Tannenbaum, 1962

LEARNING STYLES

--Dunn and Price, 1980
--Henderson and Gold, 1983
--Sigler, 1983

OTHER CHARACTERISTICS

--Bear, 1983
--Khatena, 1978
--Schaefer, 1969
--Torrance and Reynolds, 1978

GENERAL

Callahan, C.M. "Superior Abilities." In Kaufmann, J.M., and Hallahan, D.P. (Eds.). *Handbook of Special Education.* Englewood Cliffs, NJ: Prentice Hall, 1981. 49–86.

This is a survey piece on the characteristics of students with superior abilities. A unique part of this chapter is a table in which there are three columns: "Differentiating characteristics" (of individuals with superior abilities), "Examples of related needs" and "Possible concomitant problems." For example, one differentiating characteristic that is listed is: "extraordinary quantity of information, unusual retentiveness." As an example of a related need, the author writes: "to be exposed to new and challenging information of the environment and the culture, including aesthetic, economic, political, educational and social aspects; to acquire early mastery of foundation skills." The author describes "possible concomitant problems" as "boredom with regular curriculum, impatience with 'waiting for the group.'"

Davis, G.A., and Rimm, S. "Identification and Counseling of the Creatively Gifted." In Colangelo, N., and Zaffrann, R.T. (Eds.). *New Voices in Counseling the Gifted.* Dubuque, IA: Kendall/Hunt, 1979. 225–236.

This paper presents a summary of traits that have been found to be characteristic of creative children; case studies of creative elementary and high school students, together with suggestions for their appropriate counseling; and the Group Inventory for Finding Talent (GIFT) which is a questionnaire for identifying gifted elementary school children.

The summary of cognitive traits includes fluency, flexibility, originality, sensitivity to problems, ability to infer implications and consequences, etc. For personality characteristics, the authors include positive characteristics (high self-confidence, independence, high energy level, not tradition-bound, etc.) as well as negative characteristics (uncooperative, demanding, egocentric, discourteous, indifferent to convention, emotional, stubborn, etc.). For biographical factors, they mention unusual hobbies, doing impersonations, magic shows, and scientific inventions, all of which may be quite obvious. They also mention subtle characteristics like creative high school students with friends younger and older than themselves, creative students with histories of living in more than one state and traveling outside the U.S., and creative students with imaginary playmates.

For counseling purposes, the authors point out that home environments may be "too restrictive" or "too permissive." In these cases counselors have to provide appropriate support systems.

The GIFT questionnaire consists of three forms for children at various grades in elementary school. It aims at independence, curiosity, perseverance, flexibility of interests in art and writing, and broad interests. It has been translated into several languages and is used in the U.S. and abroad. Validity studies are presented.

Howell, S.K. *Characteristics of Talented and Gifted Children*. Oregon State Department of Education, Northwest Regional Educational Laboratory, 1979. 21pp.

Characteristics of talented and gifted children during preschool and school years are presented. There is discussion of the underachieving gifted child, emotional problems, school programming, and the "culturally different" child. Characteristics of teachers of the gifted and talented are also presented and there are suggestions for parents of such children to help them understand their childrens' giftedness and talent.

Hunt, D., and Randhawa, B. "Personality Factors and Ability Groups." *Perceptual and Motor Skills* 50 (1980): 902.

To investigate the personalities of academically gifted and academically handicapped students, 12 male and 11 female academically handicapped students and 22 male and 13 female academically gifted students were studied with a Children's Personality Questionnaire. It was found that the high ability group tended to be excitable, assertive, enthusiastic, venturesome, and forthright. The low ability group tended to be phlegmatic, obedient, sober, shy, and shrewd.

PERSONALITY AND COGNITIVE FACTORS
IN TRANSACTION

Berman, A.; Evyatar, A.; and Globerson, T. "Mathematical Patterns and Gifted Children." In Kramer, A.H., et al. *Gifted Children: Challenging Their Potential--New Perspectives and Alternatives*. New York: Trillium Press, 1981. 71-81.

Forty gifted children in grades 5 to 7, who were attending afternoon enrichment classes at the Technion in Israel, were tested with continuation problems in mathematics and divided into three groups. The spontaneous group gave correct answers to the problems immediately or after working on a few problems. The short explanation group gave correct answers after a short explanation. The full explanation group required a full explanation before they understood the correct solution. The three groups were tested with cognitive measures and personality measures. The results indicated that neither cognitive measures nor questions based on DeBono's work differentiated among the three groups. The spontaneous group, which was regarded as the more creative one, was "somewhat younger" than the others and impressed the investigators with the possibility that they were more "daring" than the others in their responses.

While the authors consider the possibility that the cognitive measures may not have been appropriate, they conclude that "intellectual boldness (rather than risk-taking)," which they regard as a personality variable, may be critical and deserves further study.

Smith, G.J.W., and Carlsson, I. "Can Preschool Children Be Creative? An Experimental Study of 4-6 Year-olds." *Psychological Research Bulletin, Psychological Laboratory.* Sweden: Lund University, 1980. 1-27. (Mimeographed.)

Forty-seven children from four nursery schools, who fell between the ages of 4 and 6, had their creativity evaluated by an interviewer and independent judges who studied their drawings. Three tests were administered to these children. One was the percept-genetic (PG) test in which a non-threatening still-life picture is presented to the subject at short exposure levels, then at increasing levels (an ascending order of exposure time), and finally in a descending order of exposure time. The second test was the Meta-Contrast Technique (MCT) which gets at the effects of subliminal perception. The third test was a Landscape. Test, based on Piaget and Inhelder's work which was designed to get at egocentric thinking.

The results indicated that "not until the child can direct its constructive activities towards well-defined stimuli will it be able to construct subjective material in acts of creation." The test of subliminal effects indicated that the use of a threatening stimulus with artistic students tended to increase the number of subjective themes recovered or "to wake a dormant urge to create."

Smith, G.J.W., and Carlsson, I. "Creativity in Early and Middle School Years." *International Journal of Behavioral Development* 6 (1983): 167-195.

The children in this study ranged in age from 7 to 11. A younger group (chronologically) was divided into one sub-group that was immature cognitively and another that was more mature cognitively. A third group consisted of chronologically older students. All subjects were tested with the percept-genetic (PG) test which had been found to correlate significantly with a creativity-fantasy role. The results indicated that creativity decreased in the immature, chronologically younger group and increased in the others. Creativity seemed to benefit from a certain amount of anxiety but was blocked by excessive amounts or by low anxiety tolerance.

Soueif, M.I., and El-Sayed, A.M. "Curvilinear Relationahips Between Creative Thinking and Personality Trait Variables." *Acta Psychologica* 34 (1970): 1-21.

Cognitive (Guilford) measures and personality measures were administered to 216 Egyptian male students with an average age of 23.16. The data revealed that most of the intercorrelations between the cognitive tests were statistically significant as were 61% of the intercorrelations among the personality scales. But, more than 90% of the intercorrelations between the personality and cognitive measures were not significant. This is consistent with Guilford's

earlier reports of the lack of correlation between personality and
cognitive factors. All of these results, however, are based on
linear correlations. The authors then proceeded to conduct a
moderator analysis of their data and they concluded that, while
92% of the linear correlations between personality variables and
cognitive variables were not significant, nearly all of them were
significant when correlation ratios were calculated. Similarly,
while factor analyses revealed that factors did not cut across personality and cognitive data, moderator analysis revealed interaction
effects "among personality variables in determining creative thinking test performance."

SELF-CONCEPT

American Association for Gifted Children (Sponsor). *On Being Gifted.*
New York: Walker and Company, 1978.

   This book consists of papers presented by 20 teenage gifted and
talented students at the National Student Symposium on the Education
of the Gifted and Talented. They focus on what it is like to grow
up talented and gifted, including feelings, ideals, aspirations, expectations, frustrations, helpful people (parents and teachers), and
influential school programs. A major aim of the work is to show the
potential of the gifted and to help obtain better educational opportunities for them.

Borhnstedt, G.W., and Felson, R.B. "Explaining the Relations Among
Children's Actual and Perceived Performances and Self-Esteem: A
Comparison of Several Causal Models." *Journal of Personality and
Social Psychology* 45 (1983): 43-56.

   This is a report of several causal models of the relationship
between children's performances and self-esteem. Self-esteem was
measured with 5 items adapted from the scale developed by Rosenberg
and Simmons (1972). Grades were based on grades in 4 academic subjects for the semester that data were collected. Athletic performanc
data were collected only for boys in a physical education class
where the boys were tested for such tasks as dribbling, shooting,
etc. Sociometric liking data were obtained by asking classmates to
name the three boys and three girls they liked best. The score a
student received was based on these choices. Students' perceptions
of how smart they were, were based on self-ratings, as were perceptions of athletic ability. Finally, perceptions of sociometric
status were based on ratings obtained from the students by asking
them how well they were liked.
   Four hundred and fifteen students in the 6th through 8th grade
were studied. The authors summarize their results as follows:
"Models in which self-esteem affected perceptions of popularity fit
the data better than models in which reverse or reciprocal effects
were posited. It appears that for ambiguous attributes, such as
popularity, a self-consistency bias operates whereby children's
self-esteem affects how popular they think they are. For more veri-

fiable attributes (i.e., academic and athletic achievement), perceptions of achievement more strongly related to actual achievement,
and they are more likely to affect self-esteem rather than the reverse."

Dean, R.S. "Effects of Self-Concept on Learning with Gifted Children."
Journal of Educational Research 70 (1977): 315-318.

Forty-eight (24 male and 24 female) 7th and 8th grade students
living in Phoenix, Arizona, area participated in the study.
Their average age was 12.92 and their mean IQ scores (Lorge-Thorndike) were 147.9 for the girls and 138.5 for the boys. Coopersmith's
Self-Esteem Inventory was administered to all subjects and the data
on the Inventory were split at the median, establishing two subgroups within each gender. To all subjects, a verbal free recall
test and a non-verbal paired associates learning test were administered. The results were: (1) Self-concept scores were positively
related to learning scores across tasks. (2) Gifted children with
higher self-concept scores showed a greater mastery of verbal and
non-verbal learning measures and used a clustering strategy.
(3) Children with low self-concepts seemed more rigid in their recall strategy.

Ross, A., and Parker, M. "Academic and Social Self-Concepts of the
Academically Gifted." *Exceptional Children* 47 (1980): 6-10.

One hundred and forty-seven gifted Wausau, Wisconsin, students
(63 male and 84 female) in the 5th through 8th grades were studied
with the Sears Self Concept Inventory from which a social self-concept and an academic self-concept scale were obtained. No significant differences between boys and girls were obtained and no significant differences were obtained among grade levels, indicating
no variations in self-concept over this period of time. But, there
was a statistically significant difference between academic students
(who were higher) and the total group of students on the social self-
concept.

Schaefer, C.E. "The Self-Concept of Creative Adolescents." *Journal
of Psychology* 72 (1969): 233-242.

The Gough Adjective Check List was administered to eight criterion
groups. Using a compound probability level of .10, the following
adjectives were found to differentiate between the creative and the
control subjects. "The creative adolescents, significantly more
often than the controls, viewed themselves as creative (imaginative,
artistic, ingenious, original), independent (unconventional, individualistic), uninhibited (spontaneous, impulsive), iconoclastic
(assertive, outspoken, rebellious), complicated (complex, reflective,
cynical, idealistic), and asocial (aloof). In striking contrast,
the adjectives differentiating the control students present a remarkably consistent picture of passive conformity: dependable, cooperative, contented, conventional, quiet and silent." In summarizing
these data, it is suggested that the adjectives fall into three main

themes: "(a) complexity and reconciliation of opposites; (b) impulsivity and craving for novelty; and (c) autonomy and self-assertion."

Schaefer, C.E. "Follow-up Study of a Creativity Scale for the Adjective Check List." *Psychological Reports* 30 (1972): 662.

This is a five-year follow-up study of a 27-item Creativity Scale for the Adjective Check List (Smith and Schaefer, 1969) intended to see if it continues to differentiate between creativity and control subjects. There were four creativity groups and four control groups. The fields were art and writing and math-science for boys and art and writing, separately, for girls. The results indicated that the creative groups were significantly different from the control groups in all comparisons. The author says, "as creative students move from early to late adolescence they continue to report a distinctively creative self-concept. This self-image is characterized by such adjectives as artistic, imaginative, original, progressive, quick, resourceful, sharp-witted, and spontaneous." The creative groups report more creative achievements than the controls in the five-year period.

Schaefer, C.E. "A Five-Year Follow-Up Study of the Self-Concept of Creative Adolescents." *Journal of Genetic Psychology* 123 (1973): 163-170.

This is a follow-up study of the students reported on in Schaefer (1969). Follow-up data revealed a difference according to field of study. Stable self-concepts and differences between subjects, previously reported as high and low creatives, were obtained in the literary-artistic area but not among boys in mathematics and science. Creative adolescents in the literary-art fields "remain firm in viewing themselves as being open to impulse expression and desiring novel experiences. Moreover, they continue to report that they are independent of thought and action, and take a leadership role in social situations." The lack of difference in boys in the math-science area is attributed to the fact that creatives in the follow-up study responded in a conventional manner. It is suggested that creative male mathematicians have conventional personalities while creative women mathematicians and creative male artists tend to be "rebelliously independent persons who reject outside influences." The success of male mathematicians in their organizations as adults may depend on their more conventional personalities which enable them to adapt to their organizations.

Tidwell, R. "A Psycho-educational Profile of 1,593 Gifted High School Students." *Gifted Child Quarterly* 24 (1980): 63-68.

A variety of psychological characteristics of 804 male and 789 female 10th grade gifted students in California were studied with the following instruments: Piers-Harris Children's Self-Concept Scale; the Self-Esteem Inventory, Form B; Locus of Control Questionnaire; Attitude Toward School Questionnaire; Self-Concept as a Learner Questionnaire; and Tidwell's Survey Inventory. The results indicated that the gifted have positive self-concepts, and that there is a positive correlation between their self-concept and academic ability. They see themselves as being in control of their lives, and they have positive attitudes toward school, their teachers, and learning. They have plans for higher education and professional or managerial careers. Sixty-four percent of them report they are unpopular, but 74% of them see themselves as happy or very happy. On the average, they spend 6 hours a day in school; 10 hours a week studying; 7 hours a week in home responsibilities; 10 hours a week in recreational activities; 8 hours a day sleeping; and 11 hours a week viewing television.

PSYCHOLOGICAL DIFFICULTIES

Impellizzeri, A.E.; Farrell, M.J.; and Melville, W.G. "Psychological and Emotional Needs of Gifted Youngsters." *National Association of Secondary School Principals Bulletin* 60 (1976): 43-48.

This is a discussion paper based on the thesis that many times, gifted children are neglected in terms of their social, emotional, or physical development. They are hurt by teachers' and parents' lack of understanding and their peers' lack of acceptance. They need emotional support, understanding, counseling, love, and attention.

Isaacs, A.F. "The Gifted-Talented-Creative: Two Cases." *Creative Child and Adult Quarterly* 4 (1979): 77-79.

Two case studies are presented of intellectually gifted children (IQs between 145-150). They had difficult family situations and attended two different schools. One received support and approval in school, while the other resented adjustment attempts in school. At the second grade level, the first did well in adjustment and the second did poorly and lost interest in achievement.

Samuels, S. *Disturbed Exceptional Children.* New York: Human Sciences Press, 1981. 366pp.

In various parts of this book, the author considers gifted, talented, and creative children and makes the following points, which are supported with research studies. 1. Gifted children achieve less than their potential. 2. In Terman's and Oden's study of gifted children, 22.3% of the men and 25.1% of the women who were gifted when they were young showed signs of maladjustment when they were in their forties. Of the same younger population, 8.9% of the men and 9% of the women complained of "serious maladjustment" in their forties. 3. When IQ is controlled, there is a positive relationship between achievement and self-concept. 4. In early childhood, creativity may be more acceptable than in later years. 5. Children who are creative are less accepted by their peers. 6. Highly creative children with high IQs are apt to be disruptive in school and experience some anxiety. 7. The gifted learning disabled child has to use, and needs support in using, his/her stronger areas to express his/her ideas. 8. There is evidence that the incidence of the gifted in elementary and secondary schools is 3 to 5%. Those with IQs of 140 and above probably account for 1% of the population and, in a high socioeconomic community, there can be from 1 to 20% of the children who are gifted. 9. The gifted are advanced in memory, associations, reasoning, extrapolation, and evaluation. They learn quickly, are intellectually curious and have wide interests. They read well, are original, and are impatient with routine and drill. They may be uneven in ability and interest areas. The well-adjusted gifted child has good organizing ability, high motivation and very good "staying power." 10. The gifted think divergently and develop new, unique, and original ideas. 11. Creative children are high on fluency, flexibility, originality, and elaboration. 12. Gifted children do the unusual, maintain an open-ended approach, and do not seek simple solutions. 13. High intelligence may be found in creative children but high IQ children are not necessarily creative. 14. High IQs have been found in children who are creative in the verbal and semantic areas but not creative in art and music. 15. Middle class, normal, gifted children are more easily identified by intelligence tests than are lower class, educationally advantaged, learning-disabled gifted, creative, or children with leadership potential. 16. The earlier problems in the gifted are identified, the sooner they can be helped. 17. There are twice as many boys as girls among gifted underachievers. 18. Many gifted underachievers never complete high school and some of those who do, have lower aspirations and career goals than higher achievers. 19. The gifted underachiever gives evidence of being overtly aggressive and hostile and feeling inadequate. These children have poor self-concepts and a fear of failure, which results in low motivation. 20. Emotional problems of the gifted are not related to their giftedness but to their family problems. 21. Gifted underachievers withdraw and engage less in social and work-oriented situations with their peers and spend more time in nonacademic work than do their achieving peers. 22. As a result of their feelings of inadequacy, gifted underachievers are overly competitive. 23. Extremely high intelligence (IQs of 170 and higher) has been associated with greater maladjustment. These gifted children become isolated and gravitate to adults early in life. They are precociously aware of abstract ideas but they lack the emotional maturity to deal with what they know. Some also use their intellect defensively and withdraw from social relationships. 24. The gifted and nonconforming child may not be accepted by his/her peers and teachers. Teachers have as much discomfort with gifted children as with other exceptional children. Gifted children may react maladaptively to these reactions from their teachers.

ATTITUDES TO GIFTEDNESS

Ford, B. "Student Attitudes Toward Special Programming and Identification." *Gifted Child Quarterly* 22 (1978): 489-497.

Students in elementary and high school responded to a Special Program Attitude Survey. The focus of the questionnaire was on student satisfaction with program, attitudes of non-program students toward the gifted students, parents' attitudes to the program, and reactions of non-program teachers to gifted participants. Students' responses were found to be consistently positive. Gifted students reported positive attitudes on the part of parents and teachers and no difficulties with other students.

Tannenbaum, A.J. *Adolescent Attitudes Toward Academic Brilliance.* New York: Bureau of Publications, Teachers College, Columbia University, 1962. 100pp.

This is a report of the Talented Youth Project of the Horace-Mann-Lincoln Institute of School Experimentation in which adolescent attitudes toward "reputedly 'brilliant'" students and students "'average' in ability" are compared. Results suggest "that academic brilliance in and of itself is not a stigma in the adolescent world. However, when it is combined with relatively unacceptable attributes, it can penalize its possessor severely. The nonstudious athlete may demonstrate outstanding brain power without fearing social derogation by peers; but a display of brilliance by one who is studious and indifferent to sports constitutes a definite status risk. The implied impression is that the brilliant student is an exceptionally prominent target for teen-age pressures to conform to certain behaviors and values. If so, there is danger of his deliberately masking his talent in order to relieve these pressures."

LEARNING STYLES

Dunn, R., and Price, G.E. "The Learning Style Characteristics of Gifted Students." *Gifted Child Quarterly* 24 (1980): 33-36.

One hundred nine gifted students (IQ Otis Lennon or Standardized Achievement Tests) from a large Eastern school district were compared with a group of 160 students randomly selected on the Dunn, Dunn and Price Learning Style Inventory. Results indicated that the gifted preferred formal design, did not need structure, were less responsible, and more persistent than the non-gifted. The gifted also preferred learning through their tactile and kinaesthetic senses, showing less preference for their auditory sense in learning. The non-gifted, on the other hand, preferred informal design, needed structure, were more responsible but not as persistent, and preferred their auditory sense when learning. The gifted also tended to be highly individualistic in their preference for sound, silence, interaction, temperature variations, intake, mobility, and time.

Henderson, B.B., and Gold, S.R. "Intellectual Styles: A Comparison of Factor Structures in Gifted and Average Children and Adolescents." *Personality and Social Psychology* 45 (1983): 624-632.

Two studies of elementary school children were undertaken in which students reported on their curiosity and daydreaming. In addition,

demographic data and IQ data were obtained. All data were factor
analyzed and in both the gifted and the average groups, the same
factor structure was found: intellectual power (general intelligence) and intellectual style (daydreaming and curiosity) were found
to be independent factors.

Sigler, R.S. "Five Generalizations About Cognitive Development."
    American Psychologist 38 (1983): 263-277.

    The five generalizations are (1) In studying children's knowledge,
the rule is a good basic unit of study. (2) When accuracy is studied
across different environments, it is found that children use pre-
mastery rules in terms of their predictive accuracy. (3) When
children have little knowledge about concepts, their reasoning across
different concepts is more homogeneous than when they have more
knowledge. (4) Learning in children is largely a result of the
interaction between their knowledge and their experience. Their
learning is most efficient when their experiences indicate inade-
quacies in existing rules. (5) "Once children have learned that
their existing knowledge is imperfect, their encoding plays a large
role in constructing more advanced knowledge."

OTHER CHARACTERISTICS

Bear, G.G. "Moral Reasoning, Classroom Behavior, and the Intellec-
    tually Gifted." *Journal for the Education of the Gifted* 6 (1983):
    111-119.

    Fourteen intellectually gifted 6th graders were compared with 46
of their non-gifted peers. Giftedness was defined as a score above
the 95th percentile on the Vocabulary scale of the Stanford Achievement Test. The assessment of moral reasoning was based on Kohlberg's
Moral Judgment Interview, Form A (Kohlberg, Colby, Gibbs, and
Speicher-Dubin, 1978). Teachers provided data on conduct problems
by ratings on the Behavior Problem Check List (Quay and Peterson,
1979). A correlation of .36 was found between intelligence and
moral reasoning. The gifted students were approximately one-third
of a stage more advanced than their non-gifted peers. Not all
gifted students scored higher than their non-gifted peers on moral
reasoning. The gifted also had fewer conduct problems in the classroom. The classroom conduct of the gifted was less variable than
that of their peers, but their moral reasoning was equally variable.

Khatena, J. "Frontiers of Creative Imagination Imagery." *Journal of
    Mental Imagery* 2 (1978): 33-46.

    "Studies on imagination imagery have not, for the most part, dealt
with the activating energy of creativity, and a need for the study
of creative imagination imagery was emphasized. The difficulty of
measuring imagination imagery and its creative correlates was discussed, and it was noted that recent research on creative imagination
imagery has tended to move away from self-reports to measures re-

quiring production of images closely allied to the projective technique." Several ways in which creative imagination imagery might be studied are: instruments might measure single images and images in complex patterns, a study could be made of the mental health correlates of mental health imagery, a study could be made of the relationships between creative imagination imagery and brain dominance, etc.

Schaefer, C.E. "Imaginary Companions and Creative Adolescents." *Developmental Psychology* 1 (1969): 747-749.

About 15 to 30% of children between the ages of 3 and 10 report imaginary companions. Bright children are more likely to have this experience than children who are of below-average intelligence. To check these data the author collected similar information on creative children who were part of the study reported by Schaefer (1969). Frequency of imaginary companions in this study was consistent with previous research findings (12 to 31%). The speculation that the imaginary companion phenomenon is related to creativity finds partial support in this study. "For both sexes, students who produced creative works of a literary nature reported a greater incidence of the imaginary-companion phenomenon in childhood." The author concludes: "Perhaps the main implication of this study is that parents and educators should not become unduly concerned when children report the existence of imaginary companions since this phenomenon appears to favor brighter children and, more specifically, those bright children who have leanings toward literary creativity."

Chapter 8

THE DISADVANTAGED AND THE DEPRIVED

GENERAL

--Baldwin; Gear; and Lucito, 1978
--Bruch, 1978a
--Sato, 1975
--Passow, 1975
--Sisk, 1981

PHYSICALLY HANDICAPPED

--Gerken, 1979
--Meisels, 1979
--Maker, 1977

MINORITY GROUPS IN U.S.

Black

--Cooke and Baldwin, 1979
--Richmond, 1971
--Smallwood and Taylor, 1975

Asian

--Kitano, 1975

American Indian

--Kito and Lowe, 1975
--George, 1983

Spanish-speaking

--Aragon and Marquez, 1975

IDENTIFICATION

--Bruch, 1971
--Bruch, 1975
--Fitz-Gibbon, 1974
--Gay, 1978
--Reynolds, 1982
--Torrance, 1974

TEACHING

--Bernal, 1979
--Exum, 1979
--Mitchell, 1975
--Whimbey, A., and Whimbey, L.S., 1975

Baldwin, A.Y.; Gear, G.H.; and Lucito, L.J. (Eds.). *Educational Planning for the Gifted: Overcoming Cultural, Geographic, and Socio-economic Barriers*. Reston, VA: The Council for Exceptional Children, 1978. 76pp.

In the introduction to this booklet the authors state that the population on whom this work is focused "is made up of those gifted individuals who might not be identified nor have an opportunity to develop their mental capacities because of external influences such as cultural diversity, socioeconomic status or geographic isolation." Papers focused on identification as well as curriculum and methods and future directions.

Bruch, C.B. "Recent Insights on the Culturally Different Gifted." *Gifted Child Quarterly* 22 (1978): 374-393.

This paper is a review of "some changing aspects of knowledge and attitudes affecting the culturally different gifted." Because of federal intervention, there is a decrease in the "separate-but-equal" approach to the education of minority students, though there are some instances where it is still used. When it does occur, those from the separated experience "may have greater deviation from the predominant culture's experiences through their sensitive cultural awareness." Children require sufficient opportunity "to become adaptive with the several cultures which they contact regularly."

The author provides a framework of Significant Concepts in Learning about the Culturally Different Gifted. This framework contains 68 topical areas that appear in literature search-words for articles on the culturally different gifted for use with ERIC. Analysis of the journal articles obtained indicates that "no consistent plan for development of the culturally different gifted has been encompassed to date. A plan for such continuity is sorely needed, beginning at the earliest levels."

A count of the literature also indicates that, in spite of the fact that there is an emphasis on early education of the gifted in other literature, there is no such emphasis in the literature on the culturally different. In certain areas, there is a complete absence of articles. The areas are: "(1) for native American Indians—characteristics, community, counseling, females, guidance, identification, parents, teachers, and tests; (2) for Asian Americans—community, creativity, females, guidance, parents, and programs; (3) for Spanish-speaking Americans—guidance and programs." Sensitivity to the gaps is critical. Guidance as a concept was omitted in all ethnic groups except for the black gifted.

The author calls special attention to Torrance's (1977) work with the culturally different. Of special relevance are his remarks

about guidance; he calls for focusing "upon the needs of the culturally different gifted for sponsors. He states that these persons
can encourage and protect rights when the children become discouraged,
frustrated, or abused, and that sponsors can see they they 'get a
chance' to work towards their potentials." The author also presents
several pages of a selected bibliography on culturally different
gifted.

Suggestions for Further Reading

Torrance, E.P. *Discovery and Nurturance of Giftedness in the Culturally Different.* Reston, VA: CEC ERIC Clearinghouse on Handicapped and Gifted Children, 1977.

Sato, I.S. "The Culturally Different Gifted Child--The Dawning of
His Day?" In Miley, J.F., et al. (Eds.). *Promising Practices:
Teaching the Disadvantaged Gifted.* Ventura, CA: Ventura County
Superintendent of Schools, 1975. 39-45.

The culturally different child is in a difficult situation in
school. Sato recommends: "(1) a clearer definition of the term
culturally different gifted child, (2) a reexamination of identification procedures, (3) qualitatively-differentiated program provisions, (4) availability of resources (both human and otherwise)."
Sato points out that the various defining terms that have been
used (culturally disadvantaged, socially disadvantaged, culturally
diverse and culturally deprived) are all confusing and that the
term culturally different gifted has to be separated into two
parts. "Culturally different" reflects membership in a minority
group. The "gifted" part is broader than the Terman IQ-limited
definition and should broadly refer to "those individuals who excel
consistently or show the potential of excelling consistently in any
human endeavor--academic, creative, kinesthetic (performance skills),
or psychosocial (relationship and leadership skills)."
Identification procedures are presented and discussed.

Passow, A.H. "The Gifted and the Disadvantaged." In Miley, J.F.,
et al. (Eds.). *Promising Practices: Teaching the Disadvantaged
Gifted.* Ventura, CA: Ventura County Superintendent of Schools,
1975. 51-57.

The disadvantaged and the deprived constitute the "third wave of
interest in the gifted." Passow reviews several important historical
developments in dealing with the gifted and then proceeds to a consideration of matters that focus more directly on the gifted disadvantaged. He says that differentiated curricula are needed to
take individual capabilities of students into account. The staff
needs opportunities to learn and change attitudes and strategies.
The learning environment should encompass the whole inner city and
not be limited to the school itself. Strategies need to be developed
for bilingual and multicultural education. Guidance programs and
other ancillary services need to be developed that take into account
the unusual needs of the gifted and also help with affective and
financial matters. Educators and communities need to work on the
development of talent potential and the gifted, wherever they are.
One should not limit oneself to any one group, white, middle class,

poor, etc. "All educators must become advocates for increased, appropriate attention to the gifted, especially those among the disadvantaged and minorities, where discrimination and neglect have resulted in an even greater loss of talent development."

Sisk, D. "The Challenge of Educating the Gifted Among the Poor." In Kramer, A.H., et al. (Eds.). *Gifted Children: Challenging Their Potential--New Perspectives and Alternatives*. New York: Trillium Press, 1981. 309-325.

This paper was presented by the author, the former director of the Office of the Gifted, U.S. Office of Education, at the Third International Conference on Gifted and Talented Children in Jerusalem, Israel, in 1979.

Sisk does not like the euphemistic term "culturally disadvantaged" and refers to the group under consideration simply and directly as the "gifted among the poor." Looking at the role of the school in relation to the gifted poor, the author says, "To counteract the stresses and strains of poverty in the home envirnoment, the school must endeavor to reflect a positive, stimulating, and encouraging atmosphere." The children of the poor have a sense of powerlessness and low self-esteem. A teacher can be a great help in fostering a positive self-image.

Among the techniques designed to help teachers understand the poor are: the Live-In Institute under the Elementary and Secondary Education Act of 1965 in which teacher trainees lived with poor families and experienced firsthand what their lives were like, Project Aware in which teachers lived in ghetto school areas, and Operation Bootstrap in which encounter sessions between young blacks and white visitors were used.

A major challenge on the contemporary scene is to recognize the gifted among the poor. It is important to overcome teachers' resistance to the very idea that giftedness can occur among the poor. A second problem in identifying giftedness among the poor is that "the deficit appears to be cumulative." The literature shows that the longer the children of the poor stay in school, the more their IQ and achievement scores go down.

To counteract these problems and resistances, Sisk recommends the following objectives. Parents, teachers, principals, and boards of education must be sensitized to the fact that giftedness can occur among the poor. "Second, we must begin to view the positive traits among the poor and use these as general screening devices and as a viable part of a comprehensive identification procedure." One of the techniques for identifying the talented poor is through the use of theater techniques (Wolf, 1979) and the Abbreviated Binet for the Disadvantaged (Bruch, 1973).

The author discusses the following projects in the U.S. for the gifted poor: Project LEAP (Life Enrichment Activity Program) in New Haven, Conn.; HEP-UP (High School Education at the University of Pennsylvania; Project SEED (Special Elementary Education for the Disadvantaged) in California; the New Orleans Center for Creative Arts; Project CLUE (Cooperative Leadership for Urban Education) in Tennessee; and SEPE (School Enrichment Parent Education Program) in California. Foreign programs that are discussed briefly include programs in Venezuela, Brazil, and Israel (including the Boyar School and the Heled project). Sisk also enumerates specific strategies for teaching poor students.

PHYSICALLY HANDICAPPED

Gerken, K.C. "An Unseen Minority: Handicapped Individuals Who Are Gifted and Talented." In Colangelo, N., and Zaffrann, R.T. (Eds.). *New Voices in Counseling the Gifted*. Dubuque, IA: Kendall/Hunt, 1979. 321-325.

Over 454 adults have been identified as gifted and handicapped, and there may be many more. This article calls for better identification and counseling methods. Various sources that may be of use are recommended.

Meisels, S.J. *Special Education and Development, Perspectives on Young Children with Special Needs*. Baltimore, MD: University Park Press, 1979.

The basic orientation of this book is the importance of Piaget's developmental model in education. The importance of this approach to education is threefold. (1) Children are no longer viewed as members of a homogeneous cohort group but are seen as having a position on a developmental continuum. The developmental approach allows for finer gradations in ability than the usual educational models. There is also an attempt to identify similarities as well as differences between children. (2) Since, according to the developmental approach, development follows an invariant sequence or order, an educational approach should be concerned with a child's general ability to acquire skills rather than skill preparation that is externally determined. (3) In the traditional model, children are the passive recipients of knowledge. In the developmental approach, children learn best when they are actively exploring the physical and social environment. The developmental approach is oriented to individual children.

Traditionally, handicapped children have been treated in a holistic manner; if they had reduced intellectual functioning, they were called retarded and were expected to follow a specific course of education. The handicapping condition has been seen as unique and discontinuous and "distinct from 'normally developing' individuals." This results in "social isolation and segregation and educational approaches based on a concept of defect, rather than difference." "Children with special needs display differences in their development that distinguish them from nonhandicapped children. However, these differences need not be perceived as defects that somehow set the handicapped child on a course of development that is unrelated to that of the general population. On the contrary, the developmental model assumes a continuity in skills, ability, and knowledge. Equally, it assumes that every child will be treated in some respect as a unique learner with a particular learning history, learning style, and set of preferences and needs."

Maker, C.J. *Providing Programs for the Gifted Handicapped*. Reston, VA: Council for Exceptional Children, 1977. 171pp.

Two major issues are at the center of the author's attention: how to assess the abilities and potentialities of the gifted handicapped person; and how to program for the further development and education of the gifted handicapped.

For many people, "gifted handicapped" seems a contradiction, but the author argues that this should not be so. The paradox can be traced historically to Terman's original work (p. 110) and some of the research issues involved in the findings, especially the matter of the confounding of social class and overachievement with the results. She presents the history of the issue from the pre-Terman view of a gifted child as puny, isolated, and eccentric to the post-Terman stereotype of a remarkably healthy, attractive, and social one. The author raises the question: Were these characteristics characteristics of gifted children or were they associated with other phenomena? This issue is important for, obviously, the characteristics described by Terman leave out any mention of handicap among the characteristics of the gifted child. Maker claims that intelligence is no single unit when the handicapped are studied. This is a definitive work on the topic of the gifted handicapped and thoroughly covers the identification and placement of this neglected group.

Turning to the matter of identification among the handicapped, Maker suggests that one should look for potential rather than demonstrated ability. Good use can be made of Torrance's (1974) Checklist of Creative Positives; this procedure does not require any tests and teachers can be trained to be aware of the behaviors involved. The types of behavior are listed by Maker. Biographical data are also good for identifying the gifted. Two forms are mentioned by Maker though they would need some adaptation for use with the handicapped. They are Calvin Taylor's Alpha Biographic Inventory (cf. Taylor and Lunnebord, 1974) and Charlotte Malone's (1975) Behavioral Identification of Giftedness. These are both summarized in this work.

The next major area that Maker considers is the placement of the handicapped student. Indeed, one has to consider the student's individual needs and the resources that are available. It is very important to develop the handicapped person's self-concept. On the basis of interviews with people who are close to and who work with the handicapped, Maker makes a series of recommendations for educational systems, families, etc. A sample of suggestions for each area are as follows. Educational systems should train people to recognize giftedness in spite of a handicap and to expect more than mediocre performance from handicapped people. Other people should accept the person for his/her ability rather than expecting the handicap to limit him/her. Parents should be helped to deal with their guilt feelings. Families should stress independence and responsibility. If it is needed, professional help should be sought as soon as possible. Suggestions are made for affective development and a wide variety of resources are presented. There is also a chapter called "Applications to Specific Handicapping Areas"; the groups specifically considered are: the blind, the deaf and hearing impaired, the emotionally disturbed and emotionally disordered, the academically

retarded, and the physically handicapped. In addition, the book
contains a listing of gifted programs, agencies, and experts to help
with the gifted handicapped. There is also an annotated bibliography.

MINORITY GROUPS IN U.S.

Black

Cooke, G.J., and Baldwin, A.Y. "Unique Needs of a Special Population."
In Passow, A.H. (Ed.). *The Gifted and the Talented: Their Education
and Development. The Seventy-eighth Yearbook of the National Society
for the Study of Education.* Chicago: University of Chicago Press,
1979. 388-394.

The father of gifted education for Blacks is W.E.B. DuBois who
in his work, *Talented Youth* (1903), posited "that in the black race,
as in all other races, there is a hereditarily controlled elite
whose potential would blossom within the proper educational context."
It is important to identify these people and to provide them with
the best possible education. This "would result in educated black
leaders with the intellectual tools to set political, economic, and
social goals of black liberation from poverty, social malaise, and
educational deficit."

Black talent in this country has never been developed and never
been supported by the government. As a result of this, "a deficit
model surfaced and the cult of the disadvantaged and the culturally
deprived became the contemporary nomenclature." Two early programs to motivate and prepare black leaders were the National
Scholarship and Service Fund for Negro Students and the National
Achievement Scholarship Program for Negroes.

Lots of black talent has been neglected because conventional test
scores do not reflect common black abilities and potentialities
properly. It is recommended that a "kaleidoscopic approach is necessary in order to identify the gifted children who are culturally
different and to plan a suitable curriculum for such children."
The work of Bruch (1975), Torrance (1968), and Guilford (1971) are
cited to indicate the kinds of abilities and tests in which blacks
excel. In this regard, special mention is made of the work of Purcell and Hillson (1969). The authors also point to the orientations
presented by Gallagher (1975) and the Meekers (1975), and suggest
the importance of the Baldwin Identification Matrix which appears in
this chapter and in a bulletin of the N/S-LTI-G/T (1977). "The evidence from the matrix produces a total score that gives the black
child, or any child from a different culture, an opportunity to
compete for recognition in a specialized program. It also gives
the researcher a picture of the strengths and weaknesses of a particular child."

Suggestions for Further Reading

Bruch, C. "Pro-cultural Measurement: The Use of the Abbreviated
  Binet for the Disadvantaged (ABDA)." In *First National Conference*

on the Disadvantaged Gifted. Ventura, CA: Office of the Ventura County Superintendent of Schools, 1975. 18-19.

DuBois, W.E.B. *"The Talented Tenth," The Negro Problem: A Series of Articles by Representative American Negroes of Today*. New York: James Pott Co., 1903. 33-75.

Gallagher, J.J. *Teaching the Gifted Child*. Boston: Allyn and Bacon, 1975.

Guilford, J.P., and Hoepfner, R. *The Analysis of Intelligence*. New York: McGraw-Hill, 1971.

Meeker, M., and Meeker, R.J. *Strategies for Assessing Intellectual Patterns in Black, Anglo, and Mexican-American Boys or Any Other Children--and Implications for Education*. Los Angeles: Structure of Intellect Institute, 1975.

N/S-LTI-G/T Bulletin 4 (March 1977).

Purcell, F.P., and Hillson, M. "The Disadvantaged Child." In Hillson, M. (Ed.). *Education and the Urban Community*. New York: American Book Co., 1969. 129-137.

Richmond, B.O. "Creative and Cognitive Abilities of White and Negro Children." *Journal of Negro Education* 40 (1971): 111-115.

Sixty disadvantaged rural Georgia 8th grade students participated in this study. Thirty-four were black and 36 white. The Lorge-Thorndike Tests and the Torrance Tests of Creative Thinking were administered to both groups. The results indicated that: (1) white students scored significantly higher than black students on the verbal and non-verbal measures of intelligence. (2) On the creativity measures, there were no statistically significant differences between the blacks and the whites. (3) Creativity measures give educators of the disadvantaged data that cannot be obtained through the more traditional measures of intelligence.

Smallwood, G., and Taylor, O. "Black Component." In Miley, J.F., et al. (Eds.). *Promising Practices: Teaching the Disadvantaged Gifted*. Ventura, CA: Ventura County Superintendent of Schools, 1975. 22-23.

This paper focuses on black language. The authors identify four basic concepts about language and outline three main views of black English. Important points include the following: (1) Living in a dual society, children interact with all kinds of people. It is crippling to teach black children only black history, black English, etc., just as it is crippling to only teach them the standard white middle class curriculum. (2) It is wrong to say that children who speak black language cannot listen to standard English. (3) Black children who are subject to prejudiced perceptions by their teachers often fulfill these negative images. (4) Teachers who object to some of the background characteristics of their black students might want to reevaluate their own values; those teachers who think that school materials for black children are congruent with their own backgrounds might want to take another look at these

materials and their effects. The point is to focus on the characteristics and needs of the black children without prejudice.

Asian

Kitano, H. "Cultural Diversity and the Exceptional Child." In Miley,
J.F., et al. (Eds.). *Promising Practices: Teaching the Disadvantaged
Gifted*. Ventura, CA: Ventura County Superintendent of Schools,
1975. 20-21.

This paper describes the Asian family structure, the socialization
of the Asiatic child, and other related phenomena of importance to
the teacher of Asiatic students. The sociological status of the
Asian in this country is also explored.

American Indian

Kito, J., and Lowe, B. "Indian Component." In Wiley, J.F., et al.
(Eds.). *Promising Practices: Teaching the Disadvantaged Gifted*.
Ventura, CA: Ventura County Superintendent of Schools, 1975. 24-25.

The bilingual-bicultural education program in Anchorage, Alaska,
is neither a "remedial" program nor one which provides children
with compensatory education. Children are viewed as "advantaged"
and the program seeks to develop bilingualism as a precious asset
rather than a defect.

George, K. "Native American Indian: Perception of Gifted Characteristics." In Shore, B.M., et al. (Eds). *Face to Face with Giftedness*. New York: Trillium Press, 1983. 220-249.

In 1980, the United Indians of All Tribes received a $10,000,
three-year grant from the Northwest Area Foundation of St. Paul,
Minnesota. The purpose of the grant was to develop a position paper
on the identification of and programming for Native American gifted
students, and to field test a training program for the staff. This
paper is the guidepost for the project.
Because of diversity among the tribes, it is hard to generalize
about them. Consequently, it has been suggested that identification
be based on the historical and cultural realities of the local community, that local community members do the selection, and that
specific tribal values, considered as behaviors, form the basis for
gifted education criteria. Current identification procedures exclude the culturally different child. For example, in 1980, of 5150
Native American children in two counties in the state of Washington,
only 24 were identified as gifted. This is partially due to important dissimilarities between Indian and non-Indian cultures in language and semantic processing, in certain abstract and conceptual
cognitive modes, and in factors related to self-fulfillment. Unfortunately, because of the paucity of knowledge in this area,
directors of gifted programs use general characteristics lists to
identify gifted Indian children, even though these lists are in-

appropriate, or they use intelligence tests. More Indian children
will become visible if a multi-criteria approach is used.

   Native American students do not necessarily manifest their gifts
in school, but rather at home or in the community. If they do show
their gifts in school, school personnel often do not understand
their behavior. One must also consider that in some cultures,
giftedness, defined as a trait that sets one apart from one's peers,
is not a positive trait. In Native American tribal structures,
consensus and harmony among the people is important; anything that
makes one person different is not likely to be supported. Thus,
parents should be included "in defining the meaning of giftedness
for their community" and they must be provided with some orientation
on the identification and their part in it. The author suggests
that "this approach is particularly relevant to reservation-type
communities in rural settings."

   Successful identification programs use multiple assessment and
identification methods. At a conference in 1978 on curriculum for
Native Americans, there were a number of recommendations. Some of
them were: the creation of a clearinghouse for collections of
special materials for Indian students; the utilization of experts
in traditional values, such as elders, parents, grandparents, and
eminent tribal members; the creation of training institutes; the
stimulation of motivation and awareness within the community; and
the promotion of parental participation. Thus, curriculum, instruction, etc., would be culturally relevant; both convergent and divergent thinking would be taught; and curriculum would be flexible
and diversified. "We recommend a well planned experiential, enrichment or exploration approach in the first few months, then,
using an assessment approach which identifies areas of strength
and weakness (such as Meeker's SOI), building intellectual strengths
over a range of subject areas. Intellectual skillbuilding may be
accomplished by using as a motivator and vehicle for learning, the
students' interest areas which were discovered during the initial
exploration period, and intellectual strengths discovered during
screening and assessment."

   The author writes that "There is clearly a need for concentrated
and well-designed research efforts to give us more information
about the propensities and behavior patterns of gifted Native
American students, about the effectiveness and accuracy of various
identification methods and instruments in identifying Native Americans, and about the impact of existing curriculum models for high-
ability students on Native Americans."

Spanish-speaking

Aragon, J., and Marquez, L. "Spanish-speaking Component." In Miley,
J.F., et al. (Eds.). *Promising Practices: Teaching the Disadvantaged
Gifted*. Ventura, CA: Ventura County Superintendent of Schools,
1975. 26-27.

   It is important to know the similarities and differences between
Spanish-speaking and American cultures. These are reflected in
words and concepts. Such knowledge can avoid confusion and effect
mutual understanding. For example, words like "family" in English

and "familia" in Spanish appear to be the same but have different
connotations. The former refers to the nuclear family and the
latter, to the extended family. It is important that American educators become sensitive to cultural distinctions and differences
if they are to be successful.

IDENTIFICATION

Bruch, C.B. "Modification of Procedures for Identification of the
    Disadvantaged Gifted." *Gifted Child Quarterly* 15 (1971): 267-272.

    Kennedy et al. (1961) collected Binet data from 1,800 students
from grades one through six in the southeastern United States. An
item analysis of these data was utilized to determine the strengths
of these children. Four items (out of seven for the years II
through XIV) were selected because they were most successfully passed
by these students. These items then formed a new abbreviation of
the Binet "*favoring* the southeastern Black disadvantaged student."
This is called the Abbreviated Binet for Disadvantaged (ABDA).
    The form described above was used to test some of the author's
hypotheses about the strengths of black students in different cognitive abilities. The abbreviated form was analyzed utilizing
Meeker's (1969) analysis, based on Guilford's structure of intellect.
The results included the following. (1) The hypothesis that divergent production would be strong was not supported, possibly because so many of the items in the Binet have semantic content.
(2) To a degree, the hypothesis was confirmed that practical, logical
reasoning was a strength. (3) Though cognition was regarded as a
strength, it was not expected that it would test adequately in the Bi
and hence, it is not surprising that it was not supported. (4) The
expectation that transformations would be strong was not supported;
again, semantic content was the problem. (5) It was reasonably
confirmed that the black disadvantaged student would be strong in
system products. (6) The data showed that the black students had
"formidable strength in memory operations." "The finding of such
consistent memory power in content and *without* gaps in products is
an important lead in the identification of the gifted among disadvantaged Black populations." (7) Units and classes were higher
than expected.
    Tests used for identification purposes should be designated as:
(1) space relations and tests in musical form; (2) memory items on
various tests of ability and achievement; (3) logical reasoning or
problem-solving tests; (4) tests involving all but verbal (semantic
operations) single units; (5) tests requiring classification, particularly in space relations items; and (6) items requiring understanding of the integrated "whole" or the total system, primarily
of a figurative nature. Other areas in which strengths should be
noted are based on strengths observed and considered congruent with
the structure of intellect analysis. These include: art and music,
spontaneous recall, complex problem solving in daily activities,
awareness of details in descriptions, spontaneous categorizations,
and "Visual synthesis in complex drawings; multiple musical or kinaesthetic (dance or athletics) perceptions of the whole organized

system." Attention is also called to figural creativity, especially
fluency, as measured by Torrance's tests; in behavior, one should
observe social leadership and human understanding.

Suggestions for Further Reading

Torrance, E.P. "I was a block but nobody builded me." Paper prepared for The Association for the Gifted, Council for Exceptional
Children, Miami Beach, FL, 20 April 1971.

Readers who want more information about the abbreviated Binet should
write to Catherine B. Bruch, Ed.D., Department of Educational
Psychology, University of Georgia, Athens, GA 30601.

Bruch, C.B. "Assessment of Creativity in Culturally Different Children."
Gifted Child Quarterly 19 (1975): 164-174.

The author reviews a number of issues in the use of tests in the
assessment of creativity in culturally different children. She
makes a number of suggestions as to how things might be done differently. She distinguishes between the terms "disadvantaged" and
"culturally different." The former refers to "populations who are
restricted in access to mainstream cultural experiences due to econ-
nomic disadvantagement. The term 'culturally different' deals with
those cultural or sub-cultural groups whose cultural environment
differs from that of the mainstream or general culture." Keeping
these definitions in mind, the author suggests that the children's
"psycho-social distance from the mainstream should be considered in
assessment." Measurement should be culturally based, and where
equal opportunity for development is lacking, the measurement should
be culturally fair. Toward these ends, a sub-culture should assist
in the development of criteria for the measurement of creative abilities.

Four main issues are raised with respect to measurement. (1) The
tests that are used are designed for middle class populations and
for the selection of abilities relevant to the mainstream. Poor
test performance among minority group students may be related to
neglect of physical and psychological needs. "The culturally different and the disadvantaged frequently demonstrate low self-concept
and motivation on mainstream tests." (2) There is neglect on known
sub-cultural values, abilities, etc., in available assessment procedures. No studies have been made of information valued in black
culture. There is a need to change standardized instruments so
that they take into consideration the use of words in different cultural groups. (3) There are "motivational negatives" on the part
of educators, administrators, and test constructors. Staff is trained
almost exclusively to deal with middle class instruments. Educators
do not accept cultural pluralism and measures of pluralism, and
limit themselves to the IQ. Test administrators often overlook the
fact that black children may be afraid of white examiners, which
will negatively affect their scores. (4) Among the fallacies about
the measurement of abilities in culturally different groups is "that
nothing is worthwhile unless it is objectively measured." It is
also erroneous to assume that the culturally different child develops
in the same way as the mainstream child. In addition, it is a myth
that tests measure unitary abilities.

The author has several suggestions for measuring creativity in culturally different groups. There are several suggestions for each category; what follows is only a sample. (1) In terms of task construction and content, test items should be relevant to the subculture and "may contain mainstream tasks which are *equally appropriate for the main and the sub-culture*." Vocabulary should be congruent with the sub-culture as should the creative abilities tested. "Measurement tasks should consist of additional creativity components (such as Guilford's transformations and implications products as well as divergent production) for diagnostic/teaching/learning applications." Test manuals should provide examples of acceptable alternative responses. (2) Task conditions and methods should include a warm-up, especially playful warm-up sessions, time limits, and "time-outs." (3) Training sessions should be held for personnel so that the testing is done in as unbiased a manner as possible. Where necessary, members of the sub-culture can help in the training. (4) Alternatives and new directions should be pursued. Use can be made of criterion-reference evaluation systems and measurement which takes place over time. Life experiences related to creative behavior can be evaluated as well; this might include the use of: situational tasks, natural settings, or focus on the creative use of language.

Fitz-Gibbon, C.T. "The Identification of Mentally Gifted, 'Disadvantaged,' Students at the Eighth Grade Level." *Journal of Negro Education* 43 (1974): 53-56.

The purpose of this study was to develop an inexpensive, practical, and fair method of identifying mentally gifted disadvantaged students from among inner city junior high school students. Four hundred eighth grade students from a predominantly black urban area in California participated in the study.

The criterion for giftedness was how students scored on the Wechsler Intelligence Scale for Children (WISC). First, the students were screened with a variety of tests. Those who scored in the top 2% on the Standard Progressive Matrices received the Advanced Progressive Matrices, the California Test of Mental Maturity, and the California Achievement Test. These students and those nominated by the teachers were selected to take the WISC, which was individually administered by a school psychologist.

Eighteen students were selected because they had top scores on all screening tests. Four students were selected because they scored high on the individual screening test. The range in scores for this group was 94 to 136 on the WISC. Using a cut-off score of 114, nine students fell into this category. Seven of the gifted were among the top eight in the screening procedure. Five of them had been nominated as gifted by two or more teachers. The Standard Progressive Matrices (SPM) proved to be the most accurate screening procedure. For "quick, justifiable, and inexpensive" techniques, the SPM and the Advanced Progressive Matrices are recommended to select the top 2% of disadvantaged students.

Gay, J.E. "A Proposed Plan for Identifying Black Gifted Children."
Gifted Child Quarterly 22 (1978): 353-360.

To help identify black gifted children, a plan is suggested which
includes: obtaining commitment from schools to help in the identification process; locating nominees; setting up case studies; increasing
parental contact and involvement; interviewing and testing; and
administering group problem solving tasks to identify leadership
and supportive behavior. A list of 11 categories of giftedness,
culled from the literature, is compared with characteristics of
black children.

Reynolds, C.R. "The Problem of Bias in Psychological Assessment."
In Reynolds, C.R., and Gutkin, T.B. (Eds.). *Handbook of School
Psychology*. New York: John Wiley and Sons, 1982. 178-208.

This chapter focuses on the issue of test bias in psychological
and educational tests, especially as it concerns psychologists,
educators, and laymen. The author points out that the issue has
stirred emotions even among competent and objective professionals.
"The controversy over bias will likely remain with psychology and
education for at least as long as the nature/nurture controversy,
even in the face of a convincing body of evidence failing to support
cultural test bias hypotheses." The scattered and inconsistent
evidence that does exist on test bias is in support of disadvantaged,
ethnic minorities.

To help insure unbiased assessment, the author suggests two guidelines: "(1) assessment should be conducted with the most reliable
instrumentation available, and (2) multiple abilities should be
assessed. In other words, psychologists need to view multiple
sources of accurately derived data prior to making decisions concerning children." In addition, the author writes: "Test developers
are going to have to become more sensitive to the issues of cultural
bias to the point of demonstrating upon publication whether their
tests have differential content, construct, or predictive validity
across race or sex prior to publication."

Before the question of bias can be resolved diverse criteria need
to be explored. In the future, for predictive purposes, different
achievement tests and teacher-made tests need to be employed. The
differential validity of tests in the affective domain needs to be
explored. In addition, more work is necessary on psychologists'
interpretations of objective personality test data across race and
sex. "It will also be important to stay abreast of methodological
advances that may make it possible to resolve some of the current
issues and to identify common characteristics among those now seen
as irregular or random infrequent findings of bias."

Torrance, E.P. "Differences Are Not Deficits." *Teachers College
Record* 75 (1974): 471-487.

This article contains the Checklist of Creative Positives which
can be used when teachers and others observe children in a variety
of activities. It does not depend on the use of tests, and its use
requires a minimum of training. On the basis of observations, behaviors can be encouraged and taught or the children who manifest